Teacher Manual

Language and Composition

The Art of Voice

2nd Edition

Stephanie Ferree Hyatt

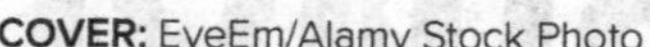

COVER: EyeEm/Alamy Stock Photo

The Internet addresses listed in the text were accurate at the time of publication. The inclusion of a website does not indicate an endorsement by the authors or McGraw-Hill Education, and McGraw-Hill Education does not guarantee the accuracy of the information presented at these sites.

mheducation.com/prek-12

Send all inquiries to:
McGraw-Hill Education
8787 Orion Place
Columbus, OH 43240

ISBN: 978-0-07-691931-4
MHID: 0-07-691931-5

Printed in the United States of America.

4 5 6 7 8 9 QVS 23 22 21 20 19

CHAPTER 1

Active Reading and Response to Texts

When students enter their first AP* English Language and Composition class, they often have no idea what to expect. Up to this point in their scholastic careers, English classes have either encompassed reading great works of literature or completing grammar exercises. Seldom have students encountered anything more than a smattering of nonfiction in their English classes.

Enter AP English Language and Composition. With a focus on nonfiction—be it memoirs, historical documents, speeches, letters, or even current events and trends—AP English Language and Composition focuses on writing and reading argument in its various forms. The course asks students to commit not just to reading for understanding but also to recognize the many layers of *why* and *how* an author sets words to a page. This produces readers who go beyond plot and summary and reach for the broader societal implications of the media we all consume.

Although AP English Language and Composition is equivalent to a college composition course, the reality of composition courses is that they frequently are as much about reading, analyzing, and appreciating *good* writing as they are about producing it. In fact, in the AP English Language and Composition course description, the College Board provides as the first objective of this course that students learn to "analyze and interpret samples of good writing, identifying and explaining an author's use of rhetorical strategies and techniques particularly in nonfiction readings." It is fitting, then, that this textbook begins with a chapter devoted exclusively to reading—and to doing so responsively and actively.

Lesson Plan 1.1

Introduction to Reading Actively

The introduction to this chapter prepares students to read differently than they have in the past. In AP class and in college, students are asked to read actively.

Class Opener

On the first day teaching this chapter, write the following question and instructions on the board for students to see as they walk into the classroom: "What does it mean to be literate? In pairs, create a one-sentence definition of *literacy*."

Give student pairs 2 to 4 minutes to complete the prompt, and then call on volunteers to share their responses. You might consider having volunteers write on a white board or post their responses under a document camera, depending on the level of technology you have available in your classroom. This activity works equally well when the answers are shared verbally. As students share their answers, you will find that most answers connect literacy with the ability to read and perhaps to write. Students will rarely include such connections as technology or media.

Activity: Discussing Key Points of Literacy

After students have shared their definitions of *literacy*, ask them to read together the chapter opener on pages 2–3 of the textbook. There are many strategies for reading in class, and most teachers have their favorites. You may call on students, allow them to call on each other, or ask for volunteers. As students read, discuss these key points:

1. **What impact does technology have on literacy?**
2. **How has reading changed in students' lifetime? Prompt students to consider digital readers and how they have redefined publishing.**
3. **What does it mean to read actively?**

Activity: Reading Actively

The first part of the chapter is titled **Reading Actively**. This section details five strategies that students must practice in order to be active readers. Do not have students read this part in advance. Instead, assign students to a group (see **Establishing Groups** on page 4 of this Teacher Manual)—you need five groups for this activity. Then assign each group one of the five strategies to overcome barriers to active reading, found on page 4 of the student textbook. Give groups five minutes to master their strategy and decide how to teach it to the class. Each group will be responsible for defining a "what, how, why" for their strategy. (What/how/why will be important as you move through the entire course.) After students have had their five minutes of discussion, ask each group to present their findings. Look for them to address the following considerations:

About the Author

Stephanie Ferree Hyatt teaches AP English Language and Composition and AP English Literature and Composition at Lee High School in Huntsville, Alabama. In 2012, Hyatt was named Teacher of the Year for both Lee High School and Huntsville City Schools. Hyatt is actively involved with the A+ College Ready Initiative and the National Math and Science Institute, for whom she teaches AP exam prep sessions for students and curriculum workshops for teachers. Hyatt has served on the Teacher Engagement Committee of the Council of Chief State School Officers and serves on the Teacher Cabinet for the Alabama State Department of Education. Hyatt holds a Master's Degree in English from the University of Alabama Huntsville, an Educational Specialist Degree in Teaching and Learning from Liberty University, and is currently writing her doctoral dissertation for an Educational Doctorate in Curriculum and Instruction. "I owe a debt of gratitude to the countless teachers who have posted their brilliant lesson plans online and to the many professional development workshop leaders who have influenced my teaching over the years."

Table of Contents

SYLLABUS xiii

PACING GUIDES

Full-Year 50-Minute Classes xix

Semester 90-Minute Blocks xxvi

INTRODUCTION xxxii

CHAPTER 1 Active Reading and Response to Texts 1

Lesson Plan 1.1 Introduction to Reading Actively 2

Establishing Groups 4

Lesson Plan 1.2 Questioning the Text and Preparing to Read (Prereading) 4

Guidelines for Reading Actively 6

Lesson Plan 1.3 Teaching "From Ancient Greece to Iraq, The Power of Words in Wartime" 7

Two-Minute Writer Conference 8

Holistic Grading: QOEGV Approach 9

Suggested Answers "From Ancient Greece to Iraq, the Power of Words in Wartime" by Robin Tolmach Lakoff 12

Lesson Plan 1.4 Teaching "How to Read a Book" 13

Suggested Answers "How to Read a Book" by Mortimer J. Adler and Charles Van Doren 14

Lesson Plan 1.5 Annotating and Note Taking 15

Discussion Questions "The Cult of Ethnicity" by Arthur M. Schlesinger, Jr. 17

Lesson Plan 1.6 The Art of Rhetorical Analysis 18

Lesson Plan 1.7 Paraphrasing and Summarizing 23

Lesson Plan 1.8 Analyzing Visual Texts 24

OPTIC Tool 25

Suggested Answers Classic and Contemporary Images 29

CHAPTER 2 The Writing Process 30

Suggested Answers Classic and Contemporary Images 31

Lesson Plan 2.1 Planning/Prewriting 31

Suggested Answers "Freewriting" by Peter Elbow 33

Lesson Plan 2.2 Drafting Thesis Statements and Planning the Essay 35

Lesson Plan 2.3 Description, Narration, and Illustration 37

Lesson Plan 2.4 Process Analysis, Comparison and Contrast, and Causal Analysis 40

Lesson Plan 2.5 Definition, Classification, and Argumentation 42

Lesson Plan 2.6 Writing Conclusions and Revising 43

Lesson Plan 2.7 Responding to "The Maker's Eye: Revising Your Own Manuscripts" by Donald Murray 44

Suggested Answers "The Maker's Eye: Revising Your Own Manuscripts" by Donald Murray 45

Lesson Plan 2.8 Responding to "Sex, Lies, and Conversation: Why Is It so Hard for Men and Women to Talk to Each Other?" by Deborah Tannen 47

Suggested Answers "Sex, Lies, and Conversation: Why Is It so Hard for Men and Women to Talk to Each Other?" by Deborah Tannen 48

Lesson Plan 2.9 Connections for Critical Thinking 50

CHAPTER 3 Argumentation and Synthesis 51

Lesson Plan 3.1 Elements of Argumentation 51

Suggested Answers Classic and Contemporary Images 52

Lesson Plan 3.2 Appeals and "The Gettysburg Address" 54

Suggested Answers "The Gettysburg Address" by Abraham Lincoln 58

Lesson Plan 3.3 Writing Powerful Arguments 60

Lesson Plan 3.4 Recognizing Fallacies in Reasoning 63

Lesson Plan 3.5 Practicing an Argument Essay 64

Lesson Plan 3.6 Synthesizing: Making Connections 66

Lesson Plan 3.7 Teaching "The Art of Rhetoric" 69

Suggested Answers "The Art of Rhetoric" by Aristotle 69

Lesson Plan 3.6 Teaching "Common Sense" 71

Suggested Answers "Common Sense" by Thomas Paine 71

CHAPTER 4 Education and Society 73

Suggested Answers Classic and Contemporary Images 73

Lesson Plan 4.1 A Comparison of Style—Douglass and Rodriguez (Part 1) 74

Suggested Answers "Learning to Read and Write" by Frederick Douglass 75

Lesson Plan 4.2 A Comparison of Style—Douglass and Rodriguez (Part 2) 77

Suggested Answers "The Lonely, Good Company of Books" by Richard Rodriguez 78

Lesson Plan 4.3 Timed-Writing: Synthesizing the Classic and Contemporary Essays 80

Lesson Plan 4.4 Socratic Seminar on Menand's "The Graduates" 81

Socratic Seminars 81

Suggested Answers "The Graduates" by Louis Menand 82

Lesson Plan 4.5 Annotating and Questioning Gregorian's "America, Still on Top" 83

Suggested Answers "America, Still on Top" by Vartan Gregorian 84

Lesson Plan 4.6 Four Corner Debate on Mike Rose's "What College Can Mean to the Other America" 86

Suggested Answers "What College Can Mean to the Other America" by Mike Rose 87

Lesson Plan 4.7 Fishbowl Discussion on Susan Jacoby's "When Bright Girls Decide that Math Is 'a Waste of Time'" 88

Suggested Answers "When Bright Girls Decide that Math Is 'a Waste of Time' " by Susan Jacoby 89

Lesson Plan 4.8 Chapter Assessment: Answers to Rhetorical Analysis and Connections for Critical Thinking 91

Lesson Plan 4.9 Synthesizing Sources: STEM vs. Liberal Arts—Is the STEAM Movement the Solution? 92

CHAPTER 5 Family Life 94

Lesson Plan 5.1 Comparison and Contrast Essay—White and Kingsolver (Part 1) 94

Suggested Answers Classic and Contemporary Images 94

Suggested Answers "Once More to the Lake" by E.B. White 95

Lesson Plan 5.2 Comparison and Contrast Essay—White and Kingsolver (Part 2) 98

Suggested Answers "Stone Soup" by Barbara Kingsolver 98

Lesson Plan 5.3 Synthesis: Comparison and Contrast Questions for Comparison 100

Lesson Plan 5.4 Annie Dillard: A Focus on Verbs 102

Suggested Answers "An American Childhood" by Annie Dillard 103

Lesson Plan 5.5 Brooks's "Love, Internet Style"—Socratic Seminar 105

Suggested Answers "Love, Internet Style" by David Brooks 106

Lesson Plan 5.6 Alvarez's "Once Upon a Quinceañera"—SOAPSTone Analysis 109

Suggested Answers "Once Upon a Quinceañera" by Julia Alvarez 110

Lesson Plan 5.7 Chapter Assessment: Answers to Rhetorical Analysis and Connections for Critical Thinking 112

Lesson Plan 5.8 Synthesizing Sources: Helicopter Parenting 113

CHAPTER 6 History, Culture, and Civilization 115

Suggested Answers Classic and Contemporary Images 115

Lesson Plan 6.1 The Declaration of Independence—Study in Syntax 116

Suggested Answers "The Declaration of Independence" by Thomas Jefferson 118

Lesson Plan 6.2 King's "I Have a Dream"—Jigsaw Group Analysis 120

Suggested Answers "I Have a Dream" by Martin Luther King, Jr. 121

Lesson Plan 6.3 Synthesizing Classic and Contemporary Essays: Timed-Writing 123

Lesson Plan 6.4 Cofer's "The Myth of the Latin Woman"—Timed Writing with a Plan 124

Suggested Answers "The Myth of the Latin Woman: I Just Met a Girl Named María" by Judith Ortiz Cofer 125

Lesson Plan 6.5 Sen's "A World Not Neatly Divided"—SOAPSTone Analysis 127

Suggested Answers "A World Not Neatly Divided" by Amartya Sen 128

Lesson Plan 6.6 Hall's "The Arab World"—Reverse Outlining 130

Suggested Answers "The Arab World" by Edward T. Hall 131

Lesson Plan 6.7 Satrapi's "The Veil"—Envisioning Narrative 133

Suggested Answers "The Veil" by Marjane Satrapi 133

Lesson Plan 6.8 Chapter Assessment: Answers to Rhetorical Analysis and Connections for Critical Thinking 135

Lesson Plan 6.9 Synthesizing Sources: Women's Rights 136

CHAPTER 7 Business and Economics 138

Suggested Answers Classic and Contemporary Images 138

Lesson Plan 7.1 Woolf's "Professions for Women"—Analyzing Rhetoric Through Structure 139

Suggested Answers "Professions for Women" by Virginia Woolf 143

Lesson Plan 7.2 Gates's "Delusions of Grandeur"—
Analyzing Purpose Through DIDLS 145

DIDLS Analysis 145

Suggested Answers "Delusions of Grandeur" by Henry Louis Gates, Jr. 148

Lesson Plan 7.3 Synthesizing Classic and Contemporary Essays: Timed-Writing 149

Lesson Plan 7.4 Krugman's "The Death of Horatio Alger"—
Writing and Analyzing Argument 150

Suggested Answers "The Death of Horatio Alger" by Paul Krugman 152

Lesson Plan 7.5 Friedman's "Globalization: The Super-Story"—
A Research Framework 154

Suggested Answers "Globalization: The Super-Story" by Thomas L. Friedman 155

Lesson Plan 7.6 Ehrenreich's "Nickel and Dimed"—
Fishbowl Discussion 157

Suggested Answers "Nickel and Dimed" by Barbara Ehrenreich 157

Lesson Plan 7.7 Reich's "Why the Rich Are Getting Richer, and the Poor, Poorer"—Gathering Relevant Details 159

Suggested Answers "Why the Rich Are Getting Richer, and the Poor, Poorer" by Robert Reich 160

Lesson Plan 7.8 Chapter Assessment: Answers to Rhetorical Analysis and Connections for Critical Thinking 162

Lesson Plan 7.9 Synthesizing Sources: Online Shopping: Has It Affected Our Lives for Better or Worse? 163

CHAPTER 8 Media and Pop Culture 165

Suggested Answers Classic and Contemporary Images 165

Lesson Plan 8.1 Steinem's "Wonder Woman" and Barna's "Today's Leading Man"—Comparing Stereotypes 166

Suggested Answers "Wonder Woman" by Gloria Steinem 168

Suggested Answers "Today's Leading Man" by Daniel Barna 169

Lesson Plan 8.2 Bordo's "The Globalization of Eating Disorders"—
An "Appealing" Socratic Seminar 171

Suggested Answers "The Globalization of Eating Disorders" by Susan Bordo 171

Lesson Plan 8.3 Ross's "Escape from Wonderland"—
Connecting Detail to Effect 173

Suggested Answers "Escape from Wonderland: Disney and the Female Imagination" by Deborah Ross 174

Lesson Plan 8.4 Will's "Plumbing the Etiquette of Baseball" —
SOAPSTone Analysis 176

Suggested Answers "Plumbing the Etiquette of Baseball" by George Will 176

Lesson Plan 8.5 Chapter Assessment: Answers to Rhetorical Analysis
and Connections for Critical Thinking 177

Lesson Plan 8.6 Synthesizing Sources: Social Media—Has It
Empowered Us or Disenfranchised Us? 179

CHAPTER 9 Literature and the Arts 181

Suggested Answers Classic and Contemporary Images 181

Lesson Plan 9.1 Welty's "One Writer's Beginnings"—
Writing with the Senses 182

Suggested Answers "One Writer's Beginnings" by Eudora Welty 183

Lesson Plan 9.2 Atwood's "Orwell and Me"—Analysis Jigsaw 185

Suggested Answers "Orwell and Me" by Margaret Atwood 186

Lesson Plan 9.3 Updike's "Moving Along"—Timed Synthesis 188

Suggested Answers "Moving Along" by John Updike 189

Lesson Plan 9.4 Gates's "Finding Neverland"—Fishbowl Discussion
with Connections 190

Suggested Answers "Finding Neverland" by David Gates 191

Lesson Plan 9.5 Hughes's "Theme for English B"—TPCASTT 193

TPCASTT 193

Suggested Answers "Theme for English B" by Langston Hughes 196

Lesson Plan 9.6 Poe's "The Raven" and "The Philosophy of Composition" 197

Suggested Answers "The Raven" and "The Philosophy of Composition"
by Edgar Allan Poe 206

Lesson Plan 9.7 Chapter Assessment: Answers to Rhetorical Analysis
and Connections for Critical Thinking 208

Lesson Plan 9.8 Synthesizing Sources: Living and Dying
in Poetry and Art 209

CHAPTER 10 Nature and the Environment 210

Lesson Plan 10.1 Eastman's "What Can the Out-of-Doors
Do for Our Children?"—A Study in Detail 210

Suggested Answers Classic and Contemporary Images 210

Suggested Answers "What Can the Out-of-Doors Do for
Our Children?" by Charles A. Eastman 212

Lesson Plan 10.2 Lopez's "Children in the Woods"—Comparison & Contrast 213

Suggested Answers "Children in the Woods" by Barry Lopez 215

Lesson Plan 10.3 Synthesizing Classic and Contemporary Essays—Timed-Writing 217

Lesson Plan 10.4 Bass's "Why I Hunt"—Recognizing Causal Analysis 218

Suggested Answers "Why I Hunt" by Rick Bass 218

Lesson Plan 10.5 McKibben's Rhetoric—Analyzing the Appeals 220

Suggested Answers "The Environmental Issue from Hell" by Bill McKibben 221

Lesson Plan 10.6 Carson's "The Obligation to Endure"—Four Corners Debate 223

Suggested Answers "The Obligation to Endure" by Rachel Carson 224

Lesson Plan 10.7 Walker's "Am I Blue?"—A SOAPSTone Analysis 225

Suggested Answers "Am I Blue?" by Alice Walker 226

Lesson Plan 10.8 Twain's "Two Views of the Mississippi"—In-Class Essay 229

Suggested Answers "Two Views of the Mississippi" by Mark Twain 229

Lesson Plan 10.9 Diamond's "The Last Americans"—Recognizing Classification 231

Suggested Answers "The Last Americans: Environmental Collapse and the End of Civilization" by Jared Diamond 232

Lesson Plan 10.10 Chapter Assessment: Answers to Rhetorical Analysis and Connections for Critical Thinking 233

Lesson Plan 10.11 Synthesizing Sources: GMOs—Are They Good for the World or Not? 235

CHAPTER 11 AP Favorites 237

Lesson Plan 11.1 Angelou, Emerson, Plato—Debating the Nature of Education: A Four Corner Synthesis Lesson 237

Lesson Plan 11.2 Bacon and Donne—Simplifying Syntax and Diction 238

Lesson Plan 11.3 Brady and Woolf—A Woman's Place: Paired SOAPSTone 239

Lesson Plan 11.4 Edwards and King—Rhetorical Analysis of the Great Preachers 240

Lesson Plan 11.5 Elizabeth, Hobbes, Machiavelli—Examining Ethics, Reason, and Power 241

Lesson Plan 11.6 Kennedy and Lincoln—Annotating Inaugural Addresses 242

Lesson Plan 11.7 Didion, Mairs, Staples—Examining Marginalization Through Detail 243

Lesson Plan 11.8 The Things We Carry—A Creative Approach to Sentence Variety 244

Lesson Plan 11.9 Orwell and Sedaris—A Study of Diction 245

Lesson Plan 11.10 Swift—Recognizing and Analyzing Satire 246

Lesson Plan 11.11 Thoreau—Fishbowl Discussion on the Politics of Transcendentalism 249

Suggested Answers for Chapter 11 Essays:

"Graduation" by Maya Angelou 250
"Of Revenge" by Francis Bacon 252
"Of Studies" by Francis Bacon 253
"I Want a Wife" by Judy Brady 254
"Marrying Absurd" by Joan Didion 255
"Meditation (No Man Is an Island)" by John Donne 256
"Sinners in the Hands of an Angry God" by Jonathan Edwards 257
"The Golden Speech" by Queen Elizabeth I 259
"Education" by Ralph Waldo Emerson 260
"Leviathan" by Thomas Hobbes 261
John F. Kennedy's Inaugural Address 263
"Letter from Birmingham Jail" by Martin Luther King, Jr. 265
Abraham Lincoln's Second Inaugural Address 267
"The Prince" by Machiavelli 268
"On Being a Cripple" by Nancy Mairs 269
"The Things They Carried" by Tim O'Brien 270
"Shooting an Elephant" by George Orwell 272
"Allegory of the Cave" by Plato 274
"Me Talk Pretty One Day" by David Sedaris 276
"Black Men and Public Space" by Brent Staples 277
"A Modest Proposal" by Jonathan Swift 278
"On the Duty of Civil Disobedience" by Henry David Thoreau 280
"A Room of One's Own" by Virginia Woolf 281

CHAPTER 12 Sample Student Essays 282

Lesson Plan 12.1 Synthesis Essay 282

Lesson Plan 12.2 Rhetorical Analysis Essay 284

Lesson Plan 12.3 Argument Essay 287

CHAPTER 13 Writing a Research Paper 290

Lesson Plan 13.1 Finding a Research-Worthy Topic 290

Lesson Plan 13.2 Conducting Research 292

Lesson Plan 13.3 Annotating Research 293

Lesson Plan 13.4 Synthesizing the Sources 296

Lesson Plan 13.5 Peer Review 296

Lesson Plan 13.6 Writing the Research Paper 297

Lesson Plan 13.7 Writing a Surprise Synthesis Essay 299

AP LANGUAGE AND COMPOSITION PRACTICE EXAM 300

Section I Answers to Multiple Choice 300

Section II Scoring Rubrics for Essays 308

An Overview of Scoring 308

Scoring Your Synthesis Essay 309

Scoring Your Rhetorical Analysis Essay 311

Scoring Your Argument Essay 313

Syllabus

Planning Your Syllabus for AP Language and Composition

This intensive reading and writing class is equivalent to a college freshman composition course. Students will closely examine and produce texts in many different forms and styles.

First Quarter

Students will begin the first quarter by determining what it really means to actively read and respond to texts. They will also be analyzing the rhetorical choices writers make to produce a successful piece of writing. Students also will be rhetorically analyzing visual choices. Points covered in **Chapter 1** include active reading; methods of annotation; the art of rhetorical analysis; the differences between paraphrasing, summarizing, and quoting; and analyzing visual texts. Activities include discussing key points of literacy; discussion of Fishbowl questions; writing in-class essays; annotating with sticky notes; multiple-entry journaling; reviewing the rhetorical triangle; reviewing rhetorical devices; practicing paraphrasing and summarizing; and drawing conclusions about advertisements and other visuals through OPTIC. Selections include:

- Robin Tolmach Lakoff, *From Ancient Greece to Iraq, The Power of Words in Wartime*
- Mortimer J. Adler And Charles Van Doren, *How to Read a Book*
- Arthur M. Schlesinger, Jr., *The Cult of Ethnicity*
- Photo: Joe Rosenthal, Marines Raising the Flag at Iwo Jima
- Photo: Visual Rhetoric Thomas E. Franklin, Firefighters Raising the Flag at Ground Zero

Chapter 2 concentrates on modes of writing and the recursive nature of the writing process. Activities include working with tone, journaling, and freewriting. Students will draft thesis statements; write introductory paragraphs; and develop body paragraphs in various modes focusing on the characteristics of a hero, including description, narration, illustration, process analysis, comparison and contrast, causal analysis, definition, classification, and argumentation. Selections include:

- Photos: Edith Wharton and Charlie Craighead Writing
- Peter Elbow, *Freewriting*
- Donald M. Murray, *The Maker's Eye: Revising Your Own Manuscripts*
- Deborah Tannen, *Sex, Lies, and Conversation: Why Is It So Hard for Men and Women to Talk to Each Other?*

Chapter 3 focuses on argumentation and synthesis. Students will define the term argument and follow with an OPTIC activity. In addition, they will become familiar with terminology often used in studying argumentation. Using these terms, students will analyze the Gettysburg Address, recognizing the rhetorical strategies and appeals in it. Other activities include examining fallacies in reasoning, and practicing for the Synthesis and Argument essays on the AP Exam. Selections include:

- Painting: Francisco de Goya's *The Third of May, 1808*
- Photo: Eddie Adams's photo of an execution
- Abraham Lincoln, *The Gettysburg Address*
- Aristotle, *The Art of Rhetoric*
- Thomas Paine, *Common Sense*

Chapter 13 teaches how to write a research paper, emphasizing that each step in the process is as valuable as the other. This is not a linear practice. Students will find a research-worthy topic and delve into their subsequent drafts. Synthesis skills will come in handy in this process because documentation and attention to MLA style will be highly regarded. (If there is time, a few essays from Chapter 11 may be analyzed).

Second Quarter

The emphasis in this quarter will be reading essays from the textbook within grouped themes or topics. In **Chapter 4** Education and Society, students will apply all the skills they have gained in the previous chapters. They will concentrate on analyzing rhetorical elements from visual to textual. They will be writing an argument concerning American education and discrimination that will include research. Classroom activities include Socratic seminar, multiple-entry journal, Four Corners Debate, and Fishbowl discussion. Other synthesis activities look at the STEM vs. liberal arts debate, leading students to develop their own arguments using the sources. Selections include:

- Photos: Carlisle Indian School and contemporary high school
- Frederick Douglass, *Learning to Read and Write*
- Richard Rodriguez, *The Lonely, Good Company of Books*
- Louis Menand, *The Graduates*
- Vartan Gregorian, *America, Still on Top*
- Mike Rose, *What College Can Mean to the Other America*
- Susan Jacoby, *When Bright Girls Decide That Math Is "a Waste of Time"*

Synthesizing Sources: STEM vs. *Liberal Arts—Is the STEAM Movement the Solution*?

- Anne Jolly, *STEM vs. STEAM: Do the Arts Belong?*
- Albert Einstein, *"Branches of the Same Tree"*
- Graph: Average Wages for Related Jobs
- Elaina Provencio, *The Major Divide: Humanities vs. STEM Majors*
- Chart: Fastest Growing Jobs in America
- NACE, *The Key Attributes Employers Seek on Students' Resumes*
- Walt Whitman, *When I Heard the Learn'd Astronomer*

Chapter 5 focuses on Family Life. The interpretation of what the word home means is a pivotal connection in this chapter. Activities include close reading and comparison, a focus on verbs, a Socratic seminar, and a SOAPSTone analysis. Narrative, comparative, and argumentative essays are assigned in this chapter. The activities end with Synthesizing Sources: Helicopter Parenting. Students will write three thesis statements in which they defend, challenge, and qualify. Selections include:

- Painting: Pieter Brueghel the Younger, *Peasant Wedding Dance*
- Photo: Modern Wedding
- E. B. White, *Once More to the Lake*
- Barbara Kingsolver, *Stone Soup*
- Annie Dillard, *An American Childhood*
- David Brooks, *Love, Internet Style*
- Julia Alvarez, *Once Upon a Quinceañera*

Synthesizing Sources: Helicopter Parenting

- Fred Lee, *Helicopter Parenting Earns Its Wings*
- Photo: Parent helping child with homework
- Joel L. Young, M.D., *The Effects of 'Helicopter Parenting'*
- Cartoon: "Helicopter Parenting"
- Don Aucoin, *For Some, Helicopter Parenting Delivers Benefits*
- Chart: Student Mental Health

Third Quarter

Chapter 6 History, Culture and Civilization is an intellectually stirring chapter that looks closely at the power of language and how voice relates to it. The chapter begins with visual rhetoric to be analyzed. Students will work closely with syntax, identifying examples of construction through a scavenger hunt. Students will divide into groups to conduct a jigsaw analysis of "I Have a Dream." They also write a focused analysis essay showing how to make an appeal like Martin Luther King, Jr. Activities include in-class essays, SOAPSTone analysis, reverse outlining, and illustrating an essay in graphic novel form with "The Veil" serving as inspiration. Compelling rhetoric on equal rights ends the chapter's Synthesizing Sources feature. Selections include:

- Photos: Immigrants at Ellis Island, 1907, and Illegal Immigrants, 1999
- Thomas Jefferson, *The Declaration of Independence*
- Martin Luther King, Jr., *I Have a Dream*
- Judith Ortiz Cofer, *The Myth Of The Latin Woman: I Just Met A Girl Named María*
- Amartya Sen, *A World Not Neatly Divided*
- Edward T. Hall, *The Arab World*
- Marjane Satrapi, "The Veil," from *Persepolis*

Synthesizing Sources: Women's Rights

- Mary Wollstonecraft, *A Vindication of the Rights of Woman*
- J. Elizabeth Jones, *Woman's Wrongs*
- Political Cartoon: That's Beautiful Tom
- Phyllis Schlafly, *"The Fraud of the Equal Rights Amendment"*
- U.S. Supreme Court *Phillips v. Martin Marietta Corp.* (1971)
- Graph: Women's Earnings as a Percent of Men's By Industry

Chapter 7 Business and Economics focuses on equal opportunity and economic changes due to globalization. Activities include rhetorical analysis through structural analysis, analyzing purpose through DIDLS, timed writing, Fishbowl discussion, and gathering details. Students use synthesizing skills to write an essay regarding online shopping. Selections include:

- Painting: Diego Rivera labor mural
- Photo: Contemporary assembly line
- Virginia Woolf, *Professions for Women*
- Henry Louis Gates, Jr., *Delusions of Grandeur*
- Paul Krugman, *The Death of Horatio Alger*

- Thomas L. Friedman, *Globalization: The Super-Story*
- Barbara Ehrenreich, *Nickel and Dimed*
- Robert Reich, *Why the Rich Are Getting Richer and the Poor, Poorer*

Synthesizing Sources: *Online Shopping: Has It Affected Our Lives for Better or Worse?*

- Photo: Online Shopping
- Mikey Rox, *6 Strange Ways Online Shopping Has Changed the World*
- Table: Quarterly Retail E-commerce Sales
- Table: Retail Store Closures
- Sandy Skrovan, *Why Most Shoppers Still Choose Brick-and-Mortar Stores Over e-Commerce*
- Photo: Amazon Distribution Centre

Fourth Quarter

While continuing to read in the textbook, students will conduct timed writings from former AP prompts. **Chapter 8** focuses on the media and popular culture in which everyone has a point of view. Activities include comparing stereotypes, Socratic seminar, connecting detail to effect in a dialectical (reader-response) journal, SOAPSTone analysis, and in-class essay with peer review. Writing and analyzing arguments continue to be the focus. The Synthesizing Sources feature includes texts and visuals related to social media. Selections include:

- Photos: Edward G. Robinson in *Little Caesar* and James Gandolfini in *The Sopranos*
- Gloria Steinem, *Wonder Woman*
- Daniel Barna, *Today's Leading Man*
- Susan Bordo, *The Globalization Of Eating Disorders*
- Deborah Ross, *Escape From Wonderland: Disney and the Female Imagination*
- George F. Will, *Plumbing the Etiquette of Baseball*

Synthesizing Sources: *Social Media—Has It Empowered Us or Disenfranchised Us?*

- Photo: Millennials Using Social Media
- Ryanne Lau, *Social Media as Tool for Meaningful Political Activism*
- Eline Blaise, *Social Media Storm: How Social Media Helped the Hurricane Harvey Victims Survive*
- Rachel Ehmke, *How Using Social Media Affects Teenagers*
- Photo: Crowdfunding
- Elise Moreau, *The Pros and Cons of Social Networking*

Chapter 9 focuses on Literature and the Arts and their place in the world. Students will explore and write with their senses, create a DIDLS analysis through jigsaw, and analyze and describe art. Other activities include Fishbowl discussion, TPCASST, and step-by-step annotation of an essay. Students will have plenty of time to better craft their writing and prepare for the AP Exam. Selections include:

- Sculpture: Auguste Rodin's *The Thinker* and Jeff Koons's *Rabbit*
- Eudora Welty, *One Writer's Beginnings*

- Margaret Atwood, *Orwell and Me*
- John Updike, *Moving Along*
- David Gates, *Finding Neverland*
- Langston Hughes, *Theme for English B*
- Edgar Allan Poe, *The Raven* and *The Philosophy of Composition*

Synthesizing Sources: *Living and Dying in Poetry and Art*

- Billy Collins, *Picnic, Lightning*
- John Crowe Ransom, *Janet Waking*
- Painting: Edvard Munch, *The Scream*
- Adrienne Rich, *Dreamwood*
- Painting: Winslow Homer, *The Gulf Stream*
- Walt Whitman, *O Me! O Life!*

In **Chapter 10** Nature and the Environment, students will study the importance of detail, and compare and contrast. Activities include recognizing causal analysis, analyzing appeals, Four Corners Debate, SOAPSTone analysis, time-writing, and work with classification. Students will address GMOs in the Synthesizing Sources feature. Selections include:

- Painting: John Frederick Kensett, *Along the Hudson*
- Photo: Los Angeles at rush hour
- Charles A. Eastman, *What Can the Out-of-Doors Do for Our Children?*
- Barry Lopez, *Children in the Woods*
- Rick Bass, *Why I Hunt*
- Bill McKibben, *The Environmental Issue From Hell*
- Rachel Carson, *The Obligation to Endure*
- Alice Walker, *Am I Blue?*
- Mark Twain, *Two Views of the Mississippi*
- Jared Diamond, *The Last Americans: Environmental Collapse and the End of Civilization*

Synthesizing Sources: *GMOs—Are They Good for the World or Not?*

- U.S. Department of Agriculture, *What Are the Benefits of Agricultural Biotechnology?*
- Ken Roseboro, *Genetic Engineers Document Why Gm Foods Are Dangerous*
- Graph: Adoption of Genetically Engineered Crops in the United States, 1996-2017
- Mitch Daniels, *Avoiding GMOs Isn't Just Anti-Science. It's Immoral.*
- Jeffrey M. Smith, *Genetic Roulette: The Documented Health Risks of Genetically Engineered Foods*
- Photo: Genetically Modified Tomatoes

Quarters 1, 2, 3, 4

Chapter 11 contains AP Favorites that can be grouped with other essays of the book or stand alone. They comprise some of the most recognized and appreciated fiction and nonfiction, spanning time periods and genre. The "favorites" are divided into mini-units that offer diverse activities for students. An emphasis on language, style, and voice are continually reinforced. Selections include:

- Maya Angelou, *Graduation*
- Francis Bacon, *Of Revenge*
- Francis Bacon, *Of Studies*
- Judy Brady, *I Want a Wife*
- Joan Didion, *Marrying Absurd*
- John Donne, *Meditation (No Man Is an Island)*
- Jonathan Edwards, *Sinners in the Hands of an Angry God*
- Queen Elizabeth I, *The Golden Speech*
- Ralph Waldo Emerson, *Education*
- Thomas Hobbes, *Leviathan*
- John F. Kennedy, *Inaugural Address*
- Martin Luther King, Jr., *Letter from Birmingham Jail*
- Abraham Lincoln, *Second Inaugural Address*
- Machiavelli, *The Prince*
- Nancy Mairs, *On Being a Cripple*
- Tim O'Brien, *The Things They Carried*
- George Orwell, *Shooting an Elephant*
- Plato, *Allegory of the Cave*
- David Sedaris, *Me Talk Pretty One Day*
- Brent Staples, *Black Men and Public Space*
- Jonathan Swift, *A Modest Proposal*
- Henry David Thoreau, *On the Duty of Civil Disobedience*
- Virginia Woolf, *A Room of One's Own*

Pacing Guide: Full-Year 50-Minute Classes

The first 11 weeks of the course present foundational writing units Chapters 1-3 and 13.

Week 1—Chapter 1: Active Reading and Response to Texts

Tasks Establish groups. Introduce course and textbook. Conduct first timed writing.

Lesson Plans
1.1 Introduction to Reading Actively
1.2 Questioning the Text and Preparing to Read (Prereading)
1.3 Teaching "From Ancient Greece to Iraq, The Power of Words in Wartime"

Timed Writing Lesson Plan 1.3 includes a timed writing assignment.

Week 2—Chapter 1: Active Reading and Response to Texts

Tasks Discuss first timed writing with "two-minute conferences." Introduce annotation. Introduce rhetorical analysis.

Lesson Plans
1.4 Teaching "How to Read a Book"
1.5 Annotating and Note Taking
1.6 The Art of Rhetorical Analysis

Timed Writing Have students peer review and edit their first timed writing.

Week 3—Chapter 1: Active Reading and Response to Texts

Tasks Introduce summarizing and paraphrasing. Introduce visual texts.

Lesson Plans
1.7 Summarizing & Paraphrasing
1.8 Analyzing Visual Texts

Timed Writing Provide students with a timed writing prompt as a diagnostic assessment. If you are not ready to use one of the College Board prompts from AP Central, consider providing a quotation that they must defend, challenge, or qualify. Sample: Albert Einstein's claim, "Imagination is more important than knowledge."

Week 4—Chapter 2: The Writing Process

Tasks Discuss and remind students of the steps in the writing process. Begin to teach modes of development.

Lesson Plans
2.1 Planning/Prewriting
2.2 Drafting Thesis Statements and Planning the Essay
2.3 Description, Narration, and Illustration
2.4 Process Analysis, Comparison and Contrast, and Causal Analysis

Timed Writing The timed writing will be developmental writing included with the lesson plans.

Week 5—Chapter 2: The Writing Process

Tasks Continue to teach modes of development. Teach conclusions and revision.

Lesson Plans
2.5 Definition, Classification, and Argumentation
2.6 Writing Conclusions and Revising
2.7 Responding to "The Maker's Eye: Revising Your Own Manuscripts" by Donald Murray
2.8 Responding to "Sex, Lies, and Conversation" by Deborah Tannen

Timed Writing Students will finish their "hero" essays. During the timed writing period, allow students to peer edit and revise their essays before submitting a final draft.

Week 6—Chapter 3: Argumentation and Synthesis

Tasks Introduce the language of argument and Aristotle's appeals.

Lesson Plans
3.1 Elements of Argumentation
3.2 Appeals and "The Gettysburg Address"
3.3 Writing Powerful Arguments

Timed Writing A prompt on "The Gettysburg Address" is included in Lesson Plan 3.3.

Week 7—Chapter 3: Argumentation and Synthesis

Tasks Introduce the argument fallacy. Read and discuss representative essays with students.

Lesson Plans
3.4 Recognizing Fallacies in Reasoning
3.5 Practicing an Argument Essay
3.6 Synthesizing: Making Connections
3.7 Teaching "The Art of Rhetoric"
3.8 Teaching "Common Sense"

Timed Writing A prompt is included in Lesson Plan 3.8.

Week 8—A Review

Tasks Review topics covered with students.

Lesson Plan 11.6 Kennedy and Lincoln—Annotating Inaugural Addresses

Portfolio writing This week, give students one or two class periods to work on a portfolio of their best writing from the first quarter. They should choose 2 "best" essays and write an explanation of why they were good. They should choose 1 "worst" essay and revise it with an explanation of what was wrong with the initial essay.

Week 9—Chapter 13: Writing a Research Paper (OPTION: Move to the end of the year.)

Tasks Teach the research process. Work with students toward the creation of a final research document.

Lesson Plans
13.1 Finding a Research-Worthy Topic
13.2 Conducting Research
13.3 Annotating Research

Timed Writing Forego timed writing this week in favor of one or two class periods of research in the library.

Week 10—Chapter 13: Writing a Research Paper (OPTION: Move to the end of the year.)

Tasks Continue the research process. Introduce argument synthesis as a part of the process.

Lesson Plans
13.4 Synthesizing the Sources
13.5 Peer Review
13.6 Writing the Research Paper

Timed Writing Allow students time during class to write their research papers.

Week 11—Chapter 13: Writing a Research Paper (OPTION: Move to the end of the year.)

Tasks Continue the research process. Consider using at least two class periods to have students present their research papers.

Lesson Plans
13.6 Writing the Research Paper
13.7 Writing a Surprise Synthesis Essay

Timed Writing Lesson Plan 13.7 presents a timed synthesis essay.

The remaining units follow the order presented in the Student Edition. Consider mixing and matching the units as the topics appear relevant to your course and to current events.

Week 12—Chapter 4: Education and Society

Tasks Compare the styles of two writers. Read and annotate significant nonfiction selections.

Lesson Plans
4.1 A Comparison of Style—Douglass and Rodriguez (Part 1)
4.2 A Comparison of Style—Douglass and Rodriguez (Part 2)
4.3 Timed-Writing: Synthesizing Classic and Contemporary Essays

Timed Writing Lesson Plan 4.3 includes timed writing suggestions.

Week 13—Chapter 4: Education and Society

Tasks Introduce Socratic questioning. Review annotation.

Lesson Plans
4.4 Socratic Seminar on Menand's "The Graduates"
4.5 Annotating and Questioning Gregorian's "America, Still on Top"
11.9 Orwell and Sedaris—A Study of Diction

Timed Writing Use this week's timed writing period to peer review and improve student essays on Douglass and Rodriguez (Lesson Plan 4.3).

Week 14—Chapter 4: Education and Society

Tasks Introduce the Four Corner Debate strategy. Continue Socratic questioning through the Fishbowl strategy.

Lesson Plans
4.6 Four Corner Debate on Mike Rose's "What College Can Mean to the Other America"
4.7 Fishbowl Discussion on Susan Jacoby's "When Bright Girls Decide that Math Is 'a Waste of Time' "
11.1 Angelou, Emerson, Plato—Debating the Nature of Education: A Four Corner Synthesis Lesson
4.8 Chapter Assessment—Connections for Critical Thinking
4.9 Synthesizing Sources: STEM vs. Liberal Arts—Is the STEAM Movement the Solution?

Timed Writing Lesson Plan 4.9 presents a timed writing synthesis assignment.

Week 15—Chapter 5: Family Life

Tasks Teach the comparison and contrast essay. Read and annotate significant nonfiction selections.

Lesson Plans
5.1 Comparison and Contrast Essay—White and Kingsolver (Part 1)
5.2 Comparison and Contrast Essay—White and Kingsolver (Part 2)
5.3 Synthesis: Comparison and Contrast Questions for Comparison

Timed Writing Lesson Plan 5.3 includes timed writing suggestions.

Week 16—Chapter 5: Family Life

Tasks Teach relevance of grammar/syntax. Continue Socratic questioning. Teach SOAPSTone strategy.

Lesson Plans
5.4 Annie Dillard: A Focus on Verbs
5.5 Brooks's "Love, Internet Style"—Socratic Seminar
5.6 Alvarez's "Once Upon a Quinceañera"—SOAPSTone Analysis

Timed Writing Peer review and revise essays written as part of Lesson Plan 5.3.

Week 17—Chapter 5: Family Life

Tasks Continue SOAPSTone strategy. Synthesize sources.

Lesson Plans
11.3 Brady and Woolf—A Woman's Place: Paired SOAPSTone
11.7 Didion, Mairs, Staples—Examining Marginalization Through Detail
5.7 Chapter Assessment—Connections for Critical Thinking
5.8 Synthesizing Sources: Helicopter Parenting

Portfolio writing This week, give students one or two class periods to work on a portfolio of their best writing from the second quarter. They should choose 2 "best" essays and write an explanation of why they were good. They should choose 1 "worst" essay and revise it with an explanation of what was wrong with the initial essay.

If you have not already done so, consider incorporating previously released prompts from the College Board's AP Central website during your weekly timed writing period.

Week 18—Chapter 6: History, Culture, and Civilization

Tasks Continue to recognize the rhetorical significance of syntax. Use jigsaw groups to strengthen analytical skills. Read and annotate significant nonfiction selections.

Lesson Plans
6.1 The Declaration of Independence—Study in Syntax
6.2 King's "I Have a Dream"—Jigsaw Group Analysis
11.4 Edwards and King—Rhetorical Analysis of the Great Preachers
6.3 Synthesizing Classic and Contemporary Essays: Timed-Writing

Timed Writing Lesson Plan 6.3 presents timed writing suggestions.

Week 19—Chapter 6: History, Culture, and Civilization

Tasks Provide a framework for timed writing. Provide a framework for research and the process of becoming informed on world issues. Continue SOAPSTone analysis.

Lesson Plans
6.4 Cofer's "The Myth of the Latin Woman"—Timed Writing with a Plan
6.5 Sen's "A World Not Neatly Divided"—SOAPSTone Analysis

Timed Writing Consider using Lesson Plan 6.4 early in the week, then peer edit and review this essay later in the week.

Week 20—Chapter 6: History, Culture, and Civilization

Tasks Analyze writing through reverse outlining. Explore the narrative process. Create and analyze graphic depictions of information. Synthesize sources.

Lesson Plans
6.6 Hall's "The Arab World"—Reverse Outlining
6.7 Satrapi's "The Veil"—Envisioning Narrative
6.8 Chapter Assessment—Connections for Critical Thinking
6.9 Synthesizing Sources: Women's Rights

Timed Writing Timed writing assignments are available as part of Lesson Plans 6.8 and 6.9.

Week 21—Chapter 7: Business and Economics

Tasks Recognize the importance of specific rhetorical structures. Read and annotate significant nonfiction selections.

Lesson Plans
- 7.1 Woolf's "Professions for Women"—Analyzing Rhetoric Through Structure
- 7.2 Gates's "Delusions of Grandeur"—Analyzing Purpose Through DIDLS
- 7.3 Synthesizing Classic and Contemporary Essays: Timed-Writing

Timed Writing Lesson Plan 7.3 presents timed writing suggestions.

Week 22—Chapter 7: Business and Economics

Tasks Provide a framework for timed writing. Provide a framework for research and the process of becoming informed on world issues. Continue the Fishbowl strategy.

Lesson Plans
- 7.4 Krugman's "The Death of Horatio Alger"—Writing and Analyzing Argument
- 7.5 Friedman's "Globalization: The Super-Story"—A Research Framework
- 7.6 Ehrenreich's "Nickel and Dimed"—Fishbowl Discussion

Timed Writing Consider using the released question 3 from the 2009 AP Language Exam Version B. This question refers to claims made by Ehrenreich on TV viewing.

Week 23—Chapter 7: Business and Economics

Tasks Continue focusing on details. Synthesize and write about the effects of economic issues on politics.

Lesson Plans
- 7.7. Reich's "Why the Rich Are Getting Richer, and the Poor, Poorer"—Gathering Relevant Details
- 11.5 Elizabeth, Hobbes, Machiavelli—Examining Ethics, Reason, and Power
- 7.8 Chapter Assessment—Connections for Critical Thinking
- 7.9 Synthesizing Sources: Online Shopping: Has It Affected Our Lives for Better or Worse?

Timed Writing Lesson Plans 7.8 and 7.9 both incorporate timed writing.

Week 24—Chapter 8: Media and Pop Culture

Tasks Compare two texts to analyze stereotypes. Discuss rhetorical appeals through a Socratic seminar.

Lesson Plans
- 8.1 Steinem's "Wonder Woman" and Barna's "Today's Leading Man"—Comparing Stereotypes
- 8.2 Bordo's "The Globalization of Eating Disorders"—An "Appealing" Socratic Seminar

Timed Writing Consider using the released question 3 from the 2008 AP Language Exam Version A. This question asks students to analyze corporate sponsorships of high school sports teams.

Week 25—Chapter 8: Media and Pop Culture

Tasks Connect detail to effect in analytical reading. Group evidence for topic sentences.

Lesson Plans
- 8.3 Ross's "Escape from Wonderland"—Connecting Detail to Effect

Timed Writing Use your timed writing period as part of Lesson Plan 8.3. Students will need two periods to fully complete the activities.

Week 26—Chapter 8: Media and Pop Culture

Tasks Perform a SOAPSTone analysis. Review syntax and diction. Synthesize sources.

Lesson Plans
- 8.4 Will's "Plumbing the Etiquette of Baseball"—SOAPSTone Analysis
- 11.2 Bacon and Donne—Simplifying Syntax and Diction
- 8.5 Chapter Assessment—Connections for Critical Thinking
- 8.6 Synthesizing Sources: Social Media—Has It Empowered Us or Disenfranchised Us?

Portfolio Writing This week, give students one or two class periods to work on a portfolio of their best writing from the third quarter. They should choose 2 "best" essays and write an explanation of why they were good. They should choose 1 "worst" essay and revise it with an explanation of what was wrong with the initial essay.

Week 27—Chapter 9: Literature and the Arts

Tasks Create imagery through sensory information. Consider artistic inspiration. Write synthesis essays.

Lesson Plans
- 9.1 Welty's "One Writer's Beginnings"—Writing with the Senses
- 9.2 Atwood's "Orwell and Me"—Analysis Jigsaw
- 9.3 Updike's "Moving Along"—Timed Synthesis

Timed Writing Lesson Plan 9.3 provides timed synthesis practice. Consider using your timed writing period to analyze and peer critique this essay.

Week 28—Chapter 9: Literature and the Arts

Tasks Use Socratic questions through the Fishbowl strategy. Analyze poetry using the TPCASTT strategy. Analyze an author using point by point close reading analysis.

Lesson Plans
- 9.4 Gates's "Finding Neverland"—Fishbowl Discussion with Connections
- 9.5 Hughes's "Theme for English B"—TPCASTT
- 9.6 Poe's "The Raven" and "The Philosophy of Composition"

Timed Writing Consider using the released question 1 from the 2007 AP Language Exam Version B. This particular question asks students to consider the decisions made by museum curators.

Week 29—Chapter 9: Literature and the Arts

Tasks Explore the importance of sentence variety. Synthesize information through writing.

Lesson Plans
- 11.8 The Things We Carry—A Creative Approach to Sentence Variety
- 9.7 Chapter Assessment—Connections for Critical Thinking
- 9.8 Synthesizing Sources: Living and Dying in Poetry and Art

Timed Writing Lesson Plans 9.7 and 9.8 both incorporate timed writing.

Week 30—Chapter 10: Nature and the Environment

Tasks Explore the importance of specific detail to rhetorical analysis. Review methods for comparison and contrast.

Lesson Plans
- 10.1 Eastman's "What Can the Out-of-Doors Do for Our Children?"—A Study in Detail
- 10.2 Lopez's "Children in the Woods"—Comparison & Contrast
- 10.3 Synthesizing Classic and Contemporary Essays—Timed-Writing

Timed Writing Lesson Plan 10.3 provides timed synthesis practice. Consider using your timed writing period to analyze and peer critique this essay.

Week 31—Chapter 10: Nature and the Environment

Tasks Explore causal analysis (cause and effect writing). Review rhetorical appeals. Improve analysis and argument skills through Four Corners Debate.

Lesson Plans 10.4 Bass's "Why I Hunt"—Recognizing Causal Analysis
10.5 McKibben's Rhetoric—Analyzing the Appeals
10.6 Carson's "The Obligation to Endure"—Four Corners Debate

Timed Writing Consider using the released question 2 from the 2009 AP Language Exam Version A. This particular question asks students to analyze two satirical points of view on the environment.

Week 32—Chapter 10: Nature and the Environment

Tasks Use the SOAPSTone strategy to analyze rhetoric. Discuss transcendental philosophy through a Fishbowl discussion.

Lesson Plans 10.7 Walker's "Am I Blue?"—A SOAPSTone Analysis
10.8 Twain's "Two Views of the Mississippi"—In-Class Essay
11.11 Thoreau—Fishbowl Discussion on the Politics of Transcendentalism

Timed Writing Lesson Plan 10.8 provides a timed in-class essay assignment.

Week 33—Chapter 10: Nature and the Environment

Tasks Recognize the use of classification. Write to synthesize.

Lesson Plans 10.9 Diamond's "The Last Americans"—Recognizing Classification
10.10 Chapter Assessment—Connections for Critical Thinking
10.11 Synthesizing Sources: GMOs—Are They Good for the World or Not?

Timed Writing Consider using the Released question 1 from the 2011 AP Language Exam Version A. This question asks students to consider the locavore movement.

Week 34—A Focus on Satire

Tasks Recognize and analyze satire.

Lesson Plan 11.10 Swift—Recognizing and Analyzing Satire

Timed Writing Consider using the released question 3 from the 2010 AP Language Exam Version A. This question asks students to analyze the role of humorists in society.

Week 35—Chapter 12: Sample Student Essays and Part 5: Practice Exam

Tasks Practice for the AP Exam—see Part 5 of the Student Edition. Analyze others' essays.

Lesson Plans 12.1 Synthesis Essay
12.2 Rhetorical Analysis Essay
12.3 Argument Essay

Portfolio Writing This week, give students one or two class periods to work on a portfolio of their best writing from the fourth quarter. They should choose 2 "best" essays and write an explanation of why they were good. They should choose 1 "worst" essay and revise it with an explanation of what was wrong with the initial essay.

Pacing Guide: Semester 90-Minute Blocks

The first six weeks of the course present foundational writing units Chapters 1-3 and 13.

Week 1—Chapter 1: Active Reading and Response to Texts

Tasks
Establish groups. Introduce course and textbook. Conduct first timed writing. Discuss first timed writing with "two-minute conferences." Introduce annotation. Introduce rhetorical analysis.

Lesson Plans
- 1.1 Introduction to Reading Actively
- 1.2 Questioning the Text and Preparing to Read (Prereading)
- 1.3 Teaching "From Ancient Greece to Iraq, The Power of Words in Wartime"
- 1.4 Teaching "How to Read a Book"
- 1.5 Annotating and Note Taking
- 1.6 The Art of Rhetorical Analysis

Timed Writing
Have students peer review a timed writing assignment in Lesson Plan 1.3.

Week 2—Chapter 1: Active Reading and Response to Texts/Chapter 2: The Writing Process

Tasks
Introduce summarizing and paraphrasing. Introduce visual texts. Discuss and remind students of the steps in the writing process. Begin to teach modes of development.

Lesson Plans
- 1.7 Summarizing & Paraphrasing
- 1.8 Analyzing Visual Texts
- 2.1 Planning/Prewriting
- 2.2 Drafting Thesis Statements and Planning the Essay
- 2.3 Description, Narration, and Illustration
- 2.4 Process Analysis, Comparison and Contrast, and Causal Analysis

Timed Writing
Provide students with a timed writing prompt as a diagnostic assessment. Consider providing a quotation they must defend, challenge, or qualify. Sample: Albert Einstein's claim, "Imagination is more important than knowledge."

Week 3—Chapter 2: The Writing Process/Chapter 3: Argumentation and Synthesis

Tasks
Continue to teach modes of development. Teach conclusions and revision. Introduce the language of argument and Aristotle's appeals.

Lesson Plans
- 2.5 Definition, Classification, and Argumentation
- 2.6 Writing Conclusions and Revising
- 2.7 Responding to "The Maker's Eye: Revising Your Own Manuscripts" by Donald Murray
- 2.8 Responding to "Sex, Lies, and Conversation" by Deborah Tannen
- 3.1 Elements of Argumentation
- 3.2 Appeals and "The Gettysburg Address"
- 3.3 Writing Powerful Arguments

Timed Writing
A prompt on "The Gettysburg Address" is included in Lesson Plan 3.3.

Week 4—Chapter 3: Argumentation and Synthesis

Tasks Introduce the argument fallacy. Read and discuss representative essays.

Lesson Plans
3.4 Recognizing Fallacies in Reasoning
3.5 Practicing an Argument Essay
3.6 Synthesizing: Making Connections
3.7 Teaching "The Art of Rhetoric"
3.8 Teaching "Common Sense"
11.6 Kennedy and Lincoln—Annotating Inaugural Addresses

Timed Writing A prompt is included in Lesson Plan 3.8.

Week 5—Chapter 13: Writing a Research Paper

Tasks Teach the research process. Work toward the creation of a final research document. Introduce argument synthesis as a part of the process.

Lesson Plans
13.1 Finding a Research-Worthy Topic
13.2 Conducting Research
13.3 Annotating Research
13.4 Synthesizing the Sources
13.5 Peer Review
13.6 Writing the Research Paper

Timed Writing Allow students time during class to write their research papers.

Week 6—Chapter 13: Writing a Research Paper

Tasks Continue the research process. Consider using two periods for students to present research papers.

Lesson Plans
13.6 Writing the Research Paper
13.7 Writing a Surprise Synthesis Essay

Timed Writing Lesson Plan 13.7 presents a timed synthesis essay.

The remaining units follow the order presented in the Student Edition. Consider mixing and matching the units as the topics appear relevant to your course and to current events.

Week 7—Chapter 4: Education and Society

Tasks Compare the styles of two writers. Read and annotate significant nonfiction selections. Introduce Socratic questioning.

Lesson Plans
4.1 A Comparison of Style—Douglass and Rodriguez (Part 1)
4.2 A Comparison of Style—Douglass and Rodriguez (Part 2)
4.3 Timed-Writing: Synthesizing Classic and Contemporary Essays
4.4 Socratic Seminar on Menand's "The Graduates"
4.5 Annotating and Questioning Gregorian's "America, Still on Top"
11.9 Orwell and Sedaris—A Study of Diction

Timed Writing Lesson Plan 4.3 includes timed writing. Peer review and improve student essays on Douglass and Rodriguez (Lesson Plan 4.3).

Week 8—Chapters 4 and 5: Education and Society/Family Life

Tasks Introduce the Four Corner Debate strategy. Continue Socratic questioning through the Fishbowl strategy. Teach the comparison and contrast essay. Read and annotate significant nonfiction selections.

Lesson Plans
- 4.6 Four Corner Debate on Mike Rose's "What College Can Mean to the Other America"
- 4.7 Fishbowl Discussion on Susan Jacoby's "When Bright Girls Decide that Math Is 'a Waste of Time' "
- 11.1 Angelou, Emerson, Plato—Debating the Nature of Education: A Four Corner Synthesis Lesson
- 4.8 Chapter Assessment—Connections for Critical Thinking
- 4.9 Synthesizing Sources: STEM vs. Liberal Arts—Is the STEAM Movement the Solution?
- 5.1 Comparison and Contrast Essay—White and Kingsolver (Part 1)
- 5.2 Comparison and Contrast Essay—White and Kingsolver (Part 2)
- 5.3 Synthesis: Comparison and Contrast Questions for Comparison

Timed Writing Lesson Plans 4.9 and 5.3 present timed writing suggestions. Peer critique.

Week 9—Chapter 5: Family Life

Tasks Teach relevance of grammar/syntax. Continue Socratic questioning. Teach SOAPSTone strategy.

Lesson Plans
- 5.4 Annie Dillard: A Focus on Verbs
- 5.5 Brooks's "Love, Internet Style"—Socratic Seminar
- 5.6 Alvarez's "Once Upon a Quinceañera"—SOAPSTone Analysis
- 11.3 Brady and Woolf—A Woman's Place: Paired SOAPSTone
- 11.7 Didion, Mairs, Staples—Examining Marginalization Through Detail
- 5.7 Chapter Assessment—Connections for Critical Thinking
- 5.8 Synthesizing Sources: Helicopter Parenting

Portfolio Writing Give students one class period to work on a portfolio of their best writing from the first quarter. They should choose 2 "best" essays and write an explanation of why they were good. They should choose 1 "worst" essay and revise it with an explanation of what was wrong with the initial essay.

Week 10—Chapter 6: History, Culture, and Civilization

Tasks Continue to recognize the rhetorical significance of syntax. Use jigsaw groups to strengthen analytical skills. Read and annotate significant nonfiction selections. Provide a framework for timed writing. Provide a framework for research and the process of becoming informed on world issues. Continue SOAPSTone analysis.

Lesson Plans
- 6.1 The Declaration of Independence—Study in Syntax
- 6.2 King's "I Have a Dream"—Jigsaw Group Analysis
- 11.4 Edwards and King—Rhetorical Analysis of the Great Preachers
- 6.3 Synthesizing Classic and Contemporary Essays: Timed-Writing
- 6.4 Cofer's "The Myth of the Latin Woman"—Timed Writing with a Plan
- 6.5 Sen's "A World Not Neatly Divided"—SOAPSTone Analysis

Timed Writing Lesson Plan 6.3 presents timed writing suggestions. Consider using Lesson Plan 6.4 early in the week, then peer edit and review this essay later in the week.

Week 11—Chapters 6 and 7: History, Culture, and Civilization/Business and Economics

Tasks Analyze writing through reverse outlining. Explore the narrative process. Create and analyze graphic depictions of information. Synthesize sources. Provide a framework for timed writing. Provide a framework for research and the process of becoming informed on world issues. Continue the Fishbowl strategy.

Lesson Plans
- 6.6 Hall's "The Arab World"—Reverse Outlining
- 6.7 Satrapi's "The Veil"—Envisioning Narrative
- 6.8 Chapter Assessment—Connections for Critical Thinking
- 6.9 Synthesizing Sources: Women's Rights
- 7.1 Woolf's "Professions for Women"—Analyzing Rhetoric Through Structure
- 7.2 Gates's "Delusions of Grandeur"—Analyzing Purpose Through DIDLS
- 7.3 Synthesizing Classic and Contemporary Essays: Timed-Writing

Timed Writing Timed writing assignments are available as part of Lesson Plans 6.8, 6.9, and 7.3.

Week 12—Chapter 7: Business and Economics

Tasks Provide a framework for timed writing. Provide a framework for research and the process of becoming informed on world issues. Continue the Fishbowl strategy. Continue focusing on details. Synthesize and write about the effects of economic issues on politics.

Lesson Plans
- 7.4 Krugman's "The Death of Horatio Alger"—Writing and Analyzing Argument
- 7.5 Friedman's "Globalization: The Super-Story"—A Research Framework
- 7.6 Ehrenreich's "Nickel and Dimed"—Fishbowl Discussion
- 7.7 Reich's "Why the Rich Are Getting Richer, and the Poor, Poorer"—Gathering Relevant Details
- 11.5 Elizabeth, Hobbes, Machiavelli—Examining Ethics, Reason, and Power
- 7.8 Chapter Assessment—Connections for Critical Thinking
- 7.9 Synthesizing Sources: Online Shopping: Has It Affected Our Lives for Better or Worse?

Timed Writing Consider using the released question 3 from the 2009 AP Language Exam Version B. This question refers to claims made by Ehrenreich on TV viewing. Lesson Plans 7.8 and 7.9 also incorporate timed writing.

Week 13—Chapter 8: Media and Pop Culture

Tasks Compare two texts to analyze stereotypes. Discuss rhetorical appeals through a Socratic seminar. Connect detail to effect in analytical reading. Perform a SOAPSTone analysis. Synthesize sources.

Lesson Plans
- 8.1 Steinem's "Wonder Woman" and Barna's "Today's Leading Man"—Comparing Stereotypes
- 8.2 Bordo's "The Globalization of Eating Disorders"—An "Appealing" Socratic Seminar
- 8.3 Ross's "Escape from Wonderland"—Connecting Detail to Effect
- 8.4 Will's "Plumbing the Etiquette of Baseball"—SOAPSTone Analysis
- 8.5 Chapter Assessment—Connections for Critical Thinking
- 8.6 Synthesizing Sources: Social Media—Has It Empowered Us or Disenfranchised Us?

Timed Writing Use the released question 3 from the 2008 AP Language Exam Version A, which asks students to analyze corporate sponsorships of high school sports teams.

Week 14—Chapter 9: Literature and the Arts

Tasks Create imagery through sensory information. Consider artistic inspiration. Write synthesis essays. Use Socratic questions through the Fishbowl strategy. Analyze poetry using the TPCASTT strategy.

Lesson Plans
9.1 Welty's "One Writer's Beginnings"—Writing with the Senses
9.2 Atwood's "Orwell and Me"—Analysis Jigsaw
9.3 Updike's "Moving Along"—Timed Synthesis
9.4 Gates's "Finding Neverland"—Fishbowl Discussion with Connections
9.5 Hughes's "Theme for English B"—TPCASTT

Timed Writing Lesson Plan 9.3 provides timed synthesis practice. Consider using your timed writing period to analyze and peer critique this essay.

Week 15—Chapter 9: Literature and the Arts

Tasks Analyze an author using point by point close reading analysis. Explore the importance of sentence variety. Synthesize information through writing.

Lesson Plans
9.6 Poe's "The Raven" and "The Philosophy of Composition"
11.8 The Things We Carry—A Creative Approach to Sentence Variety
9.7 Chapter Assessment—Connections for Critical Thinking
9.8 Synthesizing Sources: Living and Dying in Poetry and Art

Timed Writing Lesson Plans 9.7 and 9.8 both incorporate timed writing. Consider using the released question 1 from the 2007 AP Language Exam Version B. This question asks students to consider the decisions made by museum curators.

Week 16—Chapter 10: Nature and the Environment

Tasks Explore the importance of specific detail to rhetorical analysis. Review methods for comparison and contrast. Explore causal analysis (cause and effect writing). Review rhetorical appeals. Improve analysis and argument skills through Four Corners Debate.

Lesson Plans
10.1 Eastman's "What Can the Out-of-Doors Do for Our Children?"—A Study in Detail
10.2 Lopez's "Children in the Woods"—Comparison & Contrast
10.3 Synthesizing Classic and Contemporary Essays—Timed-Writing
10.4 Bass's "Why I Hunt"—Recognizing Causal Analysis
10.5 McKibben's Rhetoric—Analyzing the Appeals
10.6 Carson's "The Obligation to Endure"—Four Corners Debate

Timed Writing Lesson Plan 10.3 provides timed synthesis practice. Consider using the released question 2 from the 2009 AP Language Exam Version A. This particular question asks students to analyze two satirical points of view on the environment.

Week 17—Chapter 10: Nature and the Environment

Tasks Use the SOAPSTone strategy to analyze rhetoric. Discuss transcendental philosophy through a Fishbowl discussion. Recognize the use of classification. Write to synthesize.

Lesson Plans
10.7 Walker's "Am I Blue?"—A SOAPSTone Analysis
10.8 Twain's "Two Views of the Mississippi"—In-Class Essay
11.11 Thoreau—Fishbowl Discussion on the Politics of Transcendentalism
10.9 Diamond's "The Last Americans"—Recognizing Classification
10.10 Chapter Assessment—Connections for Critical Thinking
10.11 Synthesizing Sources: GMOs—Are They Good for the World or Not?

Timed Writing Lesson Plan 10.8 provides a timed in-class essay assignment. Consider using the released question 1 from the 2011 AP Language Exam Version A. This question asks students to consider the locavore movement.

Week 18—A Focus on Satire/Chapter 12: Sample Student Essays/Part 5: Practice Exam

Tasks Recognize and analyze satire. Practice for the AP Exam—see Part 5 of the Student Edition. Analyze others' essays.

Lesson Plans
11.10 Swift—Recognizing and Analyzing Satire
12.1 Synthesis Essay
12.2 Rhetorical Analysis Essay
12.3 Argument Essay

Timed Writing Consider using the released question 3 from the 2010 AP Language Exam Version A. This question asks students to analyze the role of humorists in society.

Portfolio Writing Give students one class period to work on a portfolio of their best writing from the second quarter. They should choose 2 "best" essays and write an explanation of why they were good. They should choose 1 "worst" essay and revise it with an explanation of what was wrong with the initial essay.

Introduction

This AP Edition Teacher Manual was written by an AP teacher for AP teachers. It provides resources, ideas, and best practices to guide you in teaching college-level English AND to help you help your students prepare for the AP Exam. Chapters 1–3 are devoted to foundational reading and writing strategies and instruction. Chapters 4–10 provide groupings of essays related to specific themes. You can teach the thematic essays in any order, but the lesson plans that accompany the essays become increasingly more challenging as students progress through the Student Edition. Chapter 11 contains a compendium of "AP Favorites." Several hundred AP teachers were polled about their favorite essays, and Chapter 11 presents strategies to teach those favorite works. Chapter 12 includes three real students' essays—and the opportunity to help your students break down what works and seek to imitate it. After this foundational material and groupings of essays, Chapter 13 is devoted to the research paper process. Finally, answers and scoring rubrics for the AP Language and Composition Practice Exam can be found in Part 5 of this Teacher Manual.

The lesson plans were written to provide you with ample opportunities to teach synthesis, rhetorical analysis, and argument, all while helping to develop not just the test-taking skills of your students, but also their critical thinking and general writing capabilities. It is our hope that the material in this Teacher Manual, combined with the wide variety of material in the Student Edition, will enable you to teach your best course ever.

1. ***Develop Active Consciousness.*** The "what" here is that students read actively. Push them to define those terms. What does it mean to read actively? The "how" you want students to address is active engagement. If students pick up on the word "passive" as it is used in the text, encourage them to define that word. What does *passive* mean? The "why" involves the sort of questioning that will make them better readers. Students need to be pushed to recognize that their opinions are valuable. Not only do they have the right to question a text, but they have the responsibility to do so.

2. ***Read Attentively.*** The "what" of this strategy is simply the ability to maintain focus while reading. The "how" will vary widely by student. Many students claim that they simply cannot read because they fall asleep, or they *will* not read because the piece is boring. Usually, however, this conversation will involve some actual helpful discourse. Some students will find that they read better while listening to music. Others might be able to read only when the surrounding environment is absolutely quiet. The "why" can be discovered by asking students if they have ever found themselves reading a book, only to realize that they do not know what happened in the previous page or pages. Explain that every reader has "zoned out" at some time—even English teachers. Acknowledging this problem will give readers confidence to relate to the instruction.

3. ***Paraphrase.*** This is a key skill that is covered thoroughly later in this chapter. At this point, it is important that students recognize the "what" of paraphrasing involves restating what they have already read. The "how" involves jotting down notes in margins or in a reader's notebook. The "why" involves fulfilling the two strategies discussed so far—active consciousness and reading attentively. Ask students if the strategy of paraphrasing will help them stay focused. Will it help them read actively? *(Yes!)*

4. ***Ask questions.*** As students read, they must learn to talk to the text. If they are truly reading actively, there will always be moments when they wish the writer had been clearer. The "what" of asking questions encompasses the 5 W's and 1 H questions (Who? What? Where? When? Why? How?) about the content, structure, and purpose of a piece. The "how" of asking questions can involve sticky notes or margin notes or a reader's journal. The "why" of asking questions is to enable the reader to engage the material in a more thorough manner.

5. ***Control your biases.*** The "what" relates to one's prejudices. Many students believe they do not hold biases. The textbook provides a political spectrum example, but you may want to add general statements such as "All corporate CEOs are corrupt" or "All senior citizens drive too slowly" to point out that these are also biases students may hold. The "how" involves dealing with these prejudices—discovering them and setting them aside as students read the views of others. The "why" refers back to what it means to be literate. In order to be literate—and certainly to be literary—students must consider multiple points of view. In addition, this is an excellent opportunity to point out to students that part of the AP experience is learning not just facts and skills; rather, the AP experience is about becoming a richer, fuller learner. It is about developing our intellectual muscles, and reading diverse opinions helps us do exactly that.

Class Closer

Ask students to work with the same partner they had at the beginning of the class, and re-evaluate what it means to be literate. Ask pairs to expand their original definition by adding no more than 5 words to their original definition.

Homework

For homework, ask students to actively read the textbook section **Questioning the Text** on page 5, and to write three or four discussion questions they would pose to the author of the textbook. (Make sure students understand the difference between a discussion question and a fact-based, comprehension question.)

Establishing Groups
Throughout this Teacher Manual, you will find descriptions of group activities. It is helpful to define groups early in the year and to change those groups at somewhat regular intervals—every 9 or 12 weeks, for example. The composition of the groups is not important, but establishing group norms is. Here are some pointers for establishing those norms: • Do *not* allow students to establish their own groups. • Keep the groups small—a group of three or four is ideal. • Give students ownership of their group. • Allow students to name their group (within reason, of course). • Give students a folder that holds group work, and keep these folders in a single location in your classroom. • Consider establishing two separate groupings. If conflicts develop, groups will be easier to manage if students do not have to work with exactly the same people every day. (For example, establish a "stars" grouping and a "stripes" grouping. Post on a "class notes" area of the board either a large star or a series of stripes. Students will know which group to sit with when they enter the room on a given day.)

Lesson Plan 1.2

Questioning the Text and Preparing to Read (Prereading)

This lesson follows up on the previous activity about reading actively, and it incorporates the following homework assignment: Read the subsection **Questioning the Text** and write three or four discussion questions to ask the writer of the textbook. One tip to suggest to students as they attempt this for the first time is to begin one of their questions with *what*, one with *how*, and one with *why*, keeping in mind that they should not be able to point to the answer in the text. For example, "What color is Daisy's dress?" (in *The Great Gatsby*) simply requires a recall answer. However, "What is the metaphorical significance of Daisy wearing white when she meets with Gatsby?" is a far deeper question on the level of analysis. Writing good questions serves two purposes: (1) Students who write good questions are analyzing as they read and are far better equipped for class discussions. (2) Students who write good questions intrinsically understand the questions they need to answer when they are writing an essay.

The activities that follow will use those questions to introduce the **"Fishbowl" classroom strategy**, which will be repeated throughout this Teacher Manual. The idea behind the Fishbowl strategy is simple: student-generated questions go into the fishbowl; discussion comes out. You do not need an actual fishbowl to utilize this strategy, but you will require some sort of container ("cauldron," cookie jar, and so on) into which students will deposit questions on slips of paper. An Internet search shows several variations on this strategy, with most variations having a group of "listeners" and a group of "speakers." You may use any variation of the strategy you like best—the goal is simply to have students create their own questions *and* participate in group discussion.

Class Opener

In groups, students will review the questions they developed as homework. It is important that you ensure all students completed the assignment to set the pattern for successfully functioning groups for the entire year. Create a class list and walk around the room checking off names of those who wrote questions. Each group should select four questions from all submitted. Ask students to focus on questions that will invite conversation, rather than comprehension, yes/no, or absolute answer questions. Allow a minimum of 5 minutes for this discussion among group members.

Activity: Discussion of Fishbowl Questions

It is tempting to start class discussion by going over what students have read for homework, but it is advisable *not* to do that in this case. One of your goals is to hold students accountable for their reading. With some essays, you will *have* to help them grasp meaning. This is not one of those selections. If students read the text actively, they will be able to participate in a discussion.

Begin the activity by asking each group to place the questions they liked best from their discussion into the fishbowl. Make a point of mixing up the questions well. Invite a student to come forward and draw a question from the bowl. The student will then read the question aloud, and the class will discuss their interpretation of the answer. Continue until a question from each group has been selected and discussed.

Activity: Developing Questions as Guides for Reading Actively

Ask the class to read **Preparing to Read** and to look at the **Guidelines for Reading Actively** on page 10 of the text (and included on the next page). Although you are not yet teaching students rhetorical analysis, this chart provides an excellent summary of what it means to read rhetorically. When you teach rhetorical analysis, strive to help students recognize four main elements: (1) context, (2) meaning, (3) motivation, and (4) methods. In the Guidelines chart, the first three bulleted statements together define "context," or the background information. The next four bullets together define "meaning," or *what* the author writes. The next bullet addresses motivation—*why* the author is writing. The final two bulleted statements address the methods—*how* the author creates meaning and demonstrates purpose.

Guidelines for Reading ACTIVELY
• *Who* is the author? Look for connections about his or her life experiences and the topic of the piece. (*Headnotes*, or author introductions that appear at the start of the essays in this book, provide some of this information.) If there is more than one author, what is the personal or professional relationship between these writers?
• Note *when* the selection first appeared. How is that significant?
• Note *where* the selection first appeared. (This information often appears at the end of the selection in the *copyright* line.) What do you know about this publication? Is the text an entire selection, an excerpt, or part of a chapter? What difference might that make to you, the reader?
• What is significant about the title? Does the title present the author's general subject in a straightforward way, hint at the topic, or create a sense of mystery, irony, or humor?
• Determine the author's purpose *(why)*: to entertain; to evoke emotion or provoke action; to promote, teach, or investigate an idea; or some combination of these.
• How does the author organize the essay? What constitutes the introductory section, the body or middle of the essay, and the conclusion? Do subdivisions or numbered sections exist, and how are they linked logically? Do there appear to be any missing links?
• What is the author's main point, or the stated or implied answer to whatever question the essay poses or explores? The author may state the main point (also termed a *thesis* or *claim*) clearly and concisely in the introduction, place it elsewhere in the text, permit it to evolve slowly, or require you to infer it after reading the entire essay.
• Determine how well other assertions or narratives in the essay support the main point. What evidence does the author use? Does sufficient information or evidence support the main point?
• Visualize the author's original readers or "audience," and notice how the author adjusts both the argument and the elements of *style*—language, sentence structure, and complexity of thought—to this audience.
• Become conscious of how your personal experience affects your response to the author's ideas. Everyone approaches reading with a set of assumptions and biases. How do your own assumptions and biases influence your response?

For this activity, students should examine the questions in the Guidelines chart and, in their groups, distill all the bulleted guidelines into a series of four questions. Provide them with these four elements: context, meaning, motivation, and methods.

Ask them to work in their groups to create a short list of what particular question they must answer for each element. What they are designing is an understanding of the essential function of what it means to read as an engaged participant.

Class Closer

As a closing activity, ask students to provide their list of four questions to the class. After the groups have shared, develop a list of four questions that, as a class, everyone can agree are the most important questions to answer as they are reading a selection. Consider posting the list in the classroom.

Homework

For homework, ask students to read the essay "From Ancient Greece to Iraq, the Power of Words in Wartime" by Robin Tolmach Lakoff in the textbook. Have students also review the questions that follow the essay.

Lesson Plan 1.3

Teaching "From Ancient Greece to Iraq, The Power of Words in Wartime"

Time the class opener activity carefully, because you want to give students a 40-minute block for the main activity.

Class Opener

Lakoff's essay considers our need to rename those we see as "other." Although Lakoff considers renaming or categorizing in relation to war, categorizing (or classifying) is also a phenomenon that high school students will relate to. Ask students to consider the nicknames given to various groups of students. What does it mean to be a nerd, a prep, a jock, and so on? Allow no more than 5 minutes for this discussion, which may become heated but can also provide students with a starting point for the essay they will write today.

Activity: Writing an In-Class Essay

Although some teachers may want to wait longer before assigning an in-class essay, requiring students to write an argument/persuasive essay during the first week of school is an excellent way to both introduce the writing process and debunk students' fears about writing. You will not grade this writing assignment, but do plan on spending the very next class period discussing the essay in one-on-one writer conferences with very specific critique. See specific tips in the **Two-Minute Writer Conference** on page 8 of this Teacher Manual.

Provide students with the following prompt, either by writing it on the white board or projecting it. Allow students exactly 40 minutes to write a response.

> **Lakoff argues, "Bullets and bombs are not the only tools of war. Words, too, play their part." In a well-reasoned essay, defend, challenge, or qualify the claim that words can be used as "tools of war." Support your argument with specific evidence from your reading, observation, and experience.**

Two-Minute Writer Conference

Plan early in the year to talk one-on-one with your students about their writing. For some students, releasing their writing to anyone for critique is debilitating. Provide positive, constructive feedback early and often. Follow these tips for constructive writer conferences:

- Read and make notes on the essays before the conference.
- Discuss every student's writing in one class period. Do not make any student wait anxiously until the next class period for feedback. Therefore, watch your time. You may have only 2 minutes per student, which is not ideal but possible.
- Have a plan. Know what you want to discuss with your writers and cover those details quickly.
- Call up the first writer. (Tell the next writer in your stack he or she is on deck.) Ask the first writer what he/she wrote on the index card in response to the statement: "Please tell how you felt about the writing assignment yesterday."
- Start with positive feedback. Point out at least one thing the writer did well. Does the writer use a compelling example? If so, start with that.
- Focus on the basics this early in the year. If the student seems to struggle with grammar, point out one thing they need to work on related to grammar. Typical stumbling blocks for high school writers include subject-verb agreement, pronoun use, unclear referents (that ignominious "it"), use of "you" when not directly addressing an audience, over-use of linking verbs, among others.
- Next, point out one non-grammar issue related to rhetoric and the way the essay is structured. Determine whether the thesis statement and topic sentences are arguable and clear. Do the topic sentences further the argument made in the thesis? How are the paragraphs structured? Are examples relevant and well-developed? Using the QOE portion of the holistic rubric on page 9 will give you starting points for talking with student writers.
- Give your writers only two or three things to work on. No amount of instruction will help them fix every bad habit in a single try.

NOTE: If you are not ready to introduce timed writing yet, there are other ways to work with this essay. See page 10 in this Teacher Manual for **Alternative Approaches to Teaching** "From Ancient Greece to Iraq, The Power of Words in Wartime."

Class Closer

Before they turn in their essays, ask every student to go back and underline his or her main idea of the essay, or thesis statement. Then ask for volunteers to read their statements. When a student reads the thesis statement, ask other students to rate it on a point scale of 1 through 5, where 1 is not arguable and 5 is absolutely arguable. Collect the essays.

Homework

Before class ends, write the following instructions on the board: "On an index card, in two or three sentences, please tell how you felt about the writing assignment today." Explain that, during the next class, you will discuss their essays privately, and they are to bring their completed index cards.

This time, and this time only, you need to be ready to give feedback the very next day. Plan for a night of essay reading and note-making. This is the perfect time to employ holistic grading skills. See the QOEGV approach to essay grading in the chart below.

Holistic Grading: QOEGV Approach

For years, holistic grading of essays has been the holy grail of English instruction. The most cumbersome part of being an AP English Language teacher (and yet the most rewarding) is reading student work. Although most teachers enjoy reading essays, few relish the hours spent making margin notes on every page as we correct grammatical errors and strive to craft perfection out of high school-level work. In reality, only a very few students take the time to read through all those comments, and even fewer apply those comments to future writing endeavors. Holistic grading allows teachers to spend less time grading and more time focusing on the big picture. Because we are able to paint our commentary with a broad brush, students are better able to incorporate our lessons into their future writing endeavors. True holistic grading (like the scoring conducted at the College Board annual reading) requires a true internalization of the scoring guidelines. The one-read, accurate holistic scoring process does exist, but it takes practice and time. The following approach provides a level of scaffolding for teachers (and students!) working toward that internalization.

One approach to holistic grading that has been around for some time is referred to by the acronym QOEGV: Question, Organization, Evidence, Grammar, Voice. (A Google search of the acronym will quickly yield the full rubric.) The idea behind this approach is simple. Grade each essay according to three criteria. Add two additional criteria only if the essay was not written in class. Each criterion is graded on a scale of 1 to 3, and then those three scores are added together to yield a final score of 3-9. The teacher must determine his or her own grading standards, but often a score of 8 or 9 is an A, 6 or 7 is a B, 5 is C, 4 is D, and 3 is F.

A shortened, modified version of the grading works like this:	
Q (Question): How well does the student address the prompt? Is the essay focused on answering the question? Does the thesis statement make a claim related to the prompt?	✓+ = 3 ✓ = 2 ✓− = 1
O (Organization): How well does the student organize the essay? Are topic sentences arguable? Do they further the thesis? Do paragraphs follow a logical progression? Are paragraphs balanced?	✓+ = 3 ✓ = 2 ✓− = 1
E (Evidence): How well does the student incorporate evidence? Is evidence relevant? Is evidence tied to a claim? Does the student use the evidence in such a way as to prove his or her thesis?	✓+ = 3 ✓ = 2 ✓− = 1
G (Grammar): Are grammatical errors present? Do they impede the reader's ability to understand the message? **(Use only if students write outside of class or are given time to revise.)**	✓− = −1
V (Voice): Is the voice so authentic, so real, so good that you just have to give the writer bonus points? **(Use this only when extra points are truly warranted.)**	✓+ = +1
Total Points	

Activity: Alternative Approaches to Teaching "From Ancient Greece to Iraq, The Power of Words in Wartime"

Here are several ways you might prefer to teach this essay if you are not yet ready to introduce timed writing.

CLASS DISCUSSION OF PROMPT Instead of having students write an essay in response to the earlier prompt, broach it aloud in class for a discussion: How might active thinkers agree or disagree with Lakoff's assertion: "Bullets and bombs are not the only tools of war. Words, too, play their part"?

Those who agree with Lakoff's claim may do so on the grounds that propaganda is an effective tool not only for experienced politicians but also for children on the school playground. The art of propaganda has grown so sophisticated that it is no longer possible to determine whether marketers or military strategists are leading the field. Those who disagree with Lakoff's claim might make a case for the chicken vs. the egg argument. They might inquire whether it is the disposition of the species at a given time that gives rise and meaning to new language or if it is the advent of new language that cultivates the disposition of a group of people at any given time.

DISCUSSING VERBAL "IDENTITY" According to the essay, naming the Other can serve as a way to control them. "Just the fact that we can name them," Lakoff argues, "gives us a sense of superiority and control." Invite students to reflect on moments and events in their lives in which they sought to leverage control over someone using the power of language. Have students consider their own age group's use of language and how that language indicates their group's identity and location in a society's chain of command.

COMPARING "WARTIME" VERSUS "PEACETIME" VALUES AND BELIEFS It has been argued repeatedly and successfully in many cultures that, during wartime, civilian rules are secondary or suspended entirely. One claim is that the needs of the state during war supersede the needs of civil society because, in order to continue, the latter requires the protection of the former. We have, however, seen that government-sponsored murder is genocide unless one's cause can be justified (witness those in Armenia, Nazi Germany, Cambodia, Rwanda, or that against Native Americans). Language that reassures civilians and members of the military that they are working for a greater good is part of the justification process. The phrase, *the end justifies the means*, is a case in point. It is understood to mean that the outcome of an action determines its moral value. If a good consequence follows, then the action that led to said consequence was a moral one. This is how killing during war is not considered murder.

Have students list and compare values and beliefs that emerge during wartime and times of peace. Brainstorm examples of the language associated with each:

Compare Values and Beliefs		
WAR	**Values**	**Beliefs**
	Freedom	must be defended
	Life	may be sacrificed
	Accountability	to one's unit and superiors
	Conformity	essential to survival
	Success	defined as larger than personal interest(s)
PEACE	**Values**	**Beliefs**
	Freedom	must be preserved
	Life	is to be enjoyed
	Accountability	to self, one's God, family
	Conformity	not essential
	Success	largely defined by personal interest(s)

DISCUSSING CROSSOVER LANGUAGE OR CODE-SWITCHING List examples of "crossover" language in popular culture and discuss the power of appropriation. Crossover or code-switching language refers to the appropriation of a new style (especially in popular music) by combining elements of different genres in order to appeal to a wider audience. Have students generate examples of phrases coined for one purpose that were later applied in entirely different contexts. Some dated examples of slang/crossover language in popular culture include:

Phat: not 'fat'; a good-looking female
4-1-1: to get or give someone the information about someone or something
24/7: all the time
pigs/popo: cops or police officers

Code-switching gives its practitioners power. Whoever controls the meaning, controls the message. It has always been true that the more vocabulary and/or languages one masters, the more one can participate in the meaning-making process. Language has been evolving since the first word was spoken. As the contexts in which humans find themselves change, language changes to accommodate these changing contexts.

Suggested Answers

"From Ancient Greece to Iraq, the Power of Words in Wartime"
by Robin Tolmach Lakoff

Comprehension

1. Assume that the major question raised by Lakoff's essay is "How is language a tool of war?" Summarize her answer, which is the main point. HINT: Her point in this essay is NOT "we can or should abolish war," as even the author likely does not believe this.

In wartime, certain actions are taken that would in civil society be considered criminal. Soldiers and a supportive public must be conditioned to countenance atrocities that human nature inherently resists. Lakoff suggests that soldiers and civilians "need to believe that what their country is doing is just and necessary." Lakoff illustrates ways that language is used as a tool in such conditioning by discussing multiple ways in which "language developed for military purposes" reassures both groups "that war is not murder."

You might encourage students to look for evidence of the use of language in this way and discuss the consequences of successful verbal conditioning. One key area to include in any discussion of how soldiers are prepared for military service is the words used to describe soldiers themselves. What happens over time to a man, young or old, who is called a "grunt" and treated accordingly? When he is dehumanized, it becomes easier for him to dehumanize in turn. It comes then as no surprise that since the 1940s, the language used to signify "to kill" has also changed over time. According to Linguist Robert Beard in "Warspeak: Linguistic Collateral Damage" (Dr. Goodword's Office), euphemisms for the necessary evil of killing have evolved from "take care of" and "take for a ride" during World War II; to "rub out," "bump," "knock off," and "eliminate" in the 1960s; to "waste," "smoke," and "blow away" during the Vietnam War; to "off," "hit," "clip," and "whack" in the 1980s and 1990s; to the current terminology, taken from a CIA manual, of "neutralize."

2. Evidence typically consists of direct observations (verifiable facts) combined with the writer's interpretation of those observations to establish the main point. What types of evidence does Lakoff use? Distinguish her observations from her interpretations.

In her argument that each side must be made to see the other as "killable," Lakoff provides historic examples of racial epithets used to reduce members of one army in the eyes of another.

Sample Evidence:

- "An American soldier refers to an Iraqi prisoner as "it."
- "Under normal conditions, most people find it difficult to kill."
- "Just the fact that we can name them gives us a sense of superiority and control."
- "The Greeks and Romans referred to everyone else as "barbarians."

Sample Interpretations:

- "The word "enemy" itself provides the facelessness of a collective noun." (The word *enemy* has been so frequently used that it has lost much of its charge.)
- "The reasoning is: They are not really human, so they will not feel the pain." (Is that actually the reasoning?)

Rhetorical Analysis

3. **What is the tone of the essay? What can you infer from this tone about Lakoff's emotional relationship to language used in wartime?**
   Lakoff's tone is that of hopeful pessimism. The conclusion to this article restates the author's thesis that words can make the unthinkable not only thinkable but inevitable, and introduces the possibility that if a people wanted to put an end to torture and humiliation, the end of war itself would become inevitable. Further, she states the premise that "human beings are . . . genetically hard-wired to feel compassion toward others."

4. **How does Lakoff's diction—the words she herself uses rather than the authors she quotes—contribute to her tone?**
   Lakoff's use of collective nouns suggests that she believes and/or would have readers believe that all members of the human family value human life; that we would not, under normal circumstances, condone or participate in torture; and that we are receptive to well-constructed arguments about the power of language to persuade, condition, and reclaim identities both individual and national.

Lesson Plan 1.4

Teaching "How to Read a Book"

Class Opener

Describe a situation in which an individual (or yourself) left a social event and then proceeded to mentally reconstruct and analyze the conversations that had occurred throughout the evening. Ask students if they have had a similar experience. What types of questions ran through their minds as they later replayed the evening's conversations? Write students' questions and the following questions on the board: What did the person mean by what s/he said? How did the person arrive at such a particular conclusion? Which part of the conversation did the speaker stress most? What did some of the words mean? Explain that these types of questions about a verbal conversation are exactly like the questions one should ask in a "conversation with text."

Activity: Annotating with Sticky Notes

Have students take out a small stack of sticky notes, and, using the questions and ideas from the **Reading Actively** section of the chapter, read "How to Read a Book" actively, making notes (annotating the text) with sticky notes. If your students have personal copies of the textbook, have them annotate directly in the text. After they have finished reading and annotating, ask students to answer the Comprehension and Rhetorical Analysis questions in their groups.

Class Closer

At the end of class, discuss students' answers (see below). Especially take time to discuss the Rhetorical Analysis questions on the next page with students.

Homework

Have students choose an online article or essay from a popular website, and ask them to cut and paste the text into a new document. Then have them locate "Track Changes" (or a similar editing feature) in their word-processing program, and experiment with using this software to mark the article electronically. Ask students to determine whether Track Changes is as useful as the more traditional reading practices advocated by Adler. Why or why not? Which method of marking a text appeals more to students, and why? There is no single correct answer to this, but be sure students' responses are backed up by specific, detailed reasons.

Suggested Answers

"How to Read a Book" by Mortimer J. Adler and Charles Van Doren

Comprehension

1. Summarize what Adler means by "marking up a book."

Adler does not mean mere note taking but, rather, the process of what is today called "active reading," perhaps more appropriately "interactive" reading or, as Adler states, "a conversation." Adler suggests that marking a book is an evolutionary act, one that is continuously being revised as the reader gains new insight through further reading and experience.

2. In your own words, explain how you believe Adler would define the phrase "reading a book" in our modern age.

Adler alludes to a book as having a presence, something the reader can make a part of oneself.

3. What does Adler suggest the reader use the front and back endpapers for?

The back endpapers should be used as an index of the author's points in order of appearance. The front endpapers should be used as a record of the reader's thinking: a personal outline of the work.

Rhetorical Analysis

4. What is the tone of the essay? What can you infer from this tone about Adler's emotional relationship to books?

Adler's tone is that of an advocate and cheerleader. It is obvious that he is his own best example of the ideal reader.

5. Paragraph 6 lists devices for marking a book. What if Adler had written the list in paragraph form rather than numbering them? What if he had listed them with bullets? Would the tone have changed? Would your perception have changed? Why?

Adler is known for his Aristotelian bent concerning philosophy. Definition, explanation, and hard and fast rules fit within this description, as does his list for marking a book. The list also duplicates the way Adler explains how to mark a book with numbers in the margin and on other pages. For the reader who has devised or devises his or her own system of "close readings," the list may seem a bit despotic.

6. Study the rhetorical format of paragraph 4. What strategy is Adler employing?

These are examples of a persuasive style of discourse. The question is asked and then answered. This method of argumentation is effective because it demonstrates that the author already knows competing arguments surrounding his position, and, hence, can "preemptively" disarm them.

7. Adler uses the analogy that "reading a book should be a conversation between you and the author." What other analogies can you find in the essay?

Possible responses include the outline as a measure of understanding; a bookplate as intellectual ownership; marking a book as a form of respect for an author.

Lesson Plan 1.5

Annotating and Note Taking

This lesson is about annotating and questioning the text. At this point, students are working toward what will eventually be rhetorical analysis. They are learning to read actively, and it is time to move them toward the what-why-how that will enable them to truly understand complex prose. The assignments that follow will introduce a complicated version of the double-entry journal. Students have probably had some experience with double-entry journals in their earlier classes, but at this point in their academic sojourn, they will find that it is time to add a column or two and create multiple-entry journals. The multiple-entry journal format will reappear with some frequency in this Teacher Manual. This approach forces students to move past simply reading an essay for comprehension and into the realm of rhetorical analysis.

Class Opener

This activity will take longer than a traditional bellringer, but establishing the strategy of the multiple-entry journal is important. Have students return to the Lakoff essay they read earlier in the chapter. Ask them to quickly fill in the chart below (write on the white board or distribute as a worksheet—**see Chapter 1 online, Chapter Assignments, Multiple-Entry Journal).**

Multiple-Entry Journal		
Lakoff's purpose:		
A quotation that demonstrates this purpose (What)	**Your rationale for why this quotation demonstrates Lakoff's purpose (Why or Commentary)**	**A description of what is unique about the writing style (How)**

Possible Responses:

Multiple-Entry Journal		
Lakoff's purpose: To connect the power of language to the horrors of war		
A quotation that demonstrates this purpose (What)	**Your rationale for why this quotation demonstrates Lakoff's purpose (Why or Commentary)**	**A description of what is unique about the writing style (How)**
"So some terms of war are collective nouns, encouraging us to see the enemy as an undifferentiated mass, rather than as individuals capable of suffering." (paragraph 12)	Lakoff juxtaposes describing the enemy as a cancerous conglomeration of flesh, a mass, to the concept of individualism and suffering. Cancer does not suffer, it causes suffering. By choosing such charged language, Lakoff demonstrates that language, a powerful tool, can be used to dehumanize war.	Lakoff begins this sentence with the very informal word "So," making her claim seem somewhat conversational and encouraging the reader to accept her argument as just another bit of friendly discourse. Lakoff chooses words that can either be read as medical terminology or as an attempt at gross anti-individualism, "an undifferentiated mass," to demonstrate the power of words to create discomfort and even instill hatred.

Activity: Multiple-Entry Journaling of "The Cult of Ethnicity"

As a class, read "The Cult of Ethnicity" on pages 26-29 of the textbook, asking students to stop and read the marginal annotations and other markings provided at the point of contact. Challenge students to use the multiple-entry journal they used at the beginning of class to analyze this essay. In their groups, they should choose three quotations and analyze the "why" and "how" of each quotation.

Class Closer

Ask groups to share their journal entries with the class. This will be an excellent opportunity for you to help them focus on differentiating meaning, motivation, and method.

Homework

Ask students to write their favorite quotation on one side of an index card. On the other side, they should provide the how/why as they did earlier with their multiple-entry journal. In addition, they should read the section **The Art of Rhetorical Analysis**, beginning on page 15 of the textbook.

Discussion Questions

"The Cult of Ethnicity" by Arthur M. Schlesinger, Jr.

Comprehension

1. What impact on the reader do you think the author or editor of this article's headline intended to have through the use of the word *cult*?

Often the term "cult" is used to indicate the members of a group of people on the margins of society, who share a particular or particularly questionable set of beliefs. The writer of the article's headline is perhaps suggesting that the forces pushing for ethnicity are similarly marginal.

2. What might bring a historian to the conclusion that, "[e]thnic and racial conflict—far more than ideological conflict—is the explosive problem of our times"?

A survey of the origins or exciting causes of conflicts around the globe today would indicate that, at the core of most conflicts is a rivalry between factions of a shared geographic region, cultural background, or historic heritage.

3. What, according to Schlesinger, has the American nation been able to do that other countries with members from diverse ethnic groups have not yet managed to do as successfully?

Schlesinger argues that America, better than other nations, has been able to integrate, assimilate, and welcome more immigrants from disparate regions and peoples than any other nation to date. Peaceful coexistence has been America's great achievement and example to the world.

Rhetorical Analysis

4. What are some possible effects on the reader of listing many nationalities before, during, and after mention of Crevecoeur's *promiscuous breed*? How does doing so set the stage for mention of Zangwill's 1908 play, *The Melting Pot*?

Schlesinger's lists are inclusive and therefore cast no aspersions on any one group in particular. The author's use of such details adds credibility to his claim.

5. What arguments does Schlesinger employ to build the case for the existence of a cult of ethnicity?

The author provides readers with examples of healthy and unhealthy consequences to build his case for the existence of the cult of ethnicity.

6. How does the author use the contrasting of healthy and unhealthy consequences to suggest a hidden, presumed subversive, agenda on the parts of those "well-intentioned individuals" who promote, celebrate, and perpetuate distinguishing among and between ethnic identities? Does such a practice come at the expense of national unity?

The healthy consequence of the creation of a cult of ethnicity is the creation of faceted or complicated notions of identity for members of both privileged and invisible groups within society. The unhealthy consequence, Schlesinger claims, is a herd mentality among members of those groups that flies in the face of the rugged individualism upon which the nation was founded. The author suggests that this consequence plays right into a focus on *pluribus* (the many) at the expense of *unum* (the unity) of this nation's people.

7. **Is Schlesinger's use of the term *hullabaloo* to characterize the shift toward multicultural curriculum and instruction calculated to raise or lower the reader's esteem for such practices?**

   Hullabaloo is a term used to signify a "fuss," not something one might consider fundamental or foundational such as multicultural education and the esteem in which it is held by anti-racism educators. Schlesinger's use of the term indicates the side of the debate he advocates. It indicates his lack of esteem for the shift toward multicultural curriculum and instruction.

8. **Upon what historical facts might the author base his claim that Europe is "the unique source of the liberating ideas of democracy, civil liberties and human rights"?**

   Schlesinger might base his claim that the ideas of democracy originated in Europe on the dawn of the Greco-Roman enlightenment and resulting texts that capture the early yearnings of Greeks and Romans for freedom given voice in the tragedies and epics of that and subsequent periods. French writer Alexis de Tocqueville's *Democracy in America* is also standard fare in American history and social studies classes, and it discusses at length many supports for this premise.

9. **Is the author's zero-sum argument that, "[t]he balance is shifting from *unum* to *pluribus*" tenable? Are the unity and diversity conceived of by the American nation's founding fathers mutually exclusive? Explain.**

   Schlesinger's argument is tenable if one concedes that this balance is always in flux as it is the very fulcrum on which the theory and practice of democracy rests. The ideals of unity and diversity are inseparable because, in practice, one is unsustainable without the other. For "many" to exist, *pluribus* must be comprised of several single units. The more confident each unit is in its independent value to the whole, the more harmonious interactions among the several parts will be. According to Carlos Cortés, in "Limits to Pluribus, Limits to Unum" (*National Forum,* Vol. 74, Winter 1994), the "*pluribus* values as freedom, individualism, and diversity live in constant and inevitable tension with such *unum* values as authority, conformity, and commonality." This summarizes the challenge and opportunity of any viable democracy.

Lesson Plan 1.6

The Art of Rhetorical Analysis

Class Opener

As students enter the classroom, ask them to answer this question written on the board: "What is rhetoric?" Aristotle defined *rhetoric* simply as "the available means of persuasion." While some students may have negative associations with the term *rhetoric*, the original study of rhetoric is largely positive. When we study rhetoric, we are simply studying an author's attempt to persuade us to adopt a particular point of view. When we analyze rhetoric, we are pulling apart the devices, the strategies, and the modes the author has employed to convince us of their particular view of the world.

Activity: Reviewing the Rhetorical Triangle

Students may have learned about the Aristotelian or rhetorical triangle in an earlier English class. Explain that the rhetorical triangle shows how elements interact to create meaningful content. Review students' knowledge by describing the parts of the rhetorical triangle as you draw them on the board. See the completed rhetorical triangle diagram on page 21.

The First Triad refers to the three *points* of the rhetorical triangle.

- At the top of the triangle is the **writer** or **speaker**. This could also be the ***persona*** or character that the writer creates to be the voice for the piece.
- In order to write, the speaker needs something to discuss—a **subject or topic**.
- The writer must also be aware of "who" is going to read the work—the **audience** or **reader**.
- In order for authors to achieve their **purpose**, all three points of the triangle must be addressed with fairly equal attention.

It may be helpful to provide students with a scenario:

We are learning to analyze rhetoric in class today. The topic or subject is rhetorical analysis. I am here as your speaker, presenting to you a particular frame of reference for how to understand rhetoric. You are here today to learn about rhetorical analysis with an interest in doing well in this class and eventually achieving a qualifying score on your AP Exam. These are our points on the rhetorical triangle.

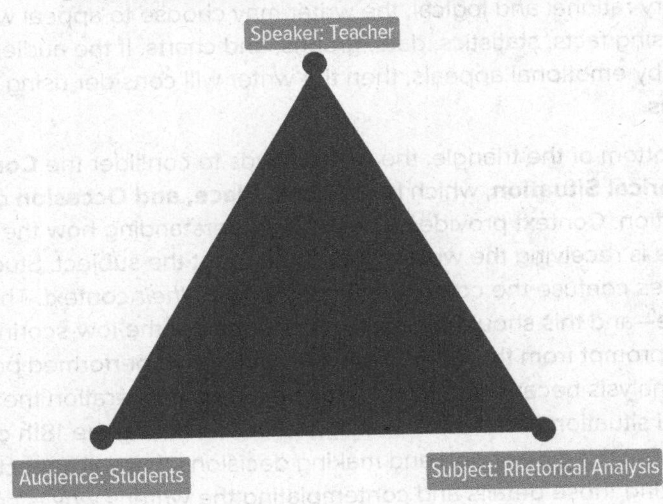

Now suppose that a single point on this triangle were ignored. What if I, as your speaker, didn't come to class today? You would still need to learn rhetorical analysis, but you wouldn't be able to achieve that purpose without a speaker. What if you, as the audience, didn't come to class today? I'd be here—talking about rhetorical analysis, but we couldn't achieve our purpose because the audience would not be present to receive the message. Similarly, what if the subject were not here? What if neither you nor I knew that we needed to discuss rhetorical analysis today? We could talk about the news. We could write a persuasive essay. We could even discuss what we had for dinner or watched on TV last night. But we couldn't achieve our purpose.

We often speak of *author's purpose* when we are teaching students to write or read critically. But the achievability of author's purpose involves the author/speaker, the audience, and the subject working in concert toward a similar goal. The author must reach the audience and must stay focused on the subject. The subject must be relevant to both the author and the audience. And the audience must have some connection to both the subject and the author. Once we've established the three points of the triangle, we must move to the sides.

The three *sides* of the triangle are called the Second Triad.

- To say something meaningful about a topic, a writer needs to have a point he or she is making. Therefore, the writer develops an **assertion**, a **thesis**, or a **main idea** about the subject. Students tend to think of thesis statements as a single sentence found in the first paragraph of a passage—after all, this is how they are taught to write! In complex writing, however, the thesis is seldom found so clearly or so cleanly. Sometimes it must be inferred. Often it is found farther down in the passage—even at the very end of a piece. Students need to consider how the author develops an argument, always considering how the thesis achieves a **purpose.**

- On the other side of the triangle, the writer needs to get the audience's attention—and keep it. To do so, the writer has to decide how best to **appeal** to the audience. The writer might establish an ethical appeal through **ethos or ethics** by showing that he is credible and trustworthy. The writer could also allude to shared values and beliefs with the audience. If the audience appears to be very rational and logical, the writer may choose to appeal with **logos or logic**—using facts, statistics, data, graphs, and charts. If the audience can be swayed by emotional appeals, then the writer will consider using **pathos or emotions**.

- At the bottom of the triangle, the writer needs to consider the **Context** or **Rhetorical Situation**, which is the **Time, Place, and Occasion** of the composition. Context provides a basis for understanding how the targeted audience is receiving the writer's message about the subject. Students sometimes confuse the context of the writer with *their* context. These are not the same—and this should be addressed. Consider the low-scoring rhetorical analysis prompt from the 2014 Exam. Many students performed poorly on this analysis because they failed to take into consideration the unique rhetorical situation of a mother writing to her son during the 18th century as he is approaching manhood and making decisions that will impact his future. Recognizing those details and contemplating the writer's *why* is critical to adequately analyzing any selection.

The *inner group* of terms is called the Third Triad. It can be completed after reading the selection.

- The author's **tone** is his or her attitude or feeling toward the subject. Students often struggle with tone. By comparing the connotative diction in a selection—that is, by isolating words that are associated with either positive or negative values—students frequently are able to better ascertain what particular tone a writer is employing.
- The **rhetorical modes** are the methods the writer uses to structure his writing. By having students jot "mode notes" in the margins of the selection they are reading, they can better navigate the multiple modes a writer employs in a particular device.

- **Rhetorical devices** are the tools the writer uses to create meaning and to deliver his or her message. Although devices are important, they must always be analyzed in terms of how they create meaning within the piece. Most students can identify rhetorical devices; however, identification alone is not enough. An essay that merely points to asyndeton, alliteration, repetition, and juxtaposition simply shows that the student has a reasonable command of domain-specific vocabulary. It is far more important for students to be able to connect a device to *effect* and *meaning*. For example, rather than merely noting that a writer uses asyndeton, the student might explain how the omission of conjunctions in an author's style has the effect of creating a melancholy tone. Students might elaborate how this style choice creates a feeling in the reader that the lists could go on forever, and that neither the writer nor the reader is to be granted closure within the passage.

Aristotelian or Rhetorical Triangle

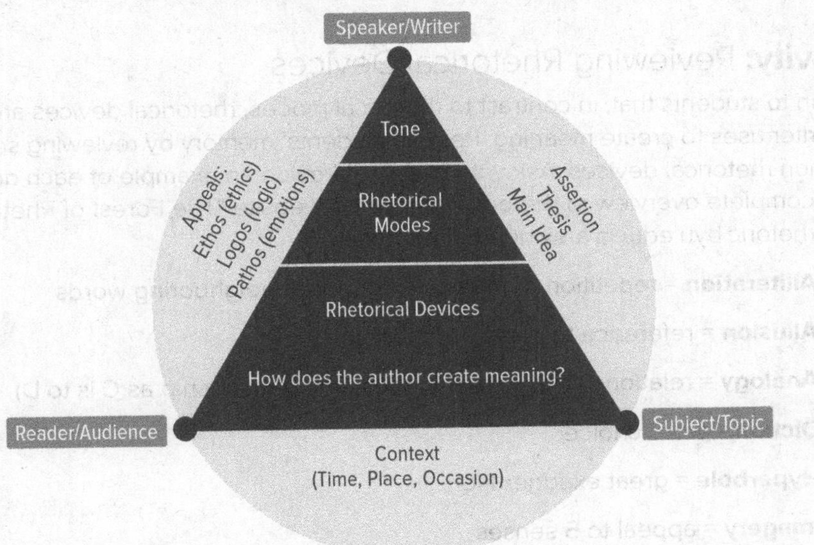

Activity: Reviewing Rhetorical Modes

Explain that rhetorical modes are just methods or patterns of speaking and writing that help a writer develop his or her ideas. Point out that rhetorical modes are linked to the writer's purpose for writing. Review with students the purposes and rhetorical modes on the next page.

Purpose	Rhetorical Mode
To narrate, to tell a story	Narration
To define, to explain what a term means	Definition
To describe	Description
To classify	Classification
To present a process; to show how something is done	Process Analysis
To give examples	Exemplification
To explain what causes a result	Cause and Effect
To compare and contrast	Comparison/Contrast
To analyze; to show how separate parts work to create the whole	Analysis
To convince or persuade	Persuasion; Argumentation

Activity: Reviewing Rhetorical Devices

Explain to students that, in contrast to rhetorical modes, rhetorical devices are tools the writer uses to create meaning. Refresh students' memory by reviewing several common rhetorical devices. Ask volunteers to provide an example of each device. For a complete overview of rhetorical terms, the website "The Forest of Rhetoric" at http://rhetoric.byu.edu/ is a wonderful resource.

- **Alliteration** = repetition of the same sounds in neighboring words
- **Allusion** = reference to history or literature
- **Analogy** = relationship (A is to B in the same relationship as C is to D)
- **Diction** = word choice
- **Hyperbole** = great exaggeration
- **Imagery** = appeal to 5 senses
- **Irony** = contradiction between what is said and what is meant
- **Juxtaposition** = side-by-side
- **Metaphor and Simile** = comparison
- **Parallel structure** = same sentence patterns
- **Personification** = giving inanimate objects human characteristics
- **Repetition** = repeating a remark
- **Satire** = to ridicule in order to elicit change
- **Symbolism** = concrete items that represent abstract ideas
- **Syntax** = sentence structure

Class Closer

Ask students to scan the **Rhetorical Table of Contents** in the front of the student textbook. Have them quiz one another in pairs as to the purpose of various essays according to their rhetorical modes.

Homework

Ask students to scan the editorials in a recent newspaper or newsmagazine. Have them find three examples of rhetorical devices used in the editorials, write the excerpts and devices in their journals, and bring them to class to share. Another homework option is to have students find song titles that exhibit rhetorical devices: "I Want You, I Need You, I Love You" (parallelism); "While My Guitar Gently Weeps" (personification); "Just Like Romeo & Juliet" (allusion); "You Ain't Nothin' But a Hound Dog" (metaphor); "Endless Love" (hyperbole); etc.

Lesson Plan 1.7

Paraphrasing and Summarizing

Class Opener

Use this activity to launch into a discussion of paraphrasing. As soon as students have entered the classroom, ask for a volunteer to relate in detail what his/her history teacher told the class yesterday. When the student has finished, ask another student to repeat what the first student related. Repeat this with a third student. Ask a fourth student to write on the board what the history class was about. (This will take less than five minutes.)

Activity: Practicing Paraphrasing

As a class, read the section **Paraphrasing** on page 30 of the text. Help students see what makes a paraphrase successful or unsuccessful. In pairs, have students revisit the essay "How to Read a Book." Each pair will be assigned a different paragraph to paraphrase. When they have completed their paraphrases, place each pair's paraphrase on the document camera to project for the class (or read aloud if a document camera is not available.) The class will determine if each paraphrase is successful or unsuccessful.

Activity: Practicing Summarizing

Read together the textbook section **Summarizing** on pages 31–32. Look at the sample summary provided and help students understand why it is useful. Make sure they recognize that the author of the summary has retold the essay in her own words.

Ask students to look back at "How to Read a Book," and then introduce the following method of summarizing similar to the **GIST method of summarizing:** Working in their groups, students must find 6 to 8 key words in the essay. Using each of those key words, the groups must write a 100-word summary of the essay. After the group has created a 100-word summary, challenge students to shorten it to 50 words. Then task them with creating a 25-word summary. Finally, ask them to summarize it in 10 words.

Class Closer

As a closing activity, ask groups to choose which summary they feel is most accurate. Discuss that summary with the class.

Homework

For homework, ask students to read **Quoting** and **Avoiding Plagiarism** on pages 33–34 in the textbook. Plagiarism will be discussed in further detail during the research paper process in Chapter 13.

Lesson Plan 1.8

Analyzing Visual Texts

Class Opener

Ask students to write a short paragraph describing the outfit they are wearing today. After they have completed this paragraph, ask them to write a second short paragraph analyzing that outfit. What argument are they making through their clothing choice? How do they want people to see them?

Activity: Learning to Analyze Visuals

Explain to students that *visual rhetoric* refers to a wide variety of analytical and pedagogical practices. In particular, it refers to the practice of analyzing and/or describing how images communicate meaning or advance arguments. It may be thought of as the rhetorical analysis of images using the familiar rhetorical vocabulary (such as *ethos, pathos,* and *logos*), but with a supplementary vocabulary unique to the analysis of the visual (e.g., with reference to color, graphic design, iconography, etc.). Although the object of visual rhetorical inquiry can be virtually limitless as long as images of some kind are involved, these subjects frequently include advertising, iconic or contemporary photography, film, maps, and Web design. And, yes, visual rhetoric can be thought of as the art of seeing.

Display a painting or an advertisement before the class. Direct students to the three points presented in the textbook on page 35, as well as the questions to ask that can guide one's analysis of visual texts (see below):

1. **The purpose of the visual**—for example, to inform, instruct, persuade, entertain
2. **The context of the subject matter**—cultural ideas associated with people or items in the image
3. **The overall emotion conveyed by the image**—pride, attraction, revulsion, fear, amusement, and so on—and how that emotional effect is created (shapes, colors, textures, and symbols used; how lines, shapes, and colors focus attention in the image)

Questions for analysis:

- What are the design elements, format, and structure of the visual? Is it black and white, or are other colors used? How does the placement of design elements affect the message?

- Is the image abstract or realistic—or both? What is the relationship among the elements making up the image?
- Does the image have a historical or cultural context necessary to understand it?
- Who is the intended audience? Does the image call for a specific audience response?
- What textual information do you immediately notice? What is the relationship between image and text?
- What is the purpose of the visual? What emotions or attitudes does the image convey?
- What thesis or point of view does the information in the visual suggest?
- What is the nature of the evidence, and how can it be verified?
- What emphases and relationships do you detect among the visual details?

Activity: Drawing Conclusions Through OPTIC

Provide students with the **OPTIC** tool for analyzing visual text. As noted in *How to Study in College* (2001) by Walter Pauk, OPTIC is a mnemonic device for remembering five key elements of analyzing visuals. This method has been used in classrooms for many years.

- **O** is for Overview. Conduct a brief initial overview of the visual.
- **P** is for Parts. Scrutinize the visual for parts that can be obvious or subtle for any further information. This is a precursor to the "**I**" that is two steps down.
- **T** is for Title (and/or captions). Read the title (or captions) and study it for meaning. What is it "saying" about the visual?
- **I** is for Interrelationships. Consider how the title and the parts are interrelated and/or connected.
- **C** is for Conclusion. Based on the steps you have taken, draw and infer conclusions about the visual's meaning.

Activity: Analyzing Advertisements

Ask students to analyze the advertisements on pages 38–39. This is an excellent opportunity to practice recognizing *ethos, pathos, logos,* and the intersectionality among these appeals in visual texts. Remind students that when writers create an appeal to *ethos*, they are attempting to persuade the audience to agree with them because they are experts in their fields and/or they are good people. When writers create an appeal to *pathos*, they are pulling at the audience's heartstrings by making the audience relate in a meaningful and personal way to the subject. They may do this by offering personal examples and narrative or by evoking sensory imagery. When writers create an appeal to *logos*, they are appealing to the audience's scientific reasoning, or innate logic that wants to prove things with numbers, hard data, and facts.

In the textbook, students are presented with a number of advertisements. Allow students to choose their own advertisement, or assign specific advertisements to groups. Provide students with the following guiding questions and graphic organizers to facilitate their analysis of visuals. **(See Chapter 1 online, Chapter Assignments, Analyzing Advertisements.)**

Guiding Questions

1. What are your eyes drawn first to in the advertisement? Describe in detail only the image you see first.
2. After taking a second look at the advertisement, what do you see? Describe in detail.
3. How does the advertisement employ color? What colors do you see, and what is the impact?
4. How does the advertisement employ text? What text is on the advertisement? Do the creators employ any recognizable rhetorical devices in their creation of the text?
5. Consider how the designers of the advertisement create an appeal to *ethos*. That is, how do they establish their credibility and make the viewer trust them? Describe the element, and then consider the effect this element has on the audience, on the presentation of the subject, and on the viewer's understanding of the nature of the "speaker."

Element from the advertisement that appeals to *ethos*	Effect on *audience*	Effect on our understanding of the *subject*	Effect on our understanding of the *speaker*

6. Consider how the designers of the advertisement create an appeal to *pathos*. That is, how do they elicit an emotional response from the audience? Describe the element, and then consider the effect this element has on the audience, on the presentation of the subject, and on the viewer's understanding of the nature of the "speaker."

Element from the advertisement that appeals to *pathos*	Effect on *audience*	Effect on our understanding of the *subject*	Effect on our understanding of the *speaker*

7. Consider how the designers of the advertisement create an appeal to *logos*. That is, what sorts of facts, statistics, or incontrovertible data do they provide? Describe the element, and then consider the effect this element has on the audience, on the presentation of the subject, and on the viewer's understanding of the nature of the "speaker."

Element from the advertisement that appeals to *logos*	Effect on *audience*	Effect on our understanding of the *subject*	Effect on our understanding of the *speaker*

8. In your opinion, which of the appeals is the most persuasive? Explain your answer in a convincing and compelling paragraph response.

Possible Responses

Appeal to *ethos*

Element from the advertisement that appeals to *ethos*	Effect on *audience*	Effect on our understanding of the *subject*	Effect on our understanding of the *speaker*
Nexium Ad: Man wearing a tie	Professional attire leads viewers to take the ad seriously.	The drug is associated with professional careers.	The drug maker is serious about its product.
Army Recruitment Ad: Stern, unsmiling woman wearing combat gear	We can entrust our national safety in the hands of this leader.	Women can be successful in the army.	The army includes tough women as leaders and soldiers.

Appeal to *pathos*

Element from the advertisement that appeals to *pathos*	Effect on *audience*	Effect on our understanding of the *subject*	Effect on our understanding of the *speaker*
Perfume Ad: In casual pose, Beyoncé with outstretched arm looks at the viewer	Viewers feel that Beyoncé is reaching for them.	The perfume will make us as attractive as Beyoncé.	The perfume maker is respected by megastars.
Pur Water Ad: Child and pet dog drinking clean water	Viewers want to keep their children and pets healthy.	Viewers believe the water filter will create healthy children and pets.	Viewers feel the water purification company really cares about their health.
Chinese Family Planning Ad: Smiling father, mother, and daughter reaching for dove	Parents will fulfill patriotic and spiritual duty by having only one child.	The one-child policy will lead to a happy family.	Smiling ancestors (on left of sign) approve of the state's family-planning policy.

Appeal to *logos*

Element from the advertisement that appeals to *logos*	Effect on *audience*	Effect on our understanding of the *subject*	Effect on our understanding of the *speaker*
Nexium Ad: Data and supportive information on both sides of the man's tie	All the lines of text look like important information.	Dire physical problems occur with this disease, which Nexium can cure.	The responsible drug maker has performed medical studies. It also provides a phone number for additional medical support.

Activity: Analyzing Graphs and Tables

Charts, graphs, and tables appear frequently as part of the Synthesis prompt on the annual AP Exam. In order to effectively use the data graphs contain, students must understand not just the data included in the visual representation, but also the data that is consciously left out. For this activity, students will create questions based on analyzing the three visual representations of data on pages 43–45 of the textbook.

Provide these instructions to students: *For this segment of class, you will be analyzing data that has been represented visually. In these visuals, a certain amount of data is provided, but there is other data that is not considered. Today you are to be a skeptic and determine any bias that seems inherent in the graphical depictions of the data. Working in groups, create 6 questions for each graphic. Your first set of 3 questions must consider the data that is included in the graphic. Your second set of 3 questions must consider data that is not included in the graphic. Remember to consider the speaker, the subject, and the audience as you write your questions.*

Students may consider questions along the following lines: Why does the age range begin at 16 years old? Where was the research conducted? Did this phenomenon only begin in 1980? After groups have a number of questions, allow them to pose their questions to the class, and discuss the graphs from the standpoint of potential bias.

Class Closer

Ask students to analyze the **Classic and Contemporary Images** feature on pages 46–47 of the textbook and consider the accompanying questions. Discuss students' analyses and share with them the answers on the next page.

Classic and Contemporary Images: Suggested Answers

1. **How does Rosenthal's photo show movement? Does Franklin's photo show the same movement? Explain.**

   Movement is shown in Rosenthal's photo through the fluttering of the flag, the soldiers' arms and bodies reaching upward and forward, and the lunge of the marine on the far right. Franklin's photo does not show the same type of movement—the flag is being raised but hangs down in the still air, while the firemen stand upward and raise the flag in sober deliberation.

2. **Where does the use of diagonal lines draw your eyes to the centerpiece of each photo?**

   The diagonal flagpole in each image draws one's eyes to the flag at first glance. Then the eye follows the flagpole to the marine (in first image) planting the pole in the ground; and to the fireman's hand (in second image) as it adjusts the ropes to the flag. The diagonal white pipe and what appears to be a piece of canvas also "contain" the firemen in the image.

3. **How do the men in each photo reveal "determination" in different ways?**

   The marines, through their upraised arms, strong hold on the flagpole, and lunging bodies, show their determination to securely plant the flag into what appears to be rocky ground. The firemen, through their respectful and careful manipulation of the ropes on the flag, and their eyes focused on the unstable flagpole, show their determination to raise the American symbol above the devastation of the building.

4. **Study the setting surrounding the group of people in each photo. What effect does the setting have on your emotional response to each image?**

   In Rosenthal's photo, the marines appear to be atop a rocky, war-torn hill above a vast plain. The vast setting makes the marines appear victorious and yet vulnerable at the same time. In Franklin's photo, the dust-coated firemen appear surrounded by debris, which rises above them and off to their sides. Even so, the firemen appear to have found a small space to proclaim that America still stands firm against terrorism, and the fact that all three people in the photo are firemen reminds the viewer that these three men honor their fallen coworkers.

CHAPTER 2
The Writing Process

In this chapter, students are introduced to the writing process and to modes of writing. The official course description for AP Language and Composition requires that students be able to "move effectively through the stages of the writing process, with careful attention to inquiry and research, drafting, revising, editing and review" (College Board). As AP English teachers, we must teach students to honor the writing process even as we are teaching them to write in abbreviated periods of time.

The first six lesson plans in this chapter create a single unit, in which you will help students discover their inner writer. By the end of the unit, students will have developed a single essay that explores nine canons of development. Special focus also will be paid to developing a strong *sense* of essay and paragraph structure.

The final three lesson plans in this chapter will involve reading professional essays about writing, and then responding to those essays.

To begin this chapter's activities, you will need to decide on a central question that students will answer and develop into an essay. This question needs to be broad enough to encompass all nine canons; in fact, this is probably the broadest question you will use all year. Some suggestions are:

- What makes someone a hero?
- What advice would you give to a new high school student to help him or her be successful in high school?
- Should cell phones be allowed in school?
- Should students be required to wear uniforms?
- Which is more important to a high school education—arts or athletics?

For the purposes of this Teacher Manual, we will explore the first question, "What makes someone a hero?" This particular topic tends to be non-controversial, and students are able to use examples from their own experiences and/or stories they have been made aware of in the news.

Teaching the Chapter

Begin the discussion of this chapter by asking students to analyze the photographs in the **Classic and Contemporary Images** feature on pages 50-51. Discuss students' analyses and share with them the suggested answers below.

Classic and Contemporary Images: Suggested Answers

1. **What would you consider the dominant impression of the writing process in each of the settings in the two photographs?**
   Wharton's photograph has a very businesslike setting (note the formal office materials on the desk). She sees writing as complete organization that appears to be quite linear. The contemporary photo, with pages everywhere and a cat on the desk, promotes writing as a messy and nonlinear process.

2. **What impressions do you get from the body language of the authors in both pictures?**
   Wharton is formally sitting at her desk with a very intent look upon her face that is quite determined and proper. In the contemporary photo, the man's body language is intense in a different way. We cannot see his face, but we do know he has his eyes fastened on the computer screen. Discuss with students how they might connect their own body language to the process of writing.

3. **How has new technology changed the way most writers write? What do these photos tell us about how formal writing has changed for most people?**
   In Wharton's day, writers held a more professional- and business-oriented stance, especially female writers who were not taken as seriously as men in the writing profession. Technology has allowed revisions to be carried out more easily than rewriting by hand, but the steps of writing are basically the same.

4. **What similarities are shared by the two photographs? Which is the strongest?**
   Both photos show writers who are committed to their craft. Both writers have multiple resources near them: books on shelves in the top photo; files and folders in the bottom photo. The different settings are inconsequential to their devotion for writing.

Lesson Plan 2.1

Planning/Prewriting

This lesson covers pages 52–58 and Peter Elbow's essay on pages 89–91 in the student textbook. Much of the information will remind students of processes they have been studying since their very first writing assignments. The text reading can be done for homework, or you can take the time to read it in class. Make sure students notice the examples of brainstorming and freewriting that are provided in the text.

Class Opener

Write the following question and instructions on the board for students to see as they walk into the classroom: "What is prewriting? In your groups, create a definition." Allow groups to discuss and then agree on a definition for the class. As groups share their answers, ask the class to expand their definition to apply to writing.

Activity: Reading "Freewriting" by Peter Elbow

Cooperatively read the essay in class, allowing time for think-along questioning and analysis. Elbow introduces the basics of his view that the best polished writing begins with a first draft composed as spontaneously as possible. According to this view, the writer is less likely to censor original and innovative thinking that might otherwise never find its way on the page.

Alternative Activity: Journaling

Elbow's essay is an excellent essay to use for teaching students to write a reader-response journal entry. This type of journal entry includes three paragraphs, and it is a starting point for rhetorical analysis. The first paragraph of this entry will focus on *what* the author says—a brief summary. The second paragraph will focus on *why* the author says it—a single paragraph analysis of the author's purpose. The third paragraph will focus on *how* the author makes his claims. Students can work together on this exercise, or they can work independently. Encourage them to write quickly and to keep the analysis to one page. By encouraging brevity, you are actually building their confidence in their ability to write on-demand and quickly. Allow students to share their response essays—especially the "how" paragraphs.

Activity: Teaching Tone

Although tone is part of the AP Language trinity (diction, syntax, tone), it is probably the piece with which students most struggle. This activity involves getting students to think about gradation of meaning by asking them to come up with synonyms for common feeling words. Write the following words on the board as the headings of columns:

Happy Sad Angry Scared Excited

Ask students to work in their groups and create a list of synonyms for each word. Give them about 5 minutes to complete this task. After they have created their lists, ask a student to come to the board as scribe. Begin with group one and ask for their Happy list. Ask the other groups if they would like to contribute. Move to the next group for a Sad list, and so on. After you have lists on the board for each term, ask students to create a "tone thermometer" for one set of words. (This part generally works best if you assign one set of terms to each group.) Tell students to place the weakest synonym at the bottom of the tone thermometer and the strongest synonym at the top. (See the example below.)

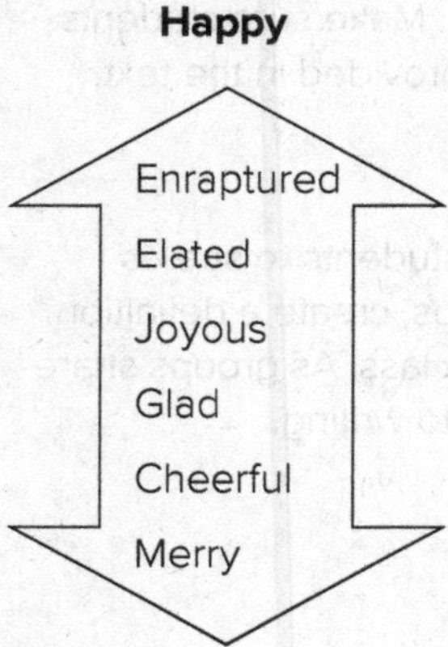

Give students a chance to collaborate about the placement of the words on the continuum. Explain to students that this is how tone works. As writers, we want to be as specific as possible in defining the tone, so that our audience truly recognizes our attitude. Conversely, as readers we want to analyze another author's tone in a given piece, and word choice is one of the strongest indicators of tone.

Suggested Answers

"Freewriting" by Peter Elbow

Comprehension

1. What is the thesis of the essay? Is it implied or stated directly in the text?

Elbow states the thesis quite clearly in the opening sentence: "The most effective way I know to improve your writing is to do freewriting exercises regularly." This is opinion, not fact, even if based on empirical evidence.

2. In paragraph 5, Elbow refers to the "producer" and the "editor." Who are they? Where are they located? How did they develop?

The producer is the part of the self or mind that is "freely" transcribing thoughts onto paper. The editor is a "voice," the writing superego, that critiques the producer's "output." Elbow claims that freewriting enables the producer to ignore the editor because the editor simply does not have the time to intervene in the freewriting process.

3. In paragraph 8, the author makes a connection between one's personal "voice" and the idea of "power." Why does Elbow focus so strongly on this connection?

Elbow adheres to the democratic idea and ideal that each individual is unique in his or her cognitive and perceptual perspective on reality, and hence one's "voice" is the engine that generates one's authenticity.

Rhetorical Analysis

4. Elbow frequently uses the "imperative" (or command) sentence form in the opening paragraph. Why? What would have been the effect had he used the simple declarative form?

Elbow uses the first paragraph to demonstrate process analysis. An analogy can be made between his instructions and those found in a recipe. This rhetorical device adds psychological authority to his thesis.

5. Writers often use examples to help illustrate their point. Does the example of a freewriting exercise Elbow provides in paragraph 3 help you to understand the method? Why or why not?

Elbow's example is apt because it is coherent. But, at the same time, it demonstrates the frustration the writer is experiencing by engaging in the freewriting exercise. It also suggests that freewriting is enjoyable as evidenced in this excerpt from the sample: "This is kind of fun."

6. The author uses colloquial terms such as "squiggle" (paragraph 1), "crazy" and "mushiness" (paragraph 3), and "lousy" (paragraph 7). How does his use of such words affect the tone of the essay? How would you describe his tone?

The author uses an informal tone to offset the physical and mental strain that writers experience while freewriting. His deliberately casual tone helps demonstrate that writing is a mix of casual and formal communication.

7. Are there any elements in Elbow's own style that suggest his essay may have started as a freewriting exercise? Consider the reasons he provides for the importance of freewriting—for example, generating ideas, discovering one's own voice, or expressing oneself succinctly and naturally.

Elbow suggests that "voice, force, and connectedness" (paragraph 9) are essential to good writing. His own essay displays these attributes through its rather relentless, focused, and succinct style. In addition, nearly all of his paragraphs introduce a new concept or instruction. As a result, the essay has a spontaneous tone even if it has been edited.

8. Elbow is himself a college writing teacher. Based on your assessment of the tone of the essay, who do you think is his intended audience? Is it broad or narrow? Specialized or general? Or could he have in mind more than one type of audience? Explain your answer.

Elbow does not make any references to college writing or academia. His only reference to "schooling" (paragraph 3) is negative. Thus, we can assume that when he states "improve your writing" in paragraph 1, the "your" refers to the general reader.

9. Note the number of times Elbow begins his sentences with coordinating conjunctions ("but," "and," "or"). For example, in paragraph 4, he makes this syntactical choice three times. Many writing teachers frown on this method of structuring sentences. Why does Elbow employ it?

Elbow is transgressing—whether intentionally or unintentionally—some of the "guidelines" of traditional writing instruction, for example, the rule that one should not start a sentence with a coordinating conjunction. In paragraph 6, he uses a vague referent: "The main thing about writing." He also uses repetition (paragraph 6). Each is a mild subversion of conventional writing methods, and implies, by example, that a student writer may do the same.

10. Compare the essay's introduction to its conclusion. Note how the introduction is rather long and the conclusion is quite short (two sentences, in fact). How do these two elements contribute to the overall "pace" of the essay?

The style of the essay mimics the tone of an enthusiastic advocate. The prose has a heightened energy which appears spent by the time the author arrives at his conclusion. It is as though Elbow has succeeded in communicating what he intended so that the conclusion has the "feel" of a speaker "winding down" with final thoughts, thereby making the conclusion achieve appropriate and effective closure.

Writing

11. During one week, complete three freewriting exercises. Wait one week, and then review what you have written. Explore any insights your freewriting gives you into your writer's "voice"—your concerns, interests, style, and "power."

Have students read their freewriting exercises aloud to the class or in groups. Have them compare freewriting assignments completed at the beginning of the term with those at the end. Have them look for commonalities in their themes and concerns as well as evolution in their style and mastery of basic writing skills.

12. Write an expository paper explaining the difficulties you have when writing an essay homework assignment or writing an essay-length response during an exam.

Have a discussion with your students before writing the assignment regarding what aspects of their writing to critique. Have them avoid general reflections such as "the topic was boring" or "I couldn't think of anything to write." You may wish to provide a checklist of common writing problems to the class and discuss them so that students have some guidelines for their essays. Emphasize that their grade will be determined by how they articulate their writing process rather than the ease or difficulty they have in writing.

13. Write a comparison and contrast essay wherein you examine the similarities and differences of speaking and writing.

A comparison and contrast paper comparing writing and speaking may be facilitated by drawing up lists of the characteristics of each mode of communication. Have students take a sheet of paper and draw a line down it vertically. On one side, have them list general attributes of speaking; on the other, list conventions of writing. This will help them organize their formal papers.

14. **Writing an Argument** Write an essay in which you support or refute the value of freewriting.

Before students begin an argument for or against freewriting, be sure that they have undertaken a representative amount of freewriting exercises.

Class Closer

After completing the tone discussion, introduce the writing topic, "What makes someone a hero?" Give students the overall question, and allow them 5 minutes for freewriting. Direct students to the freewriting samples in the textbook if necessary to get them thinking on paper about the task. Remind students to bring their freewriting with them to the next class.

Lesson Plan 2.2

Drafting Thesis Statements and Planning the Essay

Class Opener

Write a simple outline with Roman numerals I–V on the board. Ask students to take out their freewriting and use their notes from yesterday to write a brief topical outline for how they might address the topic, "What makes someone a hero?"

Activity: Writing Thesis Statements

Announce to students that they will develop thesis statements today. Explain that the main rule to the thesis statement is that it be arguable. Many students come to AP English Language classes writing "roadmap" thesis statements: *In this paper I will discuss what it means to be a hero, which includes teachers, single parents, and soldiers.* Point out that this is not an adequate thesis statement because it demonstrates poor control of the process and of language in general. Explain that in their thesis, students should avoid the words "I think" and "I believe." The reader knows that what he or she is reading is the student's opinion—the writer's name is on the top of the paper. If students start their thesis statements with "I believe," have them cross out those words to create a stronger thesis statement.

Direct Aristotelian argumentation requires a direct thesis statement. In this type of thesis statement, the student simply states directly what he believes:

> **Heroes are found all around us; whether big or small, rich or poor, the impact they have on the lives around them is what matters.**

A second type of thesis statement involves Rogerian analysis, which requires a nod to the opposing view:

> **Although society has conditioned us to believe that heroes wear capes and have superpowers, our true heroes are those marginalized members of society who put aside their own selfish interests in search of a greater good.**

Ask students to work with both models to create potential thesis statements for their argument essays. Notice that while neither thesis statement directly restates the prompt (another habit that students bring with them to class), both thesis statements do establish context. Allow the class to share their thesis statements, either in groups or as a whole class activity. For this essay, let students choose to write from someone else's thesis statement if they hear one they like better than their own. The point is to make sure that all of the thesis statements are strong enough to direct a solid essay.

Activity: Writing Introductory Paragraphs

After students have had a chance to work on thesis statements, direct them to the information on writing introductory paragraphs on page 60 of the textbook. Good introductions will provide a "hook." Read aloud the strategies here, and ask students to voice a sample statement for each.

- Offer a brief story or incident that sets the stage for your topic and frames your thesis.
- Start with a shocking, controversial, or intriguing opinion.
- Begin with a comparison or contrast.
- Use a quotation or reference to clarify and illustrate your topic and thesis.
- Ask a question or series of questions directed toward establishing your thesis.
- Offer several relevant examples to support your thesis.
- Begin with a vivid description that supports your main idea.
- Cite a statistic or provide data.
- Correct a false assumption.

Then ask students to look at their freewriting and outline for a point they can make or an anecdote they can relate that might help them begin their essay. Explain that however they choose to capture readers' attention depends on their purpose for writing, their subject, and the audience they want to reach. Students should remember that the overarching purpose of an introductory paragraph is to get to the main idea or the point of the essay, which is the thesis statement.

You might present a graphic organizer of an inverted triangle like the one on the next page to guide students' writing of introductory paragraphs. The top side of the triangle is a general or broad statement about the subject. This broad statement should not only present the subject to the reader but also engage the audience with the "hook." Each sentence after that narrows the subject until students reach the focus of their essay—or the thesis statement.

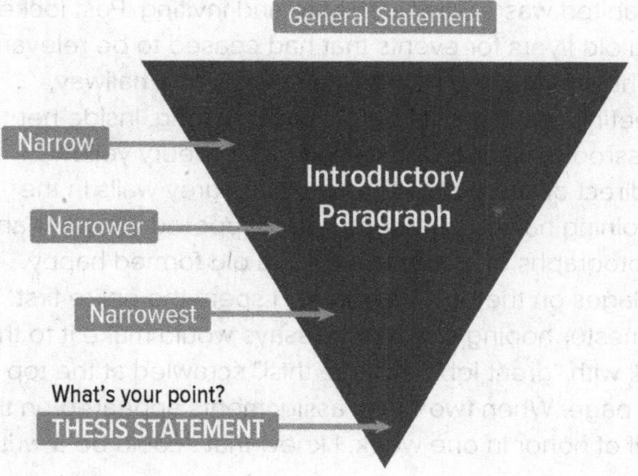

Class Closer

Sharing work is essential to building a writing community. After students have written their introductory paragraphs, give them time to share. First, let them share with their group. Then let each group share the paragraph they liked best from their offerings.

Lesson Plan 2.3

Description, Narration, and Illustration

In this lesson, students will begin writing the body paragraphs for their essays. Ask them to write each paragraph on a separate sheet of paper, as this greatly simplifies the revision process.

Explain that for all body paragraphs, students must write a topic sentence that relates the paragraph to the thesis statement. Reinforce that topic sentences should be arguable. Establish parameters for the length of body paragraphs: five sentences at a minimum. Eight sentences will yield stronger writing, but you do not want to encourage students to pad their writing, so provide some leeway.

Activity: Descriptive Body Paragraphs

Have students read the information about the rhetorical mode of **Description** in the textbook, then ask them to focus on their thesis statement and the central question you have selected in order to create a body paragraph using description. Have them pay particular attention to the idea that a descriptive paragraph uses sensory detail and focuses on spatial ordering. In our "hero" example, a descriptive paragraph might be used to describe places that house our heroes (fire stations, police departments, schools) or places where heroes will face their challenges (a grandmother in the hospital, a mother working two jobs, etc.)

The following provides an example of a descriptive paragraph that would work with the thesis statement developed earlier (see page 36):

> Teachers can serve as heroes by showing students that someone believes in them. The halls were narrow, the school was old, but the classroom Mrs. Andrews

inhabited was always welcome and inviting. Past lockers and old flyers for events that had ceased to be relevant months before, Mrs. Andrews stood in the hallway, greeting her students before the bell rang. Inside her classroom, the walls were painted a cheery yellow, in direct opposition to the battleship grey walls in the adjoining hallway. Student work peppered the walls and photographs of students new and old formed happy collages on the bulletin boards. I spent the entire first semester hoping one of my essays would make it to the wall with "great job!" or "love this!" scrawled at the top of my page. When two of my assignments appeared on the wall of honor in one week, I knew that I could be a writer.

Activity: Narrative Body Paragraphs

Have students read the information about the rhetorical mode of **Narration** in the textbook, then ask them to focus on their thesis statement and the central question you have selected to create a body paragraph using narration. Have them pay particular attention to the idea that a narrative paragraph presents details in a logical (usually chronological) order. Student writers often struggle with limiting the scope of the story and tying it back to the thesis statement.

The following provides an example of a descriptive paragraph that would work with the thesis statement developed earlier (see page 36):

> Heroes don't necessarily pull people out of burning buildings; sometimes they simply provide a safe haven for lonely children. My grandmother is my hero for providing such a place for my friends and me. Riding to my grandmother's house on the bus after school, I remember wiping the sweat from my face as I imagined the ice cold lemonade Nana would have waiting for us. As we exited the bus and walked that long half-mile to her house, we would joke around about the day at school and race each other along the broken sidewalk. Branches of trees would bow down almost to the ground, and we would snap those back at whomever was unlucky enough to be last in our little line. Nana never walked out to meet us, but she seemed to magically know when we'd appear. We'd make that last little turn off the sidewalk, trudge through her shabby yard, and find her sitting in the comforting shade of her dilapidated front porch. The boards that formed the floor were buckling, and the paint was peeling, but the lemonade was fresh and cold, and we all knew that Nana would have it waiting. Even though our neighborhood was not the safest place for kids to play, Nana created an oasis of safety for us, keeping us out of the trouble that might have otherwise found us.

Activity: Collaborative Writing with Narrative Paragraphs

Have students do narrative writing with one another. Each student should write two sentences and pass the paper around a table of four until there are two pages of a narrative. This type of collaborative writing can lead right into collaborative proofreading and revision.

Serve as navigator and, through a structured process, encourage collaborative work where equitable responsibility is shared. Some problems exist when certain students seem determined to become dictators of the collaboration, shutting down the other members of the group. In addition, there are those students who are more than ready to relinquish any active obligation.

Activity: Illustrative Body Paragraphs

Have students read the information about the rhetorical mode of **Illustration** in the textbook. Then ask them to focus on their thesis statement and the central question you have selected in order to create a body paragraph using illustration. They may choose the type of detail they wish to use for illustration, but have them select from documented facts, statistics, or quotations. (The textbook also mentions personal example, process, comparison and contrast, and case study, but we will cover those elsewhere.) You might want to provide a selection of quotations and facts that students can draw from. Otherwise, let them use computers or digital devices to find illustrative details that they like. A Google search for "hero quotation" yields an impressive assortment. You might consider assigning this third paragraph for homework, assuming students will have access to research at home.

The following provides an example of an illustrative paragraph that would work with the thesis statement developed earlier (see page 36):

> Although we always think of soldiers, firefighters, and police officers when someone mentions the word "hero," the fact is that life presents each and every one of us with opportunities for heroism. Journalist E. W. Howe once said, "The real American hero is the man who, in spite of a poor home, poor schooling, and residence in a poor neighborhood, becomes a successful and useful citizen; who somehow acquires politeness, education, and appreciation of the world's important lessons." (*The Blessing of Business*, 1918) Heroism is not defined by saving lives. Instead, heroism is demonstrated by individuals who set aside their personal desires in order to help benefit another person. Like a little boy who sees that there isn't enough pie to go around and saves the hostess embarrassment by claiming he doesn't want his slice, we each have the opportunity to make the world a little easier for others.

Class Closer

Choose a way to randomly select students (names on popsicle sticks or in a fishbowl, for example) to ensure whole class participation. Then randomly draw the name of a student to read aloud his or her descriptive paragraph. Do the same with a narrative paragraph, and end with an illustrative paragraph.

Lesson Plan 2.4

Process Analysis, Comparison and Contrast, and Causal Analysis

Continue working with students to write body paragraphs, this time using the rhetorical modes of process analysis, comparison and contrast, and causal analysis.

Activity: Process-Analysis Body Paragraphs

Have students read the information about the rhetorical mode of **Process Analysis** in the textbook, then ask them to focus on their thesis statement and the central question you have selected to create a body paragraph using process analysis. Have them pay particular attention to the idea that process analysis describes how to do something or how something has been done. In our "hero" example, a process-analysis paragraph might be used to describe how ordinary people become heroes.

The following provides an example of a process-analysis paragraph that would work with the thesis statement developed earlier (see page 36):

> Heroes are not born that way, they become remarkable in many cases through successfully navigating life's challenges. My grandfather was born the oldest of seven children into a family of poor farmers. He spent his youth struggling to stay in school while helping on the farm and taking care of his younger siblings. No one in the family ever expected to rise above the poverty of this lifestyle, but my grandfather was determined to own a business. He managed his time well, caring for his siblings and staying in school. After graduating from school, he attended a technical college while continuing to help on the farm. Eventually, he graduated and started a plumbing business. As his brothers finished school, he trained them in what became the family business. Although we don't often think of plumbers as being rich and successful, my grandfather changed the lives of his siblings through his hard work and determination.

Activity: Comparison and Contrast Body Paragraphs

Have students read the information about the rhetorical mode of **Comparison and Contrast** in the textbook, then ask them to focus on their thesis statement and the central question you have selected to create a body paragraph using comparison and contrast. They should consider both similarities and differences. In our "hero" example, a comparison and contrast paragraph might be used to compare the actions of two individuals.

The following provides an example of a comparison and contrast paragraph that would work with the thesis statement developed earlier (see page 36):

> Heroes often emerge in response to situations they never expected to encounter. In April 2011, a tornado hit my community, killing almost 300 people across the state. People responded in one of two ways—by helping those around them or by taking advantage of a terrible situation. The vast majority of people pitched in to help their neighbors by sharing food and gasoline and finding medical supplies for those in need. In contrast, looters also immediately emerged, robbing local businesses in the midst of an unprecedented crisis. The common citizen was presented with an opportunity to be a hero, and the vast majority of those in my community proved their valor.

Activity: Causal Analysis Body Paragraphs

Have students read the information about the rhetorical mode of **Causal Analysis** in the textbook, then ask them to focus on their thesis statement and the central question you have selected to create a body paragraph using causal analysis. This type of paragraph is basic cause and effect. It must be logical, and it must rely on actual evidence. If you do not have time or access to allow students to do research in class, you might consider assigning this third paragraph as a homework response.

The following provides an example of a causal analysis paragraph that would work with the thesis statement developed earlier (see page 36):

> Tragedy yields heroism. When the Twin Towers fell during the attack on 9/11, early preparation was the key to saving thousands of lives. Rick Rescorla, a retired Army Colonel, was serving as the director of security at Morgan Stanley at the time of the attacks. He took his job seriously and had intermittently required all staff to follow an evacuation plan he had developed. Due to his careful planning and his order for staff to immediately evacuate the building, more than 2500 lives were saved. Rescorla died that day, but his careful planning and attention to detail made him a hero to those he saved.

Class Closer

Again, randomly draw the name of a student to read aloud his or her process analysis paragraph. Follow with a comparison and contrast paragraph, and end with a causal analysis paragraph. Ensure whole class participation.

Lesson Plan 2.5

Definition, Classification, and Argumentation

Activity: Definition Body Paragraphs

Have students read the information about the rhetorical mode of **Definition** in the textbook, then ask them to focus on their thesis statement and the central question you have selected to create a body paragraph using definition. Definition is perhaps the most overused writing strategy, but its rhetorical significance cannot be overstated. *Definition* can be a powerful tool when a writer effectively redefines a word that the reader already knows. Think of the word "family." Now think of how that concept has been re-defined during your lifetime. Definition is an important tool when used correctly. For our purposes, students will write a paragraph defining the idea "hero." The following provides an example of a definition paragraph that would work with the thesis statement developed earlier (see page 36):

> A hero is more than a mythical being with super powers. Any ordinary person can be a hero. It doesn't matter what a person is able to do, it matters what they actually do when faced with a difficult situation. A hero is not defined by their abilities but by their actions. A hero is someone who puts others ahead of herself, whether that means risking her life or simply sacrificing her individual desires for the good of another.

Activity: Classification Body Paragraphs

Classification is a difficult skill to teach in a single paragraph. We think of classification essays—rather than classification paragraphs—for good reason: it is difficult to place any entity in a neat and tidy little box, and with classification, that is exactly what we are doing—creating order.

Have students read the information about the rhetorical mode of **Classification** in the textbook, then ask them to focus on their thesis statement and the central question you have selected to create a body paragraph using classification. Have them pay particular attention to the idea that in order to classify, they must create a system that allows things *to be* classified. This is a tall order, and you may consider allowing them to work in groups to come up with their own examples. The following is an example of a classification paragraph that would work with the thesis statement on page 36:

> Actions fall into two categories—selfish or selfless. When we consider heroism, we are considering actions that qualify as being selfless. A father takes on a second job to ensure that his children can afford to play Little League. A mother stays up all night working on her daughter's wedding gown to make sure it is perfect. A police officer steps into the line of fire to rescue an ordinary citizen. These people are not making choices that benefit them; instead, they put aside their own wants and needs in order to guarantee the happiness of another. These are selfless deeds, and they form the backbone of heroism.

Activity: Argumentation Body Paragraphs

Additional information about argumentation will be provided later in the textbook and Teacher Manual. At this point, students should recognize that in the context of writing, an argument is not a disagreement. Instead, an argument is an ordered set of claims, counterclaims, and evidence that is designed to persuade. The following is an example of an argument paragraph that would work with the thesis statement on page 36:

> Heroes are simple, everyday people who make a difference. <claim> Although there are those who will argue that this definition dilutes the concept of heroism <counterclaim>, the reality is that society is built upon the idea that individuals must willingly work to a common good. When people work individually toward that greater good, they must be rewarded. Part of this reward is by allowing to society to view them as better or higher than those who put individual needs first. We reward these individuals and perpetuate this positive activity by considering those who engage in such behavior as heroes. <evidence>

Class Closer

Again, randomly draw the name of a student to read aloud his or her definition paragraph. Follow with a classification paragraph, and end with an argument paragraph. Ensure whole class participation.

Lesson Plan 2.6

Writing Conclusions and Revising

Class Opener

At this point, students have written more than a complete essay, but they have not put it together yet. As a class opener, ask students to take out each paragraph they have written so far.

Activity: Concluding Paragraphs

Students should choose which paragraphs they want to include in their essays. First, they should review their introductory paragraphs. After they have reminded themselves what they set out to say, they should review each of the body paragraphs they have written and determine which of these they want to include in their essay and in which order.

After this has been accomplished, they should review the information on pages 77–80 of the textbook and write the concluding paragraph. Some teachers suggest saving your best point for last. Others advise closing with a second "hook." Students should avoid simply restating their thesis. Explain that the reader, by now, should be very aware of the point students have been trying to make. Ask: Have you made that point? Note that although it is perfectly appropriate to state that point in new words, there is no reason to restate it entirely.

Activity: Reading the Sample Student Essay

As a class, read together the student essay provided on pages 81–84 of the textbook. Discuss with students what makes this a good model. (Keep in mind that this is an analysis model—not a persuasive essay.) Help students find the thesis statement and recognize the nature of the topic sentences: they are arguable and they further the thesis. Discuss what types of development the author uses.

Class Closer

If there is time, read together the section on revising; otherwise, assign it as part of the homework. For homework, students should put together their essay. They should use the revision checklist on page 85 of the textbook to create a single essay with at least five paragraphs, including an introduction and conclusion.

Lesson Plan 2.7

Responding to "The Maker's Eye: Revising Your Own Manuscripts" by Donald Murray

Murray presents the case that good writing is a methodical process, and its most important aspect is revision. This essay is its own evidence of the value of structure, form, organization, and clarity in writing. The author presents his ideas meticulously, from the completion of the first draft, through the rigors of rewriting, to the methods of self-analysis and self-criticism. His sound advice is geared for the student writer.

Class Opener

Have students write a quick-write paragraph response: *In a paragraph, define the word "writer."* Discuss student answers, and then refer to the sample answer provided for question 11 on page 46.

Activity: Compare and Contrast Murray and Elbow

In groups, students should create a Venn diagram to recognize the similarities and differences between the writing styles of Murray and Elbow. Students should recognize the more formal tone Murray employs and should recognize that his opening paragraph employs a process analysis approach. Elbow, in contrast, writes almost as an advice columnist, using informal language and sentence fragments. Create a giant Venn diagram on the board and allow groups to fill in the details they discover.

Activity: Collaborative Revising

Discuss Murray's concept that revision is "fun." Students may have a hard time accepting this notion, but they have just experienced revising one of their own papers this week. Lead them in a discussion so they can examine the processes they have undertaken. Have students exchange their essays with one another and make at least three notes to help the original authors revise their essays.

Class Closer

"Sex, Lies, and Conversation: Why Is It so Hard for Men and Women to Talk to Each Other?" by Deborah Tannen is a particularly good essay for the Fishbowl approach. Ask students to read the essay for homework, writing at least 4 questions for a Fishbowl conversation (see description in Chapter 1, p. 5). Questions should be open-ended and should not have a clear answer. (They should not be comprehension questions.) Ask students to write a reference page number on each question and write their questions on individual index cards or small pieces of paper.

Suggested Answers

"The Maker's Eye: Revising Your Own Manuscripts" by Donald Murray

Comprehension

1. In paragraph 1, what does Murray mean by the statement "When a draft is completed, the job of writing can begin"? Isn't a draft a form of writing? Do you agree with his notion of a "zero draft"?

Murray implies that the first draft is by definition not fully thought out. The writing process by its very nature confuses critical analysis of form and content. It is only in the revision process that the writer has the ability to critically evaluate and then improve the work-in-progress.

2. According to Murray, what are the major differences between student and professional writers? Why do the differences help make the "professional" more accomplished at his or her work?

Murray suggests that the professional writer has a responsibility that the student does not. The professional must keep in mind that he or she is writing for an audience with implicit assumptions of quality; therefore, the writer has an obligation to communicate clearly, deftly, and succinctly. The professional writer has the goal of presenting a finished product for consumption. The student writer is still in the process of learning how to achieve this objective.

3. What are the differences between the reading styles of novice and experienced writers? How do the differences affect their own writings?

An experienced writer has the skill to be an objective reader of his own work. Murray quotes Ciardi on this point: "The last act of the writing must be to become one's own reader. It is, I suppose, a schizophrenic process, to begin passionately and to end critically, to begin hot and to end cold; and, more important, to be passion-hot and critic-cold at the same time" (paragraph 6). This ability—Murray suggests—allows the professional writer to acquire an almost obsessive need to render the writing as nearly perfect as possible.

Rhetorical Analysis

4. Compare the introduction of this essay to that of Elbow's "Freewriting." How do they differ in tone and structure?

Elbow is instructional and encouraging without providing a rationale. Murray compares and contrasts the student and professional writer. His focus seems to be on the *role* of the writer, implying that technique is a means to attain this role.

5. Murray begins to classify various aspects of the writer's concern in paragraph 13. Why does he wait so long to begin this analysis? Why are certain key words in paragraphs 13–20 italicized?

This essay begins by generally explaining the necessary attributes and practices of the professional writer. Only when Murray has established these "ground rules" does he focus in-depth on the specific classification of the writers' concerns and the exact process of revision. The italicized words demonstrate that they are part of the writers' vocabulary. He honors the role of the writer by emphasizing that it is a profession with its own taxonomy of concerns. This may be necessary as many novice writers—and particularly students—do not think of writing as a rigorous and methodical profession along the lines of other professional activities such as medicine, engineering, graphic design, computer programming, and so on.

6. Murray uses analogy, comparing one thing with another, very different thing, to make the writing process concrete and familiar. Identify some of these analogies. Why are they models of clarity?

The major analogy compares the writer to a "maker." However, Murray specifies that the "maker" does not just spontaneously create a work, but uses various methods that go into the revision process. He also compares the writer to a chef in paragraph 18. Each must be true to his or her own "taste." He suggests that the writer is a technician, for example, in paragraph 24, where he states, "the writer employs the technical skills of language." In paragraph 30, he refers to "a piece of writing," suggesting that writing does not just transmit information but is a form of information as well.

7. Murray refers to a writer as "the maker" several times in the essay. What does he imply by this usage? What other professions might be included in this category?

Murray implies that all professional writers are "makers" since they render ideas and thoughts into concrete form. One may think of architects, software designers, and engineers as representing "makers."

8. What is the purpose of the essay? Is it to inform? To persuade? To serve as a model? Anything else? Explain your response.

Murray uses exposition and definition to explain what a professional writer is and does. He states, for example, "The writer must learn to read critically but constructively, to cut what is bad, to reveal what is good" (paragraph 8). His task is not only to "demystify" the process of writing but to emphasize that it is a rigorous and exacting procedure. The essay's short, concise sentences demonstrate that Murray is intent on representing his thesis through his own writing. It characterizes the goal of the "writer's eye," which "sees the need for variety and balance, for a firmer structure, for a more appropriate form. It peers into the interior of the paragraph, looking for coherence, unity, and emphasis, which make meaning clear" (paragraph 26).

9. Murray ends the essay with an ellipsis. Why?

"A piece of writing is never finished," Murray notes (paragraph 30). Of course, the function of the ellipses is to metaphorically reinforce this point.

10. Notice the sentence in paragraph 29 that has four consecutive words with the prefix *re*-. What is the purpose and effect of this rhetorical device?

In fact, the final word in the series has the double prefix *re*-. This emphasizes the recursive nature of writing which is constantly being reinforced in the essay, and makes reference to a key word in the title of the essay: "Revising."

Writing

11. Murray focuses on the process, craft, and purpose of the writer, but he does not define "writer." Write an extended definition explaining what he means by this occupation or profession.

Try to avoid reductionist responses to the question of what defines a writer such as "someone who writes" by having your students list the activities of a writer and the purpose of the writer's process: the finished piece of writing. Students may begin by listing aspects of the writer mentioned in the essay, and encourage them to think of their own. You may try to aid your students by focusing on a genre of writing, for example, the magazine journal, newspaper article, novel, textbook, and so on.

12. Write an essay explaining your own writing process. Do not be intimidated if it is not like the one described by Murray. Compare and contrast your method with that of one or more of your classmates.

This process of self-reflection may best be encouraged through brainstorming. After your students have exhausted all the steps involved in their own writing, have them either rank them in order of importance or list them chronologically. You can suggest that they finish their essay with a critique of their own writing process by discussing what steps they either avoid or neglect—referring to the various rubrics mentioned by Murray.

13. Writing an Argument Murray suggests that revision is actually "fun" (paragraph 24). Do you agree or disagree? Write an essay defending your position.

Be sure that students read the rest of paragraph before deciding whether revising is "fun." They might not consider revising "fun," but they might agree that it is "immensely satisfying."

Lesson Plan 2.8

Responding to "Sex, Lies, and Conversation: Why Is It So Hard for Men and Women to Talk to Each Other?" by Deborah Tannen

Tannen has claimed that she was utterly surprised when her book *You Just Don't Understand* made the best-seller lists across the country. Who would have thought that a sociolinguistic study would elicit the same buying frenzy as popular novels or spiritual guidebooks? This fact demonstrates the growing and deepening interest about gender relations in our society. This essay, a summary of her work, combines the methodology of social science—statistics, reports of research, personal observation and research, and terminology—that helps define behavior previously unarticulated.

Class Opener

Students should come to class with prepared Socratic questions related to the topic. In their groups, have them take five minutes to remove any questions that have a definite answer (comprehension or fact-based questions.) Then, as a group, they should choose their 5 favorite questions.

Activity: Discussing Tannen's Essay

Using the Fishbowl approach, draw questions (or have students draw questions) to discuss the text. The discussion is likely to be very opinion-based with a healthy dose of battle of the sexes thrown in. Be prepared to draw students back into a discussion of the rhetorical implications of Tannen's essay.

Activity: Writing a Narrative Paragraph About Male-Female Communication

After the student discussion, ask students to look at Tannen's opening to the essay. Tannen begins with an anecdote (narrative writing) to set the stage for her argument. Ask students to write a single paragraph in which they write a story that illustrates the intrinsic difficulties (or lack thereof) in male-female communication. (Consider writing one yourself. Students love to hear their teachers share their writing.)

Class Closer

Spend the last part of class allowing students to share the paragraphs they have written.

Suggested Answers

"Sex, Lies, and Conversation: Why Is It so Hard for Men and Women to Talk to Each Other?" by Deborah Tannen

Comprehension

1. What is the thesis or claim of this essay? Where does Tannen most clearly articulate it?

The thesis is best articulated in the first sentence of paragraph 8, in which the author makes an analogy of "talk between men and women" and "cross-cultural communication."

2. To advance her argument, the author cites political scientists and sociologists, while she herself is a linguist. What do professionals in the first two fields do? Why does Tannen use their observations in developing her argument?

Political scientists research political systems and make generalizations and analyses about political ideas, trends, and behaviors. Sociologists study societies and social behavior. There are a number of methods that political scientists, sociologists, and linguists use in their research. These methods strengthen their arguments. By learning them, students will better be able to judge fact versus opinion and considered argument versus emotional dogmatism.

3. Why does the author employ a question in her title? What other device does she employ in her title to capture the reader's attention?

Using a question in the title draws the reader into the essay because he or she assumes it will provide the answer. She references a movie titled *Sex, Lies and Videotape*, a film that explored the ability of video to elicit personal confession that ordinarily remained secret in everyday conversation.

Rhetorical Analysis

4. Tannen begins her essay with an anecdote. Is this an effective way of opening this particular essay? Why or why not?

Using an anecdote is a standard way to make one's readers or audience "warm up" to a topic that might be, on the surface, a bit dry.

5. Besides anecdotes, the author uses statistics, social science research, appeals to authority, and definition in advancing her argument. Find at least one example of each device. Explain the effectiveness of each.

Like many writers on human interaction, Tannen must be creative in describing events and activities. For example, in paragraph 18, she creates the term "participatory listenership" and, in paragraph 13, she uses the term "topical alignment." Appeals to authority are particularly persuasive since she cites observers as far back as the 1970s, a long period of time in social science research.

6. Where and how does the author imply that she is an authority on the subject? How does this contribute to or detract from her ability to win the reader's confidence?

The initial suggestion of her authority comes in the very first sentence when the author states, "I was addressing a small gathering in a suburban Virginia living room."

7. Tannen divides her essay into four sections: one untitled and three with headings. How does each section relate to the others structurally and thematically?

If the introductory section had a title, it might make the reader wary of the "empirical" nature of the essay. The following three sections conveniently divide discourse into three major categories: speech, body language, and the use of silence. These categories are not new to sociolinguistics, but most likely are to a general readership.

8. Concerning the lack of proper communication between men and women, Tannen states, "Once the problem is understood, improvement comes naturally" (paragraph 24). Is this statement supported with evidence? Explain.

Tannen offers only one example of improvement (the young man who recognizes that he must face his girlfriend and not lie on the floor during conversations). But Tannen does not cite other examples of evidence to substantiate the claim that "improvement comes naturally." It appears that "understanding" but not "improvement" may occur, however.

Writing

9. Two other linguists, Dr. Eva Berger and Isaac Berger, wrote a book titled *The Communication Panacea: Pediatrics and General Semantics*, which argues that much of what is blamed on lack of communication actually has economic and political causes. Argue for or against this proposition in light of the ideas advanced in Tannen's essay.

Tannen does not deal with such issues as wage inequities between men and women, limited resources available to only a small percentage of the population, political ideology, religion, differing values, and a host of other phenomena that cause conflict in general, and conflict between the sexes, specifically. You may wish to narrow this assignment so that students focus on one example that either supports or contradicts Tannen's assertion.

10. Using some of the observational methods described in the essay, conduct your own ethnographic research by observing a couple communicating. Write a short essay discussing your findings.

You may wish to develop an "instrument" with your students before assigning this exercise. It may be simply done by writing the nature of the communicative act on the top of a page, for example, "eye contact," "switching topics," and so on, and have student mark each time they observe such conduct during the course of a conversation. You may also wish, for the sake of expediency, to divide your class into groups of three, and have one observer take notes while a pair converses about a predetermined theme.

11. Writing an Argument **Tannen states, "Once the problem is understood, improvement comes naturally." Argue for or against this proposition.**

This assignment may be handled in several ways. You may wish to assign it as a "personal experience" styled essay, based on anecdotes from your students' lives or as an exercise in persuasion, arguing that Tannen has either hit upon a "magic bullet" solution to conflict or as a reductionist view of human conflict.

Lesson Plan 2.9

Connections for Critical Thinking

Have students turn to the **Connections for Critical Thinking** questions on page 103 in the textbook. Tell students to choose one of the options and write for a minimum of 30 minutes. After students have finished writing, use the remainder of the class period to group students according to the option they chose. Students should read and comment on each other's essays, offering a positive comment, a critical comment, and a question for each essay read.

Sample Answers

1. **Examine the "how-to" aspect of the essays by Elbow and Murray. What general strategies do they use to develop a comprehensive process analysis of an elusive subject—for example, reading or writing? Write an essay in which you compare the tactics these writers employ to demonstrate their processes.**
   Elbow and Murray use a different style to organize their strategies. Elbow identifies his basic strategies in the introduction. Then he expands on each one in the subsequent paragraphs. Murray's style is more in-depth and academic. He spends multiple paragraphs on each feature of his suggested strategy.

2. **Study the tone of Schlesinger's essay "The Cult of Ethnicity" (in Chapter 1). How does he remain "civil" while arguing against a contemporary view he seems to abhor? Next, study Tannen's "Sex, Lies and Conversation" and examine the tone she uses in addressing the complex subject of language. Make some general observations about how the stylistic elements of an essay contribute to the ability of the author to communicate difficult subjects in a manner that is appealing to the reader.**
   Schlesinger does not attack in his essay. Instead his diatribe is directed more toward general facts and observations. Then, he says that he is optimistic that America will evolve to a higher state. He believes that the ethnic fragmentation in this country is just a stage in this young country's growth and maturity and that the United States is still an example to be admired and emulated by other countries. Tannen's approach to the topic deals with genders and gender differences. Tannen explains how certain language (in this case, marriage) hurts that relationship, that clarity in the differences between men and women will improve language, and that language will improve the communication and the relationship itself. She does not come across as insulting to either gender. These essays are excellent examples of persuasion without insult or attack. They show how a more subtle effect can be created by language choices.

3. **Synthesize the ideas in Elbow's "Freewriting" and those in Murray's "The Maker's Eye: Revising Your Own Manuscripts" so that you can write a coherent essay on writing that takes into account the transition from inspiration to craft.**
   This exercise will result in a variety of approaches, but students should consider writing stages. Explain that their favorite writers do not simply sit down and write a masterpiece. Bring in novels and share the "Acknowledgments" section to show the team effort. Have the students work with each other in answering questions such as "What was my best piece of writing and why? What went into it to make it so good? Did I simply write it out and it was perfect? Did I walk around thinking about it for days before I started writing? Students should grasp the stages of writing, including brainstorming, freewriting, proofreading, editing, proofreading, editing, rewriting, proofreading, freewriting, proofreading, editing, and so on. Elbow and Murray deal with their respective phases and students are given an "inside look" at these stages through these essays.

CHAPTER 3
Argumentation and Synthesis

This chapter offers instruction on reading and creating argumentative essays and includes several core essays that students must analyze. Students will be challenged with writing argument-driven essays and with analyzing examples of argument-driven prose.

Teaching the Chapter

Lesson Plan 3.1

Elements of Argumentation

This particular section of text is rich with vocabulary and information your students need to be familiar with. Much time during this lesson will be spent reading and annotating—practicing those skills they learned in Chapter 1.

Class Opener

In groups or pairs, have students define the term *argument*. Allow time for class discussion and allow for various interpretations of the various types of argument. Another option is to use Monty Python's skit "The Argument Clinic" as entry point into this conversation. You can locate the clip on YouTube by searching for "argument clinic." This video offers a humorous way of diving into a conversation about the difference in argument and arguing.

Activity: Argument About "War"

Have students analyze the **Classic and Contemporary Images** feature on pages 106–107 in the textbook. Then review the OPTIC steps with students:

- **O** is for Overview. Conduct a brief initial overview of the visual.
- **P** is for Parts. Scrutinize the visual for parts that can be obvious or subtle for any further information. This is a precursor to the *I* that is two steps down.
- **T** is for Title (and/or captions). Read the title (or captions) and study it for meaning. What is it "saying" about the visual?
- **I** is for Interrelationships. Consider how the title and the parts are interrelated and/or connected.
- **C** is for Conclusion.

From *How to Study in College* (2001) by Walter Pauk

Based on these steps, have students analyze the ways the artist and photographer have visually constructed an argument about "war." Discuss the questions in the textbook. See suggested answers on the next page.

Classic and Contemporary Images: Suggested Answers

1. **In the Goya painting, why do you think that the man being executed is illuminated?**

   Dressed like an average Spanish worker, he appears Christ-like as his clothes jump out against the dark background. He is kneeling, with his arms outstretched in the shape of a crucifix. If you look closely, you can see the piercing in his palms. He reflects holy, heroic defiance.

2. **Is the "enemy" clearly defined in either image? Explain.**

   The "enemy" appears to be clearly defined. The French soldiers who make up the firing squad appear to be the enemy in the Goya painting because the Spanish workers are portrayed sympathetically. However, a historical analysis would make this scene far more ambiguous. The military executioner appears to be the enemy in the Eddie Adams photograph. The fact that the man being shot is wearing civilian clothing would indicate that he is an innocent victim, yet he is not. He is a Viet Cong guerrilla, a leader of a sophisticated assassination team who had all the top South Vietnamese leaders on their hit list. He was guilty of beheading and gunning down many South Vietnamese civilians and was paying the price for his actions.

3. **Thinking about question 2, give several reasons why the persecuted are portrayed as sympathetic figures.**

   In Goya's painting, the line of the rifles directs our eyes to the pain and despair in the faces and body language of the Spanish workers being executed. From the central man with arms raised, our eyes are then drawn to the anguish and fear of those who are next in line to be executed and finally to those who have already been shot. Their visible emotions make them sympathetic. However, we do not see the faces of the persecutors. They all stand in an almost robotic line, uniform in both dress and stance, with rifles lunging at the Spanish workers. The French soldiers' rigidness and apparent voracity for the task of killing makes them unsympathetic. In Adams's photo, the perpetrator, who is in military uniform, is faceless but has a well-muscled, outstretched arm holding a revolver to the head of a young, smallish Vietnamese suspect. With his arms tied behind his back and his face in full view, the boy appears defenseless and innocent.

4. **What "argument" do the painter and the photographer make about war?**

   Paintings and photographs such as these capture the ugliness and pain of war, no matter whose side one is on. They personify the inhumanity of war and give war a real face. Goya's painting is set at Principe Pio hill in western Madrid, which is one of the city's highest and most focal points. Adams's photo was shot on the streets of Saigon at a very focal point. One could surmise that these settings tell us that war is not about battle lines and battlefields, but rather war ravages everywhere and no one is safe.

Activity: Vocabulary Quiz

Have student work in groups to annotate the textbook subsections of **Elements of Argumentation**. Much of the terminology may be new to students, but the ideas should "click" with what they inherently know to be true about writing. After they have completed their group annotation, allow for an oral quiz of argumentation vocabulary. Provide students with the following definitions and ask them to write the terms being described:

- A series of statements intended to justify some opinion; usually has a minimum of three parts *(argument)*
- A statement to be justified or upheld. It is the main idea or position that you plan to present in an argument *(claim)*
- An alternative interpretation of evidence that challenges rather than supports a claim *(counterargument)*

- Similar to a claim in that each is an opinion statement or declaration to be supported with evidence and interpretation (*thesis, main idea, point, proposition, assertion)*
- Bridge between widely-accepted evidence and widely-debated claims *(interpretation, warrant, backing)*
- The evidence and reasons presented to support your claim *(grounds)*
- A stated or unstated belief, rule, or principle that underlies an argument *(warrant)*
- A broad principle that serves as the foundation for a warrant *(backing)*
- The main point of an argument that is supported by the minor propositions *(general or major proposition)*
- The reasons offered in support of the major proposition *(minor propositions)*
- The part of the argument that supports the minor propositions; based on accurate and true facts, examples, statistics, or on accepted opinions *(evidence)*
- A verifiable statement *(fact)*
- A judgment based on the facts and careful deductive or inductive reasoning *(opinion)*
- A process of reasoning by which you develop evidence in order to reach a useful generalization *(induction)*
- A process of reasoning that proceeds from the general to the particular *(deduction)*
- Derives logically from the major and minor propositions *(conclusion)*
- A weak interpretation of evidence *(fallacy)*
- The acknowledgment and handling of opposing viewpoints *(refutation)*

Activity: Toulmin Model

This chapter includes a discussion of the Toulmin model of argumentation. Ask students to re-create the model and provide examples of claims, reasons, and warrants. As noted in the textbook, here is the way Toulmin presents his model:

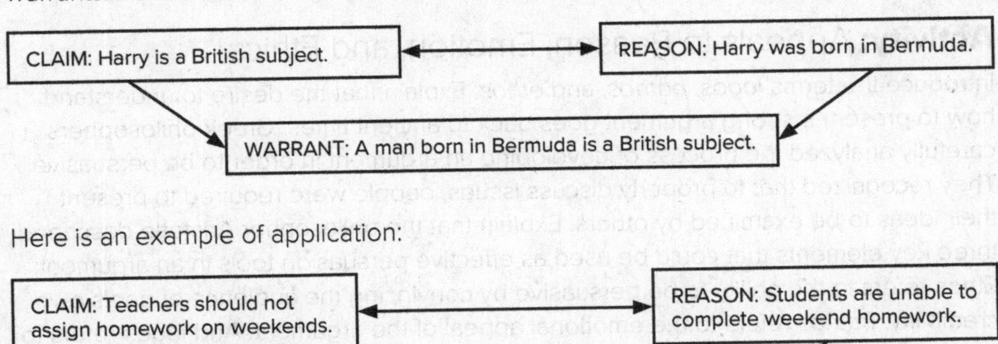

Activity: Application of Argument Vocabulary to Hero Essays

Return the "hero" essays that students wrote for Chapter 2. Ask students to find examples of and highlight the following components in their essays:

- Claim (thesis, major proposition)
- Minor proposition (hint: Look at topic sentences.)
- Evidence (facts, statistics, examples)
- Opinion
- Commentary and Interpretation (warrant, backing)
- Valid conclusion

Students should also provide justification for each label. This activity may need to be completed as homework.

Class Closer

Ask students to share which of the components listed above was easiest to find in their essays (probably thesis), and which were hardest to locate. Lead them in a discussion of what this teaches them about their own writing.

Lesson Plan 3.2

Appeals and "The Gettysburg Address"

Class Opener

Create three columns on the board with these headings: Reason/Logic, Emotion, Ethics. Ask students to work in their groups to describe elements of the **Classic and Contemporary Images** (Goya and Eddie Adams) that fall into each category. Ask students to write answers on the board.

Activity: Appeals to Reason, Emotion, and Ethics

Introduce the terms *logos, pathos,* and *ethos*. Explain that the desire to understand how to present a strong argument goes back to ancient times. Greek philosophers carefully analyzed the process of developing an argument in order to be persuasive. They recognized that to properly discuss issues, people were required to present their ideas to be examined by others. Explain that the philosopher Aristotle described three key elements that could be used as effective persuasion tools in an argument: Ethos refers to the ability to be persuasive by convincing the audience of one's own credibility. Pathos refers to the emotional appeal of the argument. And logos refers to the use of logic or reason to put forth the argument.

ETHOS Students usually have the most trouble identifying ethos. Explain that with ethos, the writer or speaker asks the reader or listener to rely on the character of the person presenting the information. The message becomes "I am trustworthy. I am someone worthy of respect." In government and politics, this message appears often in campaign ads and TV newsclips. This message also can be found in seemingly nonpolitical statements. To demonstrate, give students these facts about President Dwight D. Eisenhower: He graduated from the U.S. Military Academy. He served as the Supreme Commander of the Allied military forces during World War II. He was a conservative Republican president, and was extremely popular. Then ask: After learning some of Eisenhower's military history and conservative background, do you think he would argue *for* or *against* greater military influence? After students respond, read these excerpts from his Farewell Address, given on January 17, 1961.

> Three days from now, after half a century in the service of our country, I shall lay down the responsibilities of office as, in traditional and solemn ceremony, the authority of the Presidency is vested in my successor. . . .
>
> We now stand ten years past the midpoint of a century that has witnessed four major wars among great nations. Three of them involved our own country. Despite these holocausts America is today the strongest, the most influential and most productive nation in the world. Understandably proud of this pre-eminence we yet realize that America's leadership and prestige depend, not merely upon our unmatched material progress, riches and military strength, but on how we use our power in the interests of world peace and human betterment. . . .
>
> A vital element in keeping the peace is our military establishment. Our arms must be mighty, ready for instant action, so that no potential aggressor may be tempted to risk his own destruction. . . .
>
> . . . We recognize the imperative need for this development. Yet we must not fail to comprehend its grave implications. Our toil, resources, and livelihood are all involved; so is the very structure of our society.
>
> In the councils of government, we must guard against the acquisition of unwarranted influence . . . by the military-industrial complex. The potential for the disastrous rise of misplaced power exists and will persist. We must never let the weight of this combination endanger our liberties or democratic processes.

Farewell Address by President Dwight D. Eisenhower, January 17, 1961. www.ourdocuments.gov

After reading the excerpt, ask students the question again: True or False? Eisenhower hoped the military-industrial partnership would continue to gain influence. Explain that this statement is false. In his Farewell Address, Eisenhower stated: "In the councils of government, we must guard against the acquisition of unwarranted influence by the military-industrial complex. . . . We must never let the weight of this combination endanger our liberties or democratic processes." Point out that Eisenhower used ethos in his message. The listener trusts him because he is not campaigning. In fact, his term as president is almost over. In addition, including his time in the military, Eisenhower served the country for more than 50 years. He has credibility when he talks about the "grave implications" of war, because he's been on the battlefield personally. Eisenhower depends on the audience believing in his credibility as he presents his arguments against the military-industrial complex.

PATHOS Explain that the second element of persuasion—pathos—uses language and visuals to tug at the emotions of the audience. Vivid examples, and images or words that show strong feelings, are intended to persuade the audience by emotional appeal. Tell students to think about ads on television that ask people to support one candidate over another or to donate to relief efforts. Showing photographs of human suffering enhances the argument for support. Point out that pathos is also used in written speeches or essays. Instead of showing actual photos, essays paint a mental picture with words.

Read aloud this excerpt from "A Nation at Risk," the 1983 report of the National Commission on Excellence in Education by the U.S. Department of Education. As you read, ask students to look for pathos used in the argument to reform the educational system.

> Our nation is at risk. . . . We report to the American people that while we can take justifiable pride in what our schools and colleges have historically accomplished and contributed to the United States and the well-being of its people, the educational foundations of our society are presently being eroded by a rising tide of mediocrity that threatens our very future as a Nation and a people. . . .
>
> If an unfriendly foreign power had attempted to impose on America the mediocre educational performance that exists today, we might well have viewed it as an act of war. As it stands, we have allowed this to happen to ourselves. . . .
>
> . . . America's position in the world may once have been reasonably secure with only a few exceptionally well-trained men and women. It is no longer.
>
> The risk is not only that the Japanese make automobiles more efficiently than Americans and have government subsidies for development and export. It is not just that the South Koreans recently built the world's most efficient steel mill, or that American machine tools, once the pride of the world, are being displaced by German products. . . .
>
> Our concern, however, goes well beyond matters such as industry and commerce. It also includes the intellectual, moral, and spiritual strengths of our people which knit together the very fabric of our society.

"A Nation at Risk: The Imperative for Educational Reform," National Commission on Excellence in Education, U.S. Department of Education, 1983. https://www2.ed.gov/pubs/NatAtRisk/risk.html

Then ask students the following questions about the report: Which statements emphasize the importance and urgency of the issue? *("Our nation is at risk"; "threatens our very future as a Nation and a people")* Which statement provides an image of our educational system being washed out to sea? *("educational foundations of our society are presently being eroded by a rising tide of mediocrity")* Which words heighten the tension of the situation? *("an act of war"; "America's position in the world. . . is no longer [secure]")* Which adjectives conjure up mental images and an emotional response? *("the intellectual, moral, and spiritual strengths of our people"; "knit together the very fabric of our society")*

LOGOS Finally, explain that logos was Aristotle's favorite method to use in developing an argument, because he thought it was the most important. He believed logical appeal called for a "clear claim," supported by effective reasons and a consistent message. Then read aloud this excerpt written in 1901 by M. Carey Thomas, dean of Bryn Mawr College. Have students consider how she uses logic in her argument that males and females should have access to the same common curriculum in higher education.

> [W]hat is the best attainable training for the physician or the lawyer, man or woman? There is no reason to believe that typhoid or scarlet fever or phthisis can be successfully treated by a woman physician in one way and by a man physician in another way. There is indeed every reason to believe that unless treated in the best way the patient may die, the sex of the doctor affecting the result less even than the sex of the patient. The question needs only to be put for us to feel irrevocably sure that there is no special woman's way of dealing with disease.

"Should the Higher Education of Women Differ from That of Men?" by M. Carey Thomas. *Educational Review* 21, 1901. http://greenfield.brynmawr.edu/items/show/1492

Then ask students the following questions about the piece: What is the main question being argued? *(whether female physicians and lawyers should receive training that is different from male physicians and lawyers)* What evidence does Thomas cite? *(Logic does not support that a disease will respond differently to male physician tactics versus female physician tactics. Logic says that if a patient is not treated, the patient may die, whether the doctor is male or female. Logic says if the sex of a patient does not determine reaction to treatment, the sex of the physician providing the treatment should not matter.)* What is the importance of the last phrase? *(Thomas answer her main question in paragraph: that female doctors should be trained the same as male doctors)* Ask students if they think Thomas's argument would have been more effective had she utilized ethos or pathos instead of logos in her statement. Point out that Thomas's argument was directed toward male educators at the time. She deliberately did not want to use pathos, or emotion, to persuade. And although Thomas was herself dean of Bryn Mawr College, she faced the limitations of male-dominated society. Her argument would not have been able to gain as much credibility through ethos as it would in today's world.

Activity: Analyzing the Gettysburg Address

Have the class read the textbook section **Appeals to Reason, Emotion, and Ethics** on pages 113–116 together. Help students to recognize the appeals to reason, ethics, and emotion used in the sample paragraphs. Then ask a student to read aloud the Gettysburg Address. Because the address is one of the most famous works of spoken or written English in the United States, many students may not be aware of its elegant structure, style, or heightened diction. And because it is so short—surprisingly short when seen in print—it lends itself to rhetorical microanalysis on the sentence- and paragraph-levels of discourse, as well as an excellent piece to study for overall unity. Using the same column headings you used to analyze the photographs at the beginning of the chapter, ask students to recognize elements of logos, ethos, and pathos. Note that while logos and ethos are abundantly and immediately evident in this short passage, pathos is not as readily apparent. The students may find pathos in Lincoln's mention of the dead; although they may equally see this as ethos.

Suggested Answers

"The Gettysburg Address" by Abraham Lincoln

Abraham Lincoln: Complete Works, Volume One. Edited by John G. Nicolay and John Hay. New York: The Century Co. 1920

Comprehension

1. Although this speech was supposed to be a "dedication," Lincoln states that "we cannot dedicate." What does he mean by this?

When Lincoln states "we cannot dedicate" (paragraph 3), it is the third time he uses the term. The first mention of the term is in paragraph 1 when he makes a reference to the Declaration of Independence. The second time is in paragraph 2 when he reiterates this concept of the dedication of America to freedom. In paragraph 3, he is suggesting that although the Constitution was a form of dedication to an ideal by living men, one cannot dedicate the willing sacrifice of the fallen soldiers because the act of giving one's life is in itself the ultimate dedication. Nor can one dedicate the survivors for their brave action is, in itself, a contribution (or dedication) to the cause of the Union. Lincoln uses the term two more times in paragraph 3 to suggest that the living must dedicate themselves to what has not as yet been achieved. The forfeiture of one's life and the dedication of one's life in the battle for the Union is a completed achievement.

2. Lincoln uses abstract words such as *liberty, freedom,* and *nation*. What does he mean specifically by each of these terms?

Lincoln is directly relating the concept of "Liberty" to the liberation of the United States from the oppression of British rule so that it might be self-governing. His use of the term "freedom" also implies self-determination of the American people to create their own form of government, unencumbered by an external ruling power. His reference to "a new nation" suggests the metaphor of the birth of the United States as a country with a unique destiny, which is reiterated in the final sentence.

3. What exactly happened "Fourscore and seven years ago" in the context of the speech? Why is this reference so significant to the purpose of Lincoln's address?

Lincoln is referring to the Declaration of Independence, which may be analyzed in Chapter 8 of the textbook to compare and contrast themes that run throughout the Gettysburg Address. Lincoln is directly linking the sacrifice of the soldiers at Gettysburg to the defense of the spirit and values implicit in the original Declaration.

Rhetorical Analysis

4. Note the progression of imagery from that of "death" to that of "birth." How does this structure contribute to the claim and coherence of the speech?

Actually, the Address moves from birth—"conceived in liberty" (paragraph 1)—to death—"final resting-place" (paragraph 2)—to resurrection in the phrase "new birth of freedom" (paragraph 3). This is a theological structure found in the Christian and other religious traditions.

5. **How do the syntax (arrangement of words within a sentence), punctuation, and choice of the first-person plural form of address contribute to our understanding that this message was intended to be spoken rather than written?**

   Lincoln removes his personal role in the defense of the Union by "absorbing" himself within the greater context of the American people. Although he is the commander-in-chief and president, he subsumes these roles for the role of a member of a cause. This humility is emphasized when he states "The world will little note . . . what we say here." Note that the pronoun "I" is never mentioned in the speech. This is an effort to unify himself with his audience. Because the speech was intended to be heard, Lincoln probably made an effort to repeat key phrases for mnemonic purposes. Even the length of the speech contributes to the audience's ability to recall it, and, at the same time suggests he is limiting the amount of his rhetoric as deference to the actions of the men he is commemorating.

6. **Note how Lincoln refers to the combatants as "brave" and "honored." How does he suggest that their struggle was distinguished from that of "us the living"? How does this comparison and contrast create clear similarities and differences between those who fought and those who are present to carry on the soldiers' work?**

   The soldiers have demonstrated ultimate bravery and, for many, the ultimate sacrifice. They have made it possible for the living to complete the "unfinished work." This contrasts with those who are prepared to devote themselves ("increased devotion"—paragraph 3) to restoring the Union through less sacrificial acts. He is suggesting that the combatants' sacrifice is a prerequisite to the ongoing work of the living. However, the reverse is not true. Restoring the Union through peaceful means could not begin without their sacrifice. However, the noncombatants do have in common the goal of freedom.

7. **The American Civil War was a battle between the North and the South, as were the opponents at the Battle of Gettysburg. However, Lincoln does not mention this. What is the reason behind this omission? How does it make the speech focus on more comprehensive issues?**

   Lincoln is more abstract in his address; he does not discuss political issues surrounding the Civil War. Rather, he is describing a tale of morality between good and evil. The speech has religious overtones. Note terms such as "consecrate," "hallow," and "devotion." He also makes reference to the democratic ideology upon which the United States was founded, which, like religion, transcends the temporal moment. Lincoln knows that there are hard feelings on both sides of the war and that if the states are to successfully reunite as a nation, it will be incumbent upon him as a leader to help them find common ground. In recognizing the dead of both sides and reminding them of their common heritage, he is enabling people to focus on their similarities rather than on their differences.

8. **Besides being president, Lincoln was by definition a politician. In what ways can we determine that this is a political speech as well as a dedication?**

   Lincoln reiterates common themes in American thought and draws on traditional American values. As a politician, this is essential for maintaining status and authority. He also ends his speech optimistically, another requirement for a political address. By linking his speech with the Declaration of Independence, he is placing the event (and, by implication, himself) within the context of history.

9. **Speeches are intended to be heard. What are some elements in this speech—for example, vocabulary, syntax, length or brevity of the sentences, and juxtaposition of sentences—that appeal to the sense of sound?**

   Lincoln develops his argument inductively, placing his major theme at the end of the speech. This is important for communication intended to be heard and recalled, as he does not have the luxury of the printed word that would allow his audience to review his major argument. The third paragraph begins with a parallel structure via the repeated use of the phrase "we cannot" as a means of rhetorical emphasis. He also deftly constructs his speech to alternate images of life and death that creates a rhetorical melody to his theme, thereby contributing to a dramatic juxtaposition. Finally, the repetition of the words "that" and "people" has obvious rhetorical effect both aurally and thematically. It contributes to rendering indivisible the idea of "people" and "government."

10. Does this speech appeal primarily to the intellect or the emotions, or equally to the two? What are two or three sentences that demonstrate one or both of these appeals? What was the rationale behind your selections? Does Lincoln include any ethical appeals?

Lincoln expertly combines abstract ideas with the concreteness of the moment. The way he uses terms such as "liberty" and "freedom," however, conveys both an intellectual and emotional tenor in the speech. Terms such as "hallow" and "consecrated" are complemented with more palpable expressions such as "resting-place" and "battlefield." What also must be considered within the historical context of the speech is setting. Lincoln conveys an appropriate tone for the dedication of a cemetery. It is somber but uplifting, offering hope despite tragedy.

Writing

11. Research the actual historical events that occurred during the Battle of Gettysburg. Write an argumentative essay in which you discuss the significance of this particular speech at this point in the Civil War. Use a minimum of three secondary source materials.

A historical analysis of the circumstances of the Gettysburg Address could entail voluminous work. You may wish to abbreviate the students' task by identifying the role of the Battle of Gettysburg in the overall war effort and/or focusing on Lincoln's political role and position at this particular point in the Civil War.

12. Read the speech three times. Then write a paraphrase of it. Examine your paraphrase to discover what elements you recalled. Then reread the speech and write an expository essay focusing on how the structure of the speech contributed to your understanding of the subject.

Because the speech is so famous, students may assume they already "know it." This makes it even more crucial to demand a critical reading of its rhetoric. By writing a paraphrase, the student can better understand the method and function of the speech's rhetorical devices, teasing out which elements are geared toward style and which toward information.

Class Closer

Finalize class by asking students to recognize the appeals used in both Lincoln's Gettysburg Address and the classic/contemporary image pairing. Each dealt with war. How did each argue differently against the horrors of war?

Homework

Ask students to read and annotate the textbook section **Writing Powerful Arguments**.

Lesson Plan 3.3

Writing Powerful Arguments

Class Opener

Have students work in groups and think of examples of argument and evidence they have encountered since the previous English class. Ask them to consider events in other classes and on the news. Allow students to share pertinent examples. Be prepared to share one or two examples yourself from a recent newscast.

Activity: Discuss Argument "Steps"

Discuss with students the basic steps to writing an argument essay. Point out that when they write an argument essay, their main purpose is to convince readers to accept the writer's particular view or opinion on an issue or topic. In addition, at times, a second purpose may be to persuade the audience to take some sort of action.

To convince readers in an argument essay, it is important to provide them with a clear main point and plenty of logical evidence to back it up. Say, for example, that students want to argue that public schools should require students to wear uniforms. In this case, students should research to gather as much evidence as possible to support the point. They may check to see if uniforms are cheaper than the alternative. Perhaps they could find out if schools with uniforms have a lower rate of violence than those without them. They may even look for studies to see if students' academic performance improves when school uniforms are adopted. Remind students as they search for evidence to be sure that it clearly links to their topics and supports the main point they are trying to get across to their audience.

Explain that although consideration of audience is important for all essay forms, it is absolutely critical to the success of an argument essay. Depending on the main point students choose, their audience may be firmly opposed to their view or somewhat supportive of it. As students begin planning their argument essay, they need to ask themselves what objections an audience may hold to the argument. Why would people not support the student's main point? What, if anything, are the merits of the opposing point of view? To "get inside the head" of the opposition, students need to research all possible angles of the topic.

Activity: Create an Outline I

Give students the following comments and prewriting instructions.

Comments:

- Television has proved to be one of the worst inventions of modern times.
- Giving students grades does more harm than good.
- To protect the larger society, the age at which a boy can earn a driver's license should be raised to eighteen.

Prewriting instructions:

a. Take a few minutes to think about the three options. Which one in particular are you for or against, and why? Develop a thesis statement that highlights your position.

b. Make a brief outline of support for your position on one of the options. You may choose to argue against one of the three comments, as well as for it. Preparing the outline will give you a chance to think further about your position. And the outline will show whether you have enough support for your position. If you find that you do not have enough support to develop three paragraphs, choose another position and prepare another outline.

c. Decide how you will develop each of your three supporting points. Fill in the outline with a topic sentence (idea) for each supporting paragraph. Then add evidence and details for these three supporting points. In addition to preparing the outline, you may want to use other prewriting techniques, such as freewriting or creating lists or asking questions.

d. Decide in which order you want to present your paragraphs. *Emphatic order* (in which you *end* with your most important reason) is often the most effective way to organize an argument. Your reader is most likely to remember your final reason.

e. Identify several potential opposing arguments and summarize how you intend to counterargue.

f. As you write your outline, think of your audience as a jury that will ultimately believe or disbelieve your argument. Have you presented a convincing case? Do you need more details? If you were on the jury, would you be favorably impressed with this argument?

Activity: Create an Outline II

Ask students to turn to page 122 in the textbook. Using one of the three models provided for an argumentative essay, ask them to outline a response to the following prompt. Their outline should clearly detail their major points and argument format.

> In "The Gettysburg Address," one of the most famous and oft-studied speeches of history, Abraham Lincoln claims, "The world will little note, nor long remember, what we say here, but it can never forget what they did here." Lincoln's speech, one could argue, has become as much a part of our "remembering" the Civil War as any battle that was fought. In a well-reasoned essay, defend, challenge, or qualify the claim that language used to document an event can be every bit as memorable and powerful as the event itself. Consider historical events, literary examples, and personal experience in your response.

In groups, allow students to discuss their outlines. Have each group choose one essay outline to present to the class. Help students evaluate their adherence to the model chosen from the textbook.

Point out to students that the prompt does not ask them to defend, challenge, or qualify *Lincoln's speech*; instead, students are to outline a response to the claim that "language used to document an event can be every bit as memorable and powerful as the event itself." If students struggle to find relevant examples for their outline, remind them of the HELPS ME format (See page 129 of the student textbook). Some possible topics they could consider include Martin Luther King, Jr.'s "I Have a Dream" speech, the Declaration of Independence, George Bush's speech to Congress after the events of September 11, 2001, Barack Obama's speech to the 2004 Democratic National Convention, Tim O'Brien's *The Things They Carried*, or Brutus's speech in *Julius Caesar*.

Class Closer

Ask students to take a final look at their outlines and make any changes they deem necessary based on the class discussion. Students should turn in their outlines as a means of formative assessment.

Lesson Plan 3.4

Recognizing Fallacies in Reasoning

Class Opener

Explain to students that logic can be twisted for ineffective or blatantly unfair arguments. Ask students to read through the unfair emotional appeals and logical fallacies on pages 126–128 of the textbook. There are a total of 11.

Activity: Creating Examples of Fallacies

Assign the unfair emotional appeals and logical fallacies to various groups, and ask each group to either create an example of a fallacious argument or find one using the Internet.

Go around the room, and allow groups to share their fallacies. Most of these will be over the top and humorous. After they have finished sharing, have the groups exchange arguments. Have each group revise the fallacious argument to create an argument that would be considered sound.

Again, have the groups share the newly created "sound" arguments. Are these really sound? What are some common examples we see in the media of fallacious arguments? Consider "begging the question" (aka slippery slope) arguments for drug use (cigarettes lead to marijuana, which leads to harder drugs). Consider the rhetoric used during the healthcare reform debates (the idea that healthcare reform would lead to euthanasia). Consider showing political advertisements and analyzing these for fallacy.

Activity: Fallacies Quiz

Provide students with the following examples of fallacies, and have them match each to its type of fallacy.

> Throughout American history, military leaders have always made excellent presidents. Look at the examples of George Washington, Andrew Jackson, and Dwight Eisenhower. *(hasty generalization)*
>
> When a team from the NFC wins the Super Bowl, economic growth during the next year is stronger than when a team from the AFC wins the Super Bowl. Therefore, if we want economic growth, we should root for a team from the NFC to win this year's Super Bowl. *(false cause-and-effect relationship)*
>
> Employees are like nails. Just as nails must be hit on the head to get them to work, so must employees. *(weak or false analogy)*
>
> The governor must be correct in his patriotic approach to social policy; after all, the polls show that 60 percent of the people support him. *(bandwagon)*
>
> How dare my opponents accuse me of political corruption at a time when we are working to improve the quality of life for all people in the United States. *(disconnected ideas)*
>
> The head of the commerce commission has a number of interesting economic proposals, but let's not forget that she comes from a very wealthy family. (*ad hominem*)

The government must either raise taxes or eliminate services for the poor. *(oversimplification—either/or)*

Now that the TSA is allowed to use full body scanners and invasive pat-downs before letting us through security, it's only a matter of time before they strip-search every man, woman, and child who wants to fly on a plane. *(begging the question, slippery slope)*

Class Closer

Show a clip of "The Witch's Trial" from *Monty Python's Search for the Holy Grail.* While the clip is funny, it is also replete with logical fallacies. Stop the clip and let students explain each fallacy. Note that the students will often be able to relate each clip to multiple fallacies concurrently. For example, "How do you know she is a witch?" is followed by "She looks like one!" This could be identified as oversimplification, as hasty generalization, or even, arguably, as *ad hominem*. The perfectly healthy man claiming to have been turned into a newt is clearly a *non sequitur*. The argument that witches burn because they are made of wood is clearly a false cause-effect relationship, but it could also be described as a weak or false analogy.

Homework

Ask students to read the textbook section **The Argument Essay on the AP Exam** for homework. They will refer back to this section when they first write an argument essay. Reading this section now will help students start thinking about the process.

Lesson Plan 3.5

Practicing an Argument Essay

Class Opener

In the textbook, students are given the "HELPS ME" mnemonic. This activity challenges students to practice ways in which they can approach argumentation by using their background knowledge (as they will do on test day). Write the mnemonic on the board and discuss what it stands for:

HELPS ME

History
Current **E**vents
Literature and Arts
Personal Experience
Science and Technology
Money
Ethics

Activity: The Argument Essay on the AP Exam

A typical argument essay prompt on the AP Exam provides a philosophical quotation and requires students to take a position on some aspect of the abstract topic under consideration. For this activity, you will create four stations that students will rotate among in groups. An ideal group is 3-4 students. If you have a large class, consider creating two sets of the prompts.

Photocopy the brief prompts below on separate sheets of paper, or see **Chapter 3 online, Chapter Assignments, Practicing an Argument Essay.**

William Ralph Inge once said, "The aim of education is the knowledge not of facts but of values." Write an essay in which you take a position on the true nature of the aim of education.

James Lovelock claimed, "Sadly, it's much easier to create a desert than a forest." Consider the environmental implications of this claim and write an essay in which you take a position on humanity's responsibility to and relationship with the environment.

Richard Wright argued, "Men can starve from a lack of self-realization as much as they can from a lack of bread." Write an essay in which you take a position on the necessity or lack thereof for individuals to recognize their own strengths and limitations.

John Paul Jones saw a clear distinction between the cultivation of fear and the cultivation of faith, stating "If fear is cultivated it will become stronger, if faith is cultivated it will achieve mastery." Write an essay in which you take a position on what abstract concepts should be cultivated by individuals.

As students move around the room, they will work in their groups to identify elements related to the HELPS ME categories. For example, students responding to the first prompt about education might include these ideas:

Prompt:

William Ralph Inge once said, "The aim of education is the knowledge not of facts but of values." Write an essay in which you take a position on the true nature of the aim of education.

HELPS ME Categories	Information I know about the prompt topic
History	The quotation seems to be encompassing people and "learners" the world over. Education is a universal concept, and it seems that the importance of character would be a universal concept.
Current **E**vents	Several studies have shown that today's youth are facing higher levels of anxiety and depression related to their educations. Might this be happening because we as a society are putting so much emphasis on the acquisition of facts and too little focus on values?
Literature and Arts	Ralph Waldo Emerson's essay "Education" supports Inge's quote. Emerson discusses how students, if they are taught to trust in their inspiration, will flourish educationally. In contrast, if students are drilled with facts, they will lose their enthusiasm for learning.
Personal Experience	Time is something that must be managed better. If we agree as a whole that values-based education is the purpose to education, then we must make time for that proposition. The reality is that in today's world, we already have our time over-scheduled. How would we fit in classes devoted to values? Is Inge saying that we should get rid of fact-based education? Should we remove history and math from the curriculum? How do we rationalize these ideas? Maybe we could focus on how students currently use their free time. Maybe we could put more focus on student extracurricular activities, so that students have more time for things like National Honor Society.

Science and Technology	There is much to say about this education and technology. Teenagers today spend many hours a day looking at screens. What sort of education are they acquiring through this activity? What about the amount of time we spend watching Netflix and YouTube videos? Does that build our character or tear it down? There have been incidents of bullying over social media.
Money	Education is the key to better jobs. People with higher levels of education make more money and have access to more job opportunities. Conversely, education costs money, and there are many people who are struggling with paying off student loan debt. The question we then have to raise is do we gain knowledge of values from this education we are paying for? How can individuals gain knowledge of values?
Ethics	This quotation deals entirely with the idea of ethics. The writer posits that we should be more focused on values (ethics) than on facts. This means that the purpose of education should be to better ourselves through character.

After students have completed the group work, allow them to do a gallery walk where they look at the various answers each group has written.

Class Closer

When students have had a chance to read and discuss with each other informally, have students write a half-essay on one of the prompts. They should write an introduction with a thesis statement, one body paragraph, and then a brief outline for the rest of the essay. Look for evidence that they are writing claims and data, as well as warrants. Many entry-level AP Language students write evidence-centered arguments. The evidence is often adequate, but the essays usually lack claims and warrants. Help students revise by making sure they are explicitly stating each paragraph's claim, and explicitly explaining how they have proved that claim with a strong warrant.

Homework

Ask students to read the textbook section **Synthesizing: Making Connections** for homework. They will refer back to this section when they first write a synthesis essay. Reading this section now will help students start thinking about the process.

Lesson Plan 3.6

Synthesizing: Making Connections

Class Opener

This class opener requires role playing. Invite 6 students to the front of the room and seat them in desks facing the other students. Give each a card to indicate their role. You may use this football example but can easily modify the roles if desired. Prepare the following cards: (1) School Quarterback; (2) Rival School Running Back; (3) Local Newspaper Sports Editor; (4) Local TV Station Sports Reporter; (5) School Coach; (6) Rival School Coach. Use boys and girls; it does not matter if you have a girl quarterback.

After the stage is set, tell students that this week the final game will determine the champion of the season. The six "experts" at the front of the room are discussing the chances of a win this Friday night. Ask each expert (in character) what they think the home school's chances of winning are. Instruct the rest of the class to take notes.

The point of this exercise is to demonstrate how synthesis works. After each "expert" has spoken, tell all of your students that they must defend, challenge, or qualify this statement: "[School name] will beat [rival] this week." Students must write their choice as a statement. Then they must look at their notes and quote, paraphrase, or summarize one of the experts. Once they have done this, tell them to write their own *commentary* of one or two sentences in response to the quote. They cannot merely restate what was said; they must extend it in some way. Next, they must choose another expert and quote him or her using a quote they disagree with. Finally, they will write one or two sentences, probably beginning with the word "although" in response to the quote. They have just written an argument-driven synthesis paragraph. An example might look like this:

> The Generals will defeat the Jaguars this Friday night at Milton Frank Stadium. According to LHS quarterback DL, "The team is better prepared for this game than we've been since I joined the team." This commitment and preparation are sure to enable a sound victory Friday night. The Generals have been practicing at LHS every day since school let out in May, and they certainly appear ready to take on a school of this caliber. WAAY reporter, HJ, is not as sure, adding, "It's great to see the team so confident, but the Jaguars have won the state championship for the past five years. Confidence alone is not going to win this ball game." Although the Jaguars have indeed proved victorious at the state level for the past several years, previous victories do not guarantee another win. In fact, several of the Jaguars' best players graduated last year. One thing is certain: Friday night will be a memorable match-up.

Activity: Introducing the Steps of Synthesizing

Review **Synthesizing: Making Connections** on page 131 with your students. Then assign groups the 6 numbered bullet points in **Guidelines for Argumentative Synthesis** on page 133 of the textbook. Ask each group to become the master of one bullet point, creating an example and explaining their sub-point to the class.

Activity: Identifying Reliable and Unreliable Online Sources

Have students read **Critiquing Sources** on page 132 of the textbook. Explain that, as students move toward answering Synthesis prompts, it will be important that they recognize the difference between a reliable online source (*The New York Times*) and an unreliable online source (personal blogs). It is also important that they learn to be discerning in recognizing when information may simply be outdated. If time permits, access Wikipedia with students, and show them why Wikipedia is not an acceptable academic source. (It's great for solving debates at the dinner table, but it cannot be trusted as a documented source.)

Activity: The Synthesis Essay on the AP Exam

This is a technology-focused lesson as students will need access to the Internet to accomplish it. One of the strongest activities you can offer students in preparing for the AP Exam's synthesis question is to place them in the position of "question writers." Have students read the textbook section **The Synthesis Essay on the AP Exam** on pages 133–135. Then share with them any of the College Board's released exams. Note that the format changed with the 2011 exam, so exams after that date will be closest to what they will see today. As they examine the way the prompts are constructed, they should notice the pattern described below.

Each cover page includes the following:

a. **An introductory paragraph.** This paragraph first describes the situation in broad terms, and then offers the opposing viewpoints on the topic. The introductory paragraph is either 3 sentences: Overview. View A. View B. Or it is 2 sentences: Overview. View A; however, View B.

b. **A prompt paragraph.** These are virtually identical on every prompt. This is the format: "Carefully read the following X sources, including the introductory information for each source. Then synthesize information from at least three of the sources and incorporate it into a coherent, well-written essay that develops a position on <insert description of problem.>"

c. **A rules paragraph.** This is also the same on each prompt. It reads: "Make sure that your argument is central; use the sources to illustrate and support your reasoning. Avoid merely summarizing the sources. Indicate clearly which sources you are drawing from, whether through direct quotation, paraphrase, or summary. You may cite the sources as Source A, Source B, etc., or by using the descriptions in parentheses."

d. **A listing of the sources**

Finding 5-8 sources is time-consuming and probably too much for this exercise. Instead, challenge students to work in groups to identify a topic and find 3 relevant sources. Each source should be excerpted to approximately one page, and each should have an MLA-formatted header.

Students' deliverables will thus include:

- A cover page with an introduction, prompt, rules, and list of sources.
- Three sources, each cut to a page or less, with headers in MLA format.

This will give students crucial practice in identifying how the synthesis prompt works, and better prepare them for facing and writing these essays.

Lesson Plan 3.7

Teaching "The Art of Rhetoric"

Class Opener

Remind students of Aristotle's rhetorical triangle, drawing it on the board and reminding students of the interrelationships between speaker and audience; audience and subject; subject and speaker.

Activity: Discussing "The Art of Rhetoric" by Aristotle

Using think-along strategies, read and discuss the excerpt from "The Art of Rhetoric" with students. See suggested answers to questions below.

Suggested Answers

"The Art of Rhetoric" by Aristotle

The Works of Aristotle: Rhetorica, by W. R. Roberts. De rhetorica ad Alexandrum, by E. S. Forster. De poetica, by I. Bywater. Volume 11 of *The Works of Aristotle*, William David Ross. Clarendon Press, 1924.

Comprehension

1. **The last paragraph points out skills a person must hold to effectively persuade. What are other words for the three listed abilities that a person must hold?**

   Other words for the three listed abilities that a person must hold are logos, ethos, pathos. It is important that students recognize and remember these terms as they appear frequently in multiple choice questions. These devices speak to the writer's perception of the audience. Each writer must consider how the audience might best be persuaded. By employing these appeals, the author is assuming something about both the subject (do we relate most directly to the subject through ethics, logic, or emotion?) and the audience (that they will most directly relate to the subject through ethics, logic, emotion, or some combination of the three).

2. **What does Aristotle believe to be the most important means for a person to be able to persuade others?**

   Aristotle believes a man's character and his commitment to justice and truth are the most important means for a person to be able to persuade others. In other words, Aristotle believes that ethos is the highest appeal. It is the speaker's ability to establish his ethical position that will ultimately persuade an audience.

3. **Where is rhetoric's place when considering the arts?**

   Rhetoric is an art that can draw opposite conclusions based on the persuasiveness of the rhetorician (although ultimately truth will prevail). It, like the arts, is not a one-time cure for something but allows for continued awareness that results in a person's overall growth towards well-being.

4. **Aristotle begins and ends this portion of "The Art of Rhetoric" with one clear point about the misuse of rhetoric. What is that point?**

   Rhetoric can be misused when a speaker is not committed to the betterment of the human condition but is only concerned about persuading just for the sake of the speaker's ego. Those students who are familiar with the term "rhetoric" will have negative associations with it. The point that Aristotle is making is that rhetoric can be used for ill uses, but should not be. Rhetoric has as many legitimate uses.

Rhetorical Analysis

5. **How does Aristotle use exemplification to assert his position?**

   Aristotle urges orators to take human nature into account when preparing speeches. He urges orators to consider the human condition and the psychology behind it.

6. **Aristotle uses the rhetorical strategy of repetition in paragraph 3 (and once in paragraph 7). Identify it and explain why it is effective.**

   In paragraph 3, Aristotle's use of "It is clear" highlights and grounds those prevailing ideas in the reader's head, and its repetitive nature reinforces the ideas. In stating "It is clear", Aristotle suggests that he, in his persona as the writer, has already established ethos. He has established an ethical position as a trusted authority on this subject. It is as a trusted authority figure that he is able to claim "It is clear"; he is suggesting that the audience trusts him and can accept his authority directly.

7. **What effect do the numerical lists add to Aristotle's rhetorical style?**

   The numerical lists are a form of parallelism, making the points easy and logical to follow. The parallel structure keeps them level by being equally developed and equally paced. In a very real sense, Aristotle himself is appealing to logos by claiming that rhetoric follows an orderly set of rules, which are demonstrated through the numerical list.

8. **Why does Aristotle choose to write this in first person?**

   He wants to draw his audience closer to the subject and align them more readily with the points he is making. In so doing, he is establishing himself as an authority, appealing to ethos as a spokesperson of rhetoric.

Writing

9. **Write a short paraphrase of this excerpt.**

   See the Activity: Paraphrase "The Art of Rhetoric" below.

10. **Consider areas of expertise where you could be successfully persuasive. Choose three and write three premises for your arguments.**

    Answers will vary.

11. **Now consider three stumbling blocks to the arguments you listed in answer 2, and write how you would address each stumbling block.**

    Answers will vary.

Activity: Paraphrase "The Art of Rhetoric"

Ask students to write a paragraph-by-paragraph paraphrase of the excerpt from "The Art of Rhetoric." After they have finished their paraphrases, have students share them within their groups. Then ask the groups to create a multiple-entry journal in which they look at Aristotle's use of example in the text. For this, they should consider Aristotle's conveyance of rhetorical theory through the direct examples he provides throughout the article. The key to this exercise is to convince students to enter into a conversation with Aristotle. What are the claims he is making? How do they respond to those claims? In their groups, students should consider their reactions to Aristotle as the authority on rhetoric. Do they accept his judgment and clarity—"It is clear"—as much as he does?

Class Closer

Close class by allowing groups to share their paraphrases. As a whole class, consider each of Aristotle's "It is clear" claims. Are these items truly "clear"? Can they be so obviously claimed and justified?

Homework

Have students read *Common Sense* and answer the comprehension questions that accompany the selection.

Lesson Plan 3.8

Teaching "Common Sense"

Class Opener

As a class opener, review the comprehension questions for *Common Sense*. Ensure that students adequately understand the pre-1800s prose.

Activity: Point-Counterpoint

Draw a two-column chart on the board with the column headings "Point" and "Counterpoint." Read aloud *Common Sense* with students, noting how Paine brings up the British and Loyalist perspectives and arguments, and then how he deflates or completely overturns those claims with his own arguments.

Activity: Timed Essay

Give students 40 minutes to write an essay in response to the following prompt:

> **Write an essay in which you support or discourage political acts that endanger the lives of those without voices. Draw upon examples from your reading (including Thomas Paine), from personal experience, and from your knowledge of world politics and events.**

Class Closer

Work with students to "unpack the question." Ask students to share their thesis statements. Then ask them to share particular examples they employed.

Suggested Answers

"Common Sense" by Thomas Paine

Common Sense by Thomas Paine. Philadelphia: W. & T. Bradford, February 14, 1776. http://www.gutenberg.org/files/147/147-h/147-h.htm

Comprehension

1. **Paine's major complaint with the current political system between Great Britain and America centers on what idea?**

   The citizens of America came to America to be a separate system. They had been encouraged to be independent, but Great Britain now wants to gain any benefits that the commerce in America can afford them. The Americans resent taxation without representation.

2. **How does Paine feel about "every quiet method for peace"?**

   He says it has been "ineffectual" due to the fact that the King's vanity and obstinacy have made him unwilling to care or act upon America's wishes.

3. **What is one of the largest obstacles for Great Britain to remain in control of America?**

   The largest obstacle is the sheer distance between the two regions as well as the fact that America is a large continent, not a small island like Great Britain.

Rhetorical Analysis

4. Why was Paine's *Common Sense* so effective in getting people to act?

He spoke in a language familiar to the masses. His use of first person pulls each reader into the text and allows each person to have a larger, more resounding, voice. The pamphlet became a rallying cry to all citizens in America, not just the privileged. Paine's very claim that he was presenting "common sense" called Americans to band together to support an unquestionable ideology.

5. Why does Paine include the quote by Milton in paragraph 25?

The wounds of Great Britain's debasement of the American colonies are so sharply felt that reconciliation is now out of the question. Great Britain's blind eye must make the colonies openly rebel. This quote can also be viewed as an appeal to ethos. Although Paine claims to be proffering "common" sense, Milton represents the literature of the educated elite, extending Paine's argument beyond the masses to the upper echelon as well.

6. How does the title influence the emotions of the readers?

Thomas Paine, reinforcing the fact that he is but a standard citizen of the American colonies, labels his ideas as "common sense" because he wants his inflammatory solutions and ideas to appear as the logical next step for America. Compare this to Aristotle's style. Paine, like Aristotle, attempts to establish himself as the voice of ethos.

7. What would you consider Paine's greatest emotional appeal?

Answers will vary. Many students may refer to Paine's statement that "Even brutes do not devour their young, nor savages make war upon their families. . . ." He also makes the point in paragraph 4 that the issue under discussion is global and timeless.

Writing

8. Think about a situation in which you have felt oppressed. Then write a logical appeal to right the wrongs of that oppression.

Answers will vary. Remind students to focus on logos instead of pathos or ethos.

9. Brainstorm other political situations that could create a document such as *Common Sense*. Give the historical, sociocultural, or economic background of a chosen political situation and justify why the wrongs should be righted.

Answers will vary.

10. Writing an Argument Write an essay in which you support or discourage political acts that endanger lives.

Answers will vary.

CHAPTER 4
Education and Society

Beginning with this chapter, the student textbook consists of readings grouped together within a single topic or theme. Chapter 4's focus is on education. The lesson plans contained within each chapter of this Teacher Manual will endeavor to provide you with a variety of strategies for teaching essays; you will find that there are multiple approaches that will work for any particular essay. In some cases, essays will be paired to encourage students to recognize similarities and differences between voices and styles on a given topic.

Teaching the Chapter

Before discussing any essays in this chapter, have students analyze the photographs in the **Classic and Contemporary Images** feature on pages 150–151. Discuss the questions in the textbook. See suggested answers below.

Classic and Contempory Images: Suggested Answers

1. **How are the settings for the photographs different, and what does that imply, if anything, about the level of education exhibited in each photo?**
   The Native American photo represents a traditional classroom, complete with a blackboard, desk, and student tables. The focus is as much on the setting as it is on the students. The contemporary photo shows a modern laboratory that focuses mostly on the students.

2. **How are the photos similar, and what do those similarities show about education?**
   Both photos show male and female students interested in learning and involved in hands-on experiments. Within an encouraging teaching atmosphere, students want to learn.

3. **Are there gender divisions in the photos? Explain.**
   In the Native American photo, three women are on the outskirts of the photo. All of them are wearing the same dress with the same hairstyle. The six men are in the center of the room and are wearing suits. Although both males and females are in the same classroom, the females appear more as observers than as active participants in the experiments, including the teacher who oversees from the center of the classroom. The contemporary photo shows all students in different attire, but wearing safety goggles and aprons. They are all prominent figures in the photo, and all seem actively engaged in the experiment. The teacher herself is actively involved.

4. **How do the perspective and visual elements of each photograph reveal expressive content, or purpose?**
   The distant perspective of the Carlisle photo shows many actions occurring simultaneously. The angle of the table in the foreground draws the eye to the open desk drawers and the experiment being conducted on the desk. In the center of the classroom, the older teacher observes the students performing the experiments. The scene is one of controlled, almost stilted, learning. The contemporary photo and its closer focus make it appear that students are more actively involved in a single experiment. The focus of their eyes, their looks of expectation, and the angle of the teacher's arm and hand draw the viewer's eye to what is occurring in one spot on the lab table. The contemporary photo also shows safety gear on all of the students, which makes them appear more engaged with their task than the students in the Carlisle photo.

5. Give descriptive titles for each of the photos and explain why you decided on those titles.

   After discussing photo titles, ask students to select one individual in either photo with whom they feel the most connection. Then have them explain why.

Lesson Plan 4.1

A Comparison of Style—Douglass and Rodriguez (Part 1)

Class Opener

When students enter the classroom, have the following two sentences displayed on the board:

> **I lived in Master Hugh's family about seven years.**
>
> **From an early age I knew that my mother and father could read and write both Spanish and English.**

Ask students to work in their groups to determine three things that must be true about the writer of the first sentence, and three things that must be true about the writer of the second sentence. From just these sentences, they should recognize that Frederick Douglass (the writer of the first sentence) was enslaved and saw himself as an outsider to a family. Students should also recognize that Richard Rodriguez (writer of the second sentence) was raised in a bilingual household and that he saw himself as a member of the family. Students should also recognize that both models are written in a narrative mode.

Activity: Analyzing Rhetorical Elements in "Learning to Read and Write"

After students have had a chance to critically examine a single sentence from the text, assign them to work in seven groups to read and annotate a single paragraph from Douglass's essay. (There are eight paragraphs in "Learning to Read and Write.") Paragraph 3 is short, however, so model the activity with paragraph 3 before assigning the other paragraphs to groups.

Have groups read their assigned paragraph carefully for meaning and for rhetorical significance. As this may be one of the first times they have worked with rhetoric, give students very specific instructions. Each group should:

1. Write a one sentence summary of the paragraph.
2. Make a short list of important details from the paragraph.
3. Make a list of the main verb of every sentence in the paragraph.
4. Count the number of words in each sentence.
5. Make a list of sentence starters (prepositional phrase, subject, introductory dependent clause, etc.)
6. Make a list of any "unusual" words the author uses in the paragraph.

After the groups have finished reading and analyzing their individual paragraphs, go around the room and allow students to share their findings. What they will quickly determine is that this essay is written with an elevated vocabulary, with an extensive use of sentence variety, and with complex sentences conveying a simple meaning with complex undertones.

Class Closer

Ask groups to define the tone Douglass conveys in this piece. They should write their tone word on one side of an index card, and on the back, they should justify the word they chose.

Homework

Assign students to read the entirety of the Douglass selection and answer the accompanying questions.

Suggested Answers

"Learning to Read and Write" by Frederick Douglass

From *Narrative of the Life of Frederick Douglass: An American Slave*, Written by Himself. 1845.

Comprehension

1. **What strategies does Douglass use to continue his education after his mistress's abandonment?**

   Douglass endeavors to continue his learning by bribing poor white boys to teach him, secreting newspapers and books that come his way and reading them over and over, imitating the markings of the shipyard crates, challenging other neighborhood boys to exhibit their own skills so he can copy them, and copying lessons from his young master's notebooks.

2. **Why did the author's mistress find his reading newspapers particularly threatening?**

   Douglass's mistress did not want him to learn of the events going on outside his own sphere, particularly events relating to the role of slaves and possible inflammatory news about the work of abolitionists.

3. **Why does Douglass call learning to read "a curse rather than a blessing" (paragraph 6)?**

   Douglass was inflamed by his discovery of the possibilities denied to him and the limitations of his position. Had he never learned to read, he would have remained ignorant and would have accepted his position more easily.

Rhetorical Analysis

4. **What is Douglass's thesis? Paraphrase two points Douglass makes to support his thesis.**

   Douglass's implied thesis is that learning to read opened up his mind to the possibility of freedom (paragraph 6). It is supported by the paragraphs because they describe in detail the processes by which he accomplished his goal of educating himself and trace how this drove him to seek his freedom.

5. The first couple of sentences in the story, though simple, are very powerful. How do they serve to set up the mood of the piece and the reader's expectations?

The first two sentences establish Douglass's position in life (the mention of Master Hugh's family), and the reader understands that education that most children receive automatically is not easily attainable for the narrator. The reader is then ready to discover how such a young boy managed to achieve this goal.

6. Cite examples of Douglass's use of metaphors, and discuss how they help Douglass achieve his purpose.

Douglass uses metaphors such as "heart became stone" (paragraph 2); "bread of knowledge" (paragraph 4); "horrible pit" (paragraph 6); and "trump of freedom" (paragraph 6). Students' answers will vary as to why these images work. By making abstract ideas more concrete, the reader is able to visualize what the writer experiences.

7. How would you describe Douglass's writing style and level of language? Does it reveal anything about his character? Justify your response.

Students' responses to this question may vary. In general, the style and language used are graceful, grammatical, and metaphoric, using both concrete and figurative phrasing. Students' explanations of what the writing reveals about Douglass will also vary; some possible responses may include: proud, kind, intelligent, humble, religious, dedicated, and so on.

8. Explain the way in which the author uses comparison and contrast.

Douglass uses comparison and contrast in several places; for example, to describe his mistress's change in behavior (paragraph 2), or when he describes the benefits he derived from reading different sections of "The Colombian Orator" (paragraph 5).

9. What is Douglass's definition of *abolition*, and how does he help the reader define it? How does this method contribute to the reader's understanding of the learning process?

Douglass defines the word *abolition* in paragraph 7; students may find their own dictionary definition of the word. Douglass uses the context in which the word is placed to help define it. When he cites the escape of a slave as "the fruit of *abolition*," he aids the reader in discovering its meaning. He shows the reader that learning is a methodical process; curiosity and one's perseverance can lead to discovery.

Writing

10. What does Douglass mean when he writes that "education and slavery were incompatible with each other" (paragraph 2)? Write an essay in which you consider the relationship between the two.

When considering what the Douglass quote means, students should think about the end results of education, the process of learning and how this knowledge can be used in society, specifically in the writer's situation as well as in today's world.

11. Both Douglass and his mistress were in inferior positions to Master Hugh. Write an essay in which you compare and contrast their positions in society at the time.

Douglass's mistress was instructed by her husband not to teach the slave child. Students should compare and contrast Douglass's position to that of his mistress. Were they both equally enslaved? What advantages did one have over the other? What opportunities would be available to each if both escaped to the North? What obstacles would each encounter? Students may do some research about society at that time.

12. Illiteracy is still a problem in the United States. Write an account of what your day-to-day life would be like if you couldn't write or read. What impact would this deficiency have on your life? Use concrete examples to illustrate your narrative.

    Students should be as exact and detailed as possible when pondering what their daily lives would be like without literacy—from reading street signs to getting a well-paying job to reading to their children.

13. **Writing an Argument** Write an essay in which you argue for or against the proposition that American education continues to discriminate against minority groups.

    For students to render an effective argument, they should research this topic to understand what studies have been done to both prove and disprove this claim.

Lesson Plan 4.2

A Comparison of Style—Douglass and Rodriguez (Part 2)

Class Opener

When students enter the room, have the following quick-write displayed on the board:

What is a rhetorical question and why might an author choose to use one?

Give students a few moments to respond, and then discuss the question as a class. Explain that the Rodriguez essay they are about to encounter uses multiple rhetorical questions. In fact, paragraph 7 is comprised entirely of rhetorical questions.

Activity: Analyzing Rhetorical Elements in "The Lonely, Good Company of Books"

Once again, assign students to work in groups to read and annotate a single paragraph from Rodriguez's essay "The Lonely, Good Company of Books." It includes 12 paragraphs, but some are too short to work well for this lesson. Assign paragraphs 1, 3-6, and 8-12 (skip paragraphs 2 and 7). Students should work within their groups to read their assigned paragraph carefully for meaning and for rhetorical significance. Again, give groups these specific directions:

1. Write a one sentence summary of the paragraph.
2. Make a short list of important details from the paragraph.
3. Make a list of the main verb of every sentence in their paragraph. (NOTE: Stylistically, Rodriguez uses a number of sentence fragments. Let the students figure this out.)
4. Count the number of words in each sentence.
5. Make a list of sentence starters (prepositional phrase, subject, introductory dependent clause, etc.)
6. Make a list of any "unusual" words the author uses in the paragraph.

After the groups have finished reading and analyzing their individual paragraphs, go around the room and allow students to share their findings. They should quickly surmise that Rodriguez writes in a more modern style, incorporating sentence fragments and a somewhat self-deprecating humor. Discuss how, in his efforts to become "educated," Rodriguez attacked books with a passion. He did not always understand what he read, sometimes missing the subtleties of the text; dismissed books he considered unimportant; and forfeited the benefits of reading a book more than once. Nevertheless, he began to understand that there was a world of value and richness between the covers of a book.

Class Closer

As a group, create a large Venn diagram in which you compare the tone and diction of Douglass's and Rodriguez's essays.

Homework

For homework, students should read the entirety of the Rodriguez selection and answer the accompanying questions.

Suggested Answers

"The Lonely, Good Company of Books" by Richard Rodriguez

Comprehension

1. What was Rodriguez's parents' attitude toward reading? How did it influence his attitude? Cite examples from the essay that support your opinion.

Rodriguez's parents have an offhand attitude toward reading (paragraph 1), using their skills simply for practical purposes. This attitude caused the writer to feel disconnected from the world around him when he read ("lonely"). Students may provide additional examples.

2. What does Rodriguez mean by the "fellowship between a reader and a writer" (paragraph 4)? Why does he differentiate between "intimate" and "personal" forms of communication?

In paragraph 4, the writer makes this reference to experiencing books as a message aimed directly at him with nothing in the way. The difference between "intimate" and "personal" is that between speaking and reading. Speaking involves sharing the day-to-day events and trivialities that commonly involve the speakers with similar connections. Reading is personal because although you do not know the writer or share his background or experiences, you are linked with him in an effort to understand his thoughts and intentions. It is both simpler and more complex than speech.

3. Rodriguez hoped that reading would fill "the hollow" inside him. What was the cause of his emptiness? Why did he find reading a lonely experience?

Rodriguez found reading lonely because he was trapped in silence with the writer, without any connections to the outside world (paragraph 3).

Rhetorical Analysis

4. What is the thesis of Rodriguez's essay? Is it stated or implied? Explain.

Rodriguez's thesis is implied rather than stated: he began reading because he associated it with academic success, but he ended up appreciating the fact that books could offer much more.

5. **How does the author's use of narrative advance his views on reading and education?**

The author uses a personal story to convey his ideas without lecturing, which helps him to communicate with the reader more personally, enabling others to identify with his point of view.

6. **What is the writer's tone? How effective is it in conveying his point of view?**

Rodriguez's tone is subjective, relying on his own personal perceptions of the events he relates. There is an ironic, self-mocking tone in his narrative as he looks back on an attitude he no longer holds.

7. **Rodriguez uses uppercase letters (small capitals) when referring to signs advocating reading. Why does he use this device? How does it support his point of view?**

In paragraph 3, the writer uses uppercase letters to convey the association he made between reading and education. These signs guided him toward reading and suggested that his society held books in great esteem and would only admit him if he felt the same.

8. **The essay ends with an ironic anecdote. Why did Rodriguez choose to conclude this way? Does it satisfactorily illustrate his attitude? Explain how it ties into his earlier question, "Did one learn something only by reading it?"**

Rodriguez's closing anecdote reinforces his point that his attitude toward reading was still focused on acquiring information and making himself educated in terms that society would recognize. The final sentence in the essay is humorous and drives home this point even more strongly.

9. **What words or phrases imply that there is an ethnic component in Rodriguez's conflict? Is the subtlety effective? Justify your response.**

References to the ethnic component appear in the first paragraph in which he refers to his Hispanic background. It can also be found at the end of the third paragraph (albeit subtly) when he is considered a remedial reader. In paragraph 11, there is also a hint of ethnicity ("... reading made me a confident speaker and writer of English."). The subtlety works because it allows the reader to come to his own conclusions about why reading and education were especially important for a boy like Rodriguez.

Writing

10. **Rodriguez's parents had a pragmatic attitude toward reading. What was the attitude in your home as you were growing up? Did your parents encourage your interest in reading? Did they read themselves? What is the first book you remember reading by yourself? Write an essay in which you describe your reading history, and how it has impacted your life.**

In a personal narrative, students should focus on how reading was approached in their homes, and give an account of their reading history using Rodriguez's essay as a model.

11. **Is reading still a significant source of information and entertainment, or has it been usurped by television or the Internet? Write an essay explaining why it is important (or necessary) to be a reader today.**

Students may approach this topic from either side and argue their points. They may compare and contrast what TV or the Internet offers by way of information or entertainment that books do not offer.

12. **Writing an Argument** **Rodriguez believed reading would make him "educated." Do you agree or disagree? Is reading vital to a person's education? How do you define *education*? Can it be acquired only through reading, or are there other contributing factors? Write an argumentative essay on this topic.**

Students should write an argumentative essay on the connection between reading and education using examples and observations, and they may quote from the Rodriguez essay.

Lesson Plan 4.3

Timed-Writing: Synthesizing the Classic and Contemporary Essays

Have students turn to the synthesis questions that appear after these two essays on page 163 in the textbook. Tell students to choose one of the options and write for a minimum of 30 minutes.

After students have finished writing, use the remainder of the class period to group students according to the option they chose. Students should read and comment on each other's essays, offering a positive comment, a critical comment, and a question for each essay read.

Homework

Have students read Louis Menand's "The Graduates" and ask them to prepare for a Socratic seminar on the essay. (See below.)

Socratic Seminars
Socratic seminars require students to question each other, to take notes on the discussion, and perhaps to write a conclusion paragraph after the seminar. These types of seminars encourage active participation in class while holding students accountable for that participation. The key to a successful seminar is found in the accountability. To hold students accountable and to foster a positive seminar, consider the following requirements: • Clearly assign the reading in advance. Students must have already read the essay in order for a seminar to occur. • Require students to come with a defined number of prepared questions (two or three is usually sufficient.) • Review with students the types of questions that are allowed. If you allow comprehension questions, make sure students write only one comprehension question. Other questions must make connections within the text, between multiple texts, or between the text and a bigger idea. • Clearly define your expectations for participation and grade accordingly. Depending on the size of the class, require each student to contribute meaningfully to the conversation at least once, if not twice. • Require documentation at the end of the seminar. Students should be told that they will be required to turn in their list of questions, notes they take during the seminar, and a clear and concise conclusion paragraph as follow-up to the seminar. • Always allow time at the end of class for students to prepare their concluding paragraphs; otherwise you risk reading "shared" responses rather than individual work.

Lesson Plan 4.4

Socratic Seminar on Menand's "The Graduates"

Class Opener

Before class begins, organize the room in such a way that will foster discussion. Many teachers choose to place desks in a large circle.

Activity: Holding the Socratic Seminar

This is largely a student-driven process with the teacher acting as facilitator as needed. Allow the student-generated questions to be the focus of the seminar and step in only if the discussion goes far afield. The questions that accompany the essay provide a good jumping-off point if necessary.

There are a number of good videos on YouTube that show Socratic seminars. Many teachers prefer to have an inner and an outer group, with only the inner students participating at any given time. Some teachers add a hot seat so that if a student in the outer circle has something they want to contribute, they have the opportunity. Some use the Harkness Table approach (a Socratic variation). The key is that this is a student-driven, question-driven discussion. One strategy is to have all students write and bring to class a WHAT question, a HOW question, and a WHY question. Then those questions become the basis for the discussion. For grading purposes, use a checklist like the one below:

Name	Questions	Contribution 1	Contribution 2	Contribution 3

Students receive 50 points simply for turning in their three questions at the door. (Check the questions as students walk in.) When students contribute to the discussion in a meaningful way for the first time, the 50 points turn into 80 points. When they contribute for a second time, 80 points become 90 points. The third time, they are up to 100 points. As soon as one student reaches 100 points, tell all the students their scores and invite those with 100 points to listen quietly while other students catch up. Some teachers hand out coins each time a student speaks. However you manage it, make sure everyone has an opportunity to be heard.

Class Closer

At the end of the discussion, allow students enough time to write a paragraph synthesizing their thoughts on the topic. Five minutes should be sufficient.

Suggested Answers

"The Graduates" by Louis Menand

Comprehension

1. What is Menand's opinion of the American system of education? Do you think he is biased? Why or why not?

Menand's argument only includes discussion of the college experience at American institutions of higher education and is written in a way that suggests he is writing about native-born Americans in that context. He does not appear to take into consideration first-generation or immigrant experiences in American colleges and universities, although his last paragraph suggests that "more than fifty percent of Americans spend some time in college." If biased is understood as exclusionary, Menand's opinion may be considered biased.

2. According to Menand, what are some of the reasons why a college education has become devalued?

The increasing tuition and the pointless and escalating stress-inducing competition to enter and survive a college education are making the venture less appealing.

3. Explain what Menand means by *meritocracy.* Would you say that the fact that he teaches at Harvard and refers to this institution in his essay explains his focus on this concept? Justify your response by referring to the text.

For Menand, the term *meritocracy* is used to avoid admitting that talent is in the eye of the admissions officer in institutions like Harvard. The fourth paragraph in the text supports this view when the author discusses the anxiety-producing reality of institutions that rely on systems of merit-based admissions.

Rhetorical Analysis

4. Menand wrote this brief essay for a well-known and decidedly urbane publication. How does he address his audience? What elements of Menand's style would appeal to *The New Yorker* readers?

Menand varies use of the first-, second-, and third-person forms of address, and the assumption that his readers can relate to the college experience throughout his essay. Doing so casts a rather elite experience in a common garment, and underscores his point that what some may consider common experiences can be uncommon.

5. What is Menand's purpose in creating an analogy in his introductory paragraph? Do you find this strategy effective? Why or why not?

Menand uses the sleepover analogy to connect his argument to something familiar. His use of this analogy is effective because it invites the reader to question her own filters and recall a time when her view of reality was thrown off-kilter by circumstances.

6. Where does Menand state his claim? What are his main supporting points, and what types of evidence does he present?

Menand states his claim at the end of the second paragraph. He supports his argument that college is stressful by providing a string of numbers and percentages comparing the ratio of applicants to those accepted; enrollees to graduates; and business majors to those in other disciplines.

7. Does Menand rely largely on appeals to reason, emotion, or ethics, or does he combine these approaches? Justify your response.

Menand combines various appeals in his argument in order to make unfamiliar an experience that is largely taken for granted—attending college. Appealing to reason invites readers with chips on their shoulders to set their burdens down while he takes aim at other readers' indifference, using moral arguments about grade inflation and the cost of tuition. He begins and ends his essay with an appeal to the readers' emotions.

8. How does Menand link his opening and concluding paragraphs? Why does he use the word *vertigo* in the last paragraph?

Menand links his introduction and conclusion with reference to a sleepover experience. He uses the term *vertigo* to suggest a desirable state of imbalance that he wishes might be part of every college student's experience. Such an experience, he argues, would temper the confidence of graduates with the sobering recognition that their reality is not the standard by which all others must be judged.

Writing

9. Write a causal essay in which you analyze the reasons why college can be a stressful experience.

Student responses will vary. Remind students that they must include a thematic statement that can be supported by three claims (or topic sentences), which in turn are supported by evidence, details, and ideas.

10. Compose your own extended definition of meritocracy and how this relates to the American educational system.

Provide students with this statement from Menand's essay if they have trouble getting started on their writing: "You can't learn when you're afraid of being wrong."

11. Writing an Argument **Write a rebuttal to Menand, arguing that a college education is in no way comparable to one's first sleepover.**

Students may use examples and observations from adults who have attended college, and students may quote from the Menand essay.

Lesson Plan 4.5

Annotating and Questioning Gregorian's "America, Still On Top"

This lesson will be an exercise in rhetorical analysis, using the dialectical journal format to annotate the Gregorian essay. This is a relatively short essay, making it an excellent choice for in-class annotation. Although annotating is a common homework assignment, occasionally allowing students to annotate while in-class allows you to monitor whether students are annotating correctly.

Class Opener

Review the dialectical journal format covered in Chapter 1.

Activity: Multiple-Entry Journal

The multiple-entry journal approach encourages students to move past simply reading an essay for comprehension and into the realm of rhetorical analysis. Aloud, have volunteers read Vartan Gregorian's "America, Still on Top." Challenge students to use the multiple-entry journal to analyze this essay.

Then, working in their groups, students should choose three quotations and analyze the "why" and "how" of each quotation. Provide students with the graphic organizer shown below. (Photocopy the chart, or see **Chapter 4 online, Vartan Gregorian: Multiple-Entry Journal.)**

Gregorian's Purpose:	
A quotation that demonstrates this purpose **(What)**	
Your rationale for why this quotation demonstrates Gregorian's purpose **(Why or Commentary)**	
A description of what is unique about the writing style **(How)**	

Activity: Using Journal Entries to Write a Paragraph

Ask students to take a single row from the chart they created and write a single paragraph that answers this question: "What is Gregorian's purpose in writing this essay? Provide textual evidence to support your position." Explain that students' paragraphs should follow this format: topic sentence, quotation, commentary (multiple sentences), conclusion.

Class Closer

Discuss the suggested answers to the questions accompanying the essay in the textbook.

Homework

Students should read and be ready to discuss Mike Rose's essay, "What College Can Mean to the Other America."

Suggested Answers

"America, Still on Top" by Vartan Gregorian

Gregorian, Vartan, "America, Still on Top," *Newsweek,* August 20-27, 2007. Reprinted by permission of the author.

Comprehension

1. According to Gregorian, what are the strengths of American higher education? What are the weaknesses?

For the author, American higher education has benefited from its affordability; accessibility; and hybrid, public-private funding mechanisms.

2. According to Gregorian, why is American higher education, on balance, superior to those in Europe, Asia, Africa, and Latin America?

Gregorian argues that the informal design, local control, and public and private options that comprise the educational landscape in the United States are its strengths. Other continents and cultures evolved systems of higher education from the top down and benefited from relatively little cross-fertilization from the contributions of foreign scholars.

3. Explain the "collision course" that Gregorian mentions in this essay.

The author uses this phrase to indicate the tension between Old and New World ways of meeting their cultures' and citizens' needs and expectations for higher education. Both must find effective ways of stemming brain drain and cultivating a competitive edge in a globalized economy.

Rhetorical Analysis

4. What is the purpose of Gregorian's introductory paragraph? How effective do you find this strategy? Justify your response with reference to the text.

On the one hand, Gregorian's statement that the strength of American higher education derives from its informal design is effective because it is disarming. On the other hand, if what follows is a recipe for future success, it is limited because one cannot set out to reform or replace an existing system "informally."

5. What is Gregorian's claim, and where does he present it most clearly?

The author makes his claim that America's system of higher education is exemplary most clearly in his opening, closing, and penultimate paragraphs. In each of these paragraphs, he illustrates the strengths and weaknesses of American higher education.

6. How does Gregorian use comparison and contrast to structure this essay? What points of comparison does he develop?

Gregorian compares the origins of educational systems in the United States with those in communist countries, on the African continent, and in Latin America. He compares their quality, strategies for increasing enrollment, and fund-raising.

7. What types of evidence does Gregorian provide to support his argument? Do you find this evidence to be sufficient? Why or why not?

Gregorian effectively discusses the difference between systems of education in the United States and other countries and their evolution through time. His evidence is sufficient because his argument itself is conditional. America is once again on top, but only for a short time if her institutions do not evolve the way institutions in other countries have been forced to do.

8. What is Gregorian's purpose in referring to the post-9/11 and increasingly globalized world? Does this motif reinforce his argument or detract from it? Explain.

Gregorian uses 9/11 to indicate the historic moment that American higher education lost its edge over institutions in other countries, although he notes that interest in obtaining American degrees is once again on the rise. He refers to the globalized world to underscore the context in which competition for brainpower now exists and to illustrate new or virtually absent boundaries for that battlefield.

Writing

9. Write a brief essay on what you perceive as the strengths of American higher education.

Student responses will vary.

10. Compare and contrast the thesis of Gregorian's essay with the thesis of Louis Menand's "The Graduates."

Students should use examples from both the Gregorian essay and Menand's essay to support their claims.

11. **Writing an Argument** Argue for or against the proposition that in a globalized world, foreign educational systems will ultimately catch up with American higher education.

Require students to introduce at least three claims to support their arguments.

Lesson Plan 4.6

Four-Corner Debate On Mike Rose's "What College Can Mean to the Other America"

This particular lesson uses a classroom debate to force students to take a position on an issue and to defend that position in class. As the name implies, students will be sent to the four corners of the room to craft and prepare their positions. Do not allow students to choose their sides. Assign students to each of the four corners, and then tell them what position they will be arguing. Rose argues that socioeconomic forces divide class distinction. Thus, the impoverished are prevented from academic and career advancement. Allowing students to work on the debate for two days will give them time to pull together some research, but this debate also can be done effectively in just one class period.

Class Opener

Sort your students into four groups and have them physically move to the four corners of the room. Assign the four corners these four positions:

1. Broad monetary cuts to formal education are a historical fact of life; *other means beyond technology* must be implemented to achieve equal socioeconomic status.
2. *More money and attention* must be allocated to improve the educational status of the impoverished by *cutting other unnecessary programs.*
3. *Technology is the answer* to this educational problem; there are non-monetary ways to implement technology.
4. The problem cannot be altered; *this is the "normal."*

Activity: Preparing for the Debate

Assuming that this will be a one-period debate, give students 15–20 minutes (set a timer) to devise compelling arguments that prove the position they were given. They must come up with relevant examples. Using media in the room or the library will help students prepare better responses.

Activity: Conducting the Debate

Conduct the debate. There are many ways to do this, but primary concerns should be that the groups take turns, limited by equal time. An effective strategy is to let the first group present their most compelling argument in two minutes or less, then give the other groups one minute each to provide a rebuttal. Repeat this strategy three more times by letting the next group present for two minutes, followed by a one-minute rebuttal from the other three groups.

Class Closer

Ask the groups to determine which group won the debate. The "catch" is that they cannot vote for their own group.

Homework

Students should read Susan Jacoby's essay and prepare three questions for a Fishbowl discussion. Remind students to avoid fact-based questions.

Suggested Answers

"What College Can Mean to the Other America" by Mike Rose

"What College Can Mean to the Other America" by Mike Rose for *The Chronicle of Higher Education*, September 11, 2011. Reprinted by permission of the author.

Comprehension

1. **Note all references that Rose makes to Michael Harrington and his book. Explain the importance that Rose gives to Harrington's study and its relevance to his topic.**

   Rose makes the point that the cultural gap between the privileged and underprivileged has been observed but never truly acted upon. In fact, the situation continues to grow even more intense.

2. **Summarize Rose's perception of the current state of educational policy for the poor in the United States.**

   He asserts that current educational policies are not helping the poor get ahead in life. The underprivileged remain "visible in a terrible recession although invisible in most public policy."

Rhetorical Analysis

3. **Examine Rose's introductory paragraph. How does he structure this opening unit?**

   The opening sentence is a rhetorical question appealing to pathos by asking what "kind of society do we want to become?" He metaphorically alludes to the "invisibility" of the poor who are, in fact, "drifting further back into the dark underbelly of American capitalism."

4. **How does Rose tailor his message to his audience of college administrators?**

   He discusses the irony of using technology to solve the economic problem when, in fact, this action is not prudent or realistic. Although intended for school administrators, his argument extends beyond them, addressing multileveled policymakers whose decisions impact education.

5. **Explain Rose's tone and voice in this essay. Where does he personalize his argument, and what is the effect?**

   Rose's voice resonates with the reader by metaphorically introducing the idea of the "invisible" culture of poverty. In a later paragraph, he personalizes it by his recent experience "spending time" in an inner-city community college known for its highly regarded occupational programs. Through personal experience in this environment, he argues that students, stigmatized by lack of economic privilege, have the same capacity to be engaged in learning as those who are educationally privileged. He appeals to ethos, logos, and pathos by urging the reader to not accept complacency. These rhetorical devices are highlighted by his appeal to this morally based central argument (ethos), sound reasoning (logos), and personal experience (pathos) associated with the subject.

6. **How does Rose use a problem-solution pattern of organization in developing his argument? Point to specific passages where this pattern becomes apparent.**
The writer uses specific details to illustrate that although people and agencies in power recognize the unfair effects of the impoverished's lack of education and career opportunities, they really do nothing realistically useful about it. They acknowledge words, but rarely put deeds into action (lip-service).

7. **What is the relationship of Rose's concluding paragraph to his claim and to the evidence that he offers in the body of his essay?**
Rose points out the "long-term consequences" affecting society as a whole, illustrating the denial of equal opportunities for all. This supports his earlier claim that society needs to pull the curtain back on invisible poverty through reform, thus supporting Harrington's assertion, 50 years prior to this essay, that educational opportunities drive individual economic success. He offers historical, political, and personal experiences, attributed to additional resources such as *The Economist* and President Barack Obama, to argue the dual nature of the evidence.

Writing

8. **In a personal essay, explore your own place in American society—or in the nation where you were born and raised—and how this molded your educational experience.**
In this essay, have students consider where they stand in regards to their own economic status and how this position has enhanced or hindered their academic opportunities, both personally and professionally. Have them forecast how these opportunities, or lack thereof, will affect their futures. They may also focus on their environmental background as a contributing factor in this position.

9. **Writing an Argument** Argue for or against the proposition that the U.S. Congress should provide a solid education for the poor.
This argument rests on the idea that educational opportunities are skewed towards economic position, giving the poor an unfair hindrance. The argument can be made that those holding governmental power allow the status quo to exist because it benefits their own agendas, or those in government are rendered powerless due to a system that blocks any real educational reform.

Lesson Plan 4.7

Fishbowl Discussion on Susan Jacoby's "When Bright Girls Decide that Math Is 'a Waste of Time' "

Class Opener

Students were to have read Susan Jacoby's essay and prepared three questions for a Fishbowl discussion. Remind students of the ground rules for the Fishbowl strategy (see page 5 of this Teacher Manual). Ask them to pass their questions to the group member to their right. That group member will choose a favorite question among the three presented. Each group will submit only one question to the fishbowl.

Activity: Interpreting the Essay

Make a point of mixing up the questions. Invite a student to come forward and draw a question from the bowl. The student will then read the question aloud, and the class will discuss their interpretation of the answer. This particular essay usually sparks a lot of conversation; hence, you may find that you are able to sustain a full-period Fishbowl discussion. If the discussion reaches a lull, discuss the questions that accompany the essay in the textbook.

Activity: Writing Narrative Mini-Essays

After the Fishbowl discussion, take an opportunity for narrative writing. Ask students to write a narrative mini-essay/paragraph about facing a personal fear.

Class Closer

Ask students to reflect on their ideas of what education means to them. On an index card, ask them to write a quotation—original, from one of the essays in this unit, or from other sources—that defines what they believe to be most important about education.

Suggested Answers

"When Bright Girls Decide that Math Is 'a Waste of Time'" by Susan Jacoby

Comprehension

1. What reasons does Jacoby give for girls' deficiency in math and science?

As well as blaming a society that still discourages girls' interest and proficiency in particular fields, Jacoby also blames the girls themselves for not pursuing excellence in these areas.

2. Why does Jacoby call it a "self-inflicted female disability" (paragraph 3)?

Jacoby applies this term because the disability is caused by the girls themselves, both consciously and subconsciously. For example, a girl may decide to feign ignorance in order to be more appealing to boys. Jacoby illustrates this situation with a personal example.

3. According to Jacoby, what are the consequences of being math- and science-illiterate?

The consequences of being math- and science-illiterate include, among other things, narrowed career choices; being unprepared for a technologically advanced job market; and reinforcing dependent, helpless behavior patterns in girls.

Rhetorical Analysis

4. Explain the main idea of Jacoby's essay in your own words.

Jacoby's thesis is that girls hinder their chances of competing in the job market and contribute to their own ignorance by remaining math- and science-illiterate, although this process may be caused by subconscious forces.

5. Does the writer use abstract or concrete language in her essay? Cite examples to support your response.

For the most part the writer uses concrete language to advance her ideas. Students may find evidence of this in the essay.

6. What technique does Jacoby use in paragraphs 1 and 2? How does it aid in setting up her argument?

Jacoby dramatizes the subject by using a detailed example that is very specific, and at the same time illustrates a common scenario possibly happening in many American homes. Her example aids in understanding as the reader is able to picture the situation and can identify with it.

7. What rhetorical strategies does the writer use in her essay?

The author uses causal analysis, argumentation, and elements of narration (personal experience, dialogue, etc.) to express her views. Students should point out where these strategies are clear in the essay.

8. How does the use of dialogue aid in developing paragraph 10? What effect does the general use of dialogue have on Jacoby's point?

In paragraph 10, Jacoby uses dialogue to dramatize the problem. Dialogue is very effective in clarifying certain points and in drawing the reader's attention. He or she is able to identify readily if the dialogue echoes similar ideas in his or her mind. Dialogue is also an effective way to "humanize" an essay by making abstract ideas more concrete.

9. How is Jacoby's conclusion consistent in tone with the rest of the essay? Does it supply a sense of unity? Why or why not?

Jacoby's conclusion works because it alludes to the situation depicted in the introduction, which lends unity to the essay. In addition, Jacoby creates a relationship with the reader by offering direct advice and using the pronoun "we."

Writing

10. Write an essay describing a school-related phobia you once had or continue to have (for example, in math, writing, physical education, or biology). Explain where you think that fear came from, how it affected your performance in school, and what you did (or are doing) to cope with the problem.

In this personal narrative, students will examine a fear they had (or have) about school that interfered with their ability to function well. It may be the same problem discussed in Jacoby's essay or a different one (such as test-taking, speaking in class, failure). They should give a brief history of the problem, describe how it manifests itself, how they feel, and how they cope with it or got rid of it. Students should use concrete examples to illustrate their ideas.

11. Write an essay about the need for math and science literacy in today's world. Use support from Jacoby's essay.

Jacoby feels that math and science proficiency is crucial in today's world. In a well-organized expository essay, students will expand on this theme. They must provide examples as well as personal experience or research to help illustrate and support their points.

12. Writing an Argument Write an argumentation essay proposing that math and science phobia is not "self-inflicted" but is caused primarily by the continued presence of sexism in society.

Jacoby's essay concentrates mostly on the limitations girls impose on themselves. In this argumentative essay, students will argue that this "self-inflicted disability" springs from society's refusal to treat girls fairly. Thus, this disability can be viewed as a survival tactic. Students should quote from Jacoby's essay and provide examples to support their opinions.

Lesson Plan 4.8

Chapter Assessment

Rhetorical Analysis Answers

1. A
2. E
3. B
4. C
5. B
6. C
7. B
8. B
9. A
10. D

Connections for Critical Thinking

Have students turn to the questions that appear on page 183 in the textbook. Tell students to choose any one of the options and write for a minimum of 30 minutes.

After students have finished writing, use the remainder of a 45–50 minute period to group students according to the topic they chose. Students should read and comment on one another's essays, offering a positive comment, a critical comment, and a question for each essay read.

Answers

1. **Compare and contrast the rhetorical devices of a personal essay as represented in Rodriguez's "The Lonely, Good Company of Books" with the rhetoric of an argumentative essay like Rose's "What College Can Mean to the Other America."**

   For this exercise, students should be able to compare the language choices and the audience approach between the essays by Richard Rodriguez and Mike Rose. These differences are based on approach. Rodriguez writes a lighthearted story in first person, about reading books and learning, which takes the reader through his childhood introduction to books through high school and how his attitude toward reading evolves. Rose's approach to the topic of the poor and education is harsh in places. It is direct and sometimes harsh, but makes a strong point.

2. **Analyze an event in your education when you had a disagreement with a teacher, administrator, or another authority figure. Explain and explore whether the differences in viewpoint were based on emotional perspective, intellectual perspective, or both.**

   This response will vary greatly, depending on the individual student.

3. **Select the essay in this chapter you find most pertinent to your life as a student. Explain why you selected the essay, and explore your intellectual and emotional responses to it.**

   This response will also vary and will depend on personal choice. The students will need to read through all the essays in the chapter and annotate for clear understanding of each.

4. **Does your high school seem to support Jacoby's views regarding the educational lives of women? Explain why or why not.**

   Again, the responses here will vary, but it would be helpful for the students to work on this question together in small groups because it will likely spawn debate and individuals may be more open to discussion in smaller groups.

5. **It is 2050. Write an essay in which you explore the demographics of a typical high school classroom. Refer to the ideas contained in the Gregorian and Jacoby essays.**

   Jacoby explores the issue of females sabotaging their futures by continuing to show poor results in math and science subjects. Students should focus on the relationship of these issues in education with an eye to where these issues might end up by the year 2050. What will colleges and their student bodies be like by then, considering patterns from the past?

6. **Write an essay that categorizes at least three educational issues that the authors in this chapter examine. Establish a clear thesis to unify the categories you establish.**

   Students have several education options here, including the importance of reading and writing and how those traits assist in learning; affirmative action; classroom technology; gender issues involving math and science, including peer pressure and expectations; and ethnic diversity.

7. **Analyze the patterns and techniques used by Menand, Rose, and Jacoby to advance their claims about education today.**

   Students will need to consider who the intended audience is for each essay. This will help them see the patterns and techniques and understand the authors' choices. All three essays (Menand, Rose, and Jacoby) are strongly written arguments. Rose uses personal observations from visits with inner-city students who are poor. He is direct and honest. Jacoby is also direct and straightforward as she writes to the parents of girls who are making choices about math and science that can negatively affect them later in life. Menand combines various appeals in his argument in order to make unfamiliar an experience that is largely taken for granted—attending college. Appealing to reason invites readers with chips on their shoulders to set their burdens down while he takes aim at other readers' indifference, using moral arguments about grade inflation and the cost of tuition. He begins and ends his essay with an appeal to the readers' emotions.

Lesson Plan 4.9

Synthesizing Sources: STEM vs. Liberal Arts—Is the STEAM Movement the Solution?

Remind students that the synthesis essay is simply an argument essay with sources. Give students an entire class period to read and write a synthesis essay incorporating the sources on "STEM vs. Liberal Arts—Is the STEAM Movement the Solution?" on pages 184–189 in the textbook. In the next class period, have students work in their groups to read, respond to, and even attempt to score each other's essays using the holistic grading method described on page 9 in this Teacher Manual.

Applying Your Synthesis Skills: Suggested Answers

Comprehension

1. **Summarize the inferred arguments made in each source.**

   Sample reponses: **Source A:** Although on the surface it appears the two movements can be joined through STEAM, proponents of both movements have adversarial viewpoints on the two joining. Many associated with STEM believe the addition of the arts would "water down" their program, and Liberal Arts proponents view STEM as something that can be benefited only by a strong base in Liberal Arts. **Source B:** Albert Einstein, perhaps the most recognized and celebrated scientist and philosopher in modern centuries, argues that both Liberal Arts and STEM are "branches from the same tree." Thus, they grow tangentially with one another and come from the same base. **Source C:** The given statistics are a strong argument for the financial benefits of occupations associated with STEM. **Source D:** A real value exists in all realms of critical thinking skills that focus on socio-cultural issues. The world embodies humanity, and this embodiment can only grow through empathy and awareness—something STEM doesn't focus on. **Source E:** The "fastest growing jobs" encompass occupations in both technical and nontechnical fields, but median pay is higher for STEM-related occupations. **Source F:** Employers look for skills that reflect both a science/technical background and a humanities background. **Source G:** Whitman makes the point that although astronomers are "learn'd," charts and diagrams cannot explain the beauty of viewing the stars "in perfect silence." Nature sometimes needs to be admired and unexplained.

Rhetorical Analysis

2. How does Source A personify STEM and STEAM?

STEM and STEAM have been personified as two warring opponents having a "tug of war" that will go back and forth until fortitude declares an eventual winner.

3. What is the metaphorical effect of Source B, and how is this achieved?

The metaphor centers on the proverbial tree of life that branches into the areas of "religions, arts and sciences." The branches "lift" a person intellectually, leadings to "freedom," meaning, and a life well-lived.

4. How do Sources C and E make a convincing argument using logos?

Both sources use income data to compare occupations. Source E includes percentages showing growth rates for select occupations. Both graphics conclude that STEM occupations earn more than social science and other Liberal Arts occupations. Source E provides a rationale for entering various non-STEM occupations.

5. Source D provides a paradoxical argument. What is this argument?

The author discusses the absurdity of everyone focusing solely on STEM jobs. She questions what this world would be like if no one pursued Humanities, giving examples of the benefits of the arts: social services, schools, films, and literature. She asks the reader to imagine life if these components were removed.

6. How does the arrangement of the material in Source F give greater clarity?

The bulleted format makes concise arguments that are easier to follow.

7. Compare and contrast the "learn'd astronomer's" evidence to Whitman's visual epiphany when he leaves the lecture and walks outside (Source G).

The explanation of the nighttime universe connects Whitman to his ethereal appreciation of the "perfect silence of the stars." He implies that charts and diagrams, mathematically and scientifically derived, cannot sufficiently explain the spiritual resonance that impacts the human eye, heart, and spirit.

Writing an Argument

8. Using examples from the sources, write an essay explaining why you do or do not support the STEAM movement.

Answers will vary. The more successful essays will focus on whether the arts have a place in current society. Many students will recognize the importance of the "Renaissance person" who embodies the ideals of both sciences and arts. Others will argue that the sciences solidify a person's financial and personal success.

CHAPTER 5
Family Life

The essays in Chapter 5 provide a wide range of points of view on the nature of family in contemporary society. Some of the essays provide excellent platforms for classroom discussion, such as David Brooks's essay on Internet dating, while others allow focused teaching on language skills, such as Annie Dillard's writing style in "An American Childhood." The lesson plans for teaching the essays include strategies for teaching comparison and contrast, analyzing vivid language, and using the College Board's SOAPSTone strategy as a framework for rhetorical analysis.

Teaching the Chapter

Lesson Plan 5.1

Comparison and Contrast Essay—White and Kingsolver (Part 1)

Class Opener

To put students into the right frame of reference, refer them to the **Classic and Contemporary Images** feature on pages 192–193. Working in their groups, students should answer the questions in the textbook. Then have groups come together as a class, with each group discussing a different question.

Classic and Contemporary Images: Suggested Answers

1. **Describe the settings and perspective of each wedding.**

   The first wedding takes place outside in what appears to be the center of a rural village. We see trees, cottages, and tables set up. The guests are dressed in their country finest, and one supposes the whole village has shown up to celebrate this wedding. The second wedding takes place in what appears to be a judge's chamber or a room in a courthouse without any fanfare. Computers and boxes are in the background, and a wire hangs loosely out of an office desk. There is an informality about each of the weddings, but the settings are vastly different since one is filled with community celebration and the other is not.

2. **Compare and contrast the tone of each visual text.**

   The tone of the Brueghel painting is festive, bordering on almost bawdy. Devoid of a recognizable bride and groom, the country folks are in the midst of celebration: dancing, drinking, and embracing. The tone of the other text is far more serious and shows very little celebration, if at all. It is solemn and dispassionate, especially where the "guests" are concerned. It appears to be almost an afterthought because, except for the minister, the wedding party is casually dressed and quite removed from the equally casually dressed bride and groom.

3. **Note where each person is standing in the contemporary wedding photograph and explain the significance of each person's position and stance.**

   Students will see that the focus is on the couple getting married. Obviously the man is African American and the woman is Caucasian. We can assume that the children are from previous relationships, although the young boy may be biracial and possibly the wedding couple's child. Although the couple is focused upon each other, the children surrounding them are not. They are standing very casually with somewhat disinterested looks on their faces. We can see the minister behind the couple looking dutiful. Thus, the couple, whose hands are locked together and whose eyes are upon each other in what is obviously some type of courtroom, are the only engaged persons in the photograph.

4. **What do weddings say about culture?**

   Weddings come in many shapes and forms. Through the centuries, weddings can take on different types of ritualistic viewpoints. They can be filled with rustic celebration or performed in a tiny courtroom with only three witnesses. Most people have choices of how they want to get married, so weddings will often show historical and sociocultural influences.

Activity: Close Reading of White and Kingsolver

In order to use White's and Kingsolver's essays as the basis for students' comparison and contrast essays, provide the students with a question in advance of their reading. For this essay assignment, students will consider what the essays by White and Kingsolver reveal about the authors' attitudes toward family. To prepare for writing the essay, students will work in their groups to create a multiple-entry journal focused on the idea of "family" as it is portrayed in each essay. Begin with the White essay, allowing students sufficient time to absorb the essay and analyze it through the multiple-entry annotation approach.

Class Closer

Allow groups to discuss significant quotations and findings in White's essay. Make sure that the class has focused on the idea of "family," as this will be important for the rest of the assignment. You may want to discuss answers to the textbook questions (see below).

Homework

Assign students to read the Kingsolver essay and independently create a multiple-entry journal focused on Kingsolver's depiction of family.

Suggested Answers

"Once More to the Lake" by E.B. White

Comprehension

1. **At what point in the essay do you begin to sense White's main purpose? What is his purpose? What type of reader might his purpose appeal to?**

   Answers will vary. Paragraphs 8 and 9 evoke a highly nostalgic recollection of a vanished time that White struggles to regain. Yet some students might maintain that White's ultimate purpose—to reveal the impossibility of recapturing the past—is not stated completely until the last paragraph.

2. What motivates White to return to the lake in Maine? Explain the "simple transposition" that he mentions in paragraph 4. List the illustrations that he gives of this phenomenon. What change does he detect in the lake?

Nostalgia motivates White to return to the lake. He contrasts two sets of images: the ocean with its tides and chill, and the lake with its calm "placidity." The ocean suggests adult life; the lake the simplicity of childhood. He wishes to return to quiet. Because his son does virtually the same things he did years before, White identifies with him. See paragraph 5 in which he watches a dragonfly on the end of his fishing rod; paragraph 11, in which he and his son explore the town and woods for other instances of identification. The key difference is the popularity of outboard motorboats, paragraph 10, but there are others: paragraph 4, the tarred road; paragraph 7, the absence of the third (horse) track; paragraph 7, waitresses with washed hair; paragraph 11, the slightly different details of courting and soda parlors.

3. Explain the significance of White's last sentence. Where are there foreshadowings of this statement?

White identifies with his son and with his father; the latter identification underscores his mortality. In paragraphs 12–13, the thunderstorm and bathing in the rain are familiar to him, but new to his son. He is experienced, his son innocent and young. Like his father before him, White is growing old. Some day, his son will stand where he is standing and identify with his son. The chain of sons (and youth) is parallel to the chain of fathers (and age). Every time White senses change, he recognizes the passage of time, and mortality becomes an issue. In paragraph 1, the "fearful cold" of the sea suggests death.

Rhetorical Analysis

4. Describe White's use of figurative language in paragraphs 2, 10, and 12.

In paragraph 2, the key metaphor is in the final sentence: "the stillness of the cathedral." He has already called the place a "holy spot." Like a cathedral, the lake is sacred; separated from everyday life. It contains a hint of eternity and holiness. In paragraph 10, figurative language contrasts the inboard and outboard motorboats. Inboard motors "throbbed and fluttered" or "purred and purred." Outboard motors made "petulant, irritable sound"; they "whined...like mosquitoes." Finally, he describes a boat lunging "bull-fashion" into a dock. In paragraph 12, he describes a thunderstorm in theatrical terms: "the second-act climax" which is "still the big scene." Thunder becomes a "kettle drum, then the snare, then the bass drum and cymbals." The big scene is the recognition scene of the essay. The image shifts to "the gods grinning and licking their chops in the hills."

5. Identify those words and phrases that White invokes to establish the sense of mystery about the lake. Why are these words and their connotations important to the nature of the illusion that he describes?

Some of the images mentioned above: lake as "cathedral" and as "stage" suggest that it is not part of the everyday world. In paragraph 3, the lake is "infinitely remote and primeval." In paragraph 6, it is "an utterly enchanted sea." The lake stands for mystery; that is, its effect on White is greater than one would expect. It seems more meaningful and is more elusive than any object literally is. The lake makes time stand still, allows White to change identities, and is magical.

6. Explain the organization of the essay in terms of the following paragraph units: 1–4, 5–7, 8–10, and 11–13. Explain the function of paragraphs 8 and 12.

Paragraphs 1–4 are introductory: they establish the scene and the thesis. Paragraphs 5–7 describe the details of daily life there. Paragraphs 8–10 generalize about the American recreation, precious for its eternal desire for peace and escape. Paragraphs 11–13 conclude the essay. It connects White's vacation with the national desire for vacations, American innocence, and the American love of "nature." Paragraph 12 describes the moment when White sees clearly the difference between his son and himself: he has seen thunderstorms and bathed in the rain; his son has not. Paragraph 12 introduces the theme of mortality.

7. **There are many vivid and unusual descriptive details in this essay—for example, the dragonfly in paragraph 5 and the two-track road in paragraph 7. How does White create symbolic overtones for these descriptive details and others? Why is the lake itself a complex symbol? Explain with reference to paragraph 6.**

Relating details to feelings and ideas is part of the essay's theme. Many of the key details—the dragonfly, the wisps of moss, a discarded fishhook—are ephemeral; nevertheless, they are constant parts of lakeshore summers. Thus, they suggest both eternity and mortality. They are crucial illustrations of themes of the essay. White relates the lake to words such as "enchanted" because it is so placid. The water is transparent, a symbol of the clarity of nature. The pattern of the mussel prepares the reader for the design of American summer vacation in paragraph 8.

8. **Describe the persona that White creates for himself in the essay. How does this persona function?**

The speaker is more sensitive than most of us could be and of course far more articulate. He records numerous details and relates them to irrational desires for youth and fears of death. He is dizzy with sensation and feels drama (almost melodrama) in his visit to the lake.

9. **What is the relation between the introductory and concluding paragraphs, specifically in terms of irony of statement? Explain the irony between the two paragraphs.**

A couple of instances of irony appear in paragraph 1: "none of us ever thought there was any place in the world like that lake in Maine" and the fact that they "always" vacationed there. White talks about visiting "old haunts." He is haunted; he becomes his father's ghost and his own. In paragraph 13, the irony creates a "chill" for his son of an exciting kind; for White it is the "chill of death."

Writing

10. **Explore in an essay the theme of nostalgia apparent in "Once More to the Lake." What are the beauties and the dangers of nostalgia? Can the past ever be recaptured or relived? Justify your answer.**

Nostalgia is defined in the dictionary as "homesickness." It is derived from the Greek *nostos,* from return, and *algoa,* for pain or grief. It has acquired negative connotations because it is usually connected with sentimentality and a lack of objectivity. To be nostalgic is to be un-examining. For White, the trip feeds his "homesickness" for his own youth until the end of the essay, when it becomes clear that he cannot recapture his youth. In class discussion, some students may deny that they are drawn by nostalgia, so ask them whether they have returned to their elementary or middle schools to visit former teachers. If they have, suggest that they may have been acting nostalgically.

11. **Referring to revisiting a site on the lake that he had visited years before with his father, White remarks in paragraph 4, "I could tell that it was going to be pretty much the same as it had been before." In an essay, analyze the strategies White uses to indicate the unchanging role and function of the family.**

White is a highly evocative prose stylist. Ask students to identify sentences that they find especially appealing, and then to explain their responses.

12. **Writing an Argument** **Argue for or against the proposition that nostalgia can obscure the true nature of family relationships and even suppress painful memories that should be confronted.**

Draw on the discussion cited in the first writing assignment to have students consider what nostalgia means.

Lesson Plan 5.2

Comparison and Contrast Essay—White and Kingsolver (Part 2)

Class Opener

Have students write a summary of the Kingsolver essay in 25 words or less. After they have had a chance to finish, ask them to revise their summary. It now may be only 10 words. Ask them to revise it one final time. The final product can be only 3 words. Discuss the three words they chose.

Activity: Discussion of Journal Entries

Students will have read the Kingsolver essay for homework, creating a multiple-entry journal focused on family. In their groups, ask students to discuss the journals they created and to choose one entry from each group to share with the class. After students have had sufficient time to confer, ask each group to share the entry they chose. As they share, write down common themes on the board. You may also want to discuss answers to the accompanying questions in the textbook (see below).

Activity: Venn Diagram of White and Kingsolver

Now have groups create a Venn diagram to differentiate and find commonalities between the ideas of family put forth by White and those conveyed by Kingsolver.

Class Closer

Create a huge Venn diagram on the board. Ask each group to contribute something to add to the analysis.

Homework

Assign students to write a comparison and contrast essay, using the information from their classwork as the basis for their analysis.

Suggested Answers

"Stone Soup" by Barbara Kingsolver

Comprehension

1. **What is the essay's thesis?**

   Although not expressed explicitly, through imagery and metaphor Kingsolver expresses her thesis best in the final paragraph, championing the idea that if adults are sensitive and rational regarding the needs of children, the structure of family composition can have a greater latitude than has been traditionally thought.

2. **According to Kingsolver, why is our society so apt to condemn divorce?**

   Kingsolver suggests that it is traditionalists, who have not had to face the challenge of reformatting the family constellation, that are the major critics of divorce. In paragraph 7, she facetiously refers to this group as the "Family-of-Dolls Family Values crew."

3. What is the author's view of family symmetry (paragraph 19)?

The idea of symmetry (that is, that one side of an entity is the mirror image of the other) is challenged by Kingsolver when she claims that such a symmetry was an illusion for it did not take into account the underlings who buttressed the middle-class family such as the maids, factory workers, and other members of the exploited classes. In other words, Kingsolver is accusing would-be critics of political and economic naiveté regarding the way society was structured to afford the minority an affluent lifestyle.

Rhetorical Analysis

4. What rhetorical function does the opening anecdote serve in introducing the essay's subject matter?

Kingsolver demonstrates that unconventional family "kinship systems" can serve the same supportive function as traditional ones. She also introduces the reader to the rhetorical manner in which she is about to challenge assumptions about the family: not merely in rational, argumentative ways, but in linguistic ones as well.

5. What is Kingsolver's purpose in capitalizing, italicizing, and placing quotation marks around certain phrases—for example, the Way It Has Always Been (paragraph 4), *failed* and *the children of divorce* (paragraph 7), and "family values" (paragraph 18)?

Kingsolver seems to be trying to persuade her audience of two main issues: the first, which is her primary one, that family constellations do not have to conform to traditional structures in order to be successful; and second (and this is the way she uses her playful use of punctuation), that many of our assumptions about families are simply unchallenged clichés that when analyzed turn out to be empty slogans.

6. What is the author's purpose in creating a gap between paragraphs 15 and 16? What is the focus of her argument after this break?

Until paragraph 15, Kingsolver is on the defensive; that is, she tries to demonstrate how families of divorce must constantly defend themselves against criticism. Beginning with paragraph 16, Kingsolver sounds more proactive. For example, in paragraph 17, she states, "the main problem with our reorganized family is that other people think we have a problem" and again in paragraph 18 she asks, "Why is it surprising that a child would revel in a widening family and the right to feel at home in more than one house?"

7. Compare the introductory paragraph with the concluding one. How do they differ? How are they similar? How do they help set the boundaries of the essay?

The opening paragraph is an anecdote that serves to introduce Kingsolver's main thesis with an example. Her conclusion is her thesis, which she states confidently through a process of adducing. The introduction is intended to set a compassionate tone with the reader. After all, it celebrates the new American sports pastime, soccer. The tone of the conclusion is upbeat, nurturing and colloquial, using such terms as "stew," "heck of a," and "nourish."

8. This essay contains personal observations, personal experiences, historical data, and anecdotes. How would you describe the author's rhetorical mode to a person who has not read the essay?

The mode is a combination of narration, illustration, and comparison and contrast. Because Kingsolver is so adept at combining imagery, tales, colloquialisms, and popular psychology, her tone is fairly extemporaneous. Her conversational voice seems one that the reader can trust for its honesty and sincerity, even if he or she ultimately does not agree with the conclusions.

9. **Unlike the titles of most essays, the title "Stone Soup" gives no hint at the essay's content. What is the rhetorical purpose in keeping the meaning of the title a mystery until the very end?**

Kingsolver is relating a tale, the tale of the modern family. In this regard, it seems rhetorically prudent and natural to reserve a sense of mystery for the conclusion. In fact, the title "Stone Soup" has the tone of a parable, not quite comprehensible, but inviting.

10. **In paragraph 2, Kingsolver asks the question, "Why are our names for home so slow to catch up to the truth of where we live?" Does the author suggest an answer to this question either implicitly or explicitly during the course of the essay? If so, where?**

One can infer the answer in the opening of paragraph 4 when Kingsolver discusses her initiation from childhood to adulthood, "now I've replaced the dolls with a life." It seems that Kingsolver is suggesting that Americans (at least middle-class ones) tend to be overprotective of their children, and try to delay their awareness of the world's inevitable cruelties. So, the answer may be at least in our culture, although one would suspect the same process occurs in other cultures as well.

Writing

11. **Interview two individuals at least 25 years apart in age. Compare and contrast their views on divorce.**

Kingsolver offers the readers a portrait of the family as being resilient and adaptable. But are all families this way? You may wish to have your students compare and contrast a positive family outcome and a negative one that might result from a divorce or other family breakup.

12. **Describe the dynamics of a blended family with which you are familiar. It may be your own or a friend's.**

You may have to ask your students to find couples who were married during the early 1960s to find families that established themselves before the modern divorce phenomenon. Have your students discuss not only the respondent's view on divorce but also have them ask what was the general social view of divorce. You may also wish to contrast the perception of the divorced man versus the divorced woman.

13. **Writing an Argument** Kingsolver makes many positive assertions in the essay. In a well-written essay, take a position on one of Kingsolver's claims. Use evidence from your reading, personal experience, and observation.

You might wish to have your students not limit the concept of "blended family" to those family members who live together but to include any family group that shares time together even if they do not live in the same house. You might also wish to have your students write about families with alternative primary caretakers, such as aunts and uncles, grandmothers, or older siblings.

Lesson Plan 5.3

Synthesis: Comparison and Contrast Questions for Comparison

Class Opener

Use the synthesis questions that appear after these two essays to encourage students to analyze further and deeper than they did in their group discussions. Allow students to choose any one of the three options.

Activity: Writing

Have students write a response to the option they chose for a minimum of 30 minutes. After students have finished writing, use the remainder of a 45–50 minute period to group students according to the topic they chose. Students should read and comment on one another's essays, offering a positive comment, a critical comment, and a question for each essay read.

Homework

Assign students to read Annie Dillard's "An American Childhood."

Synthesizing the Classic and Contemporary Essays: Suggested Answers

1. Compare and contrast the tone of each writer. How does tone affect purpose? How does it affect mood? Select at least three passages from White and three from Kingsolver that demonstrate how their tones differ. Do they offer any hints as to the "voice" or personality of the writers? Why or why not?

White's essay is a meditation on the intergenerational transmission of experience from father to son, and an attempt to maintain a nostalgic attitude toward "sacred places" despite the inevitability of change. Implicit in his essay is the focus on patrilineal society. The activities he describes—fishing, camping, hiking, and boating—seem harnessed to the initiation into male adulthood. White demonstrates his mastery of narration and description throughout the essay, and the emotional tone of the essay is affirmative, secure, and conservative. Note, for example, his description of "the fadeproof lake, the woods unshatterable, the pasture with the sweetfern and the juniper forever and ever, summer without end" (paragraph 8). White does suggest the change that "modern times" have wrought: outboard motors replacing one-cylinders; Coca-Cola bottles replacing root beer. But relative to the rapid technological and social change of the twenty-first century, these alterations seem phenomenally sluggish. White employs images that evoke serenity: "Peace and goodness and jollity" (paragraph 10). However, despite the calm, White suggests the inevitability of death. But even death, although bringing a "chill" (paragraph 13) to the author, is presented subtly and faintly. This pertains to White's style, which is restrained, suggestive, and implicit. Kingsolver's writing, by contrast, reflects a society with a speedy, radically changing social and technological structure. It is one in which "Prince Charming" may become "a princess" (paragraph 10), in which the "prototypical family has "family-assigned" names, and in which the coherence of the nuclear family may be a mere façade for "the Family of Dolls." What makes White and Kingsolver so radically different is that White is operating under the central mythological narrative that life requires death, where each generation replaces the next in ecclesiastical fashion. Kingsolver ignores these assumptions, suggesting that generational change can be evolutionary if not revolutionary. Kingsolver is the Darwinian, while White is the traditional religionist.

2. What contemporary issues does Kingsolver address that White either ignores or is unaware of? Consider that White was born 56 years before Kingsolver, so his world was quite a different one. Are there other variables that might help us distinguish their concerns and outlooks—for example, gender, class, and environment?

Kingsolver suggests that it is a positive attribute that humans are malleable in their adaptation to family, culture, gender roles, and class. In this regard, she is very much enlightened by contemporary cultural studies. She remarks how the Victorian family could have a comfortable life because of "an Irish or German girl scrubbing floors" (paragraph 19). White does not address class at all, as though there is an implicit assumption that the world operates according to a *New Yorker* readership worldview. Issues of gender identification and alternative family structures barely existed in White's era, so it is not surprising they would not be topics of interest for a meditative essay. Kingsolver seems much more aware of privilege regarding things that White seems to take as prerogatives. Note even the title of the essay, "Once More to the Lake," has an implicit assumption of entitlement. "Stone Soup," by contrast, is a metaphor for adaptability, sacrifice, and community despite scarcity.

3. **What central values does each author have regarding the family? How are they similar? How do they differ? How do their values reflect their times?**

   White suggests that change always has an element of loss. His son will not have the experience of the nostalgic days of White's own youth, and will miss out on some of the father/son interaction that made his own development so rich. And, by implication, White suggests that each succeeding generation will suffer a similar diminishment in quality of life. Kingsolver suggests that change is for the better, that it is a restorative and remedy for family traditions that have been romanticized by ideologues and elites. It should be apparent—and if not, made apparent—to students that White is a man and Kingsolver is a woman. This is not a facetious statement, but it is the experience of many teachers that students often read assigned essays without knowing even minimal details about an author.

4. **At what point in Kingsolver's essay does the life experience E.B. White writes about enter into her essay? Explain.**

   In paragraphs 3 and 10, Kingsolver waxes a bit nostalgic about growing up—discussing dolls from her childhood and contrasting them with reality.

Lesson Plan 5.4

Annie Dillard: A Focus on Verbs

Class Opener

Ask the class to write a brief paragraph (5 sentences) in which they write personal descriptions of themselves. When they have finished, ask them to look back at the paragraph and underline or highlight every use of a *being* verb. Next, ask them to revise their paragraphs by removing every *being* verb. It is a natural inclination when describing ourselves to use *being* verbs to describe who we *are*. However, in her beautiful writing, Dillard does not fall into this trap when describing her mother. The goal in this lesson is to teach students that vivid verbs make their writing powerful.

Activity: Reading Actively for Verbs

In their groups, ask students to re-visit this essay, assuming they read it the night before for homework. Groups should make a list of at least 25 verbs that Dillard uses in this essay. (People are stirred and moved; they brighten mornings; father eschews; etc.)

When they have finished the list, ask each group to choose just one favorite and write that sentence on the board. Revise the sentence with them by making the verb boring. For example, "One kind relative brightened our morning by mentioning why she'd. . . ." could be written as "One kind relative said why she'd. . . ." Make the sentences worse to show how vivid Dillard's writing really is.

Activity: Writing Actively with Verbs

After you have helped students understand the strength of Dillard's style, ask them to write in the style of Dillard. Have students write an anecdote in which they provide insight into a family member by telling a story about that person. They may not use *being* verbs. Each story should be only two to three paragraphs. Point them to Dillard's anecdote about the zoo (paragraphs 21-22) as an example of a short anecdote.

When they have finished their anecdotes, have students share their stories with their groups. Ask them to work within their group as editors to make each essay even more vivid.

Homework

Students should read "Love, Internet Style" and write three questions in preparation for a Socratic seminar on this essay.

Suggested Answers

"An American Childhood" by Annie Dillard

Comprehension

1. Dillard creates a picture of her mother's personality through a number of anecdotes and explanations. How would you sum up the mother's personality?

The mother displays what psychologists often label a "metacommunicative" awareness of life. She understands that the codes and conventions of living are fixed but dictated by the environment, and therefore, can be playfully transgressed without fear of retribution. This is assuming one uses the proper tact and strategies.

2. Dillard's mother appears to have a special appreciation for words and language. What effect does it have on her family and acquaintances?

The mother's high level of "verbal intelligence" to appreciate the sounds of language, as is evident in her fascination with the phrase, "Terwilliger bunts one," and the multiple meanings of language, which enables her to skillfully play on words at the expense of the unenlightened. For example, her response to the checkout clerk in the supermarket provides her with much satisfaction by making the ordinary extraordinary. Through this influence, the family and particularly the narrator develop an appreciation for "alternative readings" of everyday life, thus making it richer, more challenging, and open to questioning.

3. What values does the mother hold? What behaviors and attitudes does she abhor and discourage?

The mother addresses everyday life as though it were a bit lazy in its proceedings, and in need of some liveliness. Although she does not effect change on a large scale—for example, politically or economically—she succeeds on a personal one. She instills this value in her family by making them the brunt of her creative energies, and in doing so has the effect of keeping "us all awake." She hates "torpid conformity" and predictability.

Rhetorical Analysis

4. In paragraph 7, Dillard explains that the highway from Tampa to Miami is referred to either as "Tamiami Trail" or "Alligator Alley." What is the connotation of each of these terms? Why does her mother prefer to call it "Tamiami Trail"?

"Tamiami Trail" connotes a certain dramatic attitude on the part of those who named it, an irony not lost on the mother (as the trail is now a highway) but most likely lost on others. In addition, it has a certain *ersatz* aesthetic and cleverness to it, which the mother most likely appreciates. "Alligator Alley" sounds more colloquial and modest, and therefore not as easily made fun of.

5. The author herself seems to have inherited a special fascination for language. Study her use of dashes and semicolons in paragraphs 26 and 27. How do they help contribute to energetic writing?

The staccato rhythms in these paragraphs serve as syntactic metaphors for the mother's driving force and quickness of mind and body. In Dillard's prose, we see the challenge to standard prose just as her mother displayed her challenges to standard conformism.

6. **What are the functions of the spaces between paragraphs 19 and 20, 22 and 23, and 32 and 33? How do these divisions contribute to the structure of the essay as a whole?**

The paragraph cluster 20 through 22 sets off a flashback, and helps to focus the anecdote in the zoo. The division between paragraph 32 and 33 functions to separate the mother's critical attitude and interaction with everyday objects with that of her attitude toward acquiring personal knowledge and opinion, a more abstract level of thinking.

7. **How does Dillard use her writing talents to create paragraph 8 out of one long sentence? What other examples can you provide of long sentences in the essay? What is her purpose in using these long sentences? How do they contribute to the overall style of the writing?**

Paragraphs 3 and 37 are one sentence each. Although most students do not have the sophistication to construct such complex structures, an analysis of how Dillard uses punctuation, particularly the dash and semicolon, can help them in mastering these two syntactic tools. You may wish to inject a "mini-lesson" on the relationship of style and punctuation at this point, focusing on the merits of the short declarative sentence versus the longer, intricate one.

8. **What is the overall emotional "tone" of the writer toward her subject—admiring, or loving, or cautionary? What adjectives does she use in describing her mother that provides the reader with clues to the tone?**

The reader can infer the endearing attitude of the writer toward her mother in the tone in which she relates anecdotes. The mother's pranks are often self-serving and harsh, yet Dillard appreciates their uniqueness, and understands they are means for her mother to display affection. The description of her mother playing bridge in paragraph 25 provides a particularly detailed portrait of her mother in action and Dillard's admiration.

9. **Dillard quotes her mother directly on several occasions. Can we assume that she is quoting precisely, given that the essay was written years after the incidents described? Does it matter?**

"The New Journalism" now allows writers to take liberties with fact. It is taken for granted that specific details in nonfiction may be inexact so long as the overall truth of the subject is honored. You may wish to discuss this stylistic technique in class; it can also be used to generate a discussion about the differences between the writing of journalism and memoir.

10. **The final paragraph not only provides closure to the essay but transmits a lesson the mother wants her family to learn. How do the style and structure of this paragraph contribute to the ultimate message of the essay? In other words, how does the form help convey the meaning?**

The final paragraph begins with the author blurting out a thoughtless political pronouncement—an action antithetical to the mother's values—but ends with an understanding of the ultimate value which the mother wishes to instill in her children. This paragraph summarizes the significance of the entire essay, and perhaps demonstrates the uniqueness of "An American Childhood."

Writing

11. **Write a descriptive essay about someone you know very well, using at least five anecdotes from that person's life, so that by the end of the essay, we have a mental picture of your subject's personality, values, and attitudes. This could be someone in your family, or someone else you are or were very close to.**

Some scholars claim that dense, descriptive writing is an anachronism, a remnant from nineteenth-century novelists who could not depend on their readers to have a mental picture of what they were describing. As the theory goes, as a result of the proliferation of visual media, essayists and fiction writers alike have adopted a more terse use of physical description because they assume the reader's mind conjures up images much more accurately and vividly. You may wish to explore the form and function of character description by comparing student samples on the board, focusing on the combination of physical description and character action.

12. Describe an incident or person in your life when the unexpected taught you an important lesson.

Students may use an example where the unexpected occurred by chance, or by a predetermined challenge. However, it should not be an experience that was fleeting or automatic; for example, learning to be more cautious when crossing streets as a result of almost being hit by a car.

13. Writing an Argument Argue for or against the proposition that an effective parent should have—at least—a touch of unconventionality. Alternatively, take a position on the role of conformity in life.

Organize a prewriting discussion around the delicate balance of fostering independence and responsibility in children, and the influence of role modeling in encouraging these values. Does one suffer by emphasizing the other? It may be helpful to refer to the tactics used by Dillard's mother.

Lesson Plan 5.5

Brooks's "Love, Internet Style"—Socratic Seminar

Class Opener

In their groups, ask the class to write definitions for the words *family*, *home*, and *love*. Ask students to share their definitions. The point that you want to draw out for them is how some of our definitions have changed. While "family" to some students might mean a mother, a father, and two children, another student will not relate to this experience at all. Help students understand the rhetorical impact of definition. When writers say to us that they are defining, or better yet "re-defining" a word we believe we own, they are making a very powerful rhetorical statement. They are forcing a position of *ethos* in which they are purporting a stronger claim on the word than the reader possesses. Brooks, in this essay, is defining a certain kind of love—"Internet love."

Activity: Socratic Seminar

Allow the student-generated questions to be the focus of the seminar and only step in if the discussion goes far afield. The questions that accompany the essay provide a good jumping off point if needed. Because this essay is based on rather adult material (high school students will not have had experience with sites like match.com), you might want to consider having a few questions ready to keep the conversation focused.

- How does Brooks define Internet love?
- Does he portray this "love" as a good thing or a bad thing?
- How is it different than the definitions of "love" you wrote at the beginning of class?
- Is Brooks writing from a subjective or objective viewpoint?

Class Closer

At the end of the discussion, make sure you allow enough time for students to write a paragraph synthesizing their thoughts on the topic. Five minutes should be sufficient.

Homework

Students should read "Once Upon a Quinceañera" and be prepared to analyze it as a class. They should create a three-entry multiple-entry journal in which they consider the voice of the speaker in the essay.

Suggested Answers

"Love, Internet Style" by David Brooks

Comprehension

1. How does Brooks describe Internet "love"? What does he mean by his opening sentence, "The Internet slows things down"?

David Brooks describes online dating as "a real estate market where people go to fulfill their most sensitive needs. It is at once ruthlessly transactional and strangely tender" (paragraph 5). For Brooks, the anonymity afforded by the Internet has allowed Internet "love" to be characterized by a broader category of potential mates that require sorting (paragraph 6), extreme examples of honesty and dishonesty (paragraph 11), and the potential for the acceleration of "social stratification" (paragraph 7). The irony of the essay's opening sentence is, of course, that general descriptions of the Internet tend to focus on how technology has increased the speed with which we can access information and communicate with one another. Obviously, this is important to the thesis of Brooks's essay, in that Internet relationships dependent upon (for the most part) written communication and the necessity of functioning within a realm of physical remoteness, has slowed down the process through which people become acquainted, familiar, and intimate.

2. What features of Internet culture does the writer identify as facilitating human relationships?

Brooks notes the importance of the gradual process facilitated by dating over the Internet. The gradual nature of repeated e-mailings is a remedy to what Brooks perceives as the breakdown of traditional courtship rituals. The Internet "imposes the restraints they need to let relationships develop gradually" (paragraph 4). In addition, students may also note that human relationships are facilitated through streamlined access to issues of importance in dating, such as a potential partner's educational or cultural background, and so on.

3. According to Brooks, how do men and women differ in their approach to online relationships?

Although both men and women tend to project images of themselves as both sensual and intelligent, women tend to focus their descriptions on features that suggest self-confidence (paragraphs 9 and 10). Men are more aggressive in their pursuit of potential mates than are females, usually being the first to make "contact" (paragraph 11). Men are also more likely to be "predators looking for sex" (paragraph 12). In contrast, women tend to steer clear of males who engage in sexual rhetoric, and women tend to be the ones who control the ultimate "pace" of a relationship's development (paragraph 12).

Rhetorical Analysis

4. What is Brooks's purpose in beginning his essay with a single-sentence paragraph? Is this sentence the thesis? Why or why not?

From a rhetorical standpoint, Brooks's first sentence functions as a provocative "hook" for his essay, challenging the reader with an ironic reversal of contemporary statements about the Internet and general technological advancement. Although the opening sentence certainly sets the stage for the conditions that the author wishes to discuss, the development of his thesis and consideration of why "slowing things down" is desirable are most clearly delineated in paragraphs 3, 4, and 5.

5. How would you describe the writer's stance? What is his attitude toward his subject? Offer examples to support your answer.

Although balanced in his treatment of Internet dating as he understands it, Brooks generally approves of the changes the Internet has made to courtship rituals. However, students should be directed to break down the stages of development in Brooks's essay in order to more clearly understand the author's stance on the subject. The essay's hook and direct-address springboard into the thesis and process description developed in paragraphs 6 through 9. The general observations made in paragraphs 10 through 12 allow the opinions expressed in paragraphs 13 and 14 to have greater resonance. Although students should notice that Brooks approves of the "new restraints" (paragraph 5) of Internet dating, careful attention should be paid to the possibility of dishonesty and "crass competition" (paragraph 13) inherent in dating and selecting partners online. In considering Brooks's "objectivity," students may focus on paragraphs 13 and 14, in which generalizations about the prolongation of the courting process are tied to assertions about "love" and the "heart." Students should be encouraged to compare the logic and tone of paragraph 14 with what they have read elsewhere in the essay. Perceptive students may find Brooks's final statements to be vague or indicative of the tone normally associated with advertising campaigns.

6. What are Brooks's main reasons in support of his thesis or claim? What forms of evidence does he offer to support his claim?

Although much of Brooks's main argument is laid out in paragraphs 3 and 4, his most persuasive support is featured in paragraph 13 and in the statistical information peppered throughout the piece. Students should be encouraged to consider the plausibility of Brooks's view that the prolongation of courtship via the Internet is a much needed remedy to the breakdown in contemporary courting rituals. In addition, the potentially warped self-image that informs many Internet dating profiles can also be viewed as evidence for why the process is both appealing and daunting. However, students should be aware that the prolongation of relationship development that Brooks describes is not a product of the e-mail courtship exclusively but also is achieved through the "sorting" procedures and, most importantly, the belief that women "generally control the pace of the relationship" (paragraph 12).

7. How does the writer develop an extended definition of Internet "love"?

Brooks's extended definition of Internet love hinges upon the description of process coupled with statements regarding social and gender-specific motivations and tendencies. Although student opinions may vary as to what this form of "love" constitutes, each should be clear that it is defined by the slowness of its pace, the caution that makes such slowness attractive, and the paradoxical ease with which people can access and alter the information necessary to that process.

8. Brooks frequently structures his essay by means of comparison and contrast. Why do you think he uses this strategy? Do you find the method effective? Why or why not?

When addressing Brooks's application of comparison and contrast in his essay, students should take the time to note primary examples of this structural technique. Students may want to categorize such examples, breaking them down into constructs that compare males versus females, or honesty versus dishonesty fostered by the remote nature of Internet communication. More perceptive students may notice Brooks's balancing of elements of fantasy versus reality inherent in Internet profiles or people's motivations. This pattern of juxtaposition tends to contribute to a general sense that Brooks's essay is itself balanced in its approach to the subject matter. However, students should be encouraged to consider if such a structure is confusing, perhaps because it is too subtle, or unconvincing because Brooks's pairing of opposites relies too heavily on stereotypes and random statistical information.

9. Does the final paragraph provide a solid conclusion? Justify your answer.

In evaluating Brooks's final paragraph, students should consider if the application of the terms "love" and "heart" resonate with the assertions made about the tendencies of the Internet dating process. Although students may agree that Internet dating is ultimately motivated by a need for love, however one may define it, they may question whether Brooks has fully developed the role of the "heart" in the process he has described. Students may also wish to consider issues raised earlier in the essay, such as social stratification or the dishonest and predatory behavior enabled by Internet courtship. If students are in agreement that an essay's conclusion should bring a sense of general closure to the topic at hand, perhaps going so far as summarizing or restating complex points developed in the essay, then students may decide that Brooks's essay does not have a "solid" conclusion.

Writing

10. Write a definition essay on "Internet love." Be certain to provide examples and utilize other rhetorical strategies like comparison and contrast to develop this extended definition.

Students attempting to define "Internet love" may wish to frame such a definition through an analysis of participant motivations, the terminology or rhetoric people use when they "chat" on the Internet, or perhaps attempt such a definition through process writing, using personal experience to show how that definition developed and changed through experiences over a period of time.

11. Writing an Argument Write a persuasive essay about the dangers and/or harmless effects of online dating. Provide at least three minor propositions and sufficient evidence to support your position.

Although students may consider the basic examples provided by Brooks as they develop their own argument about the danger or harmlessness of Internet dating, such an assignment can function as an excellent opportunity to develop study support skills in the area of research, source management, and documentation. Encourage them to expand their application of statistical information and editorial pieces drawn from both print and electronic media sources.

Lesson Plan 5.6

Alvarez's "Once Upon a Quinceañera"—SOAPSTone Analysis

This lesson introduces the SOAPSTone strategy, a pre-AP teaching tool developed by the College Board and widely taught at workshops and on the Internet. Although it is labeled pre-AP, it forces students to begin shaping their analysis of a text and to consider a multitude of details beyond simply what the text says.

This particular essay is deceptive in its complexity. At first, it reads as though it is a straightforward narrative essay. It is not. Students will be lulled into the ease of reading this piece with its relatively comfortable diction and syntax. However, there is more at work in this essay, and it is fun to see understanding emerge. This essay is ideal for a full-class discussion.

Class Opener

Ask students to write a short paragraph (5-8 sentences) describing a coming of age ritual. If they struggle with defining one, you might consider asking them to simply write about what it means to be an adult.

Activity: A SOAPSTone Discussion

SOAPSTone is an acronym developed by the College Board for teaching rhetorical analysis. It stands for:

Speaker—Students must determine who is speaking. Who is narrating the essay? In this case it seems straightforward. Alvarez seems to make clear that she, Alvarez, is the speaker. However, students can and should dig deeper. Who is Alvarez? Why is she there? She does not know this family; she is a reporter. Is she writing this objectively or subjectively? Is she writing as a participant in this culture, as an observer of the culture, or as a critic of the culture? All of these questions define her as a speaker. Connect the idea of the speaker to *ethos*. This is where the author will position herself as having the ethical right to speak on this subject. How does she do that?

Occasion—Students must determine the context of the writing. When does this occur? Where? Why is Alvarez involved at all? Is it significant that she is acting alone in this endeavor? What *is* the occasion? Is the occasion the quinceañera, or is the occasion Alvarez's attempt to document the cultural rite of quinceañeras? Is it significant that the article ends before Alvarez finds the quinceañera? Help students recognize that the occasion is not her trip to New York to attend this particular quinceañera; instead, the occasion is the cultural experience of quinceañeras.

Audience—Students must determine the intended audience for the essay. For this essay, the question of audience goes back to the idea of the subjectivity or objectivity of the writer. Is Alvarez writing for a Latino audience—an audience who is already familiar with quinceañeras? Or is she writing for a broader audience? Look at the essay with your students to help them recognize the details she provides concerning the quinceañera. Would she have to provide so much detail, even definition, if she were only writing for an audience that is familiar with this practice?

Purpose—Students must determine the author's purpose in writing the essay. Students seem to believe that all essays are expository in nature, while teachers like to argue that all essays are persuasive in nature. It is arguable that this essay is narrative and expository and persuasive all at the same time. Write these three categories on the board and ask students to provide details that support each. Narration will be easy. She is clearly telling a story. She is writing from the first person point of view. Expository will include the detail and definition she provides about quinceañeras. Persuasive elements are found at the end as she discusses the money spent on these parties, on the potential sexist implications of the practice, and on the suggestions for how the money could be better spent.

Subject—This should be the shortest discussion point. Students spend far too much time in their rhetorical analysis essays summarizing the essay they have read. Teach them to write a one sentence summary of the article. Give them a maximum word count. Force them to summarize Alvarez's essay in 15 words or less.

Tone—Tone is probably the hardest part of rhetorical analysis for students to master. Have them find specific words that lend to the tone of the essay. This essay, after all, is not about actually attending a quinceañera—the writer never gets there. This is an essay about a practice. Is she judgmental? Is she supportive? Is she hesitant? How does the author seem to feel about the practice?

You may choose to have students write a SOAPSTone essay for homework. This is a good practice. However, the discussion practice itself is useful in helping students see the complexity of the essay.

Class Closer

Ask students to choose three words from the essay that they would argue as "defining the essay." On an exit slip, ask them to justify their choices.

Suggested Answers

"Once Upon a Quinceañera" by Julia Alvarez

Comprehension

1. Why does Alvarez inject herself into this story?

The purpose of Alvarez's use of the first person is to provide the voice of a "loyal opposition." She positions herself as knowledgeable on the subject of the quinceañera tradition but not as the definitive expert. She does this to help readers suspend judgment the better to inhabit, if even for a few pages, the fantasy and fairytale of the tradition.

2. Why, according to Alvarez, is quinceañera so important in Latino/Hispanic culture?

The "need to acknowledge and celebrate these new arrivals in the field of time" is the reason Alvarez offers for the persistence of the tradition. Her essay does not make a convincing case for its importance beyond several references to the disproportionate efforts made to continue this tradition. Only once does Alvarez suggest a girl's reluctance to participate in a quinceañera, and this is not developed. Alvarez does not set out to convince readers of the importance of the quinceañera. Rather, she intends to afford a closer-than-usual view to those interested in the tradition out of simple curiosity.

3. What, ultimately, is Alvarez's attitude toward quinceañera? How do you know? Why doesn't Alvarez's husband want to accompany her as she attends the quinceañera?

Alvarez states clearly in her closing that she shares her husband's skepticism about the practicality of such celebrations. Her husband, when invited to attend, reminds her that he has attended four quinceañeras and one would have been enough.

Rhetorical Analysis

4. Although she writes in various literary modes, Alvarez is best known as a novelist. What elements of fiction—foreshadowing and characterization, for example—do you detect in this essay? Identify specific passages to support your analysis. How effective are these strategies, and why?

Alvarez is the quintessential storyteller. Her use of narrative and description are subtle enough to draw an outsider in, yet authoritative enough to engender the ring of truth. Her scene-setting makes even a potentially unfamiliar hotel room in one of New York's less celebrated boroughs accessible to readers from the Midwest, South, Southwest, or West Coast. Her use of dialogue captures the voices of her subjects and invites one effectively into the conversation.

5. How would you describe Alvarez's audience for this essay? How successful is she in tailoring the tone and content of the selection to this audience? Does she present herself as an authority on the subject or an investigator, and what is the importance of this stance?

Alvarez positions herself as an investigator with inside information. Use of first-person references add to her credibility. Such a stance allows the reader to draw his or her own conclusions about the quinceañera tradition—whether the reader is a member of a target audience of Latinas coming of age in the United States or a member of a group of outsiders looking in.

6. Does Alvarez establish a thesis or claim about quinceañeras? Why or why not?

Alvarez's thesis is not definitive. Her essay describes her experience conducting research on a cultural tradition about which she has some firsthand experience. She relies more on narrative than argument in this essay.

7. Alvarez gradually establishes an extended or working definition of quinceañera. Locate passages where the reader receives information about this custom or ritual.

Each of the paragraphs following the first two in the essay provide some detail of a quinceañera. The reader learns details about the planning, preparation, execution, and aftermath of a quinceañera along with the author's perspective on each of these aspects.

8. How does Alvarez link her introductory and concluding paragraphs? How do these two paragraphs serve as a framing device for the body of the selection?

Alvarez links her introductory and concluding paragraphs by referring to fairytale and fantasy. They serve to remind us of the feelings surrounding the event and contrast to the facts of celebrating a quinceañera.

Writing

9. Write a narrative essay in which you tell about a ritual, custom, or celebration that is important to your family or culture.

Students may rely on personal experience and observations in developing this theme. They need to provide specific examples with details.

10. In an analysis essay, compare/contrast two coming-of-age celebrations, such as quinceañeras and sweet sixteen celebrations, or bar/bat mitzvahs.

Responses will vary depending on students' own backgrounds and experiences, as well as influences from family and friends. Students should, however, be able to support their own ideas by using material in this chapter's essays.

11. Writing an Argument Argue for or against the proposition that coming-of-age celebrations have become too expensive and ostentatious in contemporary American culture.

Responses will vary, but students should support their argument with examples from the essays, as well as their own personal experiences.

Lesson Plan 5.7

Chapter Assessment

Rhetorical Analysis Answers

1. A
2. C
3. C
4. A
5. D
6. B
7. A
8. C
9. B
10. E

Connections for Critical Thinking

Have students turn to the questions that appear on page 229 in the textbook. Tell students to choose any one of the options and write for a minimum of 30 minutes.

After students have finished writing, use the remainder of a 45–50 minute period to group students according to the topic they chose. Students should read and comment on one another's essays, offering a positive comment, a critical comment, and a question for each essay read.

Answers

1. **Both Annie Dillard's "An American Childhood" and E. B. White's "Once More to the Lake" explore the experience of childhood from a different perspective. Do they share a common voice or mood? What is distinctive about each essay? Which essay do you prefer, and why? Consider the style and emotional impact of the writing.**

   One might consider White's essay wistful. His tone is somewhat sentimental, yet to call it romantic would be to deny the reality of his former and current experiences at the lake of his childhood. Dillard, on the other hand, writes about her memories of Mother in a voice at once adoring and intimidated. You can still sense the tension in the relationship in the clip of her sentences and many words in quotation marks. It is as if she wants, above all, to be accurate. Somewhere between her recollections and White's lies a truth readers can step into and against which we might measure our own memories. Each writer's style and emotional impact emerge from the microcosm of culture and family they experienced as children of a certain family in a certain time yet resonate with readers who hail from different realities. This is possible because they tell their truth with such personal authority as to invite universal identification with their experience of childhood.

2. **Argue for or against the claim that Alvarez's portrayal of a quinceañera and Brooks's take on online dating are biased.**

   To argue against each author's "bias" would be to ignore the very subjective stance of most writing. The best writing offers enough detail for readers to form their own opinions. That each writer is a member of the group he or she describes lends credibility, but each writer's views are not to be accepted as the singular authoritative perspective possible on the issues they address. If that were the case, it would be possible to consider there is but one American view of baseball or one woman's view of tax preparation or childrearing. Bias is only a bad thing when it is presented as justification for dismissing other valid and valuable perspectives on any issue. Often, when asked to judge whether bias is present, it is a veiled way of dismissing or discounting the opinion(s) being presented. Here, questioning the question may be an illuminating exercise.

3. **Argue for or against the idea that the presentation of relatively new types of relationships like those described in the essays by Kingsolver and Brooks**

seem more highly romanticized than the "traditional" relationships described by White and Alvarez.

There is nothing idealized or unrealistic about either author's portrayal of family relationships. Both use commonplace examples from everyday life as lived in every part of this country. Divorce, remarriage, and committed partnerships are part and parcel of relationships from one end of the nation and educational food chain to another. All one needs to do is to poll principals or ride school buses in urban, suburban, and rural areas to find out what shape families take in any neighborhood.

4. Argue for or against the view that changes in society and its norms—specifically, increased geographical mobility, an evolving workplace, ideas about economic class, individual liberties—have resulted in new forms of identity. Use examples from the work of Brooks, Kingsolver, and others.

Answers will vary. Evolution changes things politically, technologically, intellectually, and personally. Humans and the nations we comprise are faced with the same challenge the dinosaurs faced millennia ago: Adapt or die. Brooks's essay illustrates that despite the pitfalls, technology has reintroduced the concept of structured courtship and has made it possible for people who want to connect to do so, even in cyberspace. The challenge is to digitize one's identity in such a way as to make it at once realistic and attractive. This re-mastering of the self for an online profile, personal ad, or autobiographical essay has consequences. According to Brooks, both opportunity and evidence exist that extreme honesty and extreme dishonesty are plentiful.

5. Write a classification essay analyzing the types of women presented in the essays by Kingsolver, Dillard, and Alvarez.

Remind students that as a pattern of writing, classification enables one to make sense of large and potentially complex concepts. You divide a concept into groups and subgroups, and you classify elements within categories. Essentially, if you classify in a rigorous and logical way, you sort out for analysis the parts and ideas within a scheme, progressing from general to specific in your treatment of the topic.

Lesson Plan 5.8

Synthesizing Sources: Helicopter Parenting

For the synthesis feature in Chapter 4, we asked students to dive in and write a synthesis essay. In Chapter 5, consider a softer landing. Instead, ask students to work in their groups and read all of the sources. After they have read the sources, have them classify each source as positive, negative, or neutral. Then, they should create three thesis statements: a defend, a challenge, and a qualify. They should briefly outline each position, listing topic sentences and sources. You may then choose to ask students to write an essay based on one of the outlines they have created.

Applying Your Synthesis Skills: Suggested Answers

Comprehension

1. Write a definition of *helicopter parenting* based on the sources. Which two sources give the most compelling viewpoint of helicopter parenting that best portray your own thoughts on this issue? Why were these sources the most successful?

Answers will vary, but a compelling feature of each example follows. **Source A:** This text gives both sides of the argument and talks about the pros and cons of the topic, showing the delicate balance between parents who do not allow students to be responsible for themselves and those parents who want students to accept more responsibility for their decisions and actions. The writer cautions people not to think in extremities when they hear the term "helicopter parenting." **Source B:** This visual text shows a parent helping with the child's homework. Both the child and parent seem intent on working together, with neither appearing annoyed or controlling. **Source C:** This text is against helicopter parenting, arguing that these parents are raising children who will possibly experience abnormal anxiety, be stunted emotionally and cognitively, and experience academic difficulties in college. **Source D:** This visual text shows an annoyed daughter who is walking to a college class while her helicopter mother phones with updates on the daughter's daily schedule. Clearly the daughter does not want her mother hovering over her now that she is in college. **Source E:** This text criticizes over-parenting but argues that helicopter parenting is positive. **Source F:** This visual text is a table listing various mental health symptoms and the percentages of males and females who experienced the symptoms in the previous year at college. The percentages are relatively high.

Rhetorical Analysis

2. How did the writer of Source A view helicopter parenting? How does his diction develop his point of view?

This text talks about the pros and cons of the topic, showing the delicate balance between parents who do not allow their children to be responsible for themselves and parents who want their children to accept more responsibility for their decisions and actions. The writer cautions people not to think in terms of extremes when they hear the term "helicopter parenting." He labels it a "mildly pejorative" term, indicating disapproval but only in a mild way. He banters about the term "poor behavior" followed by "(can you say spoiled)" in a slightly humorous way, showing that he thinks people need to calm down about the horrors of over-parenting. His "take home message" is that it is good to be involved with one's children, but in reasonable ways.

3. Compare and contrast the visuals in Sources B and D. Explain their similarities and differences.

The visual in Source B shows a father who has taken an interest in helping his son's homework. The body language of both people show a collaborative interest in working together. Source D's visual shows a daughter on her way to college class. She is clearly annoyed that her mother is hovering through the phone, calling out reminders. In both instances, the students appear to want to complete the work; in Source D, however, the mother is minimizing her child's actions and responsibilities.

4. How does the information in Source F support the argument in both Sources C and E? Do you believe the data in Source F is reliable? Why or why not?

The data in Source F (college students who experienced mental health symptoms) seem to support Source C's claim that "college-aged students whose parents are overly involved in their academic lives, or whose parents created rigidly structured childhood environments, are more likely to experience anxiety and depression." Similarly, the relatively high percentage of college students who felt overwhelmed, exhausted, very lonely, very sad, and overwhelming anxiety supports Source E's claim that "when parents are making decisions for their children all the time and protecting them, when they get out on their own they don't know a thing about disappointment." The data would seem to be reliable; the American College Health Association is a respected organization, and it conducts the National College Health Assessment every year.

5. Based on these sources, where would you draw the line between what is considered helping children and becoming intrusive?

This will be the students' call, and all of the sources can help with students' responses.

Writing an Argument

6. Write an essay detailing your views on this topic. Incorporate text evidence from all six sources as you synthesize your thoughts.

Answers will vary. The more successful essays will qualify their responses.

CHAPTER 6
History, Culture, and Civilization

Although AP students are intelligent, they are also young. Many of them are not as aware of world events and affairs as we might like. The AP English exam tests more than students' ability to write a cohesive paragraph; the exam is designed in such a way as to intrinsically test students' intellectual sophistication. You should find that this particular selection of essays engages your students' intellectual curiosity and invades their personal comfort zones, which presents a wonderful opportunity to reinforce research skills. The lesson plans accompanying this chapter's essays will reinforce the skills you are already teaching in argumentation, analysis, and synthesis, while providing opportunities to encourage students to increase their knowledge of world history, religion, and politics.

Teaching the Chapter

Before discussing any essays in this chapter, have students analyze the photographs in the **Classic and Contemporary Images** feature on pages 236–237. Discuss the questions in the textbook. See suggested answers below.

Classic and Contemporary Images: Suggested Answers

1. **What is your major impression of the two shots of the second photo?**

   Students will find the main image and inset to be eerily ghostlike. The photograph completely dehumanizes the people who are being smuggled over the border in a semi-truck. Students' impressions might also be a consideration that the people being smuggled appear like cattle in a cattle truck.

2. **How is the issue of health and personal space differentiated in the classic photo as compared to the contemporary photo?**

   The first photo shows Ellis Island authorities checking the immigrants for health issues. In what appears to be a crowded office or hallway, the authorities do not hesitate to move close to the men in order to examine heart rate and other health concerns. The contemporary photos also show a crowded, enclosed space, but the health of these immigrants is not an issue at all.

3. **Immigrants are divided into legal and illegal aliens. How do these photos support those labels?**

   The men in the first photo are clearly divided into uniformed immigration officials and partially dressed male immigrants being physically examined. Several other immigrants appear to be waiting to be examined, but they are fully clothed. These men are legal aliens going through the immigration process. In the contemporary photos, we see illegal aliens being secretly transported inside a truck. They all appear to be unclothed males who ironically exhibit alien features. The X-ray strips away all humanity by giving the immigrants a ghostlike form highlighted by the blurry, yet profound, light that emphasizes the illegal alien aspect.

4. **Examine the elements physically surrounding the people in each photo. Write a paragraph describing how these elements reflect immigration policy of the time.**

   Paragraphs will vary. Some students may point out the eye chart and open door in the classic photo, signifying an immigration policy that addressed immigrants' health and allowed diversity. Ellis Island shows a clear process for allowing immigrants into the country, although we know the conditions at the time were not that desirable. Still, the photograph shows organized methods in what appears to be a sanitary setting. Surrounding elements in the contemporary photos include packaged crates of materials, limited space in which to move, and inability of the people to stand up straight. The body language seems to reveal dejection and resignation.

Lesson Plan 6.1

The Declaration of Independence—Study in Syntax

Activity: Syntax Scavenger Hunt

One of the challenges of teaching a famous historical document is just that—it is a famous historical document that students are sure they already understand. We now have the opportunity to move them beyond the initial reading for comprehension and into a syntactical analysis. (If you feel that students first need help comprehending the text, then read it together in class using think-along strategies.)

Provide each student with a blank copy of the "Syntax Scavenger Hunt." (Photocopy the chart that follows, or see **Chapter 6 online, Thomas Jefferson: Syntax Scavenger Hunt.)** Although we teach grammar skills, we do not always pull those skills into our rhetorical discussions. In order to read analytically, students need to recognize syntactical variety and understand the effect of those structures. In this lesson, we will provide the structures and devices, and ask students to identify and explain them. You may want to point out to students the following definitions:

- **Periodic sentence:** Begins with the "additional details," and the main clause comes at the end of the sentence. (More formal)
- **Cumulative sentence:** Begins with the main clause, and the rest of the details fill in the rest of the sentence. (Less formal)
- **Anaphora:** repetition of a word or expression at the beginning of successive phrases, sentences, or clauses for poetic effect

The Declaration of Independence is a complex document, but it is important to note that Jefferson's syntactical constructions often help us to understand the hierarchy that he established among God, man, and the government. Jefferson, a Deist, focuses this document not on the idea that God gives rights to Man, but rather that Man is the recipient of these rights ascribed by God. The shift may seem subtle, but it is important. If Jefferson were to focus on "God," then he would be establishing a holy war—a "which nation does God support best?" battle. Instead, Jefferson places the importance of God in a tertiary position in order to keep his argument—that freedom and autonomy are inalienable rights—at the forefront. As students complete the scavenger hunt and discuss their answers, help them to recognize these subtleties.

Syntax Scavenger Hunt			
In the Declaration of Independence, find an example of each grammar construction listed here. Then analyze each example to determine *why* Jefferson wrote it that way. In other words, what is the **effect** of that construction on the reader?			
¶	Construction	Sentence	Effect
1	Periodic Sentence		
2	Passive Voice		
2	Sentence Fragment		
2	Repetition by phrase		
2, 3-15	Cumulative Sentence		
16	Parallel prepositional phrases		
23	Anaphora		

Sample Answers

¶	Construction	Sentence	Effect
1	Periodic Sentence	"When in the course . . . separation."	This very long opening sentence establishes a great deal of information before "getting to the point." Jefferson establishes context ("when . . . bands") and he establishes ethos ("which have connected . . . God entitle them") before calling for action. In so doing, he provides a rationale before forcefully declaring his intentions.
2	Passive Voice	"all men are created equal" "they are endowed by their Creator"	Establishes the equality of both sides under one Creator, but keeps the focus on the people rather than religion
2	Sentence Fragment	"That to secure these rights" "That whenever any Form of Government"	These are intentional fragments. Jefferson is creating a list, but he wants the focus to be on the jarring quality of this list rather than on the lovely prose constructions he is capable of writing. The demand parallels the stark nature of the writing.
2	Repetition by phrase within a sentence	"it is their right, it is their duty"	This combines parallel structure and repetition. Jefferson is writing to inspire just as clearly as he is writing to invoke change. Rights and duties carry equal weight and are dependent upon each other—to secure our rights, we must, he declares, attend to our duties.

2, 3-15	Cumulative Sentence	Any of the "He has" sentences qualify, as does "The history of the present King . . ." in paragraph 2.	This construction is direct. It is neither flowery nor ornate. Jefferson has already politely and prettily described the context and the demands; he is now listing the complaints of the colonists. This construction is important because it emphasizes Jefferson's need to "get to the point" and ensure that the Crown understands the depth of the colonists' specific dissatisfaction.
16	Parallel prepositional phrases	"For quartering. . ." "For protecting. . ." Etc.	Jefferson is enumerating the charges levied against King George by the colonists. Students should notice that the object of each preposition is a gerund. This verbal construction allows Jefferson to infuse the list with action, focusing attention on specific acted-upon infractions of the colonists' freedom. Point out that this level of specificity is exactly what makes the writing so powerful.
23	Anaphora	"Nor have We . . ." "We have . . ." "We have . . ." "We have . . ."	Jefferson has shifted the focus away from the King and back to the colonists. Having reminded them of the injustices enacted upon them, he shifts to a unifying moment. The repeated capitalization of "We" ("Nor have We . . .") places the colonists on par with the King and re-establishes their right to autonomy.

Class Closer

Ask students which particular sentence in the Declaration of Independence they found to be most powerful. Discuss why they chose those sentences.

Homework

Have students read King's "I Have a Dream" speech and independently create a multiple-entry journal finding and explaining one example of ethos, one example of pathos, and one example of logos in the essay.

Suggested Answers

"The Declaration of Independence" by Thomas Jefferson

From www.archives.gov/founding-docs/declaration-transcript

Comprehension

1. Explain Jefferson's main and subordinate purposes in this document.

Jefferson's main purpose is argumentative and persuasive: to advocate separation of America from England and to move Americans to this appropriate action. He employs subordinate expository techniques—notably causal analysis and exemplification—to reinforce his argument.

2. What is Jefferson's key assertion or argument? Mention several reasons that he gives to support his argument.

Jefferson's key argument, presented in the form of a syllogism, is that when a government proves to be despotic, it is the people's right and duty to abolish it. This proposition is stated twice in paragraph 2.

3. Summarize Jefferson's definition of human nature and government.

The "Laws of Nature and of Nature's God" (paragraph 1) create all people free, equal, and endowed with "unalienable rights." Ideally governments should "secure these rights" and derive "their just powers from the consent of the governed" (paragraph 2). Such ideas reflect the impact of John Locke, the English philosopher who emphasized natural rights, on the American mind of 1776.

Rhetorical Analysis

4. There are many striking words and phrases in the Declaration of Independence, notably in the beginning. Locate three such examples, and explain their connotative power and effectiveness.

Students will probably point to the first paragraph, a graceful periodic sentence; the parallel structure and balance of words and phrases in the famous sentences constituting paragraph 2; the parallelism in the last line.

5. Jefferson and his colleagues had to draft a document designed for several audiences. What audiences did they have in mind? How do their language and style reflect their awareness of multiple audiences?

The language is forthright yet reasonable, declaratory without being shrill, and resolute without being dogmatic. It submits "Facts . . . to a candid world" and is written out of "decent respect to the opinions of mankind." Thus Jefferson had in mind the court of world opinion and perhaps even of posterity in drafting the Declaration of Independence. At the same time, the twenty-eight "facts" enumerating the crimes of George III are designed to appeal to American colonists, especially those who wanted independence from Great Britain.

6. The Declaration of Independence is a classic model of syllogistic reasoning and deductive argument. What is its major premise, and where is this premise stated? The minor premise? The conclusion?

Students often have difficulty comprehending syllogistic or purely deductive reasoning; thus, the clarity of this logical process in the Declaration of Independence should be illuminating. The major premise, stated and restated in paragraph 2, is that when a government proves to be "destructive" or despotic, it is the right and duty of the people to abolish it. Note that a major premise is like a generality. The minor premise, a specific which fits the generality, is that the government of King George III has been despotic. Thus the logical conclusion (paragraph 24) is that the representatives of the American colonies have the right to absolve themselves "from all allegiance to the British Crown."

7. What sort of inductive evidence does Jefferson offer?

Inductive reasoning often reinforces deductive reasoning by providing evidence or needed support. Paragraphs 3–22 reveal the inductive process; here there is a specific catalogue of the "injuries and usurpations" of the tyrannical King George III.

8. Why is the middle portion, or body, of the Declaration of Independence considerably longer than the introduction or conclusion? What holds the body together?

The middle section, arranged inductively, is long because Jefferson and his contemporaries had to justify their monumental declaration of independence from Great Britain. A common fault of induction is the use of too little evidence or flimsy evidence. Jefferson avoids this pitfall in his extensive list of major crimes. The entire section is unified by parallel elements ("He has," "for quartering") and by a consistent tone that is firm and resolute.

9. **Explain the function and effect of parallel structure in this document.**

Parallel structure makes certain phrases memorable ("that all men are created equal, that they are endowed..."); provides oratorical balance and flourish to a document which after all is a declaration; occasionally adds a legalistic tone, as if Jefferson is making a case in a court of law; and finally serves to unify paragraphs and entire sections (see the previous answer).

Writing

10. **Discuss the relevance of the Declaration of Independence to politics today.**

Perhaps you will want to focus this open-ended question by asking whether perfect equality is a reality or an ideal. What social, economic, political, and educational realities corrupt this ideal?

11. **Explain in an essay why the Declaration of Independence is a model of effective prose. Analyze the choices Jefferson makes to achieve his purpose in the Declaration of Independence.**

As a prewriting exercise for this topic, ask students to connect some of the grievances listed in paragraphs 3–23 to specific situations today.

12. **Writing an Argument** Write your own declaration of independence—from family, employer, required courses, or the like. Develop this declaration as an op-ed piece for a newspaper.

Have students include a preface or introductory paragraph, a list of grievances and attempted solutions, and a conclusion.

Lesson Plan 6.2

King's "I Have a Dream"—Jigsaw Group Analysis

Class Opener

Have students watch Dr. Martin Luther King, Jr., delivering the speech. You can find the video online.

Activity: Identifying Appeals

In groups, give students a chance to discuss the examples of ethos, pathos, and logos they found in King's speech for their homework assignment. Each group should choose two examples of ethos, two of pathos, and two of logos. Place large sheets of paper labeled "Ethos," "Pathos," and "Logos," around the room. On those sheets, have students write the quotation and commentary pairings their groups have selected.

Go around the room and ask students to explain their selections. Notice whether any students or groups are confusing the appeals. Remind students that pathos is connected to emotion; ethos to ethics or authority; and logos to logic. Correct any mislabeled appeals. Using a large stamp or a marker, note the best examples on each sheet.

Activity: Writing an Analysis Essay

Ask students to move to the appeal sheet that they found most powerful. Hopefully, students will distribute themselves in a fairly equitable manner. If necessary, organize students into more balanced numbers. After students have chosen an appeal, create subgroups of 3 or 4 in support of each appeal.

In their new subgroups, students will write a rhetorical analysis essay using the appeal they chose as the most significant basis for their argument. Their thesis statements, which you may want to help them prepare, should follow a format similar to this one: "In his 'I Have a Dream' speech, Dr. Martin Luther King, Jr., relies on <pathos> to appeal to the reader's <emotions> and to create a sense of unity in the fight for civil rights." Students will then create three body paragraphs, each drawing on two examples from the textual evidence they have already posted around the room. Their essay format should look like this:

- **I.** Thesis statement
- **II.** Body paragraph one
  - **a.** Topic Sentence—Minor argument one
  - **b.** Textual Evidence
  - **c.** Commentary
  - **d.** Commentary
  - **e.** Textual Evidence
  - **f.** Commentary
  - **g.** Commentary
  - **h.** Conclusion/transition
- **III.** Body paragraph two (repeats II)
- **IV.** Body paragraph three (repeats II)

The essay will be written cooperatively, within the new jigsaw group. This is a process essay rather than a product essay. Although it might not be the best essay they will write all year, the process of focusing on a single appeal will strengthen their ability to recognize and discuss argument strategy.

Class Closer

Ask students to share their essays and discuss the collaborative writing process.

Suggested Answers

"I Have a Dream" by Martin Luther King, Jr.

Comprehension

1. What is the main purpose of this speech? Where does King state this purpose most clearly?

In paragraph 4, King states, "we have come here today to dramatize a shameful condition." Beyond this, King's speech is a rallying cry and a manifesto. More than 250,000 people were seated on the lawn of the Lincoln Memorial on August 28, 1963, and millions more were watching on television. King understood what a major opportunity this was to articulate the principles and goals of the civil rights movement for a national audience and how this speech could impact on American thought for years to come.

2. **Why does King make use of "fivescore years ago" (paragraph 2)? How is this more appropriate than simply saying "a hundred years ago"?**

The use of "fivescore" instead of one hundred is a deliberate evocation of Lincoln's Gettysburg Address, both as homage to Lincoln, at whose memorial the people were assembled, and as a way of setting the tone for King's speech as a major statement equivalent to the Gettysburg Address.

3. **Who is King's audience? Where does he acknowledge the special historical circumstances influencing his speech?**

Dr. King probably had multiple audiences in mind: the crowd at the March, Washington politicians, the media, the public. He alludes to the Framers and to Lincoln in order to frame this momentous event for his audience.

Rhetorical Analysis

4. **Identify several allusions King includes. From what sources does King adapt phrases to give his work allusive richness?**

King uses allusions from Shakespeare (paragraph 6), the Bible (paragraphs 16 and 22), hymns (paragraph 15), the Declaration of Independence (paragraph 4), and "My Country 'Tis of Thee" (paragraphs 25–35). King was enormously well-read, and his choices of these phrases were deliberate. The phrases are not only euphonious, but they also placed King in the speaking style of other great American orators, particularly Lincoln.

5. **What do the terms *interposition* and *nullification* (paragraph 21) mean? What is their historical significance?**

Interposition means "to come between." In June 1963, George Wallace blocked the path of two black students trying to desegregate the University of Alabama. *Nullification* means "to make null or void or without legal force." In U.S. history, nullification refers to a series of incidents between states and the federal government over states' rights. During the civil rights struggle in the 1950s and 1960s, "states' rights" was often little more than a pretext for opposing equal justice under the law.

6. **Why does King make use of repetition? Does this technique work well in print? Explain.**

Dr. King's oratorical style reflects his training as a minister. Repetition is a good technique to use in speaking when one wants an audience to remember points made and when one wants to ensure that an audience can follow the sequence of ideas clearly. In print, this technique is not as necessary, because everyone reads at one's own speed and one can always go back and reread abstruse points. However, even in print, repetition enhances the cadences of a piece, and mirrors the rhythms of the speaker's voice.

7. **What is the purpose of the extended metaphor in paragraphs 4 and 5? Which point in paragraph 3 does it refer to?**

Dr. King is contrasting the material wealth of America with the economic plight of black Americans. The extended financial metaphor is a way of underscoring the need, above all, for economic justice as a precursor to any other kind of justice.

8. **Why is this selection titled "I Have a Dream"? How do dreams serve as a motif for this speech?**

Paragraphs 17–23 represent the climax of King's speech, and many people consider it the most stirring section. The use of dreams as an image is in keeping with the idealistic character of this piece. Moreover, as King is outlining his hopes for the future, the invocation of the American Dream is an important device.

9. **Many people consider "I Have a Dream" to be among the greatest speeches delivered by an American. In an essay, explain how King's speech is effective.**

Unquestionably, this speech is a masterpiece of rhetoric. Perhaps it would be a good idea to listen to King's speech and contrast it to other notable speeches: John Kennedy's Inaugural Address, Mario Cuomo's 1984 Democratic Keynote Address, Douglas MacArthur's Farewell Address, or any recent address given by a local or national politician who may not have mastered the techniques of rhetoric as effectively. Discuss the relationship between content and style,.and ask your students if they can remember any speech or phrases from a politician they admire.

10. **Write your own "I Have a Dream" essay, basing it on your vision of America.**

A good prewriting activity would be to have your students focus on the conditions facing their selected group and then enumerate what achievements are desirable or possible under optimum conditions.

11. **Writing an Argument** **Prepare a newspaper editorial advocating a solution to one aspect of racial, ethnic, or sexual injustice.**

Remind your students that editorials by definition are persuasive-designed to move people from conviction to action. Have them build this element into their editorial.

Lesson Plan 6.3

Synthesizing Classic and Contemporary Essays—Timed-Writing

Have students turn to the synthesis questions that appear after these two essays on page 247 in the textbook. Tell students to choose one of the three options and write for a minimum of 30 minutes.

After students have finished writing, use the remainder of the class period to group students according to the option they chose. Students should read and comment on each other's essays, offering a positive comment, a critical comment, and a question for each essay read.

Synthesizing the Classic and Contemporary Essays: Suggested Answers

1. **Compare the Declaration of Independence with King's speech in terms of language, style, and content. Are they equally powerful and resonant? Cite specific passages from the essays to illustrate your response.**

Both essays use language effectively and compellingly in their indictment of oppression. Although Jefferson uses the style of the 18th century (capitalizing letters for emphasis, complex phrasing), King uses phrases replete with metaphors and Biblical references. In both essays the appeal is powerful: Jefferson outlines the abuses of the British monarch and warns of the States' intention to separate; King appeals to the United States government to grant its African Americans the same freedoms Jefferson's document called for. Students' choices of passages will vary. They should cite specific support for their choices.

2. **Rewrite the Declaration of Independence in modern English as you believe Dr. King might have written it, reflecting his concerns about African Americans and other minorities in this country. Include a list of grievances similar to the ones concerning British rule.**

   This assignment calls for students to rewrite the Declaration of Independence as King might have, concentrating on the African American experiences in this country. However, you may choose to allow the students a wider range of groups from which to address the issue: Native Americans (referred to in Jefferson's document as "Indian Savages"); the civil rights of gays and lesbians; women still working towardg economic and political parity. Students must attempt to imitate the format of the document and include a possible resolution or ultimatum at the conclusion.

3. **Write a research paper about the lives and times of King and Jefferson. Compare and contrast any significant events or pertinent biographical data in their backgrounds. Argue that both men were fighting for the same (or different) things.**

   After researching the lives and times (context) of Jefferson and King, students should consider what they might have in common in terms of background, social class, politics, and education. How did these men find their way into politics and the public eye? Were both men fighting for the same thing? How do they contrast?

Homework

Assign students to read "The Myth of the Latin Woman: I Just Met a Girl Named María" by Judith Ortiz Cofer.

Lesson Plan 6.4

Cofer's "Myth of the Latin Woman"—Timed Writing with a Plan

Class Opener

Ask students these questions: What does Cofer have to say about stereotypes? How pervasive are stereotypes in our society? Keep this discussion brief so that students will have enough time to write an in-class essay.

Activity: In-Class Essay

Give students 40 minutes to write a rhetorical essay based on Cofer's essay, using an explicit outline. Provide the following prompt:

> **Cofer's essay explores the idea that stereotypes pervade our society. Read and annotate the essay carefully. Then, in a well-organized essay, analyze the rhetorical devices Cofer uses to convey her attitude toward stereotypes.**

The essay should follow the outline below (which you may choose to discuss during the class opener if you have a short period).

Introduction Paragraph: This need only contain a thesis. The thesis must identify the context of the essay (Cofer and the essay title) and clearly identify Cofer's attitude toward stereotypes.

Body Paragraph 1: Begin with an arguable topic sentence that indicates one of the goals Cofer has. (For example: To establish a sense of ethos and enable her audience to identify with her struggles, Cofer fills her essay with narrative examples.) Each body paragraph should follow this structure:

1. Arguable Topic Sentence
2. Textual Evidence
3. Commentary linking evidence to argument
4. Commentary linking evidence to argument
5. Textual Evidence
6. Commentary linking evidence to argument
7. Commentary linking evidence to argument
8. Summation

Body Paragraph 2: Begin with an arguable topic sentence that indicates another goal of Cofer's. (For example: By sharing personal experiences, Cofer challenges stereotypes, identifying herself as . . . and compelling her audience to. . . .)

Conclusion Paragraph: This may be a single sentence. It need not restate the thesis, but it should clearly end the conversation.

Homework

Have students read "A World Not Neatly Divided," and write three questions in preparation for a Socratic seminar on this essay.

Suggested Answers

"The Myth of the Latin Woman: I Just Met a Girl Named María" by Judith Ortiz Cofer

Comprehension

1. **What is the thesis of the essay?**

   Through personal experience and anecdote, Cofer presents the case that ethnic stereotypes are very difficult to change, and that as an educated Latina, it is her "goal to try to replace the old stereotypes with a much more interesting set of realities." In Cofer's case, this replacement can best be rendered through her stories or more generally, her art.

2. **What does Cofer mean by the expression "cultural schizophrenia" (paragraph 3)?**

   Cofer grew up in an enclave of Hispanics around which thrived a very dominant Anglo culture. Her need to negotiate between the two gave rise to a "double bind" experience; that is, feeling as though she were doing the wrong thing ethnically regardless if she were trying to conform to Latina tradition or Anglo tradition.

3. **Define the following words: *coveted* (paragraph 1), *Anglo* (paragraph 4), *coalesced* (paragraph 5), *machismo* (paragraph 7), and *entrees* (paragraph 13).**

   Coveted here means "inordinately desired." *Anglo* refers to the dominant American culture, perhaps the one that thrived most clearly in the 1950s and 1960s. *Coalesced* means "blended together." *Machismo* is a particularly Hispanic concept referring to male toughness, dominance, and stoicism. The word *entrees* here refers to the permission to enter a particular social group.

Rhetorical Analysis

4. Cofer uses many anecdotes in her discussion of stereotyping. How does this affect the tone of the essay?

Anecdotes make the tone conversational, and it also breaks down the barrier between the authoritarian position of the writer and the passive role of the reader.

5. Who is the implied audience for this essay? What aspects of the writing led you to your conclusion?

Any educated reader would be a likely member of the essay's audience. Regardless of how "sensitive" one may believe one is regarding understanding stereotyping, "seeing through the eyes" of the person being stereotyped is perhaps the best lesson in curing it.

6. This essay is written in the first person, which tends to reveal a lot about the writer's personality. What adjectives come to mind when you think of the writer's singular voice?

Some adjectives that may come to mind are "thoughtful," "insightful," "enduring," "stoic," as well as "confused," "betrayed," and "defiant." Cofer definitely demonstrates how her life has been a negotiation between trying to be sympathetic toward people with stereotypes and enduring moments that truly hurt her feelings.

7. Although this essay has a sociological theme, Cofer demonstrates that she has a poet's sensitivity toward language. What in the following sentence from paragraph 7 demonstrates this poetic style: "It is custom, however, not chromosomes, that leads us to choose scarlet over pale pink"? Select two other sentences from the essay that demonstrate Cofer's stylistic talent, and explain why they, too, are poetic.

There is alliteration in the same sentence from paragraph 7 as well as color imagery. Another example of vivid language is the last line of paragraph 10: "I was just an Evita or a Maria: merely a character in his cartoon-populated universe." And in paragraph 12, there is a metaphor in the sentence: "I understand that my anger gave my reading fire."

8. In paragraph 8, Cofer contrasts cultural perceptions related to Hispanic and Anglo behavior. How is the paragraph structured so that this difference is demonstrated dramatically?

Cofer demonstrates how Hispanic Saturday night rituals were highly articulated events with specific rules and regulations that could not be transgressed. So, even though they contained erotic elements, there was a built-in safety valve that would prevent any sexual activities from arising. When Cofer switches to America, and describes her experience with Americans, she shows how stereotyping and not knowing cultural rules causes confusion that borders on inanity. This paragraph succinctly demonstrates the profound ignorance that is a result of stereotyping.

9. Cofer uses quotation marks to emphasize the connotation of certain words. Explain the significance of the following words: *mature* (paragraph 4), *hopeless* (paragraph 5), *hot tamale* (paragraph 6), *wronged* (paragraph 7), and *decent* (paragraph 8).

Cofer uses most of the words in quotations ironically. She implies that "mature" was a euphemism for "sexual"; "hopeless" was the attitude Anglo girls had toward their Hispanic peers because they probably felt they would just never be able to adjust to the American way of dress; "hot tamale" is another cliché which an Anglo would use to imply that Latin women were highly sexual; "wronged" in paragraph 7 refers to premarital intercourse; and "decent" in paragraph 8 refers to the idea that a young Latin woman is sexually modest.

Writing

10. In a personal essay, explore whether you have experienced or observed stereotyping. How has this experience molded your perception of the world in which you live?

A variation of this assignment might be as follows: "Argue for or against the idea that understanding cultural diversity is the sign of a truly educated individual."

11. **Writing an Argument** In an essay, write an argument about what creates cultural stereotypes, and provide suggestions on how to overcome stereotyped thinking.

You may wish to have students consider their own stereotyping to attempt an understanding of stereotyping in general. This assignment might prove fruitful by having students consult educational websites.

Lesson Plan 6.5

Sen's "A World Not Neatly Divided"—SOAPSTone Analysis

Class Opener

Provide students with the following excerpt from the essay: "When people talk about clashing civilizations, as so many politicians and academics do now, they can sometimes miss the central issue. The inadequacy of this thesis begins well before we get to the question of whether civilizations must clash." What is the "thesis" the author is referring to? Is this the thesis of the essay? In a single paragraph quickwrite, define the central argument of this essay. (You will tease the answer out in the SOAPSTone discussion to follow.)

Activity: A SOAPSTone Discussion

SOAPSTone is an acronym developed by the College Board for teaching rhetorical analysis. It stands for:

Speaker—Students must determine who is speaking. Who is narrating the essay? The speaker in this essay is Sen. Help students recognize, however, that he is speaking through an academic persona. He never uses the pronoun "I"; he never identifies himself as existing within any of the contexts he describes in the essay.

Occasion—Students must determine the context of the writing. When does this occur? Where? What particular event has motivated this writing? Sen is writing as an academic within an academic context. The occasion might be identified as the classification of the "Western World" and "Islamic World." Sen argues persuasively against this moment, suggesting that the classification is indefensible.

Audience—Students must determine the intended audience for the essay. This essay is written for the "Western" audience who defines the members of the "Islamic World" in such a way as to deem them perpetually "other." This is an excellent moment to discuss the notion of "the other" and xenophobia in culture.

Purpose—Students must determine the author's purpose in writing the essay. This is an excellent essay with which to analyze diction. Ask students to pick out particularly loaded words in this essay. Although Sen writes as an academic, he writes with great zeal and passion, as is evidenced by his choice of words like "coarsened" and "impoverished," which he uses almost anachronistically as he applies them to ideas rather than concrete entities. Sen's purpose is to persuade his audience that overt classification is both illegitimate and polarizing.

Subject—This should be the shortest discussion point. Ask students to summarize Sen's argument in 20 words or less.

Tone—The specific diction in this essay lends itself to an analysis of tone. The tone of this essay is didactic, academic, and critical. Have students identify specific words or phrases that illustrate these tones.

If you are assigning College Board AP prompts to students, this would be an excellent time to assign the 2007 Rhetorical Analysis prompt, which asked students to analyze Scott Russell Sanders's response to Salman Rushdie in a passage from *Staying Put: Making a Home in a Restless World.*

Class Closer

Ask students to choose three words that establish the tone of the essay. On an exit slip, ask students to justify their choices.

Homework

Assign students to read "The Arab World" by Edward T. Hall.

Suggested Answers

"A World Not Neatly Divided" by Amartya Sen

Comprehension

1. According to Sen, what is the "basic weakness" underlying the idea that the world is composed of "clashing civilizations" (paragraph 1)?

The basic weakness of the idea, according to Sen, is its "program of categorizing people of the world according to a unique, allegedly commanding system of classification."

2. What does the writer mean by "singular classification" (paragraph 2)? Why is classifying people in terms of their civilization "crude and inconsistent"? Why is applying singular classification to religions and other features of society wrong?

Sen argues that it is futile to understand a culture in terms of a singular classification system, because cultural identity is always the product of a number of intersecting influences.

3. What, according to Sen, is "the main hope of harmony" (paragraph 7) in the world?

The main hope, according to Sen, lies in the "plurality of our identities."

Rhetorical Analysis

4. What argumentative strategy does Sen employ in the introductory paragraph? What point of view is he arguing against?

Sen is making a clear logical appeal in his attack on an established discourse (a discourse, and a point of view, adopted by politicians and religious fundamentalists alike).

5. While arguing against a certain type of classification, Sen actually uses classification as a rhetorical strategy. How, precisely, does he employ classification to organize his argument?

Sen employs classifications as a rhetorical strategy toward the end of paragraph 2 to demonstrate their complex and contradictory nature. (For example, the fact that Sanskrit has a larger atheistic literature than exists in any other classical language.)

6. What examples does Sen use to support his argument? Why does he use them? Why does he decide not to provide illustrations near the end of the selection?

Sen offers the examples of two Muslim emperors of the Mogul dynasty in India (paragraphs 3–4), but the illustrations cease because they serve primarily to make a rhetorical point—that any attempt to illustrate an essential quality of a civilization will tend toward oversimplification.

7. What transitional devices serve to unify the essay?

Note the transition from paragraph 2 to paragraph 3, in which Sen switches from a critique of one classification (India as a Hindu culture) to consider the similarly crude classification (India as part of the "Islamic world").

8. How effective is Sen's concluding paragraph? Does it serve to confirm his claim? Why or why not?

Student responses will vary, although students should note in the final paragraph the repeated reference to the interests of religious fundamentalism.

Writing

9. Write an essay about the problems you see in your community or school. Explain how singular classification might explain some of these problems.

If students use Sen's essay as a model for generating ideas, they might see how certain groups or subcultures are lumped together and how this causes problems. Begin by having students brainstorm what classifications there are in their communities or school.

10. In an analytical essay, explain how singular classification might help explain the events of September 11, 2001.

This analytical essay has students posit ideas against Sen's essay and discuss the events of 9/11. Having students discuss the events of 9/11 will certainly bring out conflicting viewpoints. You might also want to give students the option of looking at 9/11 not as a symptom of clash of cultures but effected by failures of intelligence or a small group's grab for power.

11. Writing an Argument Write an essay in which you demonstrate that singular classification actually can be helpful in framing public discourse about groups, nations, or civilizations.

For students to argue this point, they will need to discuss how it is nearly impossible for decision makers to think of everyone as individuals. Faced with this task, decision makers must necessarily classify nations, groups, and civilizations. Although students argue this, they do not have to agree that such classifications always use the best categories and are always fair.

Lesson Plan 6.6

Hall's "The Arab World"—Reverse Outlining

Class Opener

Work in groups to determine definitions for the words *proxemic* (paragraph 1), *paradox* (paragraph 2), *inviolate* (paragraph 3), *defer* (paragraph 6), *olfaction* (paragraph 14), and *peripherally* (paragraph 17). This question also appears as one of the comprehension questions that accompany Hall's essay in the textbook. (See answer 4.) The question provides important and useful practice in defining words in context and will help with the remainder of the conversation.

Activity: Reverse Outlining

It has been said that if an essay is well-written, the reader should be able to read the introduction followed by the topic sentences and understand the gist of the essay. In this essay, Hall provides not only clear and concise topic sentences, but also headers to help guide the reading of the piece. In today's activity, students will work together to reverse outline—that is, to create an outline from something that has already been written. Provide them with the same framework they would use in writing an essay themselves, and ask them to use it to outline Hall's argument.

- **I.** Thesis
- **II.** Claim 1—Topic Sentence
    - **a.** Evidence
    - **b.** Commentary
    - **c.** Evidence
    - **d.** Commentary
- **III.** Claim 2—Topic Sentence

Continue this format until you reach the conclusion. Students will find that this essay is clearly and carefully written, following a very precise and very formal writing style.

Class Closer

Ask students to work with their groups to identify a sociological or cultural phenomenon that exists within their school. Once they have identified that phenomenon, ask them to brainstorm situations in which this phenomenon is observed, and then identify a series of questions about that phenomenon. Perhaps the phenomenon is gum-chewing. What are the contexts within which students chew gum? Do they enjoy chewing gum more if it is forbidden? Do they chew gum when they are nervous? When taking a test, for example? Ask students to be prepared to report back on their "anthropological research" during the next class period.

Suggested Answers

"The Arab World" by Edward T. Hall

Comprehension

1. This excerpt is from Hall's book *The Hidden Dimension.* What is the hidden dimension, according to the author?

The "hidden dimension" is the dimension of space. Although we are aware of it visually, we adapt to it unconsciously, according to cultural rules and regulations. It seems only when these conventions are transgressed do we actually become aware of them.

2. In paragraph 10, Hall explains that "differing concepts of the placement of the ego in relation to the body are not easily grasped." What does he mean by this statement? How is it relevant to the theme of his essay?

The term "ego" was originally devised by Freud to explain the part of the psyche that helped maintain a homeostasis between our wishes and desires and the limitations placed upon us by culture and civilization. In regard to Arabs, Hall suggests that they express their egos more openly than Westerners to compensate for the more oppressive limits of space that confine them due to geographical placement of their countries.

3. The title of this essay is "The Arab World." What does the term *world* mean within the context of the essay?

Hall believes that "culture" is the primary component that defines our "world." It determines how we perceive reality, develop and maintain relationships, and understand ourselves in relationship to the "universe."

4. Define the following words: *proxemic* (paragraph 1), *paradox* (paragraph 2), *inviolate* (paragraph 3), *defer* (paragraph 6), *olfaction* (paragraph 14), and *peripherally* (paragraph 17). How does understanding these words affect your understanding of Hall's essay?

Proxemic is a neologism created by Hall to suggest the study of humans' responses to spatial relationships. *Paradox* refers to a seemingly contradictory situation; in this case, the idea that two cultures can perceive behaviors as signaling opposite messages. *Inviolate* means "a rule or custom that is not meant to be transgressed." *Defer* means "to give way" to someone based on custom. *Olfaction* is "sense of smell." *Peripherally* refers to being off-center or away from the central concern of an issue or situation.

Rhetorical Analysis

5. How would you characterize Hall's voice, considering his style of language and method of analysis?

Because Hall utilizes anecdotes so often in his writing as supporting points to his generalizations, the author is able to establish a rapport with the reader since the reader can imagine himself in the same situation as the writer. This aspect of identification is often missing from works in anthropology, sociology, and psychology.

6. How does Hall develop his comparison and contrast of the American versus the Arab perception of manners and driving?

Hall makes excellent use of topic sentences in his paragraphs. Often they introduce the content of what is to follow by stating a fact, and at other times by stating a misconception. For example, in paragraph 14, Hall states, "olfaction occupies a prominent place in the Arab life." In paragraph 18 he states, "One mistaken American notion is that Arabs conduct all conversation at close distances." Each of these methods serves to intrigue the reader so that he will seek the answer to the proposition originally stated.

7. **People often favor their own perspective of life over a foreign perspective. Is Hall's comparison value-free, or does he seem to prefer one cultural system to another? Explain by making reference to his tone.**

Through comparison and contrast, through humor at cultural misunderstanding from both Arab and Westerner perspectives, and via his use of subheadings that suggest objective observation, Hall is able to maintain a "bird's-eye view" perspective on his subject matter. Even when he describes situations in which he was a perpetuator or victim of some cultural misunderstanding, he does so without rancor or judgment.

8. **Who is the implied audience for this essay? Explain your view.**

This excerpt from *The Hidden Dimension* was published in 1966. Although the themes incorporated in the essay may now seem obvious or commonplace, at the time of the writing, they were rather revolutionary for the average reader. Travel abroad was much less common as was international business. In addition, the concept of the nuclear family was still a strong one in the nation, and travels far beyond the home or local community were rare. There was much less understanding of even other ethnic or racial groups in America, let alone in other countries. It was also the time when the idea of the "ugly American" was prominent, a term borrowed from a Graham Greene novel but generalized to imply the idea that Americans were ethnocentric and insensitive to the customs and values of others.

9. **Hall makes use of personal anecdote in explaining his theme. What other forms of support does he offer? Cite at least two others and provide an example of each.**

Hall uses an illustration about the "spite house" built so that a neighbor could not have a view; he also uses the interview method, although he does not expressly state just how many of his findings were a result of this procedure. In fact, the major clue we have is in paragraph 21 in which he states "in the course of my interviews."

10. **Writers often have various purposes in writing—for example, to entertain, to inform, to effect change, to advise, or to persuade. What is Hall's purpose or purposes in writing this essay? Explain your view.**

Hall seems to be advancing an entirely new field of study—proxemics—which seems to be a specialized subject within anthropology. In this regard, Hall may be considered a true innovator. Besides the obvious educational value of the writing, there is an implicit sense that Hall hopes his findings will result in more intercultural cooperation and understanding. And, as many of his subsequent books demonstrate, this does become an important role in his intellectual mission.

Writing

11. **Write an essay in which you explain the use and interpretation of personal space by observing students in social situations at your school.**

Students usually enjoy "fieldwork," especially when it does not require great preparation or travel from one's environment. Students often report that although they had been in situations hundreds of times before—for example, eating in the school cafeteria—"anthropological" observation has given them considerable insight into behaviors they never previously thought about.

12. **Write a personal anecdote about a time in your life when cultural perception caused a conflict between yourself and another person.**

Nearly every student has had a situation in which misperception resulted in a conflict. You may wish to do some pre-writing activities by listing some of the many possible signals that can be misinterpreted by others. This will allow your students to develop a "vocabulary" that may be helpful in writing their essays and keep their writing from falling into generalizations or mere narrative.

13. **Writing an Argument** In a well-written essay, take a position on the importance of personal space.

You may wish to raise the issue of playing music or holding phone conversations in public, and how those actions may intrude on others' personal space.

Lesson Plan 6.7

Satrapi's "The Veil"—Envisioning Narrative

Class Opener

As interesting and amusing as comic strips and graphic novels are, what should appeal to an AP teacher is the chance, as usual, to move beyond content and talk about technique—in this case, the technique of exposition. Explain to students that a cartoonist has a story to tell. Sometimes he or she is limited by the space available—which means drawing, say, six panels and peopling them with much dialogue and casts of thousands; or perhaps producing eight or ten smaller "scenes" and walking the reader through the story in a more leisurely discursive fashion. And finally, there are often many volumes of a graphic novel, which focus less on action heroes and more on social and political commentary, often using sophisticated irony and satire to comment on contemporary issues and problems. The visual choices belong to the illustrator; what we examine is the principle of choice the illustrator employs in determining the number of scenes and the contents of each. It is a choice that every artist, especially writers of literary fiction and drama, must make.

Activity: Analyzing "The Veil"

Have students read "The Veil" to themselves three times in class. First, have them read the spread for the story. The second time, have them study its visual structure. The third time, have them analyze the tone and rhetorical devices Satrapi used. Then ask students to use the graphic novel as a basis for a short story. Or you may want to write the story together as a class. A third option is to have students work in groups, with the first person composing a paragraph about the first panel and then passing the story around the group for each student to compose a new paragraph about the next panel, with the creation of a novella as the group's joint goal.

Activity: Picturing an Essay

Ask for student volunteers who are artistically gifted to illustrate another essay from this chapter—or a favorite short story or poem—in graphic novel form. This exercise also encourages students to hone their "imagery" and their narrative muscles as they decide which essay might make for the "best" one to render visually.

Class Closer

Have students or groups discuss their interpretations of "The Veil," or read aloud the short stories.

Suggested Answers

"The Veil" by Marjane Satrapi

Comprehension

1. Comment on your experience reading Satrapi's "The Veil." Did the graphic story catch and sustain your interest? Explain.

Students' answers should reflect on both subject matter and visual interest.

2. What idea is conveyed through this graphic story?

The main idea conveyed is one of cultural change and how it is personalized through the eyes of a young, somewhat confused girl at the time.

3. What social, cultural, or political values are central to "The Veil"? What perspective on these values does the author take? How do you know?

The author addresses the social values of dress and thought as well as gender relations and the authority of males in society. Various cultural values she addresses include removing the French language from schools; highlighting the religious overtones in the country by calling the revolution "The Islamic Revolution;" and pointing out leaders' opposition to capitalism. Political values are shown in various ways: by the authoritarian figure dressed in military gear and boots; by the girls pretending to execute one another; by the inclusion of women in the Islamic Revolution but then veiled and separated during the "Cultural Revolution," etc.

Rhetorical Analysis

4. What tone is achieved through the use of black-and-white and repetition?

Answers will vary. Using black-and-white sets a deceptively simple tone at first. The more one views the cartoon, however, the black overtones begin to feel oppressive. Have students analyze the various panels for repetition (or sameness) and satire or irony. Did students recognize the satire in the first and second panels ("you don't see me")?

5. What effects are achieved with the changing perspective of close-ups; for example, the man at the podium?

Students should notice the actions of the children in the panels with a distant perspective—actions that are common to children everywhere: playful, curious, selfish. In contrast, the panels with close-up illustrations achieve an effect of dominance, fear, and power.

6. To what extent do you think Satrapi's combination of words and pictures is effective in conveying her idea? How would the story differ if told in words only?

Answers will vary. Have students try to tell the same story in words. Or have students draw a three-panel cartoon and then repeat the story in three paragraphs.

Writing

7. Write an essay comparing "The Veil" with a current cartoon or graphic novel. How does each author use the graphic story genre to present an idea or message?

Students' essays will vary.

8. Writing a Graphic Novel Create your own graphic novel from a short story or poem that you like. How difficult was it for you to "tell" the same story in a different medium?

Students' essays will vary.

Lesson Plan 6.8

Chapter Assessment

Rhetorical Analysis Answers

1. C
2. A
3. A
4. B
5. A
6. B
7. D
8. C
9. A
10. B

Connections for Critical Thinking

Have students turn to the questions that appear on page 271 in the textbook. Tell students to choose one of the five options and write for a minimum of 30 minutes.

After students have finished writing, use the remainder of the class period to group students according to the option they chose. Students should read and comment on one another's essays, offering a positive comment, a critical comment, and a question for each essay read.

Answers

1. **Compare the Declaration of Independence with King's speech in terms of language, style, and content.**

   Students should not just read the Jefferson and King pieces but should include research into both of these writers' lives, especially at the time these particular articles were written. This will add to their analysis of the writing styles, language, and content, as well as audience appeal.

2. **Write an essay exploring the topic of culture and civilization in the essays by Cofer, Hall, and Sen.**

   Essays will be different, depending on each writer's perspective. However, students should note the variety of approaches and tones taken in these specific articles. Cofer shares her experiences in the first-person narrative style that helps a reader relate to an uncomfortable life situation. Cofer faced awkward behavior brought on by stereotypes of her Latina tradition, and her story is dotted with moments of discomfort created by strangers who exposed their prejudices and ignorance. Cofer does not offer much in the way of affiliation, only orientation. The closest she comes is making eye contact then shaking hands with the woman who mistook her for a waitress. Hall's descriptions are based on personal observation. Sen believes "civilizational categories are crude and inconsistent." If we are to live together peaceably, Sen says, we need to broaden our thinking beyond the limitations of these identities and accept the plurality of all people.

3. **In an essay, describe the current position of women in our culture. Refer to any three essays in this chapter to support your main observations.**

   This exercise should be relatively easy for the students, considering the women today in politics, media, show business (including producers, writers, and directors), and so on. There are many women for students to focus on.

4. **How does one's experience of being an outsider or stranger to a culture affect one's understanding of that culture?**

   Students should be able to incorporate personal experience here. Have them brainstorm a time in their own lives when they felt like outsiders—in any capacity—and use that as an introduction to this discussion. They will then be able to use elements from these essays to make connections.

5. Select the three essays you find the most compelling or the least appealing in this chapter. Discuss why you selected them.

Responses will vary, depending on individual preference, but students should support their claims and give examples from the readings.

Lesson Plan 6.9

Synthesizing Sources: Women's Rights

This chapter's synthesis prompt involves short texts and can be handled in a single period. Give students the practice of writing a true synthesis essay using the sources provided and this prompt:

> **Women's Rights have presented a historical struggle that, in many ways, continues in spite of the 19th Amendment. Critically read and analyze the text and images, making note of the year each appeared in print, and then write an essay in which you take a position on the current status of women's rights as an affirmative issue. Synthesize and cite at least three of the texts in your response. Make sure that your argument remains central and do not merely summarize the texts.**

Applying Your Synthesis Skills: Suggested Answers

Comprehension

1. What central idea arises from each of these sources?

All of the sources reveal that the discussion of women's rights has been an ongoing argument throughout history (at least since the Enlightenment), and the argument has not been completely concluded. Strong arguments for women's rights appear in Sources A, B, and C. Anti-women's rights arguments appear in Source D, with the opinion that granting women equal rights exposes women to the draft and reduces their claim to child support and alimony. Source E emphasizes women's labor rights by highlighting a Supreme Court judgment in favor of the female petitioner. Source F reveals that women's earnings are not equal to men's earnings.

Rhetorical Analysis

2. Compare Sources A and B. Which source is written in the first person? Which discusses slavery? Which makes a reference to the Garden of Eden? Which seems more dramatic? Why?

Jones in Source B uses the word "I" throughout her address, which makes her imploring more dramatic. She bases her argument on the similar battle being waged to free enslaved men. Wollstonecraft in Source A references the Garden of Eden in her words: "by the serpentine wrigglings of cunning they mount the tree of knowledge and only acquire sufficient to lead men astray."

3. Explain the visual and textual rhetoric in Source C.

Students should notice the features that tell us the men in this cartoon are important. They are wearing wigs and ruffled shirts as men did at the time of the American Revolution. They also are posed in a way similar to a famous painting of the drafting of the Declaration of Independence. All of these caricature elements reveal that these men are some of America's "Founding Fathers." The woman in the cartoon is also a caricature. By placing her on the floor—on her hands and knees holding a scrub brush—the cartoonist is telling us that she is insignificant. The men in the room do not even notice her. Because the men are reviewing the document that resulted in the independence of the United States, we can assume that they symbolize power, freedom, bravery, and intelligence. The woman scrubbing the floor symbolizes the low status of women in the United States. Explain to students that irony is the use of words or actions that contradict what is really going on, and then have students read the caption of this cartoon. Students should recognize that Benjamin Franklin is reading Thomas Jefferson's draft of the Declaration of Independence when he says, "All men are created equal." The irony comes when he follows that up by saying: "*That's beautiful Tom*." (Mike Peters (c) Distributed by King Features Syndicate, Inc.) Here's the irony: The words "all men are created equal" are *beautiful* only if a person was a white male when the Declaration was written. Everyone else in society was evidently created "UN-equal." The cartoonist is pointing out that the Founding Fathers, while congratulating themselves on a beautifully worded document, should have considered all *humans* as equal.

4. What words and phrases does Schlafly use in Source D to support her argument that equal rights are wrong? What is her tone? Is her argument convincing? Defend your answer.

Students' responses will vary. Schlafly's argument is that women already have "special privilege" status, which would be reduced by an Equal Rights Amendment. She supports this argument by citing the rights of women not to be drafted and to legally receive child support and alimony. Her claims are based on the warrants that with an Equal Rights Amendment, men would no longer legally be required to pay child support or alimony, and that women (as well as men) would be drafted into the military if the draft were reinstated. Her tone seems to be negative.

5. Analyze Justice Marshall's rhetoric in the Supreme Court's decision in Source E. How does his diction and syntax change from the beginning of the paragraph to the end?

Students should note the initial word, "Certainly," which portrays Justice Marshall as sympathetic to the employer. He follows this word by addressing minimum work and parental performance standards. His almost tentative words "I fear that" and "fallen into the trap" and "ancient canards about the proper role of women" are somewhat sympathetic to but also mildly chastising of the employer and previous courts who heard this case. That long sentence with its hesitant reprimand is abruptly changed by the next sentence, which is short and direct: "Congress, however, sought just the opposite result." The last sentence points out the law in a clear, direct manner. (U.S. Supreme Court, Phillips v. Martin Marietta Corp., 400 U.S. 542 (1971), http://supreme.justia.com/cases/ federal/us/400/542/case.html)

Writing an Argument

6. Why is the issue of women's rights an important issue today? Support your response using these sources as well as your own arguments.

Work with students to help them develop an argumentative synthesis or an evaluative synthesis that broaches deeper issues with women's and/or minority rights, using these texts as resources, with a direction for resolution.

CHAPTER 7
Business and Economics

This chapter provides a broad selection of essays that deal with some aspect of the workforce, the economy, money, or business. In general, this tends to be an area of weakness in student knowledge. Many have not had an economics course prior to taking AP English Language; therefore, some concepts covered in this chapter may be challenging and new for them. The lessons in this chapter focus on honing students' rhetorical analysis skills—primarily through developing crucial commentary writing skills—and on continuing to develop students' sophistication in argumentation.

Teaching the Chapter

Before discussing any essays in this chapter, have students analyze the visuals in the **Classic and Contemporary Images** feature. Discuss the questions in the textbook on page 279. See suggested answers below.

Classic and Contemporary Images: Suggested Answers

1. **Compare and contrast the tone of each visual.**

   Answers will vary, but students should note that the mural exhibits a warm tone not only from the furnace at the top of the image but from the obvious hard labor of the workers. Their complete focus on their tasks shows a tone of dedication and collaboration. The photo of the auto assembly line also shows unending labor, but the fiery colors (hell?) and duplication/replication of the vehicle bodies result in a somewhat menacing tone, detached and unemotional.

2. **How do the perspective and visual elements of each image reveal movement?**

   Have students study the angles Rivera uses in the workers' limbs and machinery. The eye follows these angles and moves quickly from one worker to another, thus mimicking the actions of the laborers themselves as they heave and push and drag and lift. The eye never stands still—moving from the man in yellow in the lower portion of the mural outward and upward, following the rendering of the machinery to the man stoking the furnace at the top. The workers are shown tightly packed with no wasted space, yet their actions are synchronized, almost like dancers. In the bottom photo, movement is shown by the blurry robotic arm in the right foreground, as well as by the sparks from the welding tools splashing on the floor and reflecting in the windshield. Our mental "ears" hear the whirs, screeches, and roars of compressors, conveyor belts, and power tools.

3. **What does the lack of any images of people in the assembly line photo achieve?**

   Students may note that without any people, the assembly line photo appears much more stark, unemotional, and industrial than the mural, although both images show mechanized industry.

4. **Give descriptive titles for each of the images and explain why you decided on those titles.**

   Student responses will vary.

Lesson Plan 7.1

Woolf's "Professions for Women"—Analyzing Rhetoric Through Structure

Class Opener

To help students get in the spirit of Woolf's essay, you need to give them a cursory understanding of Coventry Patmore's poem "The Angel in the House," which was immensely popular during the Victorian period. In the book-length narrative poem, Patmore extolls his wife's virtues, largely in regard to how she creates a pleasing home environment for him. The following excerpt is from Canto IX. (The full version of the poem is available at Project Gutenberg.)

Man must be pleased; but him to please
  Is woman's pleasure; down the gulf
Of his condoled necessities
  She casts her best, she flings herself.
How often flings for nought! and yokes
  Her heart to an icicle or whim,
Whose each impatient word provokes
  Another, not from her, but him;
While she, too gentle even to force
  His penitence by kind replies,
Waits by, expecting his remorse,
  With pardon in her pitying eyes;
And if he once, by shame oppress'd,
  A comfortable word confers,
She leans and weeps against his breast,
  And seems to think the sin was hers;
And whilst his love has any life,
  Or any eye to see her charms,
At any time, she's still his wife,
  Dearly devoted to his arms;
She loves with love that cannot tire;
  And when, ah woe, she loves alone,
Through passionate duty love flames higher,
  As grass grows taller round a stone.

—London: John W. Parker and Son, West Strand, 1858

Ask students to work in groups and answer the following questions:

1. Who is the Angel in the House?
2. What is woman's purpose, according to Patmore?
3. How might a woman respond to Patmore's characterization?
4. What are the positive aspects of his analysis?
5. What might some negative aspects be?

Encourage students to recognize that Woolf sees the portrayal as limiting to women. When she describes "killing" the Angel, she is speaking of this stereotype.

Activity: Rhetorical Analysis Through Structural Analysis

This essay looks at the broad subject of professions for women from the personal perspective of a writer—Woolf herself—trying to make her way in a male-dominated world. Woolf's fiction reflects a special consciousness or awareness of the ways in which culture and society impinge on women. It is not surprising, then, that Woolf in this nonfiction essay believes that women must re-create their own images of the self in order to succeed as professionals. She employs analogy, narration, and analysis to organize her essay. Several of Woolf's paragraphs are quite long; students should be encouraged to read these paragraphs carefully for in them she elaborates the creative process.

This difficult piece presents an excellent opportunity to work through rhetorical analysis in a paragraph-by-paragraph fashion. Many students attempt to organize their analysis essays by device, but most are more successful employing a more organic "walk-through" approach. This essay is ideal for that type of analysis. For this lesson, ask students to focus on only one paragraph at a time, using the guiding questions in the chart that follows. (Photocopy the chart, or see **Chapter 7 online, Virginia Woolf: Analyzing Rhetoric Through Structure**.)

¶	Structural Analysis Question	Response to Question	Effect of Author's Choice
1a	How does the author structure the first part of this paragraph?		
1b	How does the author structure the middle section of the paragraph?		
1c	How does the author conclude the paragraph?		
2	How does the author structure this paragraph?		
3	How does the author structure this paragraph?		
4	How does the author structure this paragraph?		
5	How does the author structure this paragraph?		
6	How does the author structure this paragraph?		
7	How does the author structure this paragraph?		

Possible Responses:

¶	Structural Analysis Question	Response to Question	Effect of Author's Choice
1a	How does the author structure the first part of this paragraph?	She reminds those present that she has been invited to speak, then introduces herself, downplaying her particular expertise as she focuses solely on facts with the repeated phrase "it is true."	She presents herself as being humble and forthright.
1b	How does the author structure the middle section of the paragraph?	She suggests that hers is not an altogether unusual experience for a woman, offering an appeal to ethos in which she refers to other famous women writers.	The audience is placed in the position of recognizing that Woolf, a woman writer, is part of a continuum, therefore recognizing implicitly that writing is not a new profession for women (therefore also implying that the employment of women is not a new concept).
1c	How does the author conclude the paragraph?	She uses the word "thus" to signal that she is drawing a conclusion based on the topic given and her experience with that topic (professions for women). She then offers a defense of women writers.	Woolf seems to acknowledge that her audience (and society in general) is at this time uncomfortable with the idea of women working. Therefore, she offers a somewhat sarcastic version of why it is "okay" for women to write—it doesn't cost their families anything. Implicitly, she is criticizing the assumed idea that women are not worth investing in.
2	How does the author structure this paragraph?	She begins with the word "but," suggesting a contrast, and then offers a reductivist process analysis of how she became a writer.	Woolf makes it clear by reducing her writing career to its absolute simplest terms that she does not want to focus on "how" one becomes a writer—ostensibly the reason for her invitation. The effect on the reader, then, is to a feel a bit disconcerted—what, then, does she want to discuss?
3	How does the author structure this paragraph?	She opens with a clearly hyperbolic rhetorical question. She then continues with the hyperbole as she sets about to establish her nemesis—an imagined, metaphorical enemy who must be destroyed in order for a woman to be able to write and be fully engaged in professions for women. The Angel in the House is the symbol of women in the Victorian era; therefore, there is a certain metaphorical quality (metonymy) embodied in the use of the symbol. This paragraph focuses on figurative language and writing rather than on a discussion of her own lived experiences.	Although it seems innocuous enough, in this paragraph Woolf is wholeheartedly tackling societal norms, criticizing the venerated heroine representative of the Victorian ideal. Among her audience, there are presumed to be those who would still hold with this ideal and those who have rejected it as passé. The hyperbole is amusing, yet somehow rings true as it underscores the honest difficulty that faced a woman trying to write a literary critique of a male author.

4	How does the author structure this paragraph?	Woolf offers an answer by way of a transition paragraph. She claims she does not know the answer to the rhetorical question she poses, transitioning to paragraph 5, which returns to the process analysis strategy offered in paragraph 2.	The audience expects the writer to offer answers, but instead is provided with additional questions, suggesting that there is no pat answer to a discussion of women's employment.
5	How does the author structure this paragraph?	Woolf returns to process analysis, ostensibly offering a discussion of the next steps in her writing career, but shifting quickly to a metaphorical discussion of a woman fishing as a means of describing her stream-of-consciousness novel-writing experience.	It is fair to say that this paragraph is hard to follow. In some ways, it seems as though Woolf is waxing poetic or even flexing her creativity for the audience, who is likely to struggle with following the shifting metaphor. Nonetheless, the effect on the audience is being wowed by Woolf's prowess, recognizing a brilliance that undeniably parallels or exceeds that of contemporary male writers. In essence, she is defending women writers by being incredibly impressive as a writer.
6	How does the author structure this paragraph?	In this paragraph, Woolf posits the intellectual and philosophical paradox that she argues she has not yet solved as a woman writer: to be disembodied as a writer. She claims that one cannot write outside one's own existence.	The paragraph's effect is to quite literally stump the audience. Woolf has offered a paradox that exists within her own experience and therefore poses a question she herself cannot answer. She offers a series of three rhetorical questions, each increasing in its difficulty to consider or discuss.
7	How does the author structure this paragraph?	Woolf charges the audience of women with continuing to fight for their place in the workforce. She uses references to her own works—"rooms of your own" and "your five hundred pounds a year"—works that inspired women to see themselves as capable of employment and creativity.	Woolf's charge references stereotypical women's interests, such as decorating, juxtaposing these interests while at the same time paralleling women's lived experiences with the workforce.

Class Closer

This analysis is among the hardest students will face. In closing, allow them to stretch their creativity along the lines offered in Woolf's speech. Offer that during her lifetime, women faced difficulty and uncertainty in joining the workforce. Ask them to consider employment today. Are there still careers dominated by men? Are there careers dominated by women? Are there careers still barred to women or men? Allow students the opportunity to discuss and possibly write a quick-write response as to whether or not the "Angel in the House" still needs to be slain.

Homework

Have students read Henry Louis Gates's "Delusions of Grandeur" essay and answer the comprehension and rhetorical analysis questions after they read.

Suggested Answers

"Professions for Women" by Virginia Woolf

Comprehension

1. This essay was presented originally as a speech. What internal evidence indicates that it was intended as a talk?

Ask students to examine the first and last paragraphs. In the last lines of paragraph 7, especially, the syntax becomes quite loose, suggesting a conversational tone.

2. Who or what is the "angel" that Woolf describes in this essay? Why must she kill it? What other obstacles does a professional woman encounter?

The "angel" that Woolf describes in this essay is the feminine alter ego, a conventional, dissimulating psychic force that inhibits, according to Woolf, many women. This angel must be destroyed because it prevents women from realizing their true selves, notably in the professions. The other major obstacle that professional women encounter is "the extreme conventionality of the other sex." A third obstacle is the need to tell the truth about women's experiences.

3. Paraphrase the last two paragraphs of this essay. What is the essence of Woolf's argument?

Woolf's basic argument in the last two paragraphs is that professional women have many phantoms or angels to slay. Women must struggle to slay these phantoms—to overcome obstacles—and in this process redefine themselves and their lives and roles in society.

Rhetorical Analysis

4. There is a significant amount of figurative language in the essay. Locate and explain examples. What does the figurative language contribute to the tone of the essay?

Analogy is a variety of figurative language that is most evident in this essay (see also question 5), with Woolf likening her alter ego to an angel or phantom. Other instances of figurative language include: the metaphorical "path" cut for Woolf by other English women writers (paragraph 1); the personification of Woolf's "phantom" (paragraph 3); the remarkable figurative comparison, part metaphor and part personification, likening the imagination to the "image of a fisherman" (paragraph 5); and the extended metaphor in paragraph 7 comparing places in the professions for women to "rooms" of their own which now must be finished. Such figurative language lends a poetic, highly descriptive, and emotionally charged tone to the essay.

5. How do we know that Woolf is addressing an audience of women? Why does she pose so many questions, and what does this strategy contribute to the rapport she wants to establish? Explain the effect of the last two sentences.

Although the Women's Service League is not mentioned in the essay, we do know that Woolf is addressing an audience of women. Her subject, proposed to her and established in paragraph 1, is of direct interest to women. When she asks such questions as "What could be easier. . ." (paragraph 3) and "what then remained?" (paragraph 4), as well as the series of questions in paragraphs 6 and 7, she invites her audience to enter into her quest for a definition of the new or emerging role of women in professional life. Note also how the "I" and "you" merge in the last paragraph, forming a sympathetic bond between Woolf and her audience. The last two sentences of the essay might seem abrupt; they tend to signal that the business of this essay is largely unfinished, still in an exploratory state.

6. **How does Woolf use analogy to structure part of her argument?**

Following her introductory paragraph, which is whimsical and broadly anecdotal, Woolf begins in paragraph 3 to structure a major part of her essay around the analogy of the Angel in the House. In paragraph 3, she describes and elaborates upon the angel, permitting readers to understand the concept that Woolf seeks to clarify. This angel is alluded to again in paragraph 4 and 6, and then becomes a generalized phantom in paragraph 7. Thus a pattern of analogy both clarifies the topic and structures the essay. It also dramatically reinforces Woolf's argument that women must kill the false or self-destructive images that they hold of themselves in order to succeed in professional life.

7. **Why does Woolf rely on personal narration? How does it affect the logic of her argument?**

Woolf relies on personal narration because she has a representative story to tell: She is a professional writer addressing other professional women, and wants to share representative experience with them. To the extent that she uses narration for expository ends—to help explain the impediments, both internal and external, in women's lives—the former mode offers structural support for the logic of her position.

8. **Evaluate Woolf's use of contrast to advance her argument.**

The primary contrast is, of course, between the woman who seeks to realize her professional potential and the woman, obedient and obsequious, who submits to the Angel of the House. This pattern of contrast is internal to Woolf's assertion that women must reject conventional, domesticated images of themselves in order to succeed as professionals.

9. **Where does Woolf place her main proposition? How emphatic is it, and why?**

Woolf proceeds inductively to her main proposition, which appears in the last paragraph concerning the woman professional: "Even when the path is nominally open—when there is nothing to prevent a woman from being a doctor, a lawyer, a civil servant—there are many phantoms and obstacles, as I believe, looming in her way." This positioning is not especially emphatic, but it is an integral, organic outgrowth of her earlier observations on doing combat with "angels."

Writing

10. **How effectively does Woolf use her own example as a professional writer to advance a broader proposition concerning all women entering professional life? Answer this question in a brief essay.**

The value of personal experience in Woolf's essay is that it provides both testimonial and confessional. The audience shares with Woolf her struggle to shed a false skin and realize her full potential. Thus her struggle is emblematic of most women entering professional fields. Ask the women in the class if they have special angels whom they must kill. Do men also have phantoms to overcome?

11. **Write an essay about the problems and obstacles you anticipate when you enter your chosen career.**

This topic presupposes that students already have a career in mind; as a prewriting exercise, instruct them to develop a one paragraph analysis of the *main* obstacle that they anticipate.

12. **Writing an Argument** Argue for or against the proposition that Woolf's essay has little relevance for women planning careers today.

Introduce this topic by asking students to list the changes that they see in women's perceptions of themselves, and then ask them to connect items in the list to Woolf's observations.

Lesson Plan 7.2

Gates's "Delusions of Grandeur"—Analyzing Purpose Through DIDLS

Class Opener

The History Channel offers the surprising facts below about gladiators. Post the list and ask students to write a quick-write response to this question: **Is it fair to compare college athletes to gladiators?**

1. Gladiators didn't always fight to the death.
2. Fighting against animals was rare.
3. There were female gladiators.
4. Gladiator fights started out as a funeral ritual.
5. Roman emperors sometimes fought as gladiators.

Source: https://www.history.co.uk/shows/barbarians-rising/articles/9-surprising-facts-about-the-gladiators

Activity: Analyzing Purpose Through DIDLS

Gates's essay attempts to explode the myth that African Americans dominate the world of sports. He argues that young African Americans are not exposed sufficiently to other career choices or educated to compete in other areas. This stereotype is promulgated by schools and African American sports celebrities.

DIDLS is a popular acronym for helping students find their way into analysis. It stands for:

Diction (specific word choices made by the author)

Imagery (words and phrases that evoke any sensory experience)

Detail (specific detail—such as statistics—not linked to the senses)

Language (figurative language)

Syntax (the author's structural and grammatical choices)

In this lesson, students will focus on claims, data, and warrants. They will complete the chart that follows, which includes examples of specific textual and data choices made by Gates. Students will analyze those choices by making a claim about the choice and then completing the warrant to show how the examples prove the claim. In doing so, students should eventually be able to prove an arguable claim about Gates's purpose in writing this essay. If students are stuck on the warrant, tell them this is the "So what?" question. (Photocopy the chart, or see **Chapter 7 online, Henry Louis Gates, Jr.: Analyzing Purpose Through DIDLS.**)

Device	Textual Example (Data)	What argument can you make about Gates's purpose? (Claim)	How does the example prove the claim? (Warrant)
Diction	"failure"		
Imagery	"Standing at the Bar of an All-Black VFW post in my hometown of Piedmont, W. Va., . . ."		
Detail	Statistics provided in paragraph 6		
Figurative Language	"Until colleges stop using young blacks as cannon fodder in the big-business wars of so-called nonprofessional sports..."		
Syntax	Dialogue in paragraphs 2-5		

Possible Responses:

Device	Textual Example (Data)	What argument can you make about Gates's purpose? (Claim)	How does the example prove the claim? (Warrant)
Diction	"failure"	In paragraph 11, Gates repeats the word *failure*. In so doing, he is castigating society for creating a system in which failure is an option.	Gates makes it clear that the failure rate of Philadelphia students is indicative of a broader problem. He clearly links the public education system's inability to produce literate students to the broader issues at hand, namely a societal focus on sports and athletics rather than academics and professional workforce preparedness.

Imagery	"Standing at the Bar of an All-Black VFW post in my hometown of Piedmont, W. Va., . . ."	Gates opens the essay with this line to provide a small-town context to the argument.	He establishes that this sort of conversation could be happening all over America, and, importantly, that it is happening within the African American community. By beginning here, he establishes that the problem he chooses to address is one that the community most affected is unaware of and therefore is not yet working to solve.
Detail	Statistics provided in paragraph 6	Gates uses statistics to show how much more likely it is to become a well-paid professional than to become a professional athlete.	Gates seeks to expose the myth that African American students should focus on sports in order to be successful in life. He provides statistical evidence to stress the shift he believes must take place in advising African American students about their futures.
Figurative Language	"Until colleges stop using young blacks as cannon fodder in the big-business wars of so-called nonprofessional sports..."	Gates compares black athletes to "cannon fodder" in an effort to show the volatile and even violent nature of these activities.	Gates is aware of the toll that sports takes on the athlete, both physically and in terms of taking the athlete away from scholarly pursuits. By comparing the athlete to "fodder," he is making it clear that the athlete does not benefit from the activity, but is instead being manipulated by the college.
Syntax	Dialogue in paragraphs 2-5	Gates provides the dialogue to re-enact the conversation in an informal yet authentic manner to show the pervasiveness of the lack of knowledge about this issue.	Gates suggests that until the African American community recognizes the problem of the mis-education of young African Americans, then the problem will not be addressed or changed. The conversations have to take place in order to effect change.

Class Closer

After students have completed the chart, challenge them to write a rhetorical analysis essay. If they have completed the chart well, they have all the pre-writing they need to draft a quick essay. Remind them to address audience and purpose in their introduction, and to touch on each in most if not all body paragraphs.

Suggested Answers

"Delusions of Grandeur" by Henry Louis Gates, Jr.

Gates, Henry Louis, Jr. "Delusions of Grandeur." *Sports Illustrated*. 19 August 1991: Print.

Comprehension

1. What does Gates suggest is the general assumption made about African Americans in sports?

The general assumption (held by African Americans, as well as whites) is that the sports world is predominantly African American, an assumption belied by Gates's statistics (para. 1).

2. Why and how do American schools continue to perpetuate the myth that Gates is writing about?

Because schools do not educate athletes, preferring to emphasize sports activities, the majority of students who don't succeed in the sports world fall by the wayside, having no education or future as athletes. The schools continue to stereotype blacks in this field, which lures youngsters who dream of fame and wealth.

3. According to Gates, what should successful African American athletes do to help guide the career choices of young African Americans?

Gates would like famous African American athletes to be responsible for youngsters who idolize them by promoting education and diverse career choices available to African Americans (paragraphs 12 and 13).

Rhetorical Analysis

4. What is Gates's thesis? Where does it appear?

Gates's thesis is that young African Americans have accepted the myth that sports is the only career option available in which they can achieve success and that education is secondary (paragraph 10).

5. How does the introductory paragraph work to set up the writer's focus?

The introductory paragraph serves as an anecdotal example of the point that Gates is making: even blacks believe the stereotype that most professional athletes are African American.

6. State Gates's purpose in using statistics in his essay.

The statistics work to substantiate a belief that is deeply entrenched in American society, promoted as it is by televised events, celebrity commercials, and sports journalism.

7. What is the tone of Gates's essay? Cite specific sections where this tone seems strongest.

Gates presents his evidence in a personal format; he is not totally objective and his dismay at the stereotype comes through in some of his phrases and arguments, particularly in paragraphs 8, 11, and 12. Students can point out other places in the essay where his tone is clear.

8. Examine the accumulation of facts in paragraph 11. How does this technique underscore Gates's point?

Gates uses an accumulation of details to emphasize the problems in the public school system and its failure to educate young people, especially African Americans, to compete in the real world of employment and not just on the sports field.

9. Explain Gates's allusion to Roman gladiators in his conclusion. How does it aid in emphasizing his main point?

The allusion dramatically points out the barbarism and waste of continuing to track African American youngsters into careers in sports they can't succeed in, instead of educating them to compete in the real job market.

10. **Write a brief essay in which you analyze your personal reaction to Gates's statistics. Were you surprised by them? What assumptions did you have about the number of African American professional athletes? Why do you think most Americans share these assumptions?**

    Students will write essays based on their reactions to Gates's statistics. They should analyze why they were or were not surprised by the information and why Americans in general hold the same assumptions. They should consider the role of racism, the media, and education in their essays and provide examples.

11. **Write a biographical research paper on the life and career of an African American athlete or on one of the famous African Americans mentioned in this essay.**

    To further substantiate Gates's claim that African Americans have made names for themselves in a variety of fields, students should conduct research on the life and career of someone not in sports. It need not be anyone recognizable such as Frederick Douglass, but obviously someone who has achieved success. They should include personal statistics, family background, education, and accomplishments.

12. **Writing an Argument** Write an essay in which you argue for or against the proposition that sports and entertainment should (or should not) be a career choice for anyone.

    Students should use a speech format (directly addressing a particular crowd) and discuss their views on the various points they wish to make about education, career choices, sports, etc. They may use some of Gates's information in their speeches. They should consider the audience they are addressing when determining style and language.

Lesson Plan 7.3

Synthesizing Classic and Contemporary Essays—Timed-Writing

Have students turn to the synthesis questions that appear after these two essays on page 289 in the textbook. Tell students to choose one of the three options and write for a minimum of 30 minutes. After students have finished writing, use the remainder of the class period to group students according to the option they chose. Students should read and comment on each other's essays, offering a positive comment, a critical comment, and a question for each essay read.

Synthesizing the Classic and Contemporary Essays: Suggested Answers

1. **Examine the argumentative styles of Woolf and Gates. What are their main propositions? Their minor propositions? What evidence do they provide?**

    In this essay students are asked to compare the argumentation strategies of both writers. They will focus on the propositions of both: Gates argues that African Americans do not overwhelmingly become athletes although society tends to promote this myth while schools track young minority students into sports; Woolf proposes that in order for women to achieve success in writing and other professions they must overcome the phantoms that block their way. Gates uses statistics to support his views, as well as examples, whereas Woolf relies primarily on personal opinion and experiences to advance her ideas. Students must use proof from the essays to support their opinions.

2. **Woolf first presented her paper as a speech before an audience of women. Gates wrote his essay as an opinion piece for *Sports Illustrated.* Write a comparative audience analysis of the two selections. Analyze the purpose, tone, style, and any other relevant aspects of these essays.**

   In this essay students will focus on the audience for both essays at the time they were presented. They must analyze this audience in terms of the language and approach used by the writers. For example, who reads *Sports Illustrated*? Once they generalize about the readership of the magazine they will show how the style, language, and content may appeal to that particular group and why Gates chose this venue. The same approach should be used to analyze Woolf's speech, its content and language. How and why is it appropriate for the women she's addressing and who may these women be?

3. **Gates's essay was written in 1991. Argue for or against the proposition that there has been progress in relation to barriers to employment for women, and whether the barriers are similar for African American men. Refer to the essays by Woolf and Gates to support your position.**

   Students will write an argumentation essay based on the works of both writers. They should also use personal observations and statistics to show that black men and women face similar problems in the job market in terms of assumptions made about them and efforts to track both into stereotypical job choices. This essay may be turned into a longer research paper that probes more deeply into the topic.

Homework

Assign students to read "The Death of Horatio Alger" by Paul Krugman.

Lesson Plan 7.4

Krugman's "The Death of Horatio Alger"—Writing and Analyzing Argument

Class Opener

In groups, ask students to define the American Dream. Allow students to share their definitions, and then have them stand in the classroom. Ask students to move to one side of the room if they believe the American Dream is still attainable, to the other side of the room if they believe the American Dream is NOT attainable, and to the middle of the room if they are not sure. Give groups a few minutes to discuss their core argument for why they chose their position. After they have had a few minutes to discuss, ask one side to choose a spokesperson to offer their position. Then do the same for the other side. As people in the middle are swayed to a position, they should move to join that side. If students on one side swayed to the other, they may move. If anyone is left in the middle, give them the opportunity to present a "qualifying" position.

Activity: Writing and Analyzing Argument

Have students write an in-class essay (40 minutes) of four paragraphs in answer to the following prompt:

> **Write an essay in which you take a position on the viability of the American Dream. Is there such a thing as the American Dream and is it still attainable? Support your argument with evidence from your reading, personal experience, and outside knowledge.**

Activity: Analyzing the Argument

After students have written the essay, provide the format that follows to let them analyze their own essays or essays written by classmates. (Photocopy the format, or see **Chapter 7 online, Paul Krugman: Writing and Analyzing Argument**.)

Argument Essay Analysis Please follow the directions EXACTLY as given in the order given. Your essay was required to be at least 4 paragraphs long. If it is not, you will not be able to complete this analysis in full. Please note that for 4-paragraph essays, each paragraph will be worth 25 points. For 5-paragraph essays, each paragraph is worth 20 points. If you wrote 1 paragraph, your highest grade will be a 25 on both this assignment and the essay.

STEP 1 Highlight your essay in the following way:

a. Highlight in BLUE your thesis statement and any claims that relate solely to your main argument, including conclusion sentences.

b. Highlight in YELLOW the topic sentences that further the argument put forth in your thesis.

c. Highlight in GREEN your commentary.

STEP 2 After your entire essay is highlighted, you are ready for step 2. Copy only your thesis statement here:

____

____

Did you establish the context? ______________________________

How? ______________________________

Did you establish a single, overarching argument? ______________________________

STEP 3 Copy each of your topic sentences here.

1. ______________________________

____

2. ______________________________

____

3. ______________________________

____

STEP 4 Summarize your evidence and commentary for each topic sentence here. Each topic sentence should have two pieces of commentary to support it.

1a. ______________________________

____

1b. ______________________________

____

2a. ______________________________

____

2b. ______________________________

____

3a. ______________________________

____

3b. ______________________________

____

Class Closer

Have students exchange their analyses, discussing the structure of their essays and arguments.

Suggested Answers

"The Death of Horatio Alger" by Paul Krugman

Comprehension

1. What reasons does Krugman give for the United States becoming more of a caste society?

While Krugman writes that "the proliferation of dead-end, low-wage jobs and the disappearance of jobs that provide entry to the middle class" (paragraph 11) are partly responsible for the caste system in America, his premise is that public policies entrench it.

2. Who is Horatio Alger? Why doesn't Krugman explain who he is in his essay?

Horatio Alger was an author whose "rags to riches" stories in the late 1800s introduced members of the underclass as heroes. Because Alger's name is often used to symbolize any success story in which the protagonist demonstrates great moral courage to change his material circumstances, Krugman does not explain who Horatio Alger is.

3. Krugman alludes to the "leftist rag" *BusinessWeek*. What can you infer about the contents and political opinions of this publication?

One can infer that a "leftist rag" would include articles about equality, democracy, and freedom written by activists, theorists, and liberals if one understands that someone or something on "the right" is generally more conservative when it comes to economic and social policies.

Rhetorical Analysis

4. What is Krugman's claim, and where does he state it most clearly?

Krugman states his claim that political leaders are reinforcing the foundations for an economic caste system in paragraph 3 where he also points out the chief argument leveled against those who resist its creation.

5. **Comment on the types of evidence that Krugman uses to support his argument. Do you find this evidence to be sufficient and convincing? Why or why not?**

   Krugman effectively uses examples and empirical studies to support his argument. One statistic, taken from data provided by the Congressional Budget Office, in particular is both sufficient and convincing. This clincher begins, "between 1973 and 2000 the average real income of the bottom 90 percent of American taxpayers actually fell by 7 percent. Meanwhile, the income of the top 1 percent rose by 148 percent. . ."

6. **Krugman's style is quite impersonal. Locate examples of this style, and explain the overall effect.**

   Krugman's use of an impersonal style—making things, not people the subject of his sentences and the passive voice—balances his use of first, second, and third-person forms of address. The combined impact of these elements in phrases like "the new economic order" (paragraph 4), "According to estimates" (paragraph 5), and "A classic 1978 survey found" (paragraph 8) makes it possible for readers to suspend judgment as he constructs his argument.

7. **Much of this essay involves comparative analysis. What subjects and ideas does Krugman compare and contrast?**

   The author compares income distribution, income gaps, and government policies of thirty years ago with today's economic realities—the decrease in unions, real income, and capital gains taxes.

8. **Krugman's conclusion is very brief. Do you find it effective? Explain.**

   Krugman's conclusion is effective because it reminds readers that homeownership, as well as individual self-determination, will no longer be emblems of the American Dream if a caste system is allowed to persist.

Writing

9. **Do you think that your life will be better economically than that of your parents? Why or why not? Write a personal essay in response to this question.**

   Student responses will vary.

10. **Write your own analysis of class inequality in the United States or in another nation you are familiar with. Or respond to Krugman's assertion: "Our political leaders are doing everything they can to fortify class inequality, while denouncing anyone who complains—or even points out what is happening—as a practitioner of 'class warfare."**

    The research for this would be a great library exercise. This essay might be done with a partner and each partnership covers a different country. Then each essay could come with a presentation to the rest of the class.

11. **Writing an Argument** Write a rebuttal to Krugman, arguing that the American Dream is still alive and well.

    The essays will vary, but students need to take a side and be persuasive, as well as remember to support their claims.

Lesson Plan 7.5

Friedman's "Globalization: The Super-Story"—A Research Framework

Class Opener

Provide students with a definition for *amplification*: Amplification involves repeating a word while adding more information. For example: "They happened in the context of a new international system—a system that cannot explain everything but *can* explain and connect more things in more places on more days than anything else." What does the author accomplish with this strategy? Have students write their own example of amplification.

Activity: Analysis Through Research

For most students, Friedman's essay will provide several historical or cultural moments with which they are unfamiliar. Some students, for example, are ill-prepared to discuss the cold war. Rather than simply give students just a list of allusions to research, in this activity we will provide them with that traditional list of allusions and also with a means to develop a cultural growth plan. For the argument prompt on the AP Exam, students often struggle with crafting the right kinds of examples. This exercise is designed to help students build cultural and historical knowledge.

Provide each student with a blank copy of the chart below. (Photocopy the chart, or see **Chapter 7 online, Thomas L. Friedman: Friedman Research Framework.**) Have students use the library or a computer to research each of the historical allusions identified in chart, which are items found in Friedman's essay. Then students are to add to the chart relevant references for each historical or cultural event.

Historical Allusion	Movie or Television	Modern Book (last 5 years)	Older or Classical Book	Current Event
The Cold War				
World War II				
9/11				
Berlin Wall				
Osama bin Laden				
Wall Street				
Land Mines/ Jody Williams				

Class Closer

After students have completed the chart, discuss ways of using the chart to help them build their cultural knowledge base. One idea is to have them turn in an index card on a weekly or bi-weekly basis with information about a current event or an event from this chart.

Homework

Have students read Thomas Friedman's "Globalization: The Super-Story" and be prepared to analyze it as a class.

Suggested Answers

"Globalization: The Super-Story" by Thomas L. Friedman

Comprehension

1. What is Friedman's "super-story"? How does he define it?

Friedman's "super-story" centers on the transition from a cold war economy to a global economy in the final two decades of the twentieth century. It is a metanarrative that imposes meaning upon one historical period.

2. What are the main features of globalization? How does globalization differ from the system characterized by the cold war? Explain the "three balances" (paragraphs 8–10) that Friedman writes about.

Integration of economic industries is the most important feature of globalization. Because market forces no longer respect national boundaries, globalization has altered the traditional geopolitical paradigm that assumes the primacy of autonomous nation-states.

3. What does Friedman mean by "super-empowered" individuals (paragraph 11)?

"Super-empowered individuals" are independent "entrepreneurs" who can function as geopolitical entities unmediated by a state. These individuals are empowered by access to an unrestricted global market—including access to the Internet and access to weapons and intelligence that were once the exclusive property of states.

Rhetorical Analysis

4. What is Friedman's thesis or claim in this essay? Where does it appear?

Friedman begins the essay with an extended definition of new concepts; his thesis does not fully emerge until the final paragraph.

5. How and why does Friedman create a personal voice as well as a colloquial style in this selection? What is the effect?

Friedman's first gesture in this selection is both personal and colloquial: "I am a big believer in..." Many of Friedman's neologisms are clearly personal inventions ("what I like to call..."), and this repeated coining of new terms gives the reader the impression that the situation he describes is indeed a new development, and that no terminology exists to describe it.

6. What definitions does Friedman establish? Are the definitions too abstract, or does he provide sufficient explanations and evidence? Explain.

"Balances" may strike some students as unnecessarily abstract, especially as Friedman might easily have defined the *parties* involved rather than the more abstract relations between them.

7. Locate instances of classification and of comparison and contrast. Why does Friedman use these rhetorical strategies? How do the two methods complement each other?

Friedman employs classification to distinguish the three different "balances" within the new system, but he uses comparison and contrast within those passages to remind readers of what has changed from the cold war to the current system. For example, Friedman classifies the balance between nation-states and global markets by way of contrast: "the United States can destroy you by dropping bombs [as in the cold war], but the Supermarkets [in a globalization system] can destroy you by downgrading your bonds" (paragraph 9).

8. Friedman uses several metaphors in this essay. What are they, and how do they function to enhance meaning?

Metaphors, according to Friedman, function as paradigms—for example, the metaphor of "the wall" versus the metaphor of "the web." According to Friedman, these metaphors not only enhance meaning, they *create* meaning when people adopt them as ways of understanding the world.

9. Why does the writer discuss 9/11 in the final three paragraphs? What is the effect on the overall message and purpose of the essay?

"The events of 9/11 did not happen in a vacuum," Friedman notes in his opening paragraph, and the advent of a super-empowered individual such as Osama bin Laden can only be understood within the context of globalization—hence, Friedman's return to the topic at the end of the essay.

Writing

10. In groups of three or four, use Friedman's essay to brainstorm about globalization. Construct a list of ideas and attributes. Using this list, write a definition essay exploring the subject of globalization. Include comparison and contrast or classification, or both, to help organize the essay.

The success of this assignment rests entirely on the students' knowledge of globalization and how it has changed markets and the world. Although Friedman sketches history in broad strokes, students might need to research some of the effects and causes of globalization.

11. Write a personal essay on how you think globalization is affecting your life.

At first, this might seem difficult for some students to realize how their lives are personally affected by globalization. As an exercise, have them walk through a day and write down everything they use, buy, wear, and eat. Have them detail everyone they see or talk to. After they complete the list, have them research the nature of the items and people on it. How many of the items come from global, multinational corporations? How many people from other countries do they interact with?

12. Writing an Argument **Has globalization changed since Friedman wrote this essay in 2002? In a letter to Friedman, explain your position and support it with examples.**

Student responses will vary.

Lesson Plan 7.6

Ehrenreich's "Nickel and Dimed"—Fishbowl Discussion

Class Opener

Remind students of the ground rules for fishbowl discussion (see page 5 of this Teacher Manual). Ask them to pass the questions they wrote about Ehrenreich's essay to the group member to their right. That group member will choose a favorite question among the three presented. Each group will submit only one question to the fishbowl.

Activity: Questions and Answers

Make a point of mixing up the questions. Invite a student to come forward and draw a question from the bowl. The student will then read the question aloud, and the class will discuss their interpretation of the answer. This particular essay usually sparks a lot of conversation; hence, you may find that you are able to sustain a full-period fishbowl discussion. If the discussion reaches a lull, discuss the questions that accompany the essay in the textbook.

Activity: Writing Narrative Mini-Essays

After the fishbowl discussion, take an opportunity for narrative writing. Ask students to write a narrative mini-essay/paragraph about the nature and value of work.

Class Closer

Ask students to reflect on what the idea of work means to them. On an index card, ask them to explain what makes a job important or worth doing.

Suggested Answers

"Nickel and Dimed" by Barbara Ehrenreich

Comprehension

1. Why do women work for The Maids when they could earn more money as independent cleaners? How does Ehrenreich distinguish her cleaning practices from her coworkers'? Why do the maids emphasize "cosmetic touches" (paragraph 6)?

The only advantage to working for The Maids, Ehrenreich realizes, is that one does not need a clientele or a car (paragraph 2). The company recruits those who do not have the capital, or the basic resources, to start their business. The "cosmetic touches" emphasized by the company are those visible signs of cleanliness that the clients are most likely to notice.

2. Describe the plight of Ehrenreich's coworkers. What "signs . . . of real difficulty if not actual misery" (paragraph 10) does she detect? What, if anything, does she do to help them?

Ehrenreich notices that her coworkers often cannot afford lunch, that they conserve cigarettes, and that they have a heightened fear of minor medical problems. Ehrenreich buys lunch for her coworkers on occasion, but cannot do more for fear of blowing her cover.

3. Who is Mrs. W? What is her lifestyle like, and what does she expect of the maids? How does she treat Ehrenreich?

Mrs. W. is a stereotypical member of the upper middle class who leads a neurotically decadent bourgeois lifestyle. She treats Ehrenreich as a submissive hired worker (observation that concludes paragraph 16).

Rhetorical Analysis

4. How does Ehrenreich structure her narrative? How much time elapses? What elements of conflict develop? What transitional devices does she employ to unify the action?

Ehrenreich's narrative chronicles her experiences during one week of employment at the cleaning service, although she does not follow a strictly chronological sequence (no Day 1, Day 2, etc.).

5. Where does the writer employ description, and for what purpose? What descriptive details seem most striking to you? How, for example, does Ehrenreich bring her coworkers and Mrs. W. to life?

The most extended passage of description occurs when Ehrenreich describes the home, and the lifestyle, of Mrs. W.

6. Identify those instances where the writer uses process analysis and comparison and contrast to organize her essay. Why does she select these strategies? What is the effect of these strategies?

Ehrenreich employs process analysis to describe the content of the four instructional videos, and the detail of her analytical mode serves to highlight the absurdity of the instruction process.

7. Explain the tone of this selection. What elements of irony and sarcasm do you detect?

One typical example of Ehrenreich's humorous sarcasm is her comment (at the end of paragraph 4) that in the "hierarchy of the company's values I rank above Windex." Ehrenreich's tone tends to become more bitterly ironic when she contrasts the lifestyle of her coworkers with their employers or with the lifestyle of someone like Mrs. W.—for example, the absurd chart Mrs. W. keeps for her infant child reminds Ehrenreich of her coworker's inability to afford a proper lunch (a situation that inspires maternal pity in Ehrenreich).

8. Do you think this essay provides a straightforward account of Ehrenreich's experience working for The Maids, or does she have an argumentative point? Justify your response.

Students should pay particular attention to the concluding "scene" and its function as social critique.

9. How does the writer conclude this selection? What elements in the last paragraph capture the main purpose behind her account?

The "epiphany" that brings the selection to an end emphasizes that Ehrenreich's purpose in this profile was to find some way of empathizing with the plight of workers like those she met at the cleaning service.

Writing

10. Write a narrative and descriptive essay of a job you have held that involved menial labor. Establish a time frame. Describe any colleagues who worked with you. Have a thesis or an argument that you either state explicitly or permit to emerge from the account.

Chances are several students have held menial jobs. The key part of this assignment is to establish a time frame. Students should try to limit themselves to a day, week, or season.

11. Compare and contrast a bad job that you have held and a job that provided you with a degree of satisfaction.

As students compare these jobs, they should not only compare the type of work and physical environment but also take into account the personal and social environment. Were they treated differently at these two jobs? How?

12. **Writing an Argument** In *Nickel and Dimed,* Ehrenreich set out to find minimum-wage jobs in several parts of the United States, including a Wal-Mart in Minnesota and a restaurant in Florida. However, she knew at the outset that these jobs were temporary and that she had the luxury of going back to her comfortable life and her career as a writer and activist. Argue for or against the proposition that Ehrenreich was being unethical and exploitative in her behavior. Refer to this selection to support your position.

If students choose to argue this assignment, they will need to address how the awareness raised by Ehrenreich in writing about menial jobs and difficult lives is less important than the notion that, for Ehrenreich, this was only a temporary situation.

Lesson Plan 7.7

Reich's "Why the Rich Are Getting Richer, and the Poor, Poorer"—Gathering Relevant Details

Class Opener

Provide students with 5 minutes to do flash research using cell phones or classroom computers on Adam Smith and his philosophy. After 5 minutes, ask each group to share a fact they learned (without repeating facts). This can be turned into a game where students get credit only for facts that other groups did not mention. (Think in terms of Boggle rules—you get credit only for the words that other players didn't see.)

Activity: Filling the Boats with Details

Robert B. Reich served as Secretary of Labor in the Clinton administration. He has been an outspoken critic of the American economic system, and has consistently promoted training and free trade as means of improving the U.S. economy. Reich has been at the forefront among thinkers who claim the United States is doomed to become a nation of haves and have-nots, mainly as a result of the disparity in education between rich and poor. Reich claims that never before in human history has there been such a difference between the salaries of those who work conceptually and those who work manually. The only way to counteract this contrast, he claims, is to get the dispossessed into the mainstream of American education.

This is a long essay with many details, which makes it an excellent opportunity to help students recognize the *most relevant* details. In his analysis, Reich uses the metaphor of three boats. Draw (or have a student draw) boat shapes onto three different colors of poster board. Title the boats "Routine Producers," "In-Person Servers," and "Symbolic Analysts." Working in groups, students will record within the outline of the boat what they believe to be the most convincing evidence provided by Reich for their category. In the water below each boat, students should include additional details for what they believe might keep that boat afloat. In the air above the boat, they should record ideas and details they believe could harm the boat. For example, does a trade alliance with Mexico and Canada support the Routine Producer boat? If they believe it helps, they will place it in the supporting water. If they believe it harms, they will place this information in the air above the boat.

After students have their boat posters populated, post them for a gallery walk. Let students observe and discuss the positions developed by each group.

Class Closer

Have students write their own position on the state of the American worker. Tell them they now have their own three boats. How would they classify American workers, and what policies do they believe should be enacted in support of the American economy?

Suggested Answers

"Why the Rich Are Getting Richer, and the Poor, Poorer" by Robert Reich

Comprehension

1. To what does the title allude? Why is this allusion significant to the meaning of the title?

The title comes from a 1920s popular song, and is the basis for the thesis of Reich's essay.

2. To whom does Reich refer when he mentions "symbolic analysts"? Regardless of their occupation, what do all symbolic analysts have in common regarding the nature of their work?

Symbolic analysts are people who have developed linguistic, computational, or other abstract skills that allow them to predict trends and devise strategies for planning means of production, distribution, and general growth of product markets. In effect, they are all problem solvers.

3. What has traditionally been the image of and the nature of work among the white-collar workers to whom Reich alludes? Why are they now one of the groups in danger of losing employment opportunities?

Reich claims that white-collar workers were thought of traditionally as managers who sat behind desks and spent much of their time interacting with people. They also managed production locally. Today, with corporations relying more on computers and on managers using complex data to analyze trends, these managers are no longer needed. In addition, with the transformation from a producing society to an information society, factories and plants, where such managers oversaw production, have disappeared.

Rhetorical Analysis

4. Reich uses the central metaphor of the "boat" in describing the state of economics and employment. Why? What connotations are associated with this image in regard to financial security?

A boat can be thought of as a composite system which has many parts and a particular division of labor. As long as all parts and workers function smoothly, the boat is seaworthy and steady. Reich makes an analogy to the economy which he divides into three boats: the boat of "routine producers"; the "in-person server" boat composed of service workers, which is also sinking; and the third boat, that of the "symbolic analysts," which is thriving and growing both in components and in the demand for its labor.

5. How does Reich's introduction prepare you for the major themes he addresses in the body of his essay?

In the introduction, Reich lays forth the tripartite structure of the workforce and discusses the function of each in the changing world economy. Furthermore, he summarizes the introduction by stating that we are now at a point in economic history when the economic outlook for one type of worker differs from that of others.

6. Examine the section breaks at the start of paragraphs 3, 11, 20, 35, and 37. How does each section relate to the theme of the essay as a whole? What transitional devices does Reich use to bridge one section to the next?

Paragraph 3 begins Reich's analysis of the "routine procurers"; paragraph 11 extends Reich's discussion of the plight of routine production workers in the United States by focusing on the change to hiring workers from countries where workers accept much lower wages. Paragraph 20 begins Reich's discussion of the "in-person server" workers and demonstrates how they are in a precarious state within the global market place. Paragraph 37 begins an in-depth analysis of the role of the symbolic analysts. Because this group is the one that is benefiting the most from the change in our economic system—and is perhaps the least understood—Reich has reserved his portrait of this group for last, perhaps to dramatize their rise in power.

7. Paragraphs 5, 6, 9, and 16 cite specific and detailed examples of the effects of the changing global economy. How does this technique/strategy contribute to conveying Reich's authority regarding the subject he is discussing?

In paragraphs 5 and 6, Reich demonstrates broad knowledge in the areas of geopolitics and history, particularly as they impact economies. In paragraph 9, Reich displays his knowledge regarding the processes of technology and their influence in determining worldwide labor patterns. He also shows his knowledge and mastery of labor statistics in advancing his thesis regarding the transformation of employment. Students may note that Reich is able to warn by simply reporting a compendium of facts, in other words, "letting the facts 'speak' for themselves."

8. Reich describes a dire situation for the American worker. How would you characterize the tone of this description? Is it angry, resigned, impartial, or accusatory? You may use these or any other adjectives as long as you explain your view.

Reich's tone is characteristically dispassionate although he is describing a situation which is bound to raise passions among laypersons and specialists alike. His use of the boat as metaphor contributes to his objective analysis because—although a boat does carry people—it is itself an inanimate object. It is rather like a system. Thus, Reich treats each group of workers as though they are operating within a system and emphasizes how each of the systems is functioning within the larger context of the global economy.

9. Why does Reich open his essay with an epigraph from Adam Smith? What is the relationship of the quotation to the overall theme of the essay? How does the tone of the epigraph contrast with the tone of the title?

Perhaps the key word in the epigram is "extent." It implies size or length or limit. However, Reich seems to be using it to imply "nature." If this is true, then Reich is using the epigram to emphasize that it is the "nature" of the market that is determining the division of labor. Interestingly enough, unlike moralistic educators, Reich does not contend that one skill is necessarily "superior" to another in any absolute sense, but rather to the extent it has value in the marketplace.

10. What is the author's purpose? Is it to inform, to explain, to warn, to enlighten, to offer solutions, or a combination of any of these? Explain your view.

Reich seems to have as his purpose enlightenment. His suggestion regarding the tripartite structure of American labor has not been articulated in quite this way before. He is also warning the reader of what may become an economic crisis for many Americans, although he does not convey any personal emotional concern.

Writing

11. In a classification essay, describe three areas of academic concentration that can help prepare one for a job as a symbolic analyst.

Although many areas of concentration focus on careers that require extensive facility as a symbolic analyst, you may broaden the subject matter and request your students to explain why the field they have chosen is valued in society.

12. In an expository essay, explain whether you believe the discrepancy between high-wage and low-wage workers will increase, decrease, or remain the same. Consider changes that may have occurred since Reich wrote the essay in 1991.

You may wish to turn this essay assignment into a research project by having students examine job trends over the past twenty to thirty years. Which jobs have had substantial increases in salary and benefits? Which have stayed the same, and which have been reduced? Some interesting data may be found in looking at salaries for doctors, nurses, physicists, teachers, CEOs, and so on. A slightly altered version of this assignment might be to assign students to investigate careers that did not exist twenty years ago, for example, any job connected with the Internet.

13. Writing an Argument In an essay, argue for or against the proposition that as long as one knows which careers command the highest salaries, it is up to the individual to decide whether he or she should pursue a job in those fields.

Is financial reward the primary purpose of selecting a major? You may wish to adapt this essay question so that it reflects a comparison and contrast format wherein the student discusses the advantages of selecting a career based on economic remuneration versus one based on love of the work itself.

Lesson Plan 7.8

Chapter Assessment

Rhetorical Analysis Answers

1. A
2. D
3. B
4. D
5. A
6. B
7. B
8. A
9. B
10. E

Connections for Critical Thinking

Have students turn to the questions that appear on page 325 in the textbook. Tell students to choose one of the four options and write for a minimum of 30 minutes.

After students have finished writing, use the remainder of the class period to group students according to the option they chose. Students should read and comment on one another's essays, offering a positive comment, a critical comment, and a question for each essay read.

Answers

1. **Using the essays of Ehrenreich and Reich, compare the effects of work on human relationships.**

   The responses here will be varied; however, students should be able to identify specific issues such as class distinction and the side effects of outsourcing. Ehrenreich illustrates the difficulties faced by those in lower-paying jobs, such as cleaning services, to just deal with day-to-day pressures. The maids with whom Ehrenreich worked in her undercover assignment could not even afford to buy themselves lunch and were not allowed to perform any activities that would throw off their assembly-line assignments. To do so would risk the income to the company on the job, as well as an individual maid's employment. Reich, by contrast, explains the other side of this argument: The fact that many of these so-called menial jobs that lower-income employees in this country barely survive on can be hired out to other countries for yet even less money, but putting American workers out of work completely. Either way, the employers and the company owners become richer, while keeping their employee costs, either in this country or elsewhere, at a minimum. It can be inferred from this that both of these articles point out class distinctions, as well as failing nationalism.

2. **Write a definition essay titled "What Is Work?" Refer to any of the selections in this chapter to substantiate your opinions.**

   This essay prompt will provoke a wonderful variety of responses, which should be fun to read; however, students need to be sure and support their responses with material from the essays in this chapter and cite their sources.

3. **Describe the potential effect of the global marketplace as described by Reich and Friedman.**

   Friedman describes globalization as a necessary and inevitable evolution that has replaced the "previous international system, the cold war system." Reich, by contrast, claims that the further ensconced in globalization that the world becomes, the gap between rich and poor with widen exponentially, with no middle class, as only those with specialized skills with be in demand. Students should be able to take these basic theories and compare and contrast the effects any and all of these would have on the world's economy.

4. **Compare the methods of Ehrenreich and Reich use to point out the options of those on the lowest rungs of the economic system in Western society.**

   For Reich, those on the lowest rungs are being pushed lower and lower by the global marketplace as the rich get richer. Those who have will only gain more. Ehrenreich gives an inside look at those considered on the lower levels of society, maids. As an undercover laborer, she is able to observe and experience the disparity between those who have and those who do not, firsthand. Students should outline the similarities and differences they find in these articles on a chart, in order to determine organization for this essay assignment.

Lesson Plan 7.9

Synthesizing Sources: Online Shopping: Has It Affected Our Lives for Better or Worse?

Assign students to read the sources and answer the first four questions for homework. This will prepare them for writing the essay. Then have them use the "Writing an Argument" prompt to write the essay as an in-class timed assignment (40 minutes).

Applying Your Synthesis Skills: Suggested Answers

Comprehension

1. **Summarize the stated arguments made in each source.**

   Source A illustrates how simple and removed shopping has become. People can buy anything at any time or place via the technology they hold in their hands. It shows that online shopping is a part of our everyday society. **Source B** cites several known (and ironic) results from the online shopping movement. It discusses everything from the demise of large shopping malls and institutions to the increase in dog bites to the threat of stolen identity. It is a commentary on the ongoing shift in our shopping world that serves as a cautionary voice. **Source C** is a table that reveals the growth of e-commerce as a percentage of all retail sales. **Source D** illustrates the financial impact that online shopping has had on well-known national companies, driving many companies to file bankruptcy and close. **Source E** asserts that shoppers, especially females, still want the sensory experience of shopping in brick-and-mortar stores. They like "the ability to see, touch and feel products." They also like the immediacy of their purchases; they can take their items home right then, rather than have to wait for them to be delivered. It shows that shopping in stores still holds value to many. **Source F** gives a visual of an Amazon warehouse where the boxes and mechanisms overshadow the few employees working on the floor. Many may view it as progress, but some will be alarmed at the dehumanization process operating "behind the scenes."

Rhetorical Analysis

2. **Compare and contrast the tone of the images presented in Sources A and F.**

   Both sources provide visual images of online shopping. While Source F gives a much more "removed" image of the business of online shopping using Amazon as the example, Source A appears more personal, yet it too illustrates an image that some will consider removed because it is so technological. Others might argue that Source A provides a more positive image of online shopping because of its personal immediacy.

3. **Which sources include irony? Explain.**

   Source B includes irony about dog bites, which were an occurrence in the past when all mail was delivered by a mail carrier. The problem was reduced when the amount of letters mailed was cut sharply due to more technological communication. Online shopping, however, has increased delivery by the USPS and other carriers such as UPS. The packages are delivered to people's doorsteps, so online shopping has put a unique twist on the problem of dog bites. Source E is a bit ironic when one considers the urgency of young shoppers: ordering online is immediate, but then one must wait for the delivery.

4. **How does the use of logos in Sources C and D impact their arguments?**

   Sources C and D use statistical evidence, giving them a more authoritative edge than the other sources. Source C is a table from the U.S. Department of Commerce. It shows e-commerce as a percent of total U.S. retail sales. It also changes the percent change from the same quarter a year earlier. E-commerce has grown three to four times faster than traditional retail sales. Source D lists an alarming number of companies (and the number of their stores) that have closed in two years due to online sales.

Writing an Argument

5. **Using examples from the sources, write an essay explaining your position on whether online shopping has affected our lives for better or worse.**

   Students have a variety way to approach this essay and may use not only the sources but also their own experiences concerning shopping.

CHAPTER 8
Media and Pop Culture

This chapter focuses on pop culture, including both historical and modern examples from the movies, sports, and even a critical discussion of Disney. Students will probably find this chapter to be a fun divergence from the heavier topics they have covered. The lesson plans will give you many opportunities to hone students' rhetorical analysis and argumentation skills, with class periods devoted not just to writing, but also to analyzing what has been written. Take the time to allow students to review and rethink their writing. Make them classify their sentences and recognize when an essay falls apart—a skill they will develop by analyzing their own writing in an organized fashion.

Teaching the Chapter

Before discussing any essays in this chapter, have students analyze the photographs in the **Classic and Contemporary Images** feature. Discuss the questions in the textbook on page 335. See suggested answers below.

Classic and Contemporary Images: Suggested Answers

1. **How do these two visuals give a historic portrayal of the stereotypical American gangster kingpin?**

   Both men seem in charge. Soprano appears pensive as he is engaged in a poker game, but his attire and demeanor show a man who is in control. Robinson is in business attire as well. His surprised yet stoic expression at being shot indicates that gunfire on city streets is part of what is expected in gangster life from that era.

2. **Which visual gives a more compelling argument for the iconic gangster, and what aspects of the visual reinforce this argument as opposed to the other visual?**

   Answers will vary. The classic photo represents the term "gangster" that was created in the early 1900s. With his derby hat, long formal coat, and hand clutching his arm (indicating that he has been shot), Edward G. Robinson in *Little Caesar* represents the iconic gangster figure from the 1930s. The contemporary photo of Tony Soprano, in modern business attire, makes him seem similar to all other men of the 2000s. Because he is gambling and holding a big cigar, students might interpret that he is more of a gangster than Robinson.

3. **How much do you know about the gangster prototype beyond these photos? Do current movie gangsters have the same or different characteristics from these classic gangsters? Explain.**

   Students should describe the physical, mental, and emotional appearance of the gangster icon. Some might focus on the tough, unemotional exterior of the gangster with perhaps a more complicated interior. At least according to Hollywood, gangsters swagger with power and are ruthless, fearless, and calculating.

Lesson Plan 8.1

Steinem's "Wonder Woman" and Barna's "Today's Leading Man"—Comparing Stereotypes

Class Opener

Ask students to work independently or in groups to create a list of descriptors for the perfect leading man and the perfect leading woman. You might opt to ask them to differentiate between a romantic lead and an action lead to see if and how they would differentiate.

Activity: Reading for Contrasts and Similarities

Both Steinem's and Barna's essays deal with Hollywood's stereotyping of gender roles. Assign half of the students to read and analyze Steinem, and half to read and analyze Barna. As they read, students should create a list of positive and negative stereotypes in a T-chart like the one below. (See **Chapter 8 online, Daniel Barna: Comparing Stereotypes**.)

How does Steinem/Barna classify Hollywood's depictions of men/women?

Positive	Negative

After students have finished their T-charts, have them share their stereotypes. Then create a Venn diagram, asking students to list similarities and differences in the stereotyping.

Hollywood's Depiction of Men/Women

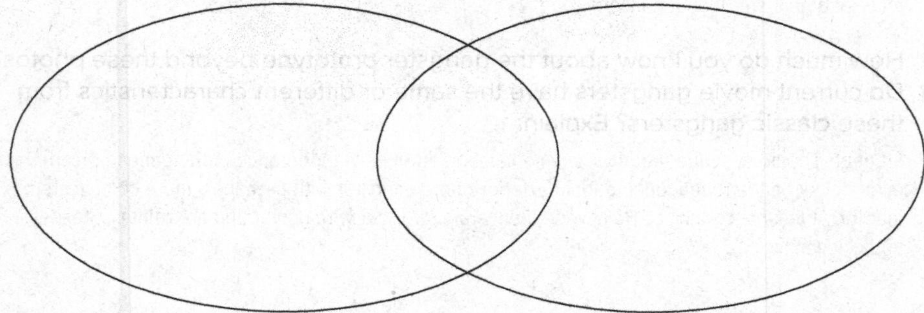

Activity: Compare and Contrast Statements

Using their diagrams, students should write a series of statements that reflect patterns and contrasts. Provide students with the following templates to complete. (See **Chapter 8 online Teacher Resources, Lesson 8.1**.)

In their essays, Steinem and Barna (agree/disagree) that men and women are portrayed

(how?)____

as evidenced by (example)________________________________.

Barna claims that _____________________________________;

however, Steinem argues _________________________________.

Both Steinem and Barna believe _____________________________.

In their analyses, Barna and Steinem relate ________________________

to the experiences evidenced by _____________________________.

While Steinem suggests ___________________________________,

Barna would argue _____________________________________.

Although Barna sees ____________________________________,

Steinem counters ______________________________________.

Activity: Topic Sentences and Body Paragraphs

After students have completed the templates, tell them they must choose three of the sentences to become topic sentences and write body paragraphs to support them, drawing textual evidence from both essays and using the body paragraph format they have been practicing:

- **I.** Body paragraph 1
  - **a.** Topic Sentence – Minor argument one
  - **b.** Textual Evidence
  - **c.** Commentary
  - **d.** Commentary
  - **e.** Textual Evidence
  - **f.** Commentary
  - **g.** Commentary
  - **h.** Conclusion/transition
- **II.** Body paragraph 2 (repeats I)
- **III.** Body paragraph 3 (repeats I)

Class Closer

Explain to students that this was a reverse essay. As a class closer, ask students to create a thesis statement for the analysis they have written. Looking back at their topic sentences, what do they share in common? What single argument can students state about the paragraphs they have written?

Homework

Have students read Susan Bordo's essay, "The Globalization of Eating Disorders." Tell students to write three questions about the essay as they read—one related to ethos, one related to pathos, and one related to logos.

Suggested Answers

"Wonder Woman" by Gloria Steinem

Comprehension

1. According to Steinem, why are children drawn to comic books and superheroes?

According to Steinem, children are drawn to comic books and superheroes because such fantasies are "psychological necessities when we have trouble tying our shoes, escaping from a worldview composed mainly of belts and knees..." (paragraph 4).

2. Why did Wonder Woman appeal especially to Steinem? What distinctions does she draw between the ways boys and girls view action heroes?

Note particularly the passage in the middle of paragraph 8, in which Steinem describes the appeal of comics from a boy's perspective: "I could stop pretending to enjoy the ridicule, bossing-around, and constant endangering of female characters."

3. The writer traces the development of Wonder Woman from her inception during the 1940s to the 1980s. How did Wonder Woman change over the years? How did she remain true to her creator's (William Marston) conception of her? What does Steinem think about these changes?

William Marston created the character partly to make a proto-feminist point, to prove "that women are superior to men because they have love in addition to force" (paragraph 18). In the 1950s, following Marston's death, Wonder Woman was slowly absorbed into the marketing paradigm for boys; and in the 1960s, the character became what Steinem describes as a "boring" female version of James Bond. It was only in the 1970s that the character revived the spirit of the 1940s conception. Steinem thinks that Wonder Woman should continue to reflect the values of a changing culture, but that the writers of the comic should respond to the demands of their audience (paragraph 32).

Rhetorical Analysis

4. What is this essay's persuasive thesis?

Steinem argues that comic books are one important reflection of cultural values.

5. At whom is this essay aimed—lovers of comic books, or women, or a general audience? On what do you base your conclusion?

The essay is aimed at a general audience. Steinem does not expect her readers to feel either defensive toward the cultural status of comic books or condescending toward them. And the essay does not seem to be addressed exclusively to women; Steinem criticizes Marston for his separatist views, which run counter to her own definition of feminism (see paragraph 18).

6. In part, this is a personal essay. How does Steinem create her persona or self-image? Does the personal element enhance or detract from the analysis? Explain your response.

Note particularly the role-playing made possible by the personal essay mode. (For example, Steinem's reading of boys' comics through the eyes of a girl—an analysis that depends on a personal point of view.)

7. **Sort out the complex cause-and-effect relationships in this essay. How does the comparative method reinforce the writer's analysis?**

Steinem compares Wonder Woman with "boys' comics" in order to suggest causal connections between representations of women and larger cultural attitudes. Her intent, in other words, is to establish causal connections through comparative analysis, rather than make a possibly reductive claim of a cause-and-effect relationship in the manner of the Congressional hearings alluded to in paragraph 8.

8. **What types of evidence does the writer provide? Is it sufficient to convince readers? Where, if anywhere, would more detail be helpful?**

Students may want more specific examples of the stereotypes Steinem notes in boys' comics of a certain period, against which Wonder Woman's changing character might be compared.

9. **Steinem divides the essay into five sections. What is her purpose? How successful is she in maintaining the essay's unity by employing this method?**

Student responses will vary.

10. **What paragraphs form the writer's conclusion? How do they recapitulate and add to the substance of the overall essay?**

Paragraphs 33–36 form Steinem's conclusion (as well as the concluding section). In this conclusion, Steinem revisits her opening meditation on the child's "need for a lost independence" as one of the appeals of comic books, but she expands the idea to include (in the case of Wonder Woman's appeal) "the adult's need for a lost balance between women and men, between humans and nature."

Writing

11. **Compare and contrast the ways in which actors have portrayed action heroes. Refer to specific icons like Batman, Spiderman, and Wonder Woman to support your assessment.**

Students should focus on what makes a hero and, in particular, how male heroes compare to female heroes. Are there differences in representation? And, are there differences in reception by both genders?

12. **Writing an Argument** Think about the numerous action heroes or superheroes that young children and adolescents encounter today in various media forms. Write an essay in which you contend that exposure to such superheroes either does or does not encourage violent behavior in young people.

Arguments about what influences violent behavior in children are always difficult to make without proper research. Encourage students to draw on research in child psychology if undertaking this assignment.

Suggested Answers

"Today's Leading Man" by Daniel Barna

Comprehension

1. **Why have critics "fallen in line and have declared Gosling one of the most important actors of this generation" (paragraph 8)? What makes Gosling important?**

Gosling was able to extricate himself from the "tween" roles that he first landed and found more mature roles that allowed him to expand his alluring independence.

2. Barna claims that Gosling has withstood the pressure to play a certain role both on and off the screen. Explain how Gosling has maintained that successful persona.

This is summed up in the last paragraph of this piece where Barna claims that Gosling has "mastered the art of drifting just under the radar, avoiding the glare of the tabloids for the most part, and emerging only when duty calls." Thus, he has achieved a successful level of independence while still building his career as a current Hollywood star.

Rhetorical Analysis

3. What is Barna's thesis? Does he state or imply his main idea? Explain.

Gosling, by choosing unconventional roles, has become a rather unconventional iconic American hero who does not fit the stereotypical male role. Barna states this idea in the last two sentences of paragraph 1.

4. Identify the allusions that Barna uses in this essay. What is his purpose in referring to other characters and works?

Barna makes allusions to Superman and John Wayne and James Bond movies (among others) to point out the fact that the modern leading man is not an "epic" sort of person any more. The new leading man's flaws have risen to the surface and do not typify the "by-the-numbers superhero" type of movie star (paragraph 1).

5. Barna makes a number of assertions regarding the cultural significance of Gosling's career. What are they, and do they effectively support his thesis? Are these assertions facts or opinions? Explain your viewpoint.

The main assertion is that Gosling's career has opened up a new type of Hollywood hero; that Gosling has redefined what it means to be a hero onscreen in current American culture, "where well-paying jobs are scarcer than ever, relationships are harder to maintain and happily ever after is just a blurry myth from our childhood" (paragraph 3). Barna also asserts that the "modern male moviegoer wants to watch someone they can relate to, someone with real-world problems, someone just like them (paragraph 4). These are opinions of the writer.

6. Which paragraphs constitute what we might consider to be Barna's conclusion? Is this conclusion effective? Why or why not?

It can be argued that Barna's conclusion is actually his first paragraph. He makes his main points and then goes on to argue for these points. Students should look at the two subheads ("Today's Man" and "The New Leading Man") and then take note of the reasons why Gosling embodies these titles. The end of the article predicts that Gosling's fame will continue, based on the previous arguments.

Writing

7. Watch a movie with Ryan Gosling in it, and then write your own critical response to it.

Encourage students to read the sample student research paper in the textbook—pages 694–715—before writing their critical response to the movie.

8. Compare-Contrast Essay **Compare Gosling to another contemporary Hollywood figure and explain how Gosling is different from that figure.**

Student essays will vary.

Lesson Plan 8.2

Bordo's "The Globalization of Eating Disorders"—An "Appealing" Socratic Seminar

NOTE: Bordo's essay should have been assigned as homework during the previous class period. Students also should have written three questions as they read—one related to ethos, one related to pathos, and one related to logos.

Class Opener

Ask students to submit their three questions to their groups. As a group, have students classify the questions by ethos, pathos, and logos. Ask each group to be ready to ask a question related to one of the appeals.

Activity: Socratic Seminar

If you have not used a Socratic Seminar, refer to page 105 in Chapter 5 of the Teacher Manual for more detail on this particular strategy. This is a largely student-driven process with the teacher acting as facilitator only as necessary. Allow the student-generated questions to be the focus of the seminar and only step in if the discussion goes far afield.

Make sure students recognize the moments of ethos, pathos, and logos in this essay. If they seem to struggle, direct them to the following:

Ethos: Paragraph 3 (could argue that the cultural construct is an appeal to ethos), Paragraph 9

Pathos: Paragraph 1, Paragraph 2

Logos: Paragraph 1 (mention of doctor's weight chart), Paragraph 4, Paragraph 6

Class Closer

At the end of the discussion, make sure you allow enough time for students to write a paragraph synthesizing their thoughts on the topic. Five minutes should be sufficient.

Homework

Have students read "Escape from Wonderland: Disney and the Female Imagination" by Deborah Ross.

Suggested Answers

"The Globalization of Eating Disorders" by Susan Bordo

Comprehension

1. **How does Bordo define the "body-image distortion syndrome" (paragraph 2)?**
   Bordo initially defines "body-image distortion syndrome" as a "perceptual and cognitive problem," and as a stereotypical disorder associated with a certain social (and socioeconomic) demographic. She later redefines it as a cultural problem.

2. **According to the essay, why have body image and weight problems become a global phenomenon? What is the main cause of this phenomenon?**

Exported media images, according to Bordo, are primarily responsible for the global phenomenon.

3. **How, according to the author, should we deal with the globalization of eating disorders?**

Bordo asks her readers to acknowledge that "we are dealing with a cultural problem" (paragraph 11).

Rhetorical Analysis

4. **How does the author establish herself as an authority on her subject? Do you think that she succeeds? Why or why not?**

In paragraph 9, Bordo mentions that she has written articles and books on the subject and that she has given talks internationally. Students' responses will vary as to the success of this gesture. You may want to ask students if they believe Bordo regards the translations of her work as a "barometer" of a trend, analogous to the phenomena she cites elsewhere (the effect of television in Fiji, for example).

5. **What is the writer's claim? Where does she place it, and why?**

"Eating and body image problems are now not only crossing racial and class lines, but gender lines. ... They have become a global phenomenon." Bordo's claim comes at the end of paragraph 3, immediately following the exemplars that serve merely to illustrate the phenomena of crossed lines.

6. **Bordo begins with an imaginary situation. Does this strategy enhance or detract from the validity of her argument? Justify your response.**

Students' responses will vary, but students should consider the opening as a dramatic illustration rather than as evidence or "case studies."

7. **How does Bordo develop this selection as a problem-solution essay? Where does the solution appear, and how effective is its placement within the essay?**

Because Bordo discusses the problem as a recent phenomenon, and a problem with remarkably clear causal mechanisms, the reader naturally expects a solution to follow as part of the pattern. The solution Bordo proposes in her conclusion—that we acknowledge the problem as cultural—may seem unexpectedly mild, given the clarity of her diagnosis.

Writing

8. **Write a causal essay analyzing the impact of mass media on your generation's vision of the ideal body.**

Before students write a causal essay, it might be helpful to point out the following: The introduction (paragraphs 1–2) of Bordo's essay is largely devoted to causal analysis—the "controlled experiment" of the Fiji Islands (paragraph 4) is only one example. Comparison-and-contrast techniques are employed (in paragraph 9, for example) to highlight the historical and generational change in attitude within cultures such as China.

9. **Why are women in the United States and around the world more susceptible to eating disorders than men? Answer this question in an analytical essay.**

For either writing assignment 8. or 9., students will need to research sociological studies on how much influence the media has over our lives and our abstract notions of beauty.

10. **Writing an Argument** Write an essay titled "Body Images, Eating Disorders, and Cultural Imperialism." In this essay, argue for or against the proposition that American media are exporting potentially unhealthy images of the human body.

Bordo obviously supports the idea that the United States is exporting eating disorders to the rest of the world. As students research this assignment, make sure that they research both sides of the issue.

If they choose to write that the eating disorders are not being exported along with Westernized culture, they must address what is making eating disorders more prevalent throughout the world.

Lesson Plan 8.3

Ross's "Escape From Wonderland"—Connecting Detail To Effect

Class Opener

Write the following prompt on the board so that students can read it and begin writing as they enter the classroom:

> **Write a single paragraph of 5–8 sentences, describing your earliest memory of a Disney movie. Include the movie title and what you remember as your first reaction to the movie.**

Activity: Analyzing Detail

Recognizing and commenting on an author's handling of detail is an important skill for rhetorical analysis. This activity will require students to recognize details and how they function in the essay. Ask students to analyze for detail as they read Ross's essay. Give students the thesis statement below, and have them fill in a dialectical journal (also known as a reader-response journal) similar to the chart that follows. (Photocopy the chart, or see **Chapter 8 online, Deborah Ross: Connecting Detail to Effect**.)

> Thesis: In her essay, Ross uses details from Disney movies to explore the impact of children's movies on children's ability to value their own imaginations and their ability to envision change. (Reference paragraph 5)

Movie/ Paragraph	Quotation/Specific Detail	Connection to Imagination/ Change

Class Closer

After the dialectical journal is complete, ask students to group the evidence they have gathered in the "Quotation/Specific Detail" column into topics, using three different colors of highlighter. They should use a different color highlighter for each of three groupings to help them see how the evidence fits together. Students should then use these groupings to write topic sentences for each color of analysis. Allow students a chance to share their work.

Suggested Answers

"Escape from Wonderland: Disney and the Female Imagination" by Deborah Ross

Comprehension

1. How does Ross define the ideology inherent in Disney's films for girls?

Ross believes that although Disney encourages a unique self-expression that builds imagination, its practice is actually a "program of control and rigid adherence to rules." Ross argues that these practices are contradictory, and this contradiction is apparent in Disney's animated films, especially those more popular to young female audiences. Young girls often fantasize about life more exciting than reality. In paragraph 7, Ross describes this dichotomy in more detail, with regard to progressive authors (what Disney claims) versus conservative authors (Disney's rigid adherence).

2. Summarize the content of the three films that Ross discusses. What similarities and differences does Ross see among them?

Students should first work, perhaps with partners, to summarize the films. Then together the class can compare and contrast Ross's summaries. For Ross's analysis, paragraphs 12–19 cover *Alice in Wonderland*. Paragraphs 20–26 cover *The Little Mermaid*. This section includes commentary regarding the original story by Hans Christian Andersen and how it was "modernized" for Disney's 1980s version. Then paragraphs 27–33 cover Ross's summary of her personal favorite, *Beauty and the Beast*.

3. According to the writer, what is a "female Quixote"? Where does she treat this concept directly and indirectly?

Ross introduces the "female Quixote" in paragraph 6. Paragraphs 9–11 talk more directly about its connection to the Disney films and Ross's own theories.

Rhetorical Analysis

4. This essay appeared in a specialized scholarly journal. What "scholarly" elements appear in the paper? How does Ross adjust her style to this specialized audience? What strategies does she use to make the essay accessible to a wider audience?

Scholarly elements include a haughtier language, a bibliography, cited sources, and the inclusion of other theorists who have written about this or similar topics. The topic invites a wider audience, and Ross brings in those readers by setting up a very clear and anticipatory introduction and thesis.

5. Where does Ross state her claim most clearly? Analyze the varieties of evidence that she uses to support her claim and the minor propositions.

Ross's main claim is culminated in paragraph 5, in which she sets up her thesis and what her plan is to support that thesis. Have the students outline the various subtopics and evidence she uses.

6. **How does the writer organize her essay? What are the main divisions, and how do they cohere?**

Organization includes a number of setup paragraphs before the thesis is given. Ross then gives a clear understanding of the "female Quixote" that she will later bring back to support her thesis. This is followed by a summary of each of her three chosen films. In each of these sections of film discussion, she supports her thesis and incorporates the "female Quixote" aspect. Her conclusion recaps.

7. **Why does Ross cite other scholars and writers? How does this strategy affect the power of her argument?**

Citing other scholars and writers strengthens Ross's own theories. She might agree or disagree with them, but she's not afraid to discuss them and this gives her a great deal of credibility as an expert on her chosen topic.

8. **Ross elaborates a definition of the Disney "program" or ideology. What rhetorical strategies does she use to create this extended definition?**

In paragraphs 3 and 4, Ross uses a causal element to explain the dichotomy between Disney's philosophy of employees with unique self-expression for a more vivid imagination versus their actual program of control and rigid adherence to strict rules. Ross explains the confusion these two polar foci create, which thus bleeds into their films.

9. **How effective do you find the concluding paragraph? Justify your response.**

Answers will vary depending on students' understanding of the essay and their agreement or disagreement with the essay's thesis.

Writing

10. **Select a Disney movie other than one discussed in this essay and write an analysis of its "program"—its ethical message or ideology.**

Either bring in several Disney films for analysis or put some of them on reserve. You may have a few students who have not seen a Disney film. It will be helpful for them to view at least portions of some for the purposes of identifying ethical messages and ideologies.

11. **In a descriptive essay, explain why children's stories or fairy tales have such a hold on young people's imaginations.**

A class discussion would open up ideas for students and be entertaining and preparatory to writing this essay. You also may want to direct students to an essay from Bruno Bettelheim's book *The Uses of Enchantment: The Meaning and Importance of Fairy Tales*—see page 731 in the textbook.

12. **Writing an Argument** **Write a persuasive essay on the benefits of children's literature and film—even the films that Walt Disney produced. Present at least three extended examples to support your claim.**

Students should be ready to write based on their individual experiences with children's literature or Disney films.

Lesson Plan 8.4

Will's "Plumbing the Etiquette of Baseball"—SOAPSTone Analysis

Class Opener

Ask students to create a code for being a successful student in your school. Give them 5 minutes to write a series of guidelines that all successful students should adhere to.

Activity: A SOAPSTone Discussion

This is an excellent essay to visit with a SOAPSTone analysis. As a reminder, SOAPSTone is an acronym developed by the College Board for teaching rhetorical analysis. It stands for:

Speaker—Students must determine who is speaking. Who is narrating the essay? The speaker in this essay is George Will, writing as a journalist as he reviews a book about baseball's unwritten codes. Differentiate between subjective and objective journalism.

Occasion—Students must determine the context of the writing. When does this occur? Where? What particular event has motivated this writing? Will is a baseball fan in addition to being a journalist, and he wants to point out the honorable as well as "dumb" codes in baseball.

Audience—Students must determine the intended audience for the essay. This essay is written for baseball fans who will either agree with or argue against the "codes" Will identifies (depending on whether the situation was for or against their team's players).

Purpose—Students must determine the author's purpose in writing the essay. Will wants to establish the sport of baseball as more respectful than other sports.

Subject— This should be the shortest discussion point. Ask students to summarize Will's argument in 20 words or less.

Tone—Through the author's diction and syntax, tone can be deciphered. Will's tone is somewhat pragmatic, although he does point out in unsympathetic terms various codes that he disagrees with or thinks are outdated.

Suggested Answers

"Plumbing the Etiquette of Baseball" by George Will

Comprehension

1. **What is the central thesis of the essay?**
   Baseball contains unwritten rules or "codes."

2. **Give two examples of "codes" and explain the rationale behind them.**
   Many examples of codes are given in the essay. The rationale behind these codes is to enforce that players be respectful toward each other and to the ethics of the game.

3. **How was Joe DiMaggio honored by a player from his team?**

The player bunted the ball to assure that DiMaggio had another chance to extend his hitting streak.

Rhetorical Analysis

4. **Analyze the statement "standards are always out of date—that is why we call them standards" (paragraph 11).**

The standards of baseball are not stagnant. They are constantly changing as evidenced by Carlton Fisk's comments about Deion Sanders.

5. **Will's essay about the codes give a certain overall impression about baseball and its players. What is the dominant impression and how is it exemplified?**

The players have a respect for the game, including a respect for other players and especially the pitcher. A time-honored tradition exists through unwritten rules that give an interesting twist to the idea of sportsmanship.

6. **Analyze the tone of the opening paragraph. What is Will's purpose in opening his essay with this tone?**

It is politically charged as if two countries are meeting to avoid a larger war or problem. A "summit" happens in a laundry room in the Metrodome, where the managers from two teams meet to discuss the breaking of an unwritten rule. "Peace" needs to be preserved between the two teams so that the sanctity of baseball will remain.

7. **Distinguish baseball from other sports, such as football and basketball, in light of the statement "traditionally baseball punishes preening" (paragraph 7).**

Football and basketball, to some extent, allow player celebrations to take place that are not humble. Baseball players do celebrate, but they celebrate in respectful ways as opposed to football players who "preen" after touchdowns, and basketball players who prance around the court. This question could be turned into an argument, because students may believe that baseball players' actions are not that contextually different from other sports' players.

Writing

8. **Writing an Argument** Write a commentary on another American sports institution and what you believe are its set of codes.

If necessary, provide students with topics, such as comparing American sports fever to Europeans' and South Americans' fanaticism with soccer, or the historical sources of American sports.

Lesson Plan 8.5

Chapter Assessment

Rhetorical Analysis Answers

1. D
2. A
3. D
4. A
5. C
6. A
7. B
8. C
9. B
10. A

Connections for Critical Thinking

Have students turn to the questions on page 375 in the textbook. Tell students to choose one of the four options and write for a minimum of 30 minutes.

After students have finished writing, use the remainder of the class period to group students according to the option they chose. Students should read and comment on one another's essays, offering a positive comment, a critical comment, and a question for each essay read.

Answers

1. **Examine the role of the media in society and journalists' responsibilities or duties to humanity. Use at least three essays from this chapter to illustrate or support your thesis.**

   The students will have much to say about this and their responses will vary, but there should be some class discussion on media issues such as news biases, political backing, privatization of the media, and so on. Remind students to use essays from this chapter and to cite their sources.

2. **Define *popular culture*, using the essays of Ross and Steinem as reference points, along with any additional essays that you consider relevant.**

   Students will have different definitions for "popular culture" other than what they look up in dictionaries, but using the two articles by Ross and Steinem, they should pick out specific characteristics that all of these essays have. Pop culture includes topics that are understood and accepted by a younger audience who, in many ways, wishes to be like or live like both fictional and nonfictional media characters.

3. **Use Barna's and Ross's essays to explore media's connections to American cultural experience. What strategies do these writers use? Are their goals similar?**

   Students need to discuss the representation of the media in these essays and how they are connected. Barna claims that "Hollywood was constantly throwing our way" "cookie-cutter action figures." He states, "As a result, men often linked heroism with masculinity." Barna uses allusion and illustration in his comparison essay of leading men then and now, and Gosling's role in changing media's view of masculinity. Ross focuses on media's damage to our ability to distinguish between reality and fantasy that creates the problems.

4. **Using at least three recent films or television episodes that you have seen, write an essay in which you agree or disagree with Bordo's claim that the media are causing "eating and body image problems" for girls and women as well as for boys and men.**

   Bordo uses research into media examples and cultural comparisons to discuss eating disorders across the globe. Students should be able to pick out some of the stereotypes assumed in these media products. Their responses will vary.

Lesson Plan 8.6

Synthesizing Sources: Social Media—Has It Empowered Us or Disenfranchised Us?

Assign students to read the sources and answer the first five questions for homework. This will prepare them for writing the essay. Then have them use the "Writing an Argument" prompt to write the essay as an in-class timed assignment (40 minutes).

Applying Your Synthesis Skills: Suggested Answers

Comprehension

1. **Summarize the inferred arguments made in each source.**

   Source A: This source begs the question: Is there any need for people to communicate vocally anymore? The three millennials, as well as the people surrounding them, appear to be living in their own worlds where their voices take the form of social media language. **Source B:** Social activism is at an all-time high thanks to the convenience and immediacy of social media. **Source C:** Thanks to social media, the speedy response to natural disasters such as Hurricane Harvey has become a positive reaction to timely and apt relief. **Source D:** Social media has driven millennials to be more image conscious in frequently superficial ways, with often unfavorable consequences. It allows for people to give out false images of themselves as well as increasing others' overall vulnerability. **Source E:** Crowdfunding is another phenomenon created by social media where the need for monetary donations reaches out to a much wider population, again increasing social awareness. Crowdfunding might also be seen as a negative because it opens up the possibility of scamming. **Source F:** The world is becoming increasingly more antisocial due to the growing use of technology and could increase people's tendency to procrastinate and avoid individual responsibilities through the instantaneous distraction of social media.

Rhetorical Analysis

2. **Explain the effectiveness of the author's use of the repeated word *activism* in Source B.**

   The author shows the immediacy of activism with social media. We no longer need to have meetings to form groups and set out times to canvass others for causes we believe in. We have all the tools at our fingertips putting the motion into play almost immediately.

3. **What is the appeal of the examples used in Source C?**

   Readers are given a direct way that social media truly impacted relief to the Houston area after Hurricane Harvey. The examples such as the nursing home, people on their rooftops, and illustrating how "social media channels were overwhelmed with pictures of scenes of devastation that the regular media couldn't get their hands on" brought proximity to the catastrophe allowing for more precise relief efforts.

4. **How does Source D use ethos to highlight the pitfalls of using social media? How does it use pathos?**

   Through a strong argument about ethical values, the author uses several scenarios of how social media may become an adolescent's pitfall. The author says that cruelty, through social media, has crossed an ethical boundary. The author appeals to our sense of moral judgment. In addition, the article appeals to a reader's pathos by discussing the cruelty inflicted on others.

5. **How do the visual elements and the perspective of Sources A and E reveal expressive content, or purpose?**

Adding the icons to the photo in Source A highlights and reinforces the purpose of the image—to show the control that social media has over Millennials' lives. Source E's image uses a "user's perspective" in looking at a tablet in front of a computer. The icons and short captions about crowdsourcing on the tablet show not only how easy it is to reach a large audience via social media, but also the limited vocabulary necessary to get across ideas.

Writing an Argument

6. **Using examples from at least three of the sources, write an essay explaining your position on whether the benefits of social media outweigh its disadvantages.**

Answers will vary. Many students will view social media benefits outweighing its disadvantages. They view social media as a way for people to react immediately to different phenomena, and they will cite the positives in these sources. Other students may note that social media's ability to immediately react is socially demoralizing. Students may share personal experiences, both good and bad, that have occurred to them through social media.

CHAPTER 9
Literature and the Arts

This chapter makes English teachers comfortable. We turn our attention to literary writers and literary topics. Studying literary nonfiction with a dash of poetry provides the perfect opportunity to ask students to think about themselves as writers. Up to this point, we have asked students to think of themselves as English students. In this chapter, however, we will ask them to think of themselves as writers and, as writers, to develop their own voices. The essays in this chapter are largely self-reflective or reflective of the lives of other artists. In the spirit of this reflection, these lesson plans will be devoted to developing authorial voice.

Teaching the Chapter

You may want to wait until students read and discuss John Updike's essay "Moving Along" later in this chapter before you ask them to analyze the photographs in the **Classic and Contemporary Images** feature. Suggested answers are below for the discussion questions in the textbook on page 385.

Classic and Contemporary Images: Suggested Answers

1. **What is the central impression created by Rodin's sculpture? How does the sculptor's technique create this impression?**

   The impression is one of philosophical contemplation. The sculpture depicts a man in sober meditation battling with a powerful internal struggle.

2. **What central impression does Koons's sculpture create? How does the sculptor's technique create this impression?**

   The impression is one of clever humor with a message that art can be created by materials that consumers use.

3. **How did Rodin utilize line and form to "contain" *The Thinker*'s thoughts? How does the classic sculpture differ from the contemporary sculpture in the use of line and form?**

   Students should recognize that no matter where on the sculpture one starts viewing *The Thinker,* the eye is continually contained on the sculpture. The viewer's eye is drawn from the head, to the hand on the chin, down to the legs and block of stone, then up the man's back and then to the head again. *Rabbit* is opposite in that the lines of the ears and hands and legs point outward, and the eye must deliberately force itself back to the body of the sculpture.

4. **If *The Thinker* could talk, what would he say? What would *Rabbit's* message be?**

   Answers will vary. *The Thinker* is contemplating serious thoughts. Some students might give him Dante's persona since the sculpture, part of a larger work, *The Gates of Hell,* supposedly represents the poet. *Rabbit's* message might be one that glorifies pop culture and possibly environmental issues since he's making use of consumer goods for the sake of art.

Lesson Plan 9.1

Welty's "One Writer's Beginnings"—Writing With the Senses

NOTE: Ask students to read and respond to the questions on this essay before class.

NOTE: This set of activities requires some teacher preparation. Bring to class three types of stimuli:

- Pieces of unusual fabrics—velvet, silky, mohair, sheer (If you do not have fabric on hand, perhaps the family and consumer sciences teacher will have remnants available.)
- Evocative music that students might not have heard (Yo Yo Ma's recording "The Silk Road" works wonderfully. Recordings of this nature are probably available at the local public library.)
- Photographs of beautiful but inaccessible places (If you have a projector in your classroom, consider going to the photo archives of *National Geographic* at http://photography.nationalgeographic.com/photography/)

Class Opener

Begin with a discussion of Eudora Welty as a writer. Ask students to relate to Welty's sense of reading and writing in her childhood home. Allow a few minutes for students to discuss this in terms of their own experiences.

Activity: Writing With the Senses

Welty's essay is a declaration of her coming-of-age as a writer. She discusses what life was like in her home, and she recalls the abundance of reading materials and opportunities she was presented with as a child. Although it is tempting to ask students to write their own "how I became a writer" story, sometimes we find that our students have come from print-poor environments and cannot relate to Welty's abundance of the written word. Instead, use this activity as a springboard to have students consider one of Welty's minor points: Welty describes her mother's "hedonism" in becoming engrossed in a book; further, she alludes to her own "sensory education."

In this lesson, use the idea of "sensory education" to encourage students to write creatively using unexpected sensory experiences as their basis for writing. Students will make use of semi-common objects and sounds in order to write creatively. These stimuli will enable them to activate prior knowledge and draw on experiences they do not usually relate to in their writing. By "freeing" their writing in this way, students will hopefully improve their abilities to craft examples for their essays.

Give students the three prompts that follow; however, the prompts will not involve an assignment of *what* to write about. Instead, students will respond first to a tactile object, second to a musical selection, and third to a visual display. With each "prompt," students will have a set period of time to write whatever comes to their minds. Explain to students that the writing pieces need not connect to one another. Students should choose to write in an expository, a narrative, or a persuasive style. They will be required to change modes with each prompt. Students must title each piece they write.

PROMPT ONE: Students will receive a small piece of unusual fabric. Students will have 10 minutes to write based on the fabric, considering associations with its color and its texture. Students should choose to write in an expository, a narrative, or a persuasive style.

PROMPT TWO: Change the prompt to music for 12 minutes. Students will listen to "The Silk Road" by Yo Yo Ma (or another piece you have chosen), and they will write as they listen. Again, tell students to write what comes into their minds. However, this time, they must choose a different mode of writing. If they wrote in the expository fashion the first time, they must now switch to either narrative or persuasive.

PROMPT THREE: Give students the third prompt. This time, students will have 15 minutes to write in the final mode. Post a photograph from National Geographic (or a photo you have chosen) and have students write a final paragraph/essay in the final writing mode based on their response to the photograph.

Class Closer

Have students share their writing, which may be the most beautiful work they produce all year. At the end of the activity, organize students into their editing groups. Each student will choose one piece of writing for their partners to critique. The student will read his/her writing aloud, and the group members will offer one suggestion and one item of praise.

Homework

Have students read Margaret Atwood's "Orwell and Me" for homework and bring with them the book they remember as being the most influential book of their childhood. (Perhaps this will be the book that they learned to read with. Perhaps it will be a favorite author they read repeatedly. Perhaps it will be their first chapter book.)

Suggested Answers

"One Writer's Beginnings" by Eudora Welty

Comprehension

1. What is the significance of the essay's title? Does Welty write about one continuous "beginning" or a series of beginnings? Explain.

The essay could be about both one continuous "beginning" and a series of beginnings. Welty writes about her childhood experience in learning to read, which led to her reading a growing variety of materials, each awakening new worlds to her developing sensibilities. She is always at a starting point to begin to learn and to explore the world.

2. What does Welty mean when she says that her mother was a "hedonist" (paragraph 6)? Does Welty also become a hedonist? Why or why not?

Welty's mother read more for pleasure and escape rather than for information. Welty herself becomes a hedonist and more. The physicality of books and the sounds of words give her a sense of pleasure, but reading has also helped her to experience the world and its wonders fully and deeply. The pleasures of reading have become the pleasures of writing for her.

3. Explain the nature of Welty's "sensory" education.

Her discussion of the moon reveals the nature of her sensory education. The word *moon* becomes palpably connected to the object to which it refers. Words become a sensory experience for Welty. Her analogy to the roundness of the concord grape is very effective and evocative.

Rhetorical Analysis

4. Welty alludes to dozens of works of literature. What does she assume about her audience's knowledge of these works? How do the allusions contribute to Welty's purpose?

Welty assumes that most of her readers are familiar with the works, but she says that probably nobody had the collection of books she had. Even if the reader is not familiar with them, one can still discover what these works mean to Welty and how they helped her develop her sensibility as a writer and as a participant in life.

5. What is Welty's thesis, and how does she develop it?

The thesis highlights the importance of reading in Welty's life, starting from childhood and providing examples of the effects of becoming an avid reader. Reading has shaped her into the person she has become and is intimately connected to her work as a writer. It honed her perceptive abilities.

6. What determines the order in which Welty organizes her essay, which she divides into three parts?

Welty starts with a discussion of formative books in her early life and the role of her parents, and then she goes on to reveal her sensory development by using single extended examples. The effects of early reading become more evident as the essay progresses.

7. Welty includes several descriptive passages in this essay. Where are these passages, and what do they contribute to the overall meaning of the selection?

The descriptions of her mother reading to her, of the illustrations in books, of the physical books themselves, of the moon and grape analogy—all are good examples of her fine-tuned sense of perception.

8. How do the last two paragraphs of the essay echo the first two paragraphs?

The last two paragraphs go back to the experience of her mother reading to her; they explain how reading awakened both her senses and an inward voice that guides her writing. Reading and writing have become one. In effect, Welty experiences life as a child with a beginner's mind.

Writing

9. Write a description of a scene or series of events from your childhood in which you were reading (or being read to), engaged in an art project, or listening to music. In your essay, explain the impact of this memory or activity on your current life.

The childhood experience may have led to the discovery of the work students love or to some other important outcome.

10. Write an essay explaining the importance of providing children with sensory stimuli involving reading, artwork, and music.

There are so many diverse art forms today; one must thoughtfully choose the appropriate "sensory" stimuli for the child.

11. Writing an Argument **Argue for or against the proposition that children today read less than those of previous generations—and suffer the consequences.**

What are the effects of poor reading skills? A person may know how to read but not know how to *actively* read.

Lesson Plan 9.2

Atwood's "Orwell and Me"—Analysis Jigsaw

Class Opener

The students we teach today had not yet been born when the events of 9/11/01 occurred. In many parts of the country, students know only spotty details about that day. To set the stage for their understanding of Atwood, consider opening class by exploring the online 9/11 Memorial Museum with them. There is an interactive online version that can be found here: https://www.911memorial.org/museum

Activity: Analysis Jigsaw

STEP ONE: For this activity, students will work in groups to create a DIDLS analysis of specific pieces of Atwood's essay. You will need to assign them to four groups: *Animal Farm,* Orwell, Atwood (or self/speaker), and *Nineteen Eighty-Four*. Each group will perform a specific DIDLS analysis using the double-entry journal format below. Each group will focus only on their assigned component of the essay. (Photocopy the chart or see **Chapter 9 online, Margaret Atwood: Analysis Jigsaw**.)

Category	Quotation	Analysis
Diction		
Imagery		
Detail		
Language (Figurative)		
Syntax		

There are many possible configurations of this information, but possible responses on Atwood might be:

Category	Quotation	Analysis
Diction	"gobbled"	Atwood describes her young self as insatiably hungry for the book.
Imagery	"I cried my eyes out"	This elaboration on simply crying provides an appeal to pathos, while offering a heightened sense of the emotional response the author had to Orwell's work.
Detail	"I was able to read it at the age of nine."	Atwood's young age suggests that she was highly impressionable and that she read the book with a level of innocence that belied the content of the book.
Language (Figurative)	"I grew up with George Orwell."	This is an example of hyperbole. The author did not truly grow up with George Orwell, but he had a significant effect on her. This overstatement helps the reader understand his impact on her.

Syntax	"I knew nothing about the kind of politics in the book—the child's version of politics then, just after the war, consisted of the simple notion that Hitler was bad but dead."	The author writes a short sentence, and then uses a dash to write an elaboration of her child-self. The choice of the dash indicates that the author sees the elaboration as being inextricably linked to the claim offered in the first part of the sentence.

STEP TWO: After groups have completed their DIDLS analysis, they will then move into new groups in which each new member is an expert in one component of the essay. For example, if you have 4 groups of 4 (ideal), you will number the members of the group 1, 2, 3, and 4. All of the 1s will then form a new group. One member will have worked on Orwell, one on Atwood, one on *Animal Farm,* and one on *Nineteen Eighty-Four.* They will bring with them their notes from their group's original conversation.

At this point, the new group has a new goal: To use the analysis they have created in their original groups to determine Atwood's overall claim in the essay. They must now consider what Atwood's primary purpose for this essay is. Instruct groups to create a single statement in which they identify Atwood's purpose.

Class Closer

Students will not necessarily come to an agreement on Atwood's purpose. For a class closer, allow students to informally debate their findings, pushing them to use the evidence charts they created to back up their claims.

Suggested Answers

"Orwell and Me" by Margaret Atwood

Comprehension

1. **This article is an edited extract of a talk that Atwood gave on BBC Radio. Why do you think her talk would be of interest to a radio audience?**

   Students will have different ideas here. Have them listen to radio news and interviews. Atwood is particularly gifted at drawing images and tells a good story.

2. **Summarize what you learn from Atwood's essay about George Orwell and his novels *Animal Farm* and *Nineteen Eighty-Four.***

   Responses here will vary, depending on students having previously read *Animal Farm* and/or *1984,* as well as their individual understandings of politics.

3. **What does Atwood learn from Orwell? What does she think all of us should learn from him today in our "post-9/11 world"?**

   In *Animal Farm,* Atwood learned not to trust those who extol themselves, their importance, and their position, but also those who are too vulnerable and weak to stand up to this. She quotes Orwell, "it isn't the labels ... that are definitive, but the acts done in their name" (see paragraph 3). Atwood saw the events analogized described in *1984* as more realistic than those in *Animal Farm* because they could happen anywhere: a world of constant surveillance, no right to speak freely, a need for war, overdone slogans, distortion of language, and the cover-up or disposal of all records of anything that is really happening to cause it all or as a result of it all. Atwood believes, in the end, that Orwell had faith in human strength and resilience. Atwood hopes this to be true of the post-9/11 world. She points out in paragraph 18 many of the elements from Orwellian stories that are in existence today. Lead the students into a discussion about these elements.

Rhetorical Analysis

4. Why does Atwood begin on a personal note: "I grew up with George Orwell"? What is the effect of beginning the essay this way?

Atwood begins by telling us about her childhood, literary influences. She shares her love of Orwell from a young age, and how at that young age, she had a somewhat limited but a clear childlike understanding of Orwell's stories. This helps the reader, especially he or she who might not ever have read Orwell, to understand what she's leading to from the most basic perspective. By doing this, Atwood introduces herself to us, as she would in a radio interview, and introduces us to the topic, as well as her knowledge of the topic. She also shares with us how she was first interested and leads us into a deeper understanding.

5. What is Atwood's main claim? What premises or warrants does she establish, and how sound is the logic? Justify your response.

Atwood's main claim is that those elements that make Orwell's imaginary stories so interesting and frightening are real now and we must not be blinded to this, nor should we ignore them (see paragraph 16).

6. Consider the appeal of ethos. Atwood seems to speak from a position of authority. How does she establish this sense of authority in the essay?

Atwood tells us of her own reading and writing experience. She supports this by detailing important elements from specific Orwell books; then explains his influences on her writing.

7. Why does Atwood summarize Orwell's two novels at considerable length? How does she use comparison and contrast to frame her discussion of the novels?

It is necessary to have a thorough summary of the two Orwell books to understand Atwood's claims. If the students have not read these, these summaries are even more important. It would be helpful for the students to read at least *1984,* then locate and identify the symbolism to which Atwood refers. She compares and contrasts *1984* and *Animal Farm* to illustrate their underlying meanings, but even more so, to better support her claim of how their meanings are especially eye-opening today, post-9/11.

8. What causes and effects does Atwood analyze in this essay? In each, what is her purpose?

There is cause and effect in Orwell's influences in Atwood's own writing. Cause and effect is clear in the *Animal Farm* pigs and their behavior after overthrowing the humans. Also, in *1984,* Winston is pushed into giving up Julia, only to discover she gave him up as well. See what other examples students can identify.

9. How does Atwood conclude her discussion of Orwell? How successful do you find the ending, and why?

In using Orwell's own created language, such as "doublethink," Atwood pays him honor and brings us back around to her main point. At the very end, she wonders what Orwell would say, then answers her own question on his behalf. Students will have different ideas of the success of this ending.

Writing

10. Read *Animal Farm* or view the film version. Then write your own analysis of Orwell's work.

Bring in the Orwell films for a class analysis of predetermined sections or reserve them at the library. Many students today will not have seen these films or read these books. They will have only a cursory knowledge of the stories' plots.

11. **Writing an Argument** Atwood raises the question of whether writers and artists should warn us about dangers confronting society. Write a persuasive essay in which you take a clear stand on this issue. Provide examples drawn from literature, art, and the media.

Students will need to research other works to proceed. Perhaps they can read and discuss the comparisons in small groups.

Lesson Plan 9.3

Updike's "Moving Along"—Timed Synthesis

NOTE: This essay is an excellent springboard to assigning the 2007 Form B synthesis essay from AP Central, which deals with museums and the decisions made by curators.

Class Opener

To put students into the right frame of reference for discussing works of art, refer them to the images at the beginning of the chapter. In their groups, ask them to answer the questions provided in the text. Go around to each group, asking each group to discuss a different question in the textbook on page 385. See the suggested answers in this Teacher Manual on page 181.

Activity: Analyzing and Describing Art

Many high school students are uncomfortable with analyzing and talking about art, but learning to describe visuals is a key skill they need to develop. The individualism associated with analyzing art is fundamental to learning to develop voice as a writer. Updike's piece is a short essay, so read it aloud in class. Then, using Paragraph 2 and Paragraph 3 as models, ask students to choose a work of art and write a detailed description of what is being depicted. If you have access to a local art museum, going there would be a worthwhile field trip. If not, most school libraries will have a good selection of books of artwork. A Google image search for "famous paintings" will also yield an amazing array of potential subjects.

Class Closer

At the end of the period, ask students to form groups based on the time periods their art represents. On an exit card, ask students to determine at least 5 characteristics that all of the works within their period share in common.

Homework

Assign David Gates's "Finding Neverland" for reading. As students read, they will come across a number of celebrities and songs with which they may not be familiar. In preparation for a Fishbowl discussion, have students prepare three questions and choose one unfamiliar song or performer to research. In addition to their fishbowl questions, ask students to bring to class a 20–50 word introduction to the person or song they chose to research.

Suggested Answers

"Moving Along" by John Updike

Comprehension

1. According to Updike, why does the idea of travel have such a hold on the collective imagination? What is the relationship of the travel motif to art?

Traveling involves movement, unsettledness, and change of environment, and the idea of travel is common in our dreams. Updike uses the word *hallucinatory* in association with travel, a state in which the imagination would be given free play. Imagination is critical to the development or movement of art.

2. Describe the two paintings that Updike analyzes in this essay. What other famous painting does he allude to in paragraph 3?

The Punjab Hills painting depicts two lovers mounted on horseback, riding through the starry moonlit night; their regard for each other suggests passion and amorous intent. The de Forest painting is populated with strange figures and images that are somewhat nightmarish and unsettling; it has a menacing quality. These images return collectively from deep within the unconscious mind. In paragraph 3, Updike alludes to the painting of George Washington crossing the Delaware.

3. Why does Updike emphasize the "eeriness" of the two paintings? What is he saying about the human psyche?

Eeriness involves the inexplicable, which can evoke the fear and mystery of the unknown elements to be encountered in movement through space and time. The human psyche has great range and depth, works in mysterious ways, and is stimulated by travel.

Rhetorical Analysis

4. How does Updike design his introductory paragraph? What is his purpose?

Updike begins the introductory paragraph with dreams and ends with the word *phantasmal*. In between is a brief historical account of men traveling, from boat travel to highway travel to space travel, introducing the change of mind one experiences through movement. The reader is prepared for the mind's trip initiated by contemplation of the two paintings.

5. What is Updike's thesis? Does he state or imply it? Explain.

Updike's thesis is implied: travel as movement renders the landscape as a series of fantastic, dream-like mental images that stimulate the mind.

6. Identify specific passages that highlight Updike's descriptive style. What types of figurative language does he employ?

Updike's descriptive style is spatial; for example, from foreground to background, as in the description of the upper third of the Punjab Hills painting at the end of paragraph 3. He also includes details of color and gesture. Figures of speech include the merry-go-round simile in paragraph 2.

7. Explain Updike's comparative method. What do the reproductions of the two paintings contribute to the overall comparative effect? Would this brief essay be as effective without these images? Why or why not?

The two paintings have quite different effects on the viewer's sensibility. Updike offers interpretive comments on the details he highlights, but leaves the reader/viewer to form his/her own conclusions. The images, therefore, are necessary.

8. **Why is Updike's concluding paragraph relatively brief when compared with the preceding paragraphs? Is this end paragraph effective? Justify your response.**

   The preceding paragraphs focused on details, requiring substantial development compared to the conclusion. The ending paragraph's effect is questionable, obtuse, but returns the reader softly to his/her bed.

Writing

9. **Consider the two paintings that Updike reproduces, and write your own comparative essay based on them.**

   Student responses will vary.

10. **Writing an Argument** Argue for or against the proposition that when viewing a work of art, it is not necessary to relate it—as Updike does—to human behavior.

    Student responses will vary.

Lesson Plan 9.4

Gates's "Finding Neverland"—Fishbowl Discussion with Connections

Class Opener

Students should have read this essay before coming to class. They should come prepared with 3 questions and a 20–50 word summary of a key person, song, or title mentioned in the essay. Make sure they put their names on the backs of their questions and summaries (so you can give them credit for their participation), and then pass the fishbowl to each group so that all questions (cut apart individually) and all summaries can be added to the bowl. Explain that for this lesson's fishbowl, students will discuss the text through both the questions and the researched connections.

Activity: Fishbowl Discussion

Draw a question or a connection (the summaries) that students prepared from the fishbowl. You might want to let individual students run the fishbowl, so you can keep a running tab of participation. Discuss the essay through these questions and summaries. As you come to a summary, read aloud the critical information the student researched. Then allow students to comment on the summary. People/titles mentioned in the text about whom students might comment include the following:

- Kurt Cobain
- Puffy
- Mariah Carey
- Céline Dion
- Beyoncé
- James Brown
- Madonna
- Jackson 5
- Wilson Pickett
- Elvis Presley
- The Beatles
- Alice Cooper
- Ozzy Osbourne
- William Carlos Williams
- Rev. Al Sharpton
- Nat King Cole
- Sammy Davis, Jr.
- Sidney Poitier
- Harry Belafonte
- Sam Cooke
- Jimi Hendrix
- Arthur Ashe
- Michael Jordan
- Oprah Winfrey

- Tiger Woods
- Barack Obama
- Jackie Wilson
- The Temptations
- Fred Astaire
- Gene Kelly
- Bill (Bojangles) Robinson
- *The Wiz*
- Ray Bolger
- Big Joe Turner
- Jay-Z
- Emmett Till
- Toni Morrison
- *A Mercy*
- Ernest Hemingway
- Merce Cunningham
- Ray Charles
- Hank Williams
- Quincy Jones
- Tommy Mottola
- *Neverland*

Class Closer

Ask students to discuss whether or not society made too much of Michael Jackson. Who do they think, if anyone, was to blame for his early death?

Suggested Answers

"Finding Neverland" by David Gates

Comprehension

1. Summarize Gates's perception of Michael Jackson. How do you interpret the title? Why does Gates call Jackson an "artificer"? What does Gates mean by Jackson's "androgynous sexuality"?

Gates perceives Michael Jackson as a consummate artist, a master of reinvention, someone who never authentically knew himself, and an unforgettable personage. The title suggests finding a place of eternal youth and innocence, a place that does not exist; in the reference to death at the end of the essay, Jackson found his Neverland. Jackson was an "artificer," constantly changing his persona and creating appearances. Jackson also did not clearly exhibit either a masculine or a feminine sexuality.

2. Gates alludes to many stars from the world of music, dance, literature, and the arts. Which celebrities can you identify? What is Gates's purpose in listing so many of them?

Answers will vary. Young students may not know many of these allusions. Gates wants to show that Jackson had wide-ranging connections to many cultural art forms in the twentieth and twenty-first centuries; parts of each of the figures named can be seen in Jackson.

3. What, in Gates's opinion, is Michael Jackson's legacy?

Jackson's legacy is an unforgettable person whose combination of artistic talent and sense of creative reinventiveness remains unsurpassed.

Rhetorical Analysis

4. Does this essay have an explicitly stated thesis? If so, where is it? If the thesis is implied, paraphrase it.

An explicit thesis statement could be the last sentence—actually a question—of the first paragraph. An implied thesis could include the idea of a tribute to Jackson's life, or the idea that this most publicly recognized figure was unknown even to himself.

5. **The first paragraph of this essay is quite long. What is Gates's strategy and purpose here? Does this lengthy opening paragraph weaken or strengthen the body of the essay? Explain.**

   The first paragraph introduces many of the topics the essay will discuss: the iconic pop star, the subject of artifice, the androgynous sexuality, and the creative musician and performer. It also introduces Gates's style of writing. All these factors serve to strengthen the essay.

6. **Identify and comment on Gates's use of figurative language in this essay. How does figurative language—and Gates's overall style—influence the essay's tone?**

   Gates uses simile and metaphor effectively, saying Jackson looked like a vampire and mummy, or describing Jackson's dangling his son off the balcony as a ritualized attempt to dispose of his younger self, or calling Jackson a chameleon. With his lists of allusions, Gates creates a dense, intertextual style and an energetic tone.

7. **What comparative points does Gates make about Jackson and other artists? How does the comparative method serve to organize the essay?**

   Jackson is like these artists in many ways, but in other ways not like them. For example, see the comparison to Elvis. Explaining similarities and differences gives substance and organization to the essay. This organization relates Jackson to many areas of American life.

8. **Explain the effect of the last paragraph, which resembles the introductory paragraph in length. Do you think this resemblance was intentional? Why or why not?**

   The similar length of the two paragraphs is not necessarily intentional. The concluding paragraph somewhat humanizes Jackson by listing the many problems he faced at the end of his life. It puts emphasis on Michael Jackson the human being rather than on his personas. It also celebrates his achievement as an artist.

Writing

9. **Write your own evaluation of Michael Jackson or another celebrity from the world of music, explaining why you think this artist's achievement is important.**

   There are many possibilities to explore here.

10. **Write a comparative essay in which you discuss two artists from the world of music, film, or television.**

    The comparison should, of course, make a valid point.

11. **Writing an Argument** **Argue for or against the proposition that the media makes too much of the deaths or lives of prominent celebrities.**

    This is a good topic for students interested in eventually majoring in communications and media. Some research would help to strengthen this paper.

Lesson Plan 9.5

Hughes's "Theme for English B"—TPCASTT

Class Opener

Ask students to write a short poem about English class. Give them 5–10 minutes to compose the poem, either in their groups or individually. Share and discuss their poems.

Activity: TPCASTT

While AP English Language teachers utilize SOAPSTone for teaching basic rhetorical analysis, AP English Literature teachers utilize TPCASTT as a framework for analyzing poetry. Although not much poetry is studied in AP English Language class, this is an excellent opportunity to introduce students to this strategy. The strategy also provides an excellent framework for analyzing this particular poem, which discusses taking a college English course.

First, explain the acronym TPCASTT to students:

TPCASTT	
T—Title	Before reading the poem, predict what you think it will be about based only on the title.
P—Paraphrase	Paraphrase the poem in your own words, looking only at the literal meaning of the words. (Do not look for additional meaning at this point.) This is an on-the-line reading.
C—Connotation	Look for deeper meaning. Consider all of the literary and rhetorical tools used by the writer. Look for details and imagery, figurative language (simile, metaphor, personification, etc.), diction, and sound devices (alliteration, onomatopoeia, rhythm, meter, and rhyme).
A—Attitude	Similar to the use of tone in SOAPStone, look for the attitude of the author toward the subject.
S—Shifts	Where are shifts in the poem? What are these shifts?
T—Title	Having analyzed the poem, revisit the title. Do you agree with your original interpretation?
T—Theme	What does this poem have to say about the world and life? What universal truths are being addressed? What truth does the poet want to convey to the audience?

Now have students or groups apply TPCASTT to Langston Hughes's poem. Provide them with the chart on the next page, and have them fill in their responses. (Photocopy the chart, or see **Chapter 9 online, Langston Hughes: TPCASTT**.)

"Theme for English B" TPCASTT	
T—Title	
P—Paraphrase	
C—Connotation	
A—Attitude	
S—Shifts	
T—Title	
T—Theme	

Possible responses:

"Theme for English B" TPCASTT	
T—Title	The title of this poem is "Theme for English B." The word *Theme* in the title can mean one of two things. Either it refers to a paper that is assigned by a professor, or it refers to the overall idea of something. The words *English B* are also interesting. The author is referring either to the second half of the course (English A, then English B), or to a subgroup of students beneath those in English A.
P—Paraphrase	The poem is written in short, mostly clear thoughts. It is not easy to paraphrase without repeating some of the phrases Hughes writes. Below is a detailed paraphrase; it may be shorter and more concise. The teacher told us to write a page when we got home. If we wrote about what came to us, it was supposed to be true. Is writing that easy? I'm 22 years old. I am African American. I was born in Winston-Salem, where I went to school. I moved to Durham, then came here to Harlem to go to college. I'm the only African American student in my class. The college is on a hill, and to get to the room I live in at the Y, I go down the hill, through a park and down a couple of streets. After I got to the Y, I took the elevator to my room, and now I'm writing this page. It's not easy to know what is real and true when you are 22. I am what my senses tell me. I hear the city speaking to me. I am speaking to it. We are talking together on this page. I hear New York, too, not just Harlem. Who am I? I like eating, sleeping, drinking, being in love, working, reading, learning, and understanding life. When people give me gifts, I like pipes and all different kinds of records. I am African American, but I like the same things people of other races like. Is this page the same color as me? It won't be white because I am not white. It will be a part of the instructor, though, and the instructor is white. Even though you are white, we are still a part of each other. That is what it means to be American. We don't always want to be connected to each other, but we are. I will learn from you and you will learn from me, even though you are my senior and have more freedom than I have. This is my writing.

C—Connotation	In this poem, Hughes uses a number of double entendres. He intentionally lacks clarity. Why is the class English *B*? He never tells. He uses the word *theme* but does not clarify which meaning he intends. This double meaning continues with word choices such as "colored." Hughes describes himself as colored, but he also describes the paper as colored. He shifts point of view several times: beginning with third person (the instructor said), then first person (I), then second person (you). Notice the frequent use of dashes, suggesting the interrupted, free-flowing thought process of a student writing a "theme" for class. Harlem is personified as an adviser or a conversational friend.
A—Attitude	The persona in this poem seems to be jaded and somewhat cynical. He seems to question the authenticity of the assignment, and he doubts that what is "true" will come as easily as the instructor assumes. He seems to feel like an outsider in many ways—race, living arrangements, social standing. He seems discontent with the genuineness of the academic world in which he finds himself.
S—Shifts	Shifts include the shifts in point of view. The poem begins with a clear assignment, which is in italics to differentiate it as being someone else's words. The poem then shifts with a question to the nature of whether "it" is "that simple." The poet does not explain what "it" is. Is "it" writing? Is "it" truth? The poet then shifts to a simple accounting of facts. A listing of all the things that are unquestionably true—place of birth, age, status of being the only "colored" student in class, and location of residence. There is a shift within the listing: the mention of race does not seem to flow from the nice, orderly list of facts. The poet then shifts as he moves from a list of facts to a questioning, again, of knowing what is true. His statement at the beginning of the third stanza parallels the question that opens the second stanza and the claim that ends the first stanza. "It" appears again and the poet references the difficulty in knowing truth, especially at age 22. He then shifts with the word "but" (line 17) to a discussion and a series of implicit questions about how he should see himself, addressing Harlem through an apostrophe and adding that he hears New York, too. He then shifts again with the word "well" (line 21), describing himself not as the confidante of major cities and cultural epicenters, but instead as an everyman. He shifts again to deal with the issue of "colored" people, papers, and writing. He shifts again to address the instructor directly and to make a very political claim that being American means we are all part of each other. His final shift occurs after he makes his argument, as he simply ends by defining his "theme" as a "page" for English B.
T—Title	The title has more significance upon analysis. The title "Theme for English B" refers not just to a short paper being written for a class. Instead, the "theme" is the overall argument and point of view of the poet. It is a truth that he wants to impart to the instructor—that even though the instructor is older and of a different race, they are the same and they have much to learn from each other.
T—Theme	There are a number of topics and ideas to address. As with much of his poetry and prose, Hughes is concerned with issues of inequality. The theme of this poem is embodied in the title. The theme is that truth is an elusive quality. It is not something we obtain just by letting words flow onto a page. Instead, we find truth by recognizing our sameness and listening to what others have to say. We find truth in exploring the critical nature of what it means to be human, whether we are white and old or young and black.

Class Closer

Allow students or groups to share their TPCASTT analysis and to debate the overall theme of the poem.

Suggested Answers

"Theme for English B" by Langston Hughes

Comprehension

1. The writer experiences an inner struggle as he tries to respond to the instructor's directive. What is the crux of his internal struggle?

He struggles with the idea that his response to the instructor will not be heard, and he sees it as a cultural struggle because his "voice" is not one that is empowered.

2. Carefully looking at each word, explain what the title of the poem implies.

"Theme from English B" implies that there is an English A comprised of intellectually brighter students.

3. In line 27, when the writer asks "will my page be colored that I write?", what is he really asking of his white instructor?

He is asking if the fact that he is African American will somehow affect what his white instructor reads. He questions if his instructor can ignore the skin color and the cultural implications that go with it when he replies to the writer's response.

Rhetorical Analysis

4. Lines 38–40 before the last declaration "This is my page for English B" deliberately slows down the pace of the poem through the use of dashes. Why do the words become more deliberate and slow?

The writer begins the stanza speaking in a matter-of-fact manner, but the dashes convey a shift in the writer's emotions as he honestly states the true differences between his instructor and him.

5. An apparently complicated connection exists between Harlem, the area of New York City where the writer feels most comfortable, and New York City itself. How does he personalize this connection?

The writer connects with Harlem because it embodied African American culture. Belonging to the city of New York is a more difficult personal acknowledgement for the writer, but he shows (through parentheses) that he "hears New York too." This choice in syntax provides a recognition of his right to feel like a New Yorker, even though he states this somewhat reluctantly, implying that he is hesitant to cross cultural boundaries.

6. What is the desired effect of the rhetorical question in line 6, "I wonder if it's that simple"? Examine the diction used in the question and Hughes's responses to the question.

The speaker poses this rhetorical question to the assignment that asks him to write a "page" that needs to come "out of [him]" which will make "it true." Hughes takes issue with this by pointing out the cultural insinuations that these words project. Hughes sees that this assignment is really not that simple, given the culturally diverse divisions that exist between his instructor and him.

Writing

7. **Describe an assignment that you have written in an extremely truthful manner. What caused you to be honest with yourself and others?**

   Student responses will vary.

8. **Writing an Argument** Argue for or against separating students into different levels of classes at school (gifted, regular, basic).

   Student responses will vary.

Lesson Plan 9.6

Poe's "The Raven" and "The Philosophy Of Composition"

Class Opener

The "meat" of this lesson is not Poe's poem "The Raven," but rather his commentary "The Philosophy of Composition" about his poem. Write the acronym TPCASTT vertically on the board. Read the poem together at the beginning of class. Do a quick version of TPCASTT to ensure comprehension.

Activity: The Poet as Critic

This pairing of poem and essay is unique in that Poe, who wrote as a critic, actually describes the writing of this poem with a critic's alacrity for detail. Students should read and annotate Poe's essay, reading it in terms of the TPCASTT analysis they performed of the poem. This is a complicated essay, and it is an excellent opportunity to teach pre-20th century nonfiction to students. The annotations here following each numbered paragraph will help you take your students step-by-step through an analysis of the essay:

> [1]CHARLES DICKENS, in a note now lying before me, alluding to an examination I once made of the mechanism of *Barnaby Rudge,* says—"By the way, are you aware that Godwin wrote his *Caleb Williams* backwards? He first involved his hero in a web of difficulties, forming the second volume, and then, for the first, cast about him for some mode of accounting for what had been done."

Above, Poe, in alluding to Dickens, is referring to an enormously successful author who made much more money than Poe himself did. AP Language students should immediately see this as an appeal to ethos and question Poe's motivation for starting in such a way. Poe is placing himself in league with Godwin and Dickens, and as part of a literary field that is incredibly well-respected.

> [2]I cannot think this the *precise* mode of procedure on the part of Godwin—and indeed what he himself acknowledges, is not altogether in accordance with Mr. Dickens' idea—but the author of *Caleb Williams* was too good an artist not to perceive the advantage derivable from at least a somewhat similar process. Nothing is more clear than that every plot, worth the name, must be elaborated to its *dénouement* before anything be attempted with the pen. It is only with the *dénouement* constantly in view that we can give a plot its indispensable air of consequence, or causation, by making the incidents, and especially the tone at all points, tend to the development of the intention.

Paragraph 2 opens with a difficult, convoluted sentence. Ask students to break it into pieces. (a) Poe denies the veracity of Dickens' claim. (b) Poe appeals to a reading of Godwin to dispute Dickens. Again, students should ask themselves why? Why does

Poe open this essay with a discrediting of Dickens? Why mention Dickens at all? (c) Although the facts are not exactly as claimed, there still would be an advantage in this sort of backwards crafting.

Poe's words "Nothing is more clear" make up an argument. Of course there are things that are "more clear," but here Poe is implying the agreement of the audience in order to guarantee it. Poe's claim, then, is that before an author can write anything, that author must know every event that will happen within the text. Poe's focus on the denouement demands that writing always be accomplished with the absolute end in focus.

> [3]There is a radical error, I think, in the usual mode of constructing a story. Either history affords a thesis—or one is suggested by an incident of the day—or, at best, the author sets himself to work in the combination of striking events to form merely the basis of his narrative—designing, generally, to fill in with description, dialogue, or autorial comment, whatever crevices of fact, or action, may, from page to page, render themselves apparent.

In paragraph 3, Poe claims that the way that writing is typically conducted is radically wrong—assuming, then, that *his* way is radically right and radically different from the norm. Poe argues that traditional writing involves beginning with a thesis in mind and then filling in the details, rather than beginning with an ending in mind and constructing a realistic way to get there. Ask students what they think of this. As teachers, we tell them to start with a thesis.

> [4]I prefer commencing with the consideration of an *effect*. Keeping originality *always* in View—for he is false to himself who ventures to dispense with so obvious and so easily attainable a source of interest—I say to myself, in the first place, "Of the innumerable effects, or impressions, of which the heart, the intellect, or (more generally) the soul is susceptible, what one shall I, on the present occasion, select?" Having chosen a novel, first, and secondly a vivid effect, I consider whether it can be best wrought by incident or tone—whether by ordinary incidents and peculiar tone, or the converse, or by peculiarity both of incident and tone—afterward looking about me (or rather within) for such combinations of event, or tone, as shall best aid me in the construction of the effect.

Paragraph 4 is the key to Poe's philosophy of composition, and it is indeed what we want our students to walk away with. The "effect" is all-important. This is important for students to pay attention to. Many times students believe that English teachers are imagining the thought that goes into good writing. And yet here is one of the greatest writers of all time describing exactly what we teach: he considers the effect and the combination of event and tone in order to write.

> [5]I have often thought how interesting a magazine paper might be written by any author who would—that is to say, who could—detail, step by step, the processes by which any one of his compositions attained its ultimate point of completion. Why such a paper has never been given to the world, I am much at a loss to say—but, perhaps, the autorial vanity has had more to do with the omission than any one other cause. Most writers—poets in especial—prefer having it understood that they compose by a species of fine frenzy—an ecstatic intuition—and would positively shudder at letting the public take a peep behind the scenes, at the elaborate and vacillating crudities of thought—at the true purposes seized only at the last moment—at the innumerable glimpses of idea that arrived not at the maturity of full view—at the fully matured fancies discarded in despair as unmanageable—at the cautious selections and rejections—at the painful erasures and interpolations—in a word, at the wheels and pinions—the tackle for scene-shifting—the step-ladders and demon-traps—the cock's feathers, the red paint and the black patches, which, in ninety-nine cases out of the hundred, constitute the properties of the literary *histrio*.

In paragraph 5, Poe moves blatantly beyond ethos and oversteps into a tone of arrogance. He is claiming that he is able to do something beyond what others have done. Even though the tone seems arrogant, he is right. However, students need to consider why he feels the need to build up for so long. He seems to spend an inordinate amount of time building, but perhaps consider—doesn't he do the same thing in order to build suspense in his short stories? Is this simply a characteristic of Poe's writing? Consider, too, Poe's use of dashes. Why so many? What is the effect? What is the effect of providing so many details? Does the writing process seem more lively by describing it in terms of "step-ladders and demon-traps"?

> 6I am aware, on the other hand, that the case is by no means common, in which an author is at all in condition to retrace the steps by which his conclusions have been attained. In general, suggestions, having arisen pell-mell, are pursued and forgotten in a similar manner.

Here, Poe's arrogance is again made clear. He claims and seems to believe that his writing process is more authentic than that of others. Is this a valid claim or is it hubris?

> 7For my own part, I have neither sympathy with the repugnance alluded to, nor, at any time, the least difficulty in recalling to mind the progressive steps of any of my compositions; and, since the interest of an analysis, or reconstruction, such as I have considered a *desideratum,* is quite independent of any real or fancied interest in the thing analyzed, it will not be regarded as a breach of decorum on my part to show the *modus operandi* by which some one of my own works was put together. I select "The Raven," as the most generally known. It is my design to render it manifest that no one point in its composition is referable either to accident or intuition—that the work proceeded, step by step, to its completion with the precision and rigid consequence of a mathematical problem.

Ask students to paraphrase the very long first sentence in paragraph 7. What he is essentially saying is that he is better than other writers, as he has the ability to remember his entire writing process and he has no problem with sharing his process by way of this essay. What comparison does he make in the last sentence? (He compares writing "The Raven" to a mathematical problem. Mathematics is the only pure science with absolute answers.) What do students think about comparing poetry and math? Are they analogous?

> 8Let us dismiss, as irrelevant to the poem, *per se,* the circumstance—or say the necessity—which, in the first place, gave rise to the intention of composing *a* poem that should suit at once the popular and the critical taste.

In other words, Poe is saying in paragraph 8: Don't ask me about writing for money! Is this a legitimate argument on his part?

> 9We commence, then, with this intention.
>
> 10The initial consideration was that of extent. If any literary work is too long to be read at one sitting, we must be content to dispense with the immensely important effect derivable from unity of impression—for, if two sittings be required, the affairs of the world interfere, and everything like totality is at once destroyed. But since, *ceteris paribus,* no poet can afford to dispense with *anything* that may advance his design, it but remains to be seen whether there is, in extent, any advantage to counterbalance the loss of unity which attends it. Here I say no, at once. What we term a long poem is, in fact, merely a succession of brief ones—that is to say, of brief poetical effects. It is needless to demonstrate that a poem is such, only inasmuch as it intensely excites, by elevating, the soul; and all intense excitements are, through a psychal necessity, brief. For this reason, at least one-half of the *Paradise Lost* is essentially prose—a succession of poetical excitements interspersed, *inevitably,* with corresponding depressions—the whole being deprived, through the extremeness of its length, of the vastly important artistic element, totality, or unity, of effect.

Claim one: A literary work should be read at one sitting. Ask students if they believe Poe believed this or if he was just incapable of writing a novel. Why does he believe you must be able to read literature in one sitting? *(He is concerned with the "unity of impression"—in other words, it should all work together at one time for the reader. There should not be a chance to forget what one has read.)*

[11]It appears evident, then, that there is a distinct limit, as regards length, to all works of literary art—the limit of a single sitting—and that, although in certain classes of prose composition, such as "Robinson Crusoe" (demanding no unity), this limit may be advantageously overpassed, it can never properly be overpassed in a poem. Within this limit, the extent of a poem may be made to bear mathematical relation to its merit—in other words, to the excitement or elevation—again, in other words, to the degree of the true poetical effect which it is capable of inducing; for it is clear that the brevity must be in direct ratio of the intensity of the intended effect—this, with one proviso—that a certain degree of duration is absolutely requisite for the production of any effect at all.

Why does *Robinson Crusoe* not require the same unity as other works of literature? Is Poe claiming that it has no art? What do students think?

[12]Holding in view these considerations, as well as that degree of excitement which I deemed not above the popular, while not below the critical taste, I reached at once what I conceived the proper length for my intended poem—a length of about one hundred lines. It is, in fact, a hundred and eight.

What length does Poe decide a poem should be? *(100 lines or so)* Why? *(To guarantee this unity of impression)*

[13]My next thought concerned the choice of an impression, or effect, to be conveyed: and here I may as well observe that throughout the construction, I kept steadily in view the design of rendering the work universally appreciable. I should be carried too far out of my immediate topic were I to demonstrate a point upon which I have repeatedly insisted, and which, with the poetical, stands not in the slightest need of demonstration—the point, I mean, that Beauty is the sole legitimate province of the poem. A few words, however, in elucidation of my real meaning, which some of my friends have evinced a disposition to misrepresent. That pleasure which is at once the most intense, the most elevating, and the most pure is, I believe, found in the contemplation of the beautiful. When, indeed, men speak of Beauty, they mean, precisely, not a quality, as is supposed, but an effect—they refer, in short, just to that intense and pure elevation of soul—not of intellect, or of heart—upon which I have commented, and which is experienced in consequence of contemplating the "beautiful." Now I designate Beauty as the province of the poem, merely because it is an obvious rule of Art that effects should be made to spring from direct causes—that objects should be attained through means best adapted for their attainment—no one as yet having been weak enough to deny that the peculiar elevation alluded to is most readily attained in the poem. Now the object Truth, or the satisfaction of the intellect, and the object Passion, or the excitement of the heart, are, although attainable to a certain extent in poetry, far more readily attainable in prose. Truth, in fact, demands a precision, and Passion, a homeliness (the truly passionate will comprehend me), which are absolutely antagonistic to that Beauty which, I maintain, is the excitement or pleasurable elevation of the soul. It by no means follows, from anything here said, that passion, or even truth, may not be introduced, and even profitably introduced, into a poem for they may serve in elucidation, or aid the general effect, as do discords in music, by contrast—but the true artist will always contrive, first, to tone them into proper subservience to the predominant aim, and, secondly, to enveil them, as far as possible, in that Beauty which is the atmosphere and the essence of the poem.

Sample questions for paragraph 13: Can a work of fiction be "universally appreciable"? Note that the word *appreciable* does not mean universally liked. It seems that Poe did indeed accomplish this goal.

Poe claims that "Beauty is the sole legitimate province of the poem." This is a famous claim. Do students agree? Is there "Beauty" (note its capitalization) in a poem like "The Raven"?

What is Beauty? Poe claims that it is not a quality but an effect—"an intense and pure elevation of the soul."

Poe claims that it is an "obvious rule of Art that effects should be made to spring from direct causes—that objects should be attained through means best adapted for their attainment." Is this an obvious effect of art? Discuss this with students. What is art?

Poe continues to define terms that the audience is well acquainted with. This is a strong rhetorical position. Whenever an author attempts to redefine our view of something we know (think in terms of what a family is), they are revising our world view. Here, Poe claims that Truth is "the satisfaction of the intellect" and Passion is "the excitement of the heart." While we might readily agree with his definition of Passion, Truth is not so easily defined.

Poe goes on to connect Truth to precision, and passion to homeliness. What do students think of these definitions? How might they define these terms? Is Poe on to something, or is he losing his audience here?

> [14]Regarding, then, Beauty as my province, my next question referred to the tone of its highest manifestation—and all experience has shown that this tone is one of sadness. Beauty of whatever kind in its supreme development invariably excites the sensitive soul to tears. Melancholy is thus the most legitimate of all the poetical tones.

Above, Poe argues eloquently that Beauty and melancholy are connected. Is his logic sound? What other tones might students argue belong in the province of poetry?

> [15]The length, the province, and the tone, being thus determined, I betook myself to ordinary induction, with the view of obtaining some artistic piquancy which might serve me as a key-note in the construction of the poem—some pivot upon which the whole structure might turn. In carefully thinking over all the usual artistic effects—or more properly points, in the theatrical sense—I did not fail to perceive immediately that no one had been so universally employed as that of the refrain. The universality of its employment sufficed to assure me of its intrinsic value, and spared me the necessity of submitting it to analysis. I considered it, however, with regard to its susceptibility of improvement, and soon saw it to be in a primitive condition. As commonly used, the refrain, or burden, not only is limited to lyric verse, but depends for its impression upon the force of monotone—both in sound and thought. The pleasure is deduced solely from the sense of identity—of repetition. I resolved to diversify, and so heighten the effect, by adhering in general to the monotone of sound, while I continually varied that of thought: that is to say, I determined to produce continuously novel effects, by the variation of the application of the refrain—the refrain itself remaining for the most part, unvaried.

What does Poe claim he contrived first in writing "The Raven? *(the refrain)* Poe argues that the monotone and repetition are key to the effect.

> [16]These points being settled, I next bethought me of the nature of my refrain. Since its application was to be repeatedly varied it was clear that the refrain itself must be brief, for there would have been an insurmountable difficulty in frequent variations of application in any sentence of length. In proportion to the brevity of the sentence would, of course, be the facility of the variation. This led me at once to a single word as the best refrain.

What does Poe decide about his refrain? *(It should be a single word so that he can offer frequent variations upon it.)*

> [17]The question now arose as to the character of the word. Having made up my mind to a refrain, the division of the poem into stanzas was of course a corollary, the refrain forming the close to each stanza. That such a close, to have force, must be sonorous and susceptible of protracted emphasis, admitted no doubt, and these considerations inevitably led me to the long o as the most sonorous vowel in connection with r as the most producible consonant.

In paragraph 17, Poe discusses the intentional uses of a sound device—the long "o" connected to an "r." Students frequently doubt that sound devices appear in poems at the intention of the author. Poe clearly argues that he chose the word "nevermore" with that end in mind.

> [18]The sound of the refrain being thus determined, it became necessary to select a word embodying this sound, and at the same time in the fullest possible keeping with that melancholy which I had pre-determined as the tone of the poem. In such a search it would have been absolutely impossible to overlook the word "Nevermore." In fact it was the very first which presented itself.

Poe claims above that the word "nevermore" was impossible to ignore. At this point, the essay starts to seem a bit unbelievable. Ask students if they believe Poe is telling the complete "truth"—at least in the way he defines it.

> [19]The next desideratum was a pretext for the continuous use of the one word "nevermore." In observing the difficulty which I had at once found in inventing a sufficiently plausible reason for its continuous repetition, I did not fail to perceive that this difficulty arose solely from the preassumption that the word was to be so continuously or monotonously spoken by a human being—I did not fail to perceive, in short, that the difficulty lay in the reconciliation of this monotony with the exercise of reason on the part of the creature repeating the word. Here, then, immediately arose the idea of a non-reasoning creature capable of speech, and very naturally, a parrot, in the first instance, suggested itself, but was superseded forthwith by a Raven as equally capable of speech, and infinitely more in keeping with the intended tone.

> [20]I had now gone so far as the conception of a Raven, the bird of ill-omen, monotonously repeating the one word "Nevermore" at the conclusion of each stanza in a poem of melancholy tone, and in length about one hundred lines. Now, never losing sight of the object—supremeness or perfection at all points, I asked myself—"Of all melancholy topics what, according to the universal understanding of mankind, is the most melancholy?" Death, was the obvious reply. "And when," I said, "is this most melancholy of topics most poetical?" From what I have already explained at some length the answer here also is obvious—"When it most closely allies itself to Beauty: the death then of a beautiful woman is unquestionably the most poetical topic in the world, and equally is it beyond doubt that the lips best suited for such topic are those of a bereaved lover."

What is the effect of Poe quoting himself in paragraph 20? Does the information seem more precise because of the quoted material? Remember his definition of truth as involving intellectual curiosity and precision.

> [21]I had now to combine the two ideas of a lover lamenting his deceased mistress and a Raven continuously repeating the word "Nevermore." I had to combine these, bearing in mind my design of varying at every turn the application of the word repeated, but the only intelligible mode of such combination is that of imagining the Raven employing the word in answer to the queries of the lover. And here it was that I saw at once the opportunity afforded for the effect on which I had been depending, that is to say, the effect of the variation of application. I saw that I could make the first query propounded by the lover—the first query to which the Raven should reply "Nevermore"—that I could make this first query a commonplace one, the second less so, the third still less, and so on, until at length the lover, startled from his original nonchalance by the melancholy character of the word itself, by its frequent repetition, and by a consideration of the ominous reputation of the fowl that uttered it, is at length excited to superstition, and wildly propounds queries of a far different character—queries whose solution he has passionately at heart—propounds them half in superstition and half in that species of despair which delights in self-torture—propounds them not altogether because he believes in the prophetic or demoniac character of the bird (which reason assures him is merely repeating a lesson learned by rote), but because he experiences a frenzied pleasure in so modelling his questions as to receive from the expected "Nevermore" the most delicious because the most intolerable of sorrows. Perceiving the opportunity thus afforded me, or, more strictly, thus forced upon me in the progress of the construction, I first established in my mind the climax or concluding query—that query to which "Nevermore" should be in the last place an answer—that query in reply to which this word "Nevermore" should involve the utmost conceivable amount of sorrow and despair.

In paragraph 21, Poe almost rewrites the poem in prose form, using long sentences, and trying to capture the essence of the poem. Does he succeed? What is the effect of the sentence length? What is the effect of Poe's correcting or clarifying himself?

[22]Here then the poem may be said to have had its beginning—at the end where all works of art should begin—for it was here at this point of my preconsiderations that I first put pen to paper in the composition of the stanza:

"Prophet!" said I, "thing of evil! prophet still if bird or devil!
By that Heaven that bends above us—by that God we both adore,
Tell this soul with sorrow laden, if, within the distant Aidenn,
It shall clasp a sainted maiden whom the angels name Lenore—
Clasp a rare and radiant maiden whom the angels name Lenore."
Quoth the Raven—"Nevermore."

According to Poe in paragraph 22, where should all works of art begin? *(at the ending)*

[23]I composed this stanza, at this point, first that, by establishing the climax, I might the better vary and graduate, as regards seriousness and importance, the preceding queries of the lover, and secondly, that I might definitely settle the rhythm, the metre, and the length and general arrangement of the stanza, as well as graduate the stanzas which were to precede, so that none of them might surpass this in rhythmical effect. Had I been able in the subsequent composition to construct more vigorous stanzas I should without scruple have purposely enfeebled them so as not to interfere with the climacteric effect.

Why does Poe write the last stanza first? *(so that by starting with the climax, he can better build to it, insuring its potency)*

[24]And here I may as well say a few words of the versification. My first object (as usual) was originality. The extent to which this has been neglected in versification is one of the most unaccountable things in the world. Admitting that there is little possibility of variety in mere rhythm, it is still clear that the possible varieties of metre and stanza are absolutely infinite, and yet, for centuries, no man, in verse, has ever done, or ever seemed to think of doing, an original thing. The fact is that originality (unless in minds of very unusual force) is by no means a matter, as some suppose, of impulse or intuition. In general, to be found, it must be elaborately sought, and although a positive merit of the highest class, demands in its attainment less of invention than negation.

Poe breaks his stride in paragraph 24 to speak more as a literary critic, focusing his discussion on versification. What is his complaint? *(that poets lack originality in versification where it should be readily sought)*

[25]Of course I pretend to no originality in either the rhythm or metre of the "Raven." The former is trochaic—the latter is octametre acatalectic, alternating with heptametre catalectic repeated in the refrain of the fifth verse, and terminating with tetrametre catalectic. Less pedantically the feet employed throughout (trochees) consist of a long syllable followed by a short, the first line of the stanza consists of eight of these feet, the second of seven and a half (in effect two-thirds), the third of eight, the fourth of seven and a half, the fifth the same, the sixth three and a half. Now, each of these lines taken individually has been employed before, and what originality the "Raven" has, is in their combination into stanza; nothing even remotely approaching this has ever been attempted. The effect of this originality of combination is aided by other unusual and some altogether novel effects, arising from an extension of the application of the principles of rhyme and alliteration.

What is ironic about Poe's claim in paragraph 25 that there is nothing original about the meter of the poem? *(He is being rather pedantic here. His meter may be definable, as he here defines it, but it is certainly original. A sonnet is unoriginal. This odd mixture of rhythm and meter is certainly original.)* In claiming a lack of originality, Poe underscores how truly remarkable the planned versification of "The Raven" is.

[26]The next point to be considered was the mode of bringing together the lover and the Raven—and the first branch of this consideration was the locale. For this the most natural suggestion might seem to be a forest, or the fields—but it has always appeared to me that a close circumscription of space is absolutely necessary to the effect of insulated incident—it has the force of a frame to a picture. It has an indisputable moral power in keeping concentrated the attention, and, of course, must not be confounded with mere unity of place.

What is Poe's major consideration for the raven and the lover? *(how to bring them together)* Why does he not choose a natural location, such as a forest or fields? (*He claims to want a smaller space.*)

[27]I determined, then, to place the lover in his chamber—in a chamber rendered sacred to him by memories of her who had frequented it. The room is represented as richly furnished—this in mere pursuance of the ideas I have already explained on the subject of Beauty, as the sole true poetical thesis.

Poe has much less to say about setting. Why does setting seem less important to him?

[28]The locale being thus determined, I had now to introduce the bird—and the thought of introducing him through the window was inevitable. The idea of making the lover suppose, in the first instance, that the flapping of the wings of the bird against the shutter, is a "tapping" at the door, originated in a wish to increase, by prolonging, the reader's curiosity, and in a desire to admit the incidental effect arising from the lover's throwing open the door, finding all dark, and thence adopting the half-fancy that it was the spirit of his mistress that knocked.

How does Poe insinuate suspense in the poem? *(He describes the bird's tapping on the door.)*

[29]I made the night tempestuous, first to account for the Raven's seeking admission, and secondly, for the effect of contrast with the (physical) serenity within the chamber.

What contrast does Poe describe in paragraph 29? *(the tempestuous night and the serenity of the chamber)*

[30]I made the bird alight on the bust of Pallas, also for the effect of contrast between the marble and the plumage—it being understood that the bust was absolutely suggested by the bird—the bust of Pallas being chosen, first, as most in keeping with the scholarship of the lover, and secondly, for the sonorousness of the word, Pallas, itself.

Why did the bird land on a bust of Pallas, as opposed to some other bust? Again, Poe claims that he was interested in the sound device as much as in the symbolism Pallas connoted.

[31]About the middle of the poem, also, I have availed myself of the force of contrast, with a view of deepening the ultimate impression. For example, an air of the fantastic—approaching as nearly to the ludicrous as was admissible—is given to the Raven's entrance. He comes in "with many a flirt and flutter."
Not the least obeisance made he—not a moment stopped or stayed he,
But with mien of lord or lady, perched above my chamber door.

The argument seems to lose focus in paragraph 31. Poe claims use of another contrast, but he is unclear in defining that contrast. He claims a contrast between "flirt and flutter" and presumably the persona of the lover. Why does he not clearly define the contrast? What is the effect in this essay?

[32]In the two stanzas which follow, the design is more obviously carried out:—

Then this ebony bird, beguiling my sad fancy into smiling
By the grave and stern decorum of the countenance it wore,
"Though thy crest be shorn and shaven, thou," I said, "art sure no craven,
Ghastly grim and ancient Raven wandering from the Nightly shore—
Tell me what thy lordly name is on the Night's Plutonian shore?"
Quoth the Raven—"Nevermore."

Much I marvelled this ungainly fowl to hear discourse so plainly,
Though its answer little meaning—little relevancy bore;
For we cannot help agreeing that no living human being
Ever yet was blessed with seeing bird above his chamber door—
Bird or beast upon the sculptured bust above his chamber door,
With such name as "Nevermore."

33The effect of the *denouement* being thus provided for, I immediately drop the fantastic for a tone of the most profound seriousness—this tone commencing in the stanza directly following the one last quoted, with the line,

But the Raven, sitting lonely on that placid bust, spoke only, etc.

Poe seems overtly conscious of the shifts in tone in the poem. Review the shifts we have identified in this essay. Is he as conscious of those shifts?

34From this epoch the lover no longer jests—no longer sees anything even of the fantastic in the Raven's demeanour. He speaks of him as a "grim, ungainly, ghastly, gaunt, and ominous bird of yore," and feels the "fiery eyes" burning into his "bosom's core." This revolution of thought, or fancy, on the lover's part, is intended to induce a similar one on the part of the reader—to bring the mind into a proper frame for the *denouement*—which is now brought about as rapidly and as directly as possible.

At this point, Poe quotes himself, identifying an obvious sound device—the g's in "grim, ungainly, ghastly, gaunt." However, for once, he does not describe his intentional use of the sound device. Why? Has he already so firmly established his use of sound device that he does not need to mention it again? Note that this omission parallels his claim that he moves rapidly to the denouement. Is he moving rapidly to the denouement in this essay as well? So rapidly that he is neglecting key points?

35With the *denouement* proper—with the Raven's reply, "Nevermore," to the lover's final demand if he shall meet his mistress in another world—the poem, in its obvious phase, that of a simple narrative, may be said to have its completion. So far, everything is within the limits of the accountable—of the real. A raven, having learned by rote the single word "Nevermore," and having escaped from the custody of its owner, is driven at midnight, through the violence of a storm, to seek admission at a window from which a light still gleams—the chamber-window of a student, occupied half in poring over a volume, half in dreaming of a beloved mistress deceased. The casement being thrown open at the fluttering of the bird's wings, the bird itself perches on the most convenient seat out of the immediate reach of the student, who amused by the incident and the oddity of the visitor's demeanour, demands of it, in jest and without looking for a reply, its name. The raven addressed, answers with its customary word, "Nevermore"—a word which finds immediate echo in the melancholy heart of the student, who, giving utterance aloud to certain thoughts suggested by the occasion, is again startled by the fowl's repetition of "Nevermore." The student now guesses the state of the case, but is impelled, as I have before explained, by the human thirst for self-torture, and in part by superstition, to propound such queries to the bird as will bring him, the lover, the most of the luxury of sorrow, through the anticipated answer, "Nevermore." With the indulgence, to the extreme, of this self-torture, the narration, in what I have termed its first or obvious phase, has a natural termination, and so far there has been no overstepping of the limits of the real.

In paragraph 35, Poe describes the conclusion of the poem, adding details. Do these details simply inform the reader as to the rest of what was on the author's mind? Or is Poe adding meaning to the poem, which we should glean from a straightforward read?

36But in subjects so handled, however skillfully, or with however vivid an array of incident, there is always a certain hardness or nakedness which repels the artistical eye. Two things are invariably required—first, some amount of complexity, or more properly, adaptation; and, secondly, some amount of suggestiveness—some under-current, however indefinite, of meaning. It is this latter, in especial, which imparts to a work of art so much of that richness (to borrow from colloquy a forcible term), which we are too fond of confounding with the ideal. It is the excess of the suggested meaning—it is the rendering this the upper instead of the under-current of the theme—which turns into prose (and that of the very flattest kind), the so-called poetry of the so-called transcendentalists.

What are Poe's stated aims in paragraph 36? *(complexity and suggestiveness)* Does he accomplish both? Why does he refer to the "so-called poetry of the so-called transcendentalists"? *(Poe seemed to be jealous of the intellectual and academic fervor for their work.)*

> [37]Holding these opinions, I added the two concluding stanzas of the poem—their suggestiveness being thus made to pervade all the narrative which has preceded them. The under-current of meaning is rendered first apparent in the line—
>
> "Take thy beak from out my heart, and take thy form from off my door!"
> Quoth the Raven "Nevermore!"

In paragraph 37, Poe feels the need to show his reader where the suggestiveness and complexity exist in the poem. He claims to have added the concluding stanzas for clarification. Does he need to point this out? What is the effect of including this stanza after criticizing the transcendentalists?

> [38]It will be observed that the words, "from out my heart," involve the first metaphorical expression in the poem. They, with the answer, "Nevermore," dispose the mind to seek a moral in all that has been previously narrated. The reader begins now to regard the Raven as emblematical—but it is not until the very last line of the very last stanza that the intention of making him emblematical of Mournful and never ending Remembrance is permitted distinctly to be seen:
>
> And the Raven, never flitting, still is sitting, still is sitting,
> On the pallid bust of Pallas just above my chamber door;
> And his eyes have all the seeming of a demon that is dreaming,
> And the lamplight o'er him streaming throws his shadow on the floor;
> And my soul from out that shadow that lies floating on the floor
> Shall be lifted—nevermore.

Poe does not really seem to tie up the loose ends of this essay, instead ending it by quoting himself. What is the effect of the ending? Because Poe has claimed that a writer must begin with the ending in mind, it would seem that the ending should be the strongest part of this essay. Is it? Why or why not? *(The ending is decidedly weak. Poe seems to assume that he has done such a fine job earlier in the essay that the essay and the poem can end in the same manner. This seems to weaken his earlier argument.)*

Class Closer

If you have the technology available in your classroom, show the version of "The Raven" that appears on *The Simpsons.* The students love it, and it's a fun way to end this lesson.

Suggested Answers

"The Raven" and "The Philosophy of Composition" by Edgar Allen Poe

The Poetical Works of Edgar Allen Poe, Together With His Essay on the Philosophy of Composition, **with introduction and notes by M.A Eaton, B.A. Copyrighted by Educational Publishing Company, 1906.**

Comprehension

1. In his essay "The Philosophy of Composition" what does Poe stress about reading a poem? How does this belief affect the length of "The Raven"?

Poe kept the poem to 108 lines because he believed the length of a poem should always insure that it could be read in one sitting.

2. What factors influenced Poe to choose a raven as the messenger in the chamber?

Poe first determined that he wanted his messenger of doom to utter only the single word "Nevermore." He chose a raven because ravens actually have the ability of repeating words and phrases, even if the words themselves seem nonsensical. Also a raven is black and symbolizes dark forebodings.

3. Explain the circumstances that lead the raven to arrive at the dwelling.

It is by chance, critical to Poe's belief that coincidence must occur in composition. The raven has escaped its owner and, driven by the storm, finds a safe haven in the lighted chamber.

4. Knowing that Pallas is the goddess of wisdom, discuss how Pallas affects the speaker's interpretation of the raven's response.

Sitting on the goddess of wisdom is yet another "sign" to the speaker that the raven has knowledgeable answers to his disconcerting questions. The speaker interprets far more into where the raven has placed itself than should actually be warranted. Pallas is the goddess of wisdom and is yet another delusional "sign" that the raven speaks the truth.

Rhetorical Analysis

5. One of the rhetorical hallmarks of "The Raven" is the effect of its diction, repetition, and alliteration. Explain the connotation of the words that lend themselves to this effect.

The use of "midnight" in the first verse, and "December" in the second symbolize endings. The location of the man in a solitary chamber emphasizes his loneliness as he bemoans his lost Lenore. The storm rages outside and mirrors the storm that permeates within the man. The raven, a symbol for the narrator's "Mournful and never-ending remembrance," continues to repeat the word "Nevermore" that further embeds the narrator's sense of isolation and despair. The alliterative effect also captures the reader's imagination. Using phrases such as "grim, ungainly, ghastly, gaunt, and ominous bird of yore" (one that Poe actually points out in "The Philosophy of Composition") establishes a repetition of consonants that resonate with the reader.

6. People often ask rhetorical questions, never truly seeking the answer. Explain how the speaker's questions allow him to fall into deeper despair.

The speaker discovers that "Nevermore" is the only word the raven will speak. Knowing this, he sinks into deeper self-pity by asking the raven questions that he knows will only be answered with "nevermore." Already knowing the answer to the questions aids in increasing the self-torture of the narrator as he allows his discourse with the raven to further deteriorate his mental well-being.

7. In paragraph 38 of "The Philosophy of Composition," Poe explains that "It will be observed that the words, 'from out my heart,' involve the first metaphorical expression in the poem." Why does he include this observation in his essay?

He combines this metaphor with the bleak answer of "Nevermore" to emphasize the futility of the narrator's situation. "From out my heart" shows his reverent desire to find a true answer that will allow him to cope with the loss of Lenore. It gives the human quality of sadness to the narrator as he desperately searches for an answer.

Writing

8. Writing either poetry or prose, imitate Poe's method by beginning with the climactic event and then building from there.

Student responses will vary.

9. Writing a Narration Write about a life event that altered your way of thinking about something.

Student responses will vary.

Lesson Plan 9.7

Chapter Assessment

Rhetorical Analysis Answers

1. C
2. A
3. B
4. E
5. A
6. C
7. E
8. A
9. D
10. D

Connections for Critical Thinking

Have students turn to the questions on page 427 in the textbook. Tell students to choose one of the four options and write for a minimum of 30 minutes.

After students have finished writing, use the remainder of the class period to group students according to the option they chose. Students should read and comment on one another's essays, offering a positive comment, a critical comment, and a question for each essay read.

Answers

1. **Write an essay comparing and contrasting literature and any other art form. What merits or limitations does each form have? Which do you find more satisfying? Which form is more accessible? Use at least three essays in this chapter to illustrate or support your thesis.**

   Opinions as to the merits and limitations of art and literature will vary depending on each student's experience and exposure to each. Some high schools do a more thorough job of introducing students to these than do others. Make sure they remember to incorporate material from at least three essays from this section and cite their sources.

2. **Write an essay exploring the importance of role models in art and literature. Refer to the essays by Welty and Gates to address the issue.**

   Both authors (Welty and Gates) give unique accounts of their own role models. They deal with different forms of art and varying reasons for their admiration and respect, as well as somewhat different definitions of "role model." Students may break these down into a chart for helpful organization to brainstorm an essay.

3. **Use the essays by Welty, Updike, and Gates to explore the question of excellence in the arts. Answer this question: How do you know the work of art is good?**

   Like anyone, students have their own ideas of how to answer the question of "how do we know when art is good?"

4. **Examine the role of the artist in society and the artist's purpose in or duty to society. How would the writers in this chapter address this issue?**

   In order for students to respond to this question, it would be helpful to have a class discussion on the definition of "artist." There may be many possibilities here, but there should be a general consensus one way or another for clarity.

Lesson Plan 9.8

Synthesizing Sources: Living and Dying in Poetry and Art

This unit's synthesis feature includes paintings and poems. Using the TPCASTT system, have students analyze the poems in groups, and then pair groups to find common traits among the poems.

Applying Your Synthesis Skills: Suggested Answers

Comprehension

1. Which of the sources address death, and what is the main message of each?

"Janet Waking" conveys in seven stanzas the poet's ironic commentary on a child's initiation into the finality and "forgetful kingdom" of death; "Picnic, Lightning" reminds the reader that life is priceless and confirms that one never knows when that priceless gift will be taken away; "Dreamwood" considers the last stages of life and the end of "touristic choices."

2. Which of the sources address life, and what is the main message of each?

"O Me! O Life!" questions the imperfections of people around the speaker and ponders if the people of the world, himself included, have anything of value to offer. The answer is yes, if opportunities are taken; "Dreamwood" is about the path of a life, starting with a child seeing patterns in wood grain and moving to the adult ("the child's older self, a poet") who wants to understand her life, who wants to know the pattern, the path, the way to go.

Rhetorical Analysis

3. Compare and contrast Munch's *The Scream* to Homer's *The Gulf Stream*. Address style, appeals, and purpose in your comparison.

The Scream (1893) indicates mental horror and isolation, although there are two people in the background. The painting shows a person terrorized by his thoughts and surroundings, which have distorted the whole world around him. In *The Gulf Stream* (1899), a man rests on a rudderless, broken-masted fishing boat surrounded by sharks, turbulent waves, and an approaching waterspout. A ship on the horizon has either abandoned or missed spotting the broken boat, although one could view the ship as a sign of hope. Although the lone man is helpless and surrounded by terror, he seems oddly at peace. Although both images were painted around the same time, *The Scream* is abstract and modernist, whereas *The Gulf Stream* shows more realism.

4. Many of the sources address life as a journey. Elaborate on ways the journey metaphor weaves itself into these sources.

Answers will vary. Whitman views the journey through life as a "struggle ever renew'd" as he questions his purpose for living. Collins hears the "rasp of the steel edge against a round stone, the small plants singing with lifted faces, and the click of the sundial as one hour sweeps into the next." Thus, he sees nature as playing a powerful role in his journey through life. Nature counts down each hour of his life in a joyous manner. Ransom gives Janet a smaller world to journey through when she is young. She runs "across the world upon the grass" only to find the "forgetful kingdom of death" when she discovers that her hen has died. Rich uses a map metaphor to accentuate the journey she is taking through "a map laid down to memorize because she may be walking it." This is not a map for tourists, but for the end of the journey.

Writing an Argument

5. Using examples from at least three of these sources, write an essay answering these questions: What is the biggest challenge you face? Why is it the biggest challenge?

Student responses will vary.

CHAPTER 10
Nature and the Environment

This chapter focuses on nature and scientific writing. As such, it provides an interesting opportunity to ask students to analyze writing that is structured with multiple strategies. We will turn our attention back to comparison and contrast, but we will also look at writing that is developed through causal and process analyses. Chapter 10 holds both classic and contemporary pieces focused on the environment, science, and the natural world around us.

Teaching the Chapter

Lesson Plan 10.1

Eastman's "What Can the Out-of-Doors Do for Our Children?"—A Study in Detail

Class Opener

To put students into the right frame of reference for discussing the natural world, have students analyze the photographs in the **Classic and Contemporary Images** feature. In their groups, ask them to answer the questions in the textbook on page 437. See suggested answers below. Go around to each group, asking each group to discuss a different question.

Classic and Contemporary Images: Suggested Answers

1. Why is it fitting that California is acting on the vehicle emission problem in that state? Why does Los Angeles epitomize the problem?

   Answers will vary, but smog—due to the geographical area of the large coastal cities, the overwhelming population, and lack of a major transit system in the Los Angeles area—is one cause of the vehicle emission problem.

2. What intentional effect does *Along the Hudson* have on the person who views this painting?

   The painting purposefully shows serenity and peacefulness through the mountains, pine trees, and beautiful, unspoiled river.

3. How is "pace" exemplified in both images?

   The Los Angeles photograph has a frenzied feel. Traffic is heavy, and everyone appears to be in a hurry to get somewhere. Large buildings sprawl around the highways. Smog, a result of this fast pace, blocks the view of what we can imagine to be hills and trees.

4. What do these visuals "say" about time and progress?

In *Along the Hudson*, time seems to have stood still as this painting exemplifies tranquility and quiet serenity. The Los Angeles photo shows time to be of the essence as vehicles hurriedly move across the intersecting highways. Although the photo represents the "progress" of today's world, one that is fast-paced and industrially inclined, the other visual makes one question whether "progress" is a positive thing.

Activity: Focusing on Contrasts and Their Effects

In this lesson, students will focus on specific contrasts Eastman uses in the excerpts from his essay. Instead of focusing on simply identifying contrasts, however, students will focus on recognizing the *effect* produced by these contrasts. This exercise is an excellent opportunity to help students focus their analysis muscles, as they are forced to create meaning from specific contrasts assigned to them.

First, produce the following list of contrasts on small pieces of paper for students:

- Multiple definitions of "raw materials"
- Animate and inanimate
- Multiple implied definitions of little trinkets
- Multiple implied definitions of jewels
- Conflicting concept of "water"
- Out-of-doors opposed to implied claim about being inside

Then, allow groups to draw three of the contrasts from a hat or fishbowl. Ask them to find quotations that apply to the contrasts they selected, using a triple-entry chart in which they identify the quotations that support the contrast, the effect of the contrast, and an analysis of the argument the contrast supports. You may wish to provide students with a sample chart like the following (Photocopy the chart, or see **Chapter 10 online, Charles A. Eastman: A Study in Detail**.):

Quotations	Specific Effect of Contrast	Extension of Effect—Connection to Argument

Sample Response:

Quotations	Specific Effect of Contrast	Extension of Effect—Connection to Argument
Examples: "Earth, and trees, and stones, uncut, unpolished, unground. That is what the white man calls raw material." "There is only one raw material, and that is fresh air coming through rich sunshine."	The first quotation, ostensibly by Eastman, offers an unvarnished, unsentimental definition of what might be considered raw materials. This definition implies a certain lack of reverence for nature—an assumption that people naturally appropriate these materials for their use. In contrast, the chief's response indicates a reverence for nature, suggesting that the only "raw material" in existence is the fully renewable resource—air.	This contrast highlights the closeness that the chief feels with nature, and criticizes the government for its assumption that all of nature is available for taking and using at will. This contrast adds to the chief's later argument that children need to be educated in sunshine—presumably, the government officials would feel and think differently about nature had they spent more time outdoors.

After students have finished the contrast charts, they should work in groups to create cooperative analysis essays focused on contrast. Using the charts they have created, ask them to walk through the passage, crafting a single body paragraph around each contrast they have analyzed. They will undoubtedly need to add further details to fully realize the essay.

Class Closer

Have students share the informal essays they wrote using their "random" contrasts. Remind students that they created meaning from contrasts assigned to them. If they can do this, then choosing their own elements will provide for easier analysis in the future.

Suggested Answers

"What Can the Out-of-Doors Do for Our Children?" by Charles A. Eastman

From *Education: A Monthly Magazine*, Volume XLI, September, 1920-June, 1921. Frank Herbert Palmer, Editor. Boston: The Palmer Company. © 1921

Comprehension

1. **How does Eastman serve as a knowledgeable intermediary between Native American and white cultures?**

   Eastman lived in Sioux territory and also was educated at Dartmouth University and Boston University, allowing him perspective of both cultures. There are other various connections students can make from his biography.

2. **What is the main point of Eastman's text?**

   Through the beginning anecdotes, the point is made that "We came from Nature, and we must return to Nature; between times we must replenish our bodies with that Nature. When we do not do it we suffer." Our reliance is on nature itself. We need to be more attuned with nature.

Rhetorical Analysis

3. How does parallel structure empower this excerpt? Use an example from the text.

Eastman employs parallel structure throughout, but particularly in the last three sentences: "They are flexible. They fit anywhere. They are magnetic." This structure serves to give clarity to the point he makes about the positive effect nature has on our "mind and soul."

4. Analyze the difference in syntax, or sentence structure, between Eastman's writing and the excerpts from the "old Indians" Eastman interviews. What does this difference in syntax suggest?

Eastman's sentence structure is fairly straightforward in construction, such as a teacher would use in a classroom. The "old Indians" speak in a more rambling way, taking the form of a parable or folktale.

5. What is ironic about the response of the "old, old chief'" to Eastman's description of "raw material"?

The chief disagrees with the description of raw material by saying that raw material originates from an even rawer material—"fresh air coming through rich sunshine." Thus "raw material" is not "material" at all.

6. Identify a metaphorical example of Native Americans' reverence for nature.

The strongest metaphor is that of God's "jewels" that spring from every blade of grass. Jewels are usually thought of as being a treasured gift. This metaphor extends itself through the last paragraph.

Writing

7. Write a 250-word essay in which you analyze the wisdom of Eastman's excerpt.

Answers will vary but most will center on God's connection with nature, and it is nature that truly teaches us to be alive.

8. Writing an Argument Argue for or against the view that teaching and learning should occur only "out-of-doors."

Student responses will vary.

Lesson Plan 10.2

Lopez's "Children in the Woods"—Comparison & Contrast

Class Opener

Ask students to freewrite about their experience(s) walking in the woods—either as part of a group or individually. Students in urban areas might not have had a hiking experience like the one Lopez describes. If not, consider using websites of national parks or Google Maps to allow students to "virtually" experience such a hike.

Activity: Contrasting Present and Past

One of the methods Lopez uses to develop this essay is that of comparison and contrast. Specifically, he describes his own early experiences in the woods as a child and his own early experiences leading children in the woods. He contrasts those early experiences to how he now acclimates children to the woods. Ask students to use a T-chart to answer the following question (See **Chapter 10 online, Barry Lopez: Comparison and Contrast**.):

How does Lopez describe his experiences in the woods?

Past	Present

As they read, students will populate the chart. Once they have finished, have them share their lists. Then create a Venn diagram on the board. Ask students to find similarities and contrasts in Lopez's experience.

Lopez's Relationship with the Woods Past and Present

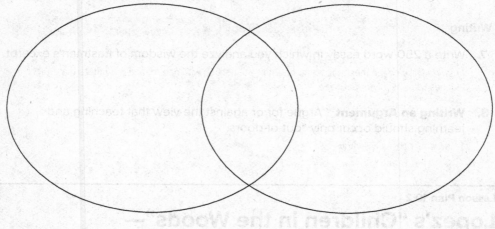

Activity: Summarizing Patterns

Using their diagrams, students should write a series of statements that reflect patterns and contrasts. Provide them with the following templates:

In his essay, Lopez portrays introducing the woods to children as ______(how)______ as evidenced by ______(example)______.

Lopez claims that in the past he ______________________;

however, now he believes ______________________.

Lopez now recognizes ______________________.

While Lopez suggests (past) ______________________,

he now believes ______________________.

Activity: Writing Body Paragraphs

After they have completed the templates, tell students that they must choose one template as a topic sentence and write a body paragraph to support that argument. They should draw textual evidence from the essay and use the body paragraph format they have been practicing:

I. Body paragraph one
   a. Topic Sentence—Minor argument one
   b. Textual Evidence
   c. Commentary
   d. Commentary
   e. Textual Evidence
   f. Commentary
   g. Commentary
   h. Conclusion/transition

Class Closer

Have students create a thesis statement for the analysis they have written. Ask: Looking back at your topic sentences, what do they share in common? What single argument can you write as a class from the paragraphs you have written?

Suggested Answers

"Children in the Woods" by Barry Lopez

Comprehension

1. What is Lopez's primary purpose in this essay? How does the title relate to the purpose?

Lopez's primary purpose is to reveal to the reader that he or she is an integral part of the texture or tapestry of life, and the title suggests that the child's perspective of and feeling for nature will keep alive this realization.

2. Does Lopez assume his audience has the same value position as he does? Why or why not?

Yes, he does; we all share the need to be reminded of our place in the order of things.

3. What, ultimately, does Lopez want children to learn about the natural world? How does he teach them?

Lopez wants children to learn that all phenomena in nature are connected, that everything fits together, and that this sense or knowledge can be kept alive throughout one's lifetime. He teaches by sharpening the power of perception, by focusing on a fragment of the whole, and by extrapolating its connections to the various elements of the whole.

Rhetorical Analysis

4. Does Lopez state his thesis or imply it? Justify your response.

The thesis is implied and cumulatively unfolds as the essay progresses; the last two paragraphs drive home the main point.

5. Why does Lopez use a personal tone or voice at the start of this essay? How does his opening paragraph connect to the body of the essay?

The personal anecdote introduces the partial focus on children's intelligence and leads the reader to recall his/her own childhood memories. The introductory paragraph points out the exceptional perceptive capabilities of children compared to adults. This observation supplies one facet of the main point that children and adults teach each other.

6. Cite instances where Lopez moves from vivid description to response and reflection.

Certainly the encounter with the partial raccoon's jaw is a good example of description and response, as is the episode with the heron's footprint.

7. Where does Lopez employ the comparative method, and toward what objective?

In paragraph 4, Lopez discusses how he taught children in the beginning compared to later expeditions. Rather than speaking broadly on a wide range of natural phenomena, he would focus on close examination of one specific object to reveal its connections to its environment.

8. What extended metaphor does Lopez establish in the final paragraph? Is this an appropriate and effective metaphor to end the essay? Why or why not?

The metaphor of the doorway through the smallest room that leads to the cathedral is effective. It represents the close examination of a single natural object that ultimately can reveal the sacred knowledge of the interconnectedness of life.

Writing

9. Write a narrative and descriptive essay in which you recount a childhood experience that taught you something about the natural world.

Student responses will vary.

10. How would you speak to children if you were taking them on a nature walk? Write a reflective essay addressing this question.

Answers will vary, but students will take many approaches to this writing prompt. They may write about the nature walk they wish they had gone on, comparing their experiences to those of Lopez leading the children in the woods. They might reflect on discoveries they had not really remembered prior to this assignment. Also, students may never have had a rural experience so it is important to point out that a nature walk could mean a walk in a park, a small garden, or a walk in an urban area where they reflect on nature.

11. Writing an Argument **Argue for or against the proposition that you can learn profound truths about yourself and the world by immersing yourself in nature.**

Student answers will vary, but they need to first think about/list their "truths." Then they can expand on those ideas by looking at the larger community and "truths" they believe have been communicated to them. Discussion should be encouraged prior to writing the argument with possible group discussion about world truths and why they have come to believe those truths. Nature's role in the discovery of these truths is a next step. Finally, they will be prepared to write their argument with specific examples as evidence.

Lesson Plan 10.3

Synthesizing Classic and Contemporary Essays—Timed-Writing

Use the synthesis questions that appear after Lopez's essay to encourage students to analyze further and deeper than they did in their group discussions. Allow students to choose any one of the three options and write for a minimum of 30 minutes.

Upon completion of students' writing, use the remainder of a 45-50 minute period to group students according to the topic they chose. Students should read and comment on each other's essays, offering a positive comment, a critical comment, and a question for each essay read.

Synthesizing the Classic and Contemporary Essays: Suggested Answers

1. **Charles Eastman and Barry Lopez consider nature as a physical and spiritual presence. In what ways are their stakes in nature the same? In what ways are they different? Does either writer have the power to effect a transformation in our attitude toward nature? Explain.**

   Both essays are powerful expressions of both authors' beliefs in the powerful interrelationship between nature and self -actualization. They begin with anecdotes that draw the reader in. Both voices are conversational, although students may feel Eastman takes a more inclusive viewpoint of nature through his recall of his discussions with various chiefs. Lopez keeps his perspective more personal throughout the essay. Both essays focus on children, although Lopez talks of his interactions with children near his Oregon home. They both believe strongly that nature is the greatest subjective way to learn the ways of the world, and to know who a person truly is. They both make the point that children learn through subjective experiences as these experiences hone critical thinking skills that open and expand paths and doors. Because Lopez is a "modern man," his efforts at restoring sanctity to the environment and to discourage its plunder have more credence today. Nevertheless, despite his authority, obvious political, social, and economic interests limit the influence of his advocacy.

2. **It has often been said that intellectual knowledge changes one's relationship with the world environment. Do Lopez's essay and Eastman's excerpt confirm that statement? Use examples from the pieces to support your argument.**

   Lopez, a student of history and philosophy, understands the geopolitical forces at work in the modern economic landscape. He can trace the relationship of humans to the environment—and comprehend how exploiting nature has been a constant factor in the equation of designing and advancing civilizations. Eastman confirms this statement by pointing out the white man's definition of "raw materials" and the young Native Americans' fascination with trinkets, and how the old chief—lacking "intellectual knowledge"—shook his head at these actions, diminishing them in the reality of true valuables—fresh air and dewdrops.

3. **Public service announcements, or PSAs, are advertisements designed to raise awareness about issues, not sell products or services. Draft a PSA that informs or educates the public about an environmental issue. Include an excerpt from both Eastman's and Lopez's essays as illustrative support for your PSA.**

   Student responses will vary.

Lesson Plan 10.4

Bass's "Why I Hunt"—Recognizing Causal Analysis

Class Opener

Have students write a paragraph quick-write in response to the following prompt:

> **Describe an occasion when you made a snap decision to do something different just because you were bored.**

Allow a few students to read their paragraphs aloud.

Activity: Recognizing Cause and Effect

Although this essay is replete with examples of causal analysis, several paragraphs stand out for their use of causal elements: paragraphs 4-5 and 7-10. Help students to recognize the causal relationships in this text, either by discussing them in a whole class setting, or by having groups first analyze and then present those relationships to the class.

Activity: Combining Development Strategies

Students may have the impression that an essay falls into a particular category—such as causal analysis or comparison and contrast—to the exclusion of other modes of writing. Bass's piece is a good essay for helping students see the strategies for development as multifaceted. Bass incorporates a significant amount of comparison and contrast into his essay as he contrasts Americans who hunt with those who buy all their food in grocery stores. Ask students to find examples of the modes of description and causal analysis. (Point out to students that discussing multiple strategies is a good way to structure a rhetorical analysis essay.)

Class Closer

Ask students to discuss Bass's overall argument. What is it? What was his most compelling evidence? How was that evidence structured? (Comparison and contrast or some other strategy altogether?)

Suggested Answers

"Why I Hunt" by Rick Bass

Comprehension

1. **Why did Bass and his wife fall in love with the Yaak Valley? What does this fondness for wild places tell us about his character and interests?**

   After feeling restless in Mississippi, Bass follows a road with no real destination. He "missed the West's terrain of space." He explains that in the Yaak, "not a single mammal has gone extinct since the end of the Ice Age." He loves to hunt and this area is full of hunters, human and otherwise. Their lives also allow them to get almost completely back to nature. There is not much in the way of phone signals or electricity. They hunt and grow their food and provide their own supplies.

2. Explain the relationship between the people residing in the Yaak Valley and their fondness for hunting.

Bass says almost everyone in the Yaak is a hunter because the hunter in this area can actually be part of the land and not so much just a visitor. He describes hunting as a "stirring of the imagination... because it is never the hunter who is in control, but always the hunted." See paragraph 8 for more of this.

3. Does Bass apologize for his fondness for hunting? Explain your response.

Bass offers no apology for his love of hunting. He does not even really feel the need to defend it. He just shares his ideals.

Rhetorical Analysis

4. Bass wrote this essay for the official magazine of the Sierra Club, of which he is an active member. Why would an organization whose goal is the preservation of wilderness and wildlife agree to publish an article expressing love for hunting? How does Bass anticipate objections to his argument?

Bass explains the act of hunting in an almost ethereal manner. Students will have a lot to say about this topic. He says, "the pursuit and the evasion of predator are shadows of the same desire" (see paragraph 9). Answers may vary here, but Bass seems to imply that hunters at this level have a special love and respect for nature and wildlife. They do not kill randomly. For Bass, the land is there to sustain him and his family. As a hunter, he is part of the environment, not a visitor in it.

5. What is Bass's claim and where does he state it? Does he rely on logical, ethical, or emotional appeal—or a combination—to advance his argument, and why?

Bass's thesis comes in the form of a question, at the end of paragraph 1. He asks the question for the reader to consider, then spends the rest of the essay trying to answer it in a way his reader will understand and relate to. In fact, his appeal is mainly emotional in that he relies on his description of the Yaak and his description of hunting, and an explanation of how those fit together to make his point.

6. What causal connection does Bass establish between landscape and human behavior? Where does he use comparison and contrast to distinguish this place and its people from other places and other Americans?

This essay has causal elements throughout, especially in paragraphs 4–5 and in paragraphs 7–10. Bass then compares and contrasts Americans who do not hunt, who live in cities and shop in grocery stores for ready-made everything, eventually causing the imagination to atrophy. Those in the minority who do hunt, according to Bass, have an understanding of the work it takes to fill the pantry to last all year, to respect nature and what it has to offer, and to not be forced to rely on someone else to take care of them.

7. Cite examples of Bass's descriptive skills and his use of figurative language. How does description and figurative language enhance the appeal of the writer's argument?

Rick Bass's descriptive skills are creative and powerful image creators. He is very good at language that brings the reader into the experience. It allows the reader to hear what the writer heard, taste what the writer tasted, see what the reader saw. He brings the reader right into the Yaak.

8. What is the dominant impression that Bass creates of the Yaak Valley region?

Responses will vary here, but students should recognize at least an almost utopian society in Bass's perspective. Students may have different terms and some may really prefer the city, so Bass's descriptions would be either foreign or of no interest.

9. **Evaluate Bass's conclusion. How does it serve as a writer's justification for hunting?**

In his conclusion, Bass states he would never force his love of hunting on someone else. He can only share with others how it makes him feel.

Writing

10. **Select a natural landscape that you know well and, including description as one rhetorical strategy, explain how this site might affect the behavior of people and/or their ethical values.**

This is an excellent writing prompt for description, especially. Students have an opportunity to be nostalgic for home or some place that is special to them and they can share this location through their descriptive language choices.

11. **Writing an Argument** **What is the difference between killing the game that you consume and buying meat in a grocery store or supermarket? Is one act more ethical than the other? Compose an argumentative essay dealing with this issue.**

This essay will vary by student, according to where and how he or she was raised—in the city or in the country, as a hunter or as a gatherer, as well as several other factors. Remind students to cite all their sources, including any interviews they might have with family members who are hunters.

Lesson Plan 10.5

McKibben's Rhetoric—Analyzing the Appeals

Class Opener

Consider showing a clip from the award-winning documentary *An Inconvenient Truth* as an opener to class. Although this film is highly controversial in some circles, the evocative opening will be a conversation starter on the topic.

Activity: Appealing to Pathos

McKibben develops his argument through appeals to *pathos* and *logos*. Remind students that an appeal to pathos involves appealing to the emotions of the reader. Have students complete a double-entry journal in which they notate only appeals to pathos. After they have compiled at least 3 examples and written commentary explaining each, go around the room and allow students to share their findings.

Activity: Appealing to Logos

Once students have completed and shared their pathos journals, repeat the activity with appeals to logos. Remind students that an appeal to logos involves using logical and factual information to support the argument. After they have compiled at least 3 examples and written commentary explaining each, go around the room and allow students to share their findings.

Class Closer

Ask students to work in groups to write a paragraph in which they use only *pathos* or only *ethos* to argue in favor of a current issue. Some issues that have sufficient gravitas and sufficient student experience include: school uniforms, funding for school sports, and arts programs in schools.

Suggested Answers

"The Environmental Issue from Hell" by Bill McKibben

"The Environmental Issue from Hell" by Bill McKibben. This article originally appeared in *In These Times* magazine (April 30, 2001).

Comprehension

1. According to McKibben, what are the causes of global warming?

Global warming is caused by raised carbon dioxide levels in the atmosphere, and McKibben attributes that rise to the general inefficiency of a "heedless, supersized society" (paragraph 10).

2. What instances of ecological disaster does the writer say will occur if we do not change our habits?

Some of the direct effects of global warming include more frequent and more damaging storms, the destruction of coral reefs, and the loss of food sources for animals such as polar bears.

3. Why is a new approach to the problem of global warming needed? What approach does McKibben suggest?

The problem of global warming is difficult to translate into a political issue partly because there are no "villains" or easily identified agents to oppose (paragraph 8). McKibben suggests the adoption of symbols for the problem—such as the widespread use of SUVs.

Rhetorical Analysis

4. How does McKibben's title capture the tone of the essay? What is his purpose in writing the essay? Does he see his readers as hostile or sympathetic to his position? How do you know?

The title captures the essay's tone of frustration, and McKibben addresses his readers with a moral injunction—note the tone of the "you" addressed in paragraphs 6 and 7. The title adapts the phrase quoted in MicKibben's opening sentence, which suggests that McKibben wants to emphasize that the figurative "hell" of global warming is a literal environmental hell and not simply a political issue.

5. How does McKibben develop his introduction? Why does he pose questions? Where does he state his claim?

McKibben's introduction, with its flurry of questions, conveys both the urgency and the difficulty of finding a solution. McKibben's claim is expressed most clearly in the single sentence of paragraph 3.

6. Does McKibben make his argument through appeals to reason, emotion, ethics—or a combination of these elements? Justify your response.

McKibben's plea is certainly an appeal to his reader's emotions, but that gesture is closely aligned with the highly pragmatic logical appeal. McKibben's point is that emotional appeals are not sufficient in the campaign against public apathy. (Hence, his somewhat cynical suggestion that we adopt the SUV rather than the coral reef as a pragmatic symbol.)

7. **How does the writer contend with possible objections to his position on global warming?**

   McKibben disagrees with fellow environmentalists over what he feels is an outmoded, ineffective strategy for bringing the issue to public awareness. Some of these strategies are dissected at the beginning of paragraph 2.

8. **Explain the pattern of cause and effect that McKibben uses to structure his essay.**

   Note especially paragraphs 5–6, which consider those parts of the world (like Bangladesh) where the effects of global warming are not absorbed into the local economy. In paragraph 2, McKibben refers to cause-and-effect patterns as a hypothetical rhetorical strategy; in paragraphs 5–6, McKibben actually employs this pattern to forward his argument.

9. **What varieties of evidence does the writer present to support his claim? What extended illustration does he provide? How effective is it, and why?**

   Recent trends—meteorological changes, ecological changes in food supply, and so on—represent the bulk of McKibben's evidence, although he also cites evidence of currently ineffective strategies for drawing attention to the problem of global warming.

10. **In the concluding paragraph, McKibben issues a call to action. How does the body of the essay prepare the reader for this persuasive appeal?**

    The body of McKibben's essay deals with the problem of making the personal political. Earlier observations about the sheltered, air-conditioned existence of the typical American commuter prepare readers for this conclusion: "[there are] many people so tied to their current ways of life that advocating change smacks of subversion."

Writing

11. **Research and write an essay in which you explain your own understanding of the causes and effects of global warming.**

    Each student will have a different sense of the science behind global warming. This writing exercise would be a good place to begin a point of inquiry that has students test their understanding not only of the science behind global warming but also how scientific theories are expounded.

12. **Research your state's policy concerning global warming. Present your findings in a summary essay.**

    If students can't find a reasonable amount of information about state policy, they should research national policy and, specifically, how national policy affects their state.

13. **Writing an Argument** **McKibben argues that SUVs are a primary cause of wastefulness and global warming and that both moral persuasion and political activism are required to change consumers' habits. Do you agree or disagree with his assertions? Write an argumentative essay responding to this issue.**

    Students will want to conduct a fair amount of research on SUVs and compare them to other autos. They should also research the SUV and its history to discover how classification as a "truck" helps it evade certain emission and fuel consumption standards.

Lesson Plan 10.6

Carson's "The Obligation to Endure"—Four Corners Debate

Recall that in a Four Corners Debate, students are given a position and then sent to the four corners of the room to craft and prepare their arguments. Randomly assign students to each of the four corners, then tell them the positions they will be arguing.

Class Opener

Tell students that Carson relies on causal analysis to examine the dangers of using insecticides carelessly. She alerts us to society's disregard for nature's plan. Her use of examples and expert testimony add strength to her argument. Assign the four corners these four positions:

1. Government regulation of environmental concerns is necessary; mankind is innately greedy and is destroying the planet out of a sense of greed.
2. Government regulation of environmental concerns is necessary; mankind is innately good and our destruction of the environment comes from a desire to improve the world—we simply need more government controls in place.
3. The scientific community, rather than the government, should regulate environmental concerns. Mankind is innately greedy and is destroying the planet out of a sense of greed, which science can help regulate.
4. The scientific community, rather than the government, should regulate environmental concerns; mankind is innately good and our destruction of the environment comes from a desire to improve the world—we simply need more scientific controls in place.

Activity: Devise Arguments

Assuming that this will be a one-period debate, give students 15–20 minutes to devise compelling arguments that prove the position they were given. They must come up with relevant examples. Using the library or computers in the room will help students prepare better responses.

Activity: Debate

Conduct the debate. There are many ways to do this, but primary concerns should be that the groups take turns, limited by equal time. An effective strategy is to let the first group present their most compelling argument in two minutes or less, then give the other groups one minute each to rebut. Repeat this strategy three more times by letting the next group present for two minutes, followed by a one-minute rebuttal from the other three groups.

Class Closer

Ask the groups to determine which group won the debate. The "catch" is that they cannot vote for their own group.

Suggested Answers

"The Obligation to Endure" by Rachel Carson

Comprehension

1. What does Carson mean by "the obligation to endure"?

This phrase appears in the title as well as in Carson's conclusion; it refers to the fact that as a species, human beings cannot survive if they pollute and disturb nature's delicate balance by forging ahead blindly and not recognizing the consequences of their actions.

2. What reasons does the author cite for the overpopulation of insects?

Carson states that Western societies (specifically America) have contributed to the overpopulation of insects by their interference with nature's control over a species. This includes the "intensification of agriculture" (paragraph 15); the introduction of species alien to an environment; and the importance of plants and the insects they harbor.

3. What remedies does Carson propose?

Carson's remedy is not the discontinuance of insecticides but a more honest approach from governmental agencies about the risks involved. She wants the public to be informed enough so that it can decide the risks it wants to take and protest against dangerous practices. The government and the public must work together for the good of the planet and their own survival.

Rhetorical Analysis

4. What tone does Carson use in her essay? Does she seem to be a subjective or an objective writer? Give specific support for your response.

As someone who is deeply committed to nature and responsible maintenance of the planet, Carson is deeply disturbed about the lack of common sense and avarice that is damaging the planet. This is evident in her use of adjectives. Students should present other examples that demonstrate her concern (and anger at humanity's ignorance).

5. How does the use of words such as *dangerous, evil, irrevocable,* and *sinister* help shape the reader's reaction to the piece? What emotional and ethical appeals do such words indicate?

The language Carson uses triggers responses of foreboding and concern within the reader. She advises the reader to have as much concern as she does.

6. Examine the ordering of ideas in paragraph 4, and consider how such an order serves to reinforce Carson's argument.

Paragraph 4 accumulates details of the way humanity tampers with nature and modifies its laws arbitrarily, forcing nature to react to this change and upsetting its design. This is monstrous creativity.

7. Paragraph 9 consists of only one (long) sentence. What is its function in the essay's scheme?

This paragraph is really one long sentence in which Carson accuses humanity of changing the environment to the extent that it will no longer support human life. The importance of this fact makes it deserve its own paragraph as the implications are far-reaching.

8. Examine Carson's use of expert testimony. How does it help strengthen her thesis?

The testimony that Carson uses helps to substantiate her claims and provide the reader with various angles on the subject. Students may refer to examples of this strategy in the essay and explain why its inclusion is effective.

9. How effectively does the essay's conclusion help tie up Carson's points? What is the writer's intent in this final paragraph? How does she accomplish this aim?

Carson's conclusion offers a remedy for the problem; perhaps her intention is to mobilize her readers. The quote at the end serves to remind the reader that our existence rests on being actively informed.

Writing

10. Write an essay in which you suggest solutions to the problems brought up in Carson's piece. You may want to suggest measures that the average citizen can take to eliminate the casual use of insecticides to control the insect population.

Although Carson's remedy is a good one, what specific solutions can reverse the damage to the environment? Students may focus on a particular aspect such as insect control or ocean dumping or may approach the topic more broadly. They should, however, be specific about changes that governments or the public can make. They may include information from Carson's essay as well as extra research if necessary.

11. Write a biographical research paper on Carson that focuses on her involvement with nature and environmental issues.

This is a straightforward biographical research paper. However, students should narrow their thesis to a concentration on Carson's interest in environmental causes and what she did in her life to advance concern for the planet.

12. Writing an Argument **Write an essay titled "Insects Are Not the Problem: Humanity Is." In this essay, argue that it is humanity's greed that has caused such an imbalance in nature as to threaten the planet's survival.**

This essay will argue that human beings are killing the planet and themselves by being greedy and short-sighted. Students should explain priorities on a personal and national basis. They should provide ample illustrations and support, including references to Carson's essay.

Lesson Plan 10.7

Walker's "Am I Blue?"—A SOAPSTone Analysis

Class Opener

Ask students to identify themselves in the following ways (allow them to move around the room to form groups): Animal lovers? (Yes on one side of the room, no on the other). Hunters? (Have them move again.) Vegetarians? (Have them move again.) Ask them which category they identify with most specifically. Ask if it is possible to be a hunter and an animal lover? Is it possible to eat meat and still love animals?

Activity: SOAPSTone Analysis

This is a more complicated essay to analyze with the SOAPSTone approach because the argument is not as immediately apparent as it is in other essays we have analyzed with this approach.

Speaker—Students must determine who is speaking. Who is narrating the essay? The speaker in this essay is Alice Walker, a writer who identifies herself in many ways, but predominantly as an African American woman writer. In this case, she is a woman on a vacation with her partner and her partner's son. (She is careful never to refer to her partner with a pronoun.)

Occasion—Students must determine the context of the writing. When does this occur? Where? What particular event has motivated this writing? Students should recognize that the occasion of this piece is an unexpected epiphany experienced by the author while on vacation.

Audience—Students must determine the intended audience for the essay. This essay is written for educated, thoughtful readers who are interested in determining the underlying nature behind what an animal might think or feel.

Purpose—Students must determine the author's purpose in writing the essay. Hopefully, students will recognize that the author is interested in breakdowns in communications among people, and between people and animals.

Subject—This should be the shortest discussion point. Summarize the argument in 20 words or less. The subject of this essay relates to communication. Walker argues that animals communicate more effectively than human beings, because such communication is vital to their survival.

Save your tone discussion for the class closer, and provide students with a list of words to use to debate.

Class Closer

Tone—Through the author's diction and syntax, tone can be deciphered.This is a difficult essay to discuss in terms of tone. The author attempts to come across as observant, simply relating details from her summer vacation. However, the tone becomes more political as she relates spitting out the steak at the end of the selection. Ask students to debate what tone words might come to mind for this particular essay from the following list: amused, benevolent, benign, compassionate, lighthearted, playful, sincere, detached, factual, impartial, argumentative, biased, disdainful, indignant.

Suggested Answers

"Am I Blue?" by Alice Walker

Comprehension

1. **What is the major thesis of the essay? Is it stated explicitly in the text, or does one have to infer it? Explain.**

   The common theme running through Walker's essay is lack of communication, whether it be between humans and animals, people of different cultures, or separate generations. The prime image she uses that distills these ideas is in relating the tragedy of Blue, who, it was assumed, would be happy living alone once his companion was separated from him.

2. **In paragraph 5, Walker states that animals are "*completed* creations (at least they seem to be, so much more than we) who are not likely *to* change." What does she mean by making this distinction between animals and humans?**

Walker suggests that animals are "programmed" to communicate and need one another for their well-being. They are not malleable or adaptable as humans are. We, on the other hand, are constantly seeking new means of adapting to the world, whether it be through philosophies, therapies, or changes in lifestyle.

3. **What is the significance of the title of the essay? Does it have more than one meaning? Explain your answer.**

Walker is suggesting that early childhood development becomes "hard-wired" and is meant to be for our own survival. By arbitrarily breaking bonds (as was done between black caregivers and white children during slavery), the "Masters" were destroying communication and encouraging alienation between the races. Walker understands that by committing to becoming a part of Blue's life, withdrawing herself from the horse would cause psychological damage and confusion.

Rhetorical Analysis

4. **In paragraph 4, Walker creates a vivid description of Blue. How does she achieve this?**

The author employs specific descriptors (primarily adjectives) that "paint" a portrait of Blue. These include "flexible dark lips," "huge cubelike teeth," and "high, broad-breasted *enormity.*"

5. **In paragraph 7, Walker makes a cognitive association between the relationship between humans and animals and the relationship between whites and blacks during slavery. Does this transition seem too abrupt, or is there a rhetorical reason for the immediate comparison? Explain.**

Walker suggests that it has been the oppressors' penchant to fear and reject difference rather than embrace it. In doing so, they have only reduced their humanity when in fact they had the opportunity to enlarge and deepen it. She illustrates this with references to the treatment of "the Indians" and to Asian women, but she could have easily widened her examples to other relationships—both human and animal.

6. **Explore the other analogies Walker makes in paragraphs 8 and 9. Are they pertinent? What is the rhetorical effect of juxtaposing seemingly different realms to convey one central idea?**

Walker attempts to transcend the perceived barrier between animal and human emotion by suggesting that it is as arbitrary as distinguishing the levels of humanity between the races. Just as many people consider animals devoid of "human" attributes such as sadness, loneliness, and empathy, historically whites "dehumanized" black people and Indians by suggesting they did not have the complex feelings that we associate with emotional depth.

7. **Walker often breaks the conventions of "college English." For example, paragraphs 8 and 9 both begin with the coordinating conjunction *and*. Paragraph 12 begins with the coordinating conjunction *but*. Paragraphs 15 and 16 are only one short sentence each. Explain the effect of each of these rhetorical devices. Find three other unusual rhetorical strategies—either on the paragraph or sentence level—and explain their effects.**

The recurrence of the coordinating conjunction "and" at the beginning of a sentence or paragraph is a device often employed by sophisticated writers to use repetition and accretion as a means of demonstrating a point. In paragraphs 8 and 9, the use of the word "and" serves to introduce illustrations of how the perception of a dominant culture is often viewed as "truth." The conjunction "but" at the beginning of paragraph 12 signals a change in Blue's world, and the single-line paragraphs (15 and 16) signal the abrupt loss of Blue's companion and are a transition to paragraph 17, where Walker describes his grief and anger, which she connects to human experience.

8. **In paragraphs 17 and 18, Walker speeds up the tempo of her writing by beginning many of the sentences with the conjunction *and*. What is the purpose and rhetorical effect of this strategy, and how does it mimic—in linguistic terms—Blue's altered emotional state?**

Walker seems to be simultaneously overwhelmed with guilt and insight. She feels guilt, knowing she has contributed in some small way to Blue's misery. She generalizes this feeling to place herself within the context of all those "people like me who have forgotten...all that animals try to tell us" (paragraph 17). As image upon image comes to the author, she uses the conjunction "and" as a rhetorical device to suggest the thought process of reaching an understanding of her own skewed relationship to nature. It is this type of relationship—that is, discounting the sensitivity of animals—that has led to Blue's anxiety.

9. **Walker seems to have a profound empathy for animals, yet it is only at the end that she is repulsed by the thought of eating meat. What rhetorical strategy is she employing in the conclusion that helps bring closure to her meditation on Blue? Does it matter whether the culminating event actually occurred in her experience, or is it all right for an essayist to use poetic license for stylistic purposes?**

Whether Walker is reporting with chronological accuracy is unimportant. What is important is that her gradual enlightenment has changed her behavior. In the concluding paragraph, she spits out her "steak." This leaves the reader the option to wonder whether her attitudes and behaviors will be permanently and/or more radically changed.

Writing

10. **Write a personal essay in which you describe your relationship with a favorite pet. Include your observations of, responses to, and attitude toward your pet. Compare and contrast this relationship to those you have with humans.**

You may wish to discuss the idea of "personification" and its role in one's relationship with a pet. Encourage your students to be observers of their pets, and avoid making assumptions about them until after the writing assignment.

11. **Some writers have argued that it matters little if certain "nonessential" endangered species become extinct if they interfere with "human progress." Argue for or against this proposition.**

The argument whether it would matter greatly if certain species of animals become extinct is a highly charged one, particularly with issues that pit businesses against environmentalists. You can suggest that your students tackle the question in several ways: aesthetically, ethically, economically, or culturally.

12. **Writing an Argument** Argue for or against one of the following practices: **(a)** hunting for the sake of the hunt, **(b)** eating meat, or **(c)** keeping animals in zoos.

Any of the three suggested topics is ripe for discussion and argumentation. If you have a culturally diverse classroom, it would be particularly interesting to study views of different groups regarding hunting, meat eating, and zoos.

Lesson Plan 10.8

Twain's "Two Views of the Mississippi"—In-Class Essay

Class Opener

Ask students to shut their eyes before asking this question: What color are the walls in the classroom? Point out that we often become so used to our surroundings that we no longer take note of them.

Activity: Defend, Challenge, or Qualify

Allow students the entire class period to first read Mark Twain's piece, then ask them to write an essay in which they respond to the following argument prompt:

> Twain concludes this essay by comparing the familiarity of the steamboat captain with the river to the familiarity of the medical doctor to the human body. Twain claims: "No, the romance and beauty were all gone from the river. All the value any feature of it had for me now was the amount of usefulness it could furnish toward compassing the safe piloting of a steamboat. Since those days, I have pitied doctors from my heart. What does the lovely flush in a beauty's cheek mean to a doctor but a "break" that ripples above some deadly disease? Are not all her visible charms sown thick with what are to him the signs and symbols of hidden decay? Does he ever see her beauty at all, or doesn't he simply view her professionally, and comment upon her unwholesome condition all to himself?"

Defend, challenge, or qualify Twain's claim that though familiarity may not breed contempt, it does induce a jaded sense of boredom with the nature of something that was once considered beautiful.

Suggested Answers

"Two Views of the Mississippi" by Mark Twain

From *Life on the Mississippi* by Mark Twain. Harper & Brothers Publishers, 1901.

Comprehension

1. Twain's experiences on the Mississippi River made him think about another profession, and Twain pities the members of that profession. Discuss what the people in this profession lose.

He pities those doctors in the medical profession because they have lost sight of the marvels of humanity when they have to work on people who are sick or dying. The appeal of helping human beings gets harder to remember when doctors are trying to heal a human condition.

2. **What does Twain "lose" as a result of his profession as a steamboat pilot?**

He loses his ability to marvel about the beauty of nature. The skies above him no longer have any appeal In fact, they serve merely as a backdrop for the work that he is doing on the boat since they only serve as tools for his work.

3. **What is Twain's strongest desire concerning his views on the world of the river?**

He desires to be able to look at the river in its simplest and most beautiful form, and to appreciate its natural beauty and not think about it as representing work.

Rhetorical Analysis

4. **What is the thesis of this essay?**

People both gain and lose something while learning. By finding out how and why something functions as it does, people learn better ways of dealing with and manipulating it. However, the focused object also loses the mystical qualities it had before you knew how it all worked. There is a natural human instinct of assigning such magical qualities to anything people do not really understand.

5. **How does the river become Twain's enemy/nemesis?**

He describes how, after becoming a pilot, he would only recognize upcoming winds from the sunset and a dissolving sand bar from the bubbles and ripples. His job was not only to navigate through, but protect his boat from, the elements.

6. **What does Twain mean when he declares that he has "mastered the language of the river"?**

It means he understands the beauty and pitfalls that await him as a steamboat pilot. He has to "read" the river and know its "language" just like anyone who is traveling in a foreign country.

7. **What images does Twain use to point out the beauty of the river and its surrounding area? Discuss the effect of these images.**

Although answers will vary, direct students to the last line of the first paragraph: "There were graceful curves, reflected images, woody heights, soft distances; and over the whole scene, far and near, the dissolving lights drifted steadily, enriching it every passing moment with new marvels of coloring." The effect is almost like watching a ballet or looking into a kaleidoscope.

8. **What function does the "tall dead tree" serve" and what saddens Twain about this tree?**

It serves as a "friendly old landmark" that he can count on to help with his navigation. Only a single branch is living on it now, and he knows the tree will not soon remain.

Writing

9. **Write a paragraph about the thrill of a new discovery you made.**

Student responses will vary.

10. **Explain a lesson that you have learned from nature.**

Student responses will vary.

11. **Writing an Argument** Argue for or against the idea that once people understand how something works, they lose their appreciation of it. Give specific examples that back up the argument.

Student responses will vary.

Lesson Plan 10.9

Diamond's "The Last Americans"—Recognizing Classification

Class Opener

Jared Diamond's argument in this essay is built upon identifying a series of misconceptions. This sort of negative argumentation strategy—identify what is wrong and not what is right—is actually a rather logical one for students to master. To get them thinking along the right lines, engage them in a bit of guy versus gal dialogue. Ask the girls to come up with 5 misconceptions that guys have about girls. And ask the guys to come up with 5 misconceptions that girls have about guys. Make them explain their choices. Then explain to the class that one strategy they might choose to employ for argumentation is to define for students those notions which are not true.

Activity: Recognizing Classification through Misconception

Classification is an underused method for development. Diamond uses a sort of reverse classification in grouping together and explaining the misconceptions that lead society to dismiss the role of a healthy environment. Those misconceptions form the topic sentences of three early paragraphs in the essay:

- Foremost among these misconceptions is that we must balance the environment against human needs.
- Another popular misconception is that we can trust in technology to solve our problems.
- The final misconception holds that environmentalists are fear-mongering, overreacting extremists whose predictions of impending disaster have been proved wrong before and will be proved wrong again.

Although it seems that Diamond makes these points, classifies them as a group of misconceptions, and then moves on, in fact the rest of the essay directly relates back to these three misconceptions.

Provide students with the three bulleted statements, then ask them to identify textual evidence from the second half of the essay in which Diamond responds to the misconception. (They may only use examples found in paragraphs 9-52 for their support.)

Class Closer

Ask students to share the evidence they have gathered from the essay to support Diamond's arguments. Do they ultimately find that they agree with him?

Suggested Answers

"The Last Americans: Environmental Collapse and the End of Civilization" by Jared Diamond

Comprehension

1. Explain the significance of Shelley's poem "Ozymandias" for Diamond's essay.

Shelley's poem delineates the ruins of a once great civilization now dead and disappearing back into the earth. This is a direct correlation to Diamond's argument that Earth has lost many civilizations due to a form of complacency.

2. What are the "three dangerous misconceptions" (paragraph 3) about the environment that Diamond discusses?

Diamond outlines three dangerous misconceptions from paragraph 3 to 8. He starts with the idea that humans need to make the environment hold up to human needs, when in fact, the environment and humanity need to work side-by-side in balanced coexistence to survive. The second misconception Diamond points out is the idea that technology will save humanity. This is based on the idea that "new technology won't create new problems." The third misconception is that those who study and report on environmental problems are overreacting and inciting panic for their own motives and that their theories have been proven wrong before and will be so again.

3. List all the civilizations that Diamond mentions in this essay. Which civilization does he emphasize? According to Diamond, why did previous civilizations fail, and how do these collapses provide guides to the state of contemporary American civilization?

Diamond discusses the fate of several civilizations that have suffered or disappeared because of environmental issues. These can be found in paragraphs 2, 8, 9, and much of the main body that talks about the Maya. He discusses the Aztecs in paragraph 19. Students should be able to point out the similarities between what happened to these ancient vanishing civilizations to issues dealt with today such as environmental damage, trade relations, aggression, and attitudes of denial so that solutions are not sought out.

Rhetorical Analysis

4. State Diamond's argument or major proposition. Where does his claim appear most clearly? What minor propositions does he develop? How does he deal with opposing viewpoints?

Diamond's major argument is in paragraph 4: "Human needs and a healthy environment are not opposing claims that must be balanced; instead, they are inexorably linked by chains of cause and effect." In supporting this argument, Diamond provides misconceptions that led to the demise of earlier cultures and are being repeated now. See if students can point out areas where he further supports his main argument. Students should be able to recognize opposing viewpoints and how Diamond focuses on them. They will find some of these beginning with paragraph 10.

5. What types of evidence does the writer provide to support his claim?

Diamond uses examples from ancient civilizations to show how mistakes are being repeated. He allows much of the essay to focus on the Maya because their culture was huge and advanced. Yet, because of the misconceptions we have today, they were eventually overcome and nearly all lost.

6. Why does Diamond divide his essay into so many sections? What relationships do you detect between and among these sections?

Discussing the experiences of these earlier civilizations forces Diamond's audience to face reality as to what is happening now. This might be a great time to bring in a film such as *An Inconvenient Truth* for discussion on this topic with regard to existing evidence and for a comparison of how this evidence is being treated.

7. Where does Diamond use comparison and contrast and causal analysis to organize parts of his essay? What is the significance or effect of these two techniques?

Comparison and contrast are rife throughout this essay, especially where Diamond connects ancient cultures with modern ones. Causal analysis makes up his main point—what caused the demise? What is being repeated? What is our future? What is causing all of this? How can we change old habits?

8. How does classification operate as a rhetorical element in this article?

Classification creates a visual historical record and it helps the reader to better understand a somewhat complex discussion.

9. Assess the relative effectiveness of Diamond's conclusion. How does the ending serve as a coda for the entire essay?

Responses here will vary. In small groups, students should discuss how they each responded to the essay, then bring their discussions back to the class as a whole. Then a consensus can be determined about Diamond's conclusion.

Writing

10. Write an essay focusing on a local environmental problem. Analyze the ways in which this environmental problem affects the lives of nearby residents.

Essays might vary, depending on the city in which this text is being used. If the local area does not have a particular issue, have students research environmental issues in other parts of the world, for example, Mexico City or Los Angeles, California. There are many options here.

11. Select one civilization that Diamond mentions. Conduct research on this civilization, and then write a report on the environmental factors that led to the decline of that society.

This is a good opportunity for a library research project. Have partners or small groups each take a different civilization discussed by Diamond and research it. They can then report back to the rest of the class in a presentation style what they learned about the decline of their respective civilization.

12. Writing an Argument **Write a persuasive essay in which you warn readers about three environmental dangers confronting the United States today.**

This essay assignment will bring out a variety of issues, depending on where the student is from and his or her understanding of environmental issues. Make sure students remember to cite sources.

Lesson Plan 10.10

Chapter Assessment

Rhetorical Analysis Answers

1. C
2. E
3. A
4. B
5. D
6. A
7. D
8. B
9. E
10. D

Connections for Critical Thinking

The writing suggestions on page 489 provide extensions to require students to synthesize these diverse essays and think of them in terms of each other. Allow students to choose one topic from the list, either for an at-home essay or an in-class response. Consider taking students to the library for this particular writing project, as many of these topics would benefit from additional research.

Answers

1. **Using support from the works of Eastman, Lopez, Carson, and others, write a causal-analysis essay tracing our relationship to the land. To what extent have history, greed, and fear helped shape our attitude? Can this attitude be changed? How?**

   The interesting relationship between humans and land is the central focus of each these three essays. They all deal with humans and their relationship to nature, to the land, but in different respects. Eastman is concerned with children's lack of time outdoors in nature. Lopez describes a specific area of land in southern California and how it has evolved through generations of "vandalism" inflicted upon it, through mining, military, and eventually suburban influences. Carson expands on this by her concerns over man's poisoning of the land through overuse of its resources, the infusion of insecticides, and other forms of contamination with no concern about the ultimate effects.

2. **Consider the empathy and sensitivity Walker has toward animals. How do her attitude and perceptions coincide with the views expressed by Bass and Eastman concerning the natural world?**

   Walker gives clarity to Blue's behavior from human perspectives. She understands what he is showing her in his eyes and in his behavior: emotions usually only accredited to humans. He is lonely, and once a new companion becomes temporary and leaves, his loneliness turns to deep sadness and frustration. Walker's compassion and empathy enlighten the reader to the reality of life, or lack thereof, for the beast. Eastman would understand this, considering his respect for nature and his traditions and beliefs that allow him to grasp the bond Walker describes. Bass corroborates this respect for nature and wildlife in his descriptions of hunter versus prey in the Yaak.

3. **Write a letter to the op-ed page of a newspaper objecting to a governmental ruling harmful to the environment. State the nature of the policy, its possible dangers, and your reasons for opposing it. Use support from McKibben, Diamond, and any other writers in this chapter. Extra reading or research may be necessary.**

   Have students research a ruling that is directly related to environmental issues. They should learn what they can about the issue itself and how the ruling came about. Then they can incorporate elements of McKibben and Diamond to support their arguments.

4. **Consider why we fear nature. Why do we consider it an enemy, an alien, something to be destroyed? How would Walker, Lopez, and Eastman respond to this question? Do you agree or disagree with them?**

   Responses to these questions may vary, depending on students' individual experiences with nature and/or wildlife. Some of them have probably been hunting. Many are probably pet owners. Some grow plants. Some students will have grown up in the country and others have rarely, if ever, seen the country. So be prepared for a broad spectrum of responses here. Students should look for how the listed writers might respond. For instance, Eastman might say that the white man fears what he cannot control or that he merely sees nature for what it can provide him, not for what it is, or what it provides simply by remaining what it is. Lopez might answer that man does not take the time to understand nature, and therefore misses out on a chance to get beyond his fears of the unknown. Walker may say that nature is more closely related to man than man would like to believe or admit. The possibility that the horse, Blue, could experience what are otherwise considered human emotions, might be too unnerving for most humans to accept because it would make them less likely to have complete control.

5. **Both Lopez and Diamond use narration and description to explore our relationship to the land. How do they approach their subject in terms of language, attitude, and style?**

   Lopez is descriptive and uses personal observation to express his deep sadness at how humans have slowly destroyed parts of the United States. The "vandalizing" actions by miners, military, developers, and other destructive forces have taken a toll on the country's history and heritage. For Diamond, the destruction to the environment began centuries ago and ultimately led to the demise of several great civilizations.

6. **Choose an author in this chapter whose essay, in your opinion, romanticizes nature. Compare his or her attitude with that of a writer with a more pragmatic approach to the subject. Compare the two views, and specify the elements in their writing that contribute to the overall strength of their arguments.**

   Essays in response to these questions will vary based on individual student opinion. Have a discussion in class that helps to define terms like *pragmatism* and *romanticizing*, so the students will have a basis from which to begin their compare and contrast.

7. **Write an essay titled "Nature's Revenge" in which you examine the consequences of environmental abuse. Consider the short- as well as the long-term effects on the quality of life. Use support from any three writers in this chapter to defend your opinion.**

   Students should consider the commonly repeated theory that "nature takes back her own." In other words, Earth's history is replete with moments of destruction when devastation or catastrophic events occur. Theories abound that modern overuse of resources and environmental damage is leading to catastrophe. Open the topic up for discussion and have students pre-write their ideas of long-term and short-term effects of environmental abuse in the name of quality of life.

8. **Write specifically about our relationship to other living creatures on our planet. Is it one of exploitation, cooperation, or tyranny? How does this relationship influence how we treat each other? Explore the answers to these questions in an essay. Use the works of Eastman, Lopez, and Walker to support your thesis.**

   Responses will vary. Have students list elements from the essays that support their individual ideas.

Lesson Plan 10.11

Synthesizing Sources: GMOs—Are They Good for the World or Not?

Assign students to read the sources and answer the first five questions for homework. This will prepare them for writing the essay. Then have them use the "Writing an Argument" prompt to write the essay as an in-class timed assignment (40 minutes).

Applying Your Synthesis Skills: Suggested Answers

Comprehension

1. **Briefly summarize the stated or inferred arguments made in each source.**

   Sample Responses: **Source A**, from the U.S. Department of Agriculture, points out the many benefits associated with agricultural biotechnology, another name for genetically modified plants. **Source B** provides scientific evidence that GMOs have toxic results that affect farmers and communities. **Source C** uses data, including a graph and statistical information, to assert that the use of GMOs has increased food production through more effective acreage production. **Source D** argues that GMOs have greatly contributed to solving the hunger problem in developing countries and are only shunned by those in more elite sectors of the world. **Source E** discusses the genetic dangers to animals and allergic reactions to humans using GMOs, and states that Monsanto covered up diseases that affected tested animals. **Source F** highlights the visual beauty of three tomatoes that have been genetically modified and appear to be healthier and more delicious than tomatoes grown without GMOs.

Rhetorical Analysis

2. Identify the emotion-laden diction in the titles of the sources. How do the titles create tone?

The word *Biotechnology* in Source A's title denotes a scholarly tone, and the word *Benefits* implies the article will be favorable toward GMOs. The word *Dangerous* in Source B provides a tone of warning. The words *Anti-Science* and *Immoral* in Source D chide public opinion that thinks GMOs should be halted. The word *Roulette* in Source E connotes risk and potential harm.

3. Compare the number of positive and negative words in Sources A, B, and E. How do the words support the purpose of each source?

Source A uses many positive words, including *benefits, safer, non-toxic, protect, saved, enhanced, innovations, invaluable,* and *wealth of opportunities.* Source B uses many negative words, including *hazards, warns, harmful, failed, concerns, crude, imprecise, outmoded,* and *toxic.* Source E also includes many negative words: *stunted, impaired, abnormal, inflamed.* Sources B and E are against the use of GMOs, whereas Source A is pro-GMO.

4. Which sources use logos to support their arguments? Which sources use pathos? Provide examples.

Sources A, B, and E use logos to support their arguments. Source C uses logos, although it does not try to persuade the audience. Source D uses pathos to support its argument. An example of logos in Source A includes: "scientists have identified the complete genetic structure of several strains of Listeria and Campylobacter, the bacteria often responsible for major outbreaks of food-borne illness in people." An example of logos in Source B includes: "Over 75% of all GM crops are engineered to tolerate being sprayed with herbicide. This has led to the spread of herbicide-resistant superweeds and has resulted in massively increased exposure of farmers and communities to these toxic chemicals." An example of logos in Source E includes: "About two dozen farmers report that GM corn varieties caused their pigs or cows to become sterile, 71 shepherds say that 25% of their sheep died from grazing on *Bt* [from *Bacillus thuringiensis*] cotton plants, and others say that cows, water buffaloes, chickens, and horses also died from eating GM crops." An example of pathos in Source D includes: ". . . consumers and farmers alike are eager to share in the life-saving and life-enhancing advances that modern science alone can bring." The use of parallel structure ("It's cruel, it's heartless, it's inhumane") also assumes a poetically moral high ground.

5. Describe the visual rhetoric in Source F.

The vibrant red of the three tomatoes indicates stunningly robust health and look tempting to eat. They are touching and posed in a similar manner, suggesting they are aligned. This creates a sense of positive unity and visual appeal. Our eye is drawn to the tomatoes because of their pleasing harmony. They are placed on a white and black background—a genetic code—which allows them to stand out. The idea that they are genetically modified, as explained by the title, seems trivial at first glance. Some students may take a different approach and assert that the vivid red is akin to the "forbidden fruit"—the apple associated with Adam and Eve.

Writing an Argument

6. Using examples from at least three of the sources, write an essay explaining who—in your opinion—benefits the most from the production of GMO plants.

Student essays will vary. Essays should focus on who benefits from GMOs—manufacturers of GMOs, farmers, consumers, developing countries, the environment. Some sources concentrate on the benefits of GMOs, citing such issues as alleviating world hunger and improving food safety. Others offer cautionary warnings of human health and environmental hazards. Both sides offer statistical evidence and authoritative research to sway the reader. The graph and captions in Source C do not try to appeal emotionally, but they indicate that GMOs are found in much of U.S. crop production, and it would be difficult to create a reversal of GMO production. Some essays will use this evidence to say GMOs are here to stay, despite negative effects.

CHAPTER 11

AP Favorites

Chapter 11 includes essays that were selected as the favorites of the hundreds of AP English teachers polled in anticipation of this book. These "favorites" do not have a single focus or a single theme or even a single time period. Instead, they are as diverse as the teachers who teach them. While you probably already have a favorite way of teaching them, this chapter of the Teacher Manual will simply provide suggestions for strategies that work well with these essays, and potential groupings and thematic pairings that will give you additional options for synthesis practice. These essays are listed in alphabetical order in the Student Edition. **Suggested answers** to the Comprehension and Rhetorical Analysis questions in the Student Edition begin on page 250.

Teaching the Essays

Lesson Plan 11.1

Angelou, Emerson, Plato—Debating the Nature of Education: A Four Corner Synthesis Lesson

This activity encompasses Maya Angelou's "Graduation," Ralph Waldo Emerson's "Education," and Plato's "Allegory of the Cave." Although two of the authors in this lesson make significant claims regarding education, the third reminds us of how much we take for granted regarding our access to education. In Angelou's "Graduation," she explores the importance of graduation within a marginalized community, a fitting reminder of the materialization of the philosophizing of Emerson and Plato. The focus of this lesson is two-fold: First, students will read, analyze, and debate the philosophy of education. Then they will read and discuss Angelou's narrative in terms of that debate.

Activity: Reading and Presenting Emerson and Plato

You probably remember reading Plato's "Allegory of the Cave," either in a philosophy of education course or a general philosophy course. This essay focuses on the need for the cave dwellers to look away from watching the shadows that play on the walls, and instead turn their attention to those devices causing the shadows. Plato's allegory through Socrates's teaching suggests that real education comes from observing and creating our own knowledge rather than accepting those images that are handed to us. Emerson's "Education" differentiates between Drill and Genius as being fundamental to learning. Organize the class into two groups and have one group responsible for reading and presenting "Education," whereas the other group is responsible for reading and presenting "Allegory of the Cave."

Activity: Four Corners Debate

After students have presented their readings of the assigned essays, divide each group into four, so that each group has an equal number of Emerson readers and an equal number of Plato readers. Then assign the following positions to the groups for a Four Corners Debate:

- Drill is necessary for education, but genius is not.
- Genius is necessary for education, but drill is not.
- Both drill and genius are necessary for education.
- Neither drill nor genius is necessary for education, as education is created based on the experiences of the participants.

Students should use examples from both Plato and Emerson as they debate. Use the standard Four Corners Debate procedures you have employed during other points in the course.

Activity: Socratic Seminar of Details in "Graduation"

While students are considering the importance of education, give them a little break from the hard-core philosophy by sharing "Graduation," a compelling narrative about the importance of graduation as a rite of passage in a poor, rural area where racism is still felt and present. This is a wonderful essay to use as a Socratic Seminar, particularly since students just read through Socrates's questioning technique in "Allegory of the Cave." Ask students to capture specific details from the text on index cards. Then on the back of each index card, have students draft a question related to that particular detail. Use either side of the card to facilitate the discussion.

Lesson Plan 11.2

Bacon and Donne—Simplifying Syntax and Diction

This activity encompasses Francis Bacon's "Of Revenge" and "Of Studies," and John Donne's "Meditation." Students are often intimidated by archaic language and syntax, causing them to "shut down" in the testing environment. These pieces are decidedly brief, offering an excellent opportunity for students to play the part of the modern editor.

Activity: Simplifying Syntax and Diction

Students can complete this activity either independently or in groups. All they need is the set of publishing guidelines listed below. Tell students they will be editing these pieces for a modern audience. They must do all of the following:

- Break each piece into multiple paragraphs.
- Simplify at least 10 sentences.
- Change at least 5 archaic words to reflect modern, academic choices.

After they have completed this task, they must write an introduction to their new, modern piece. The introduction must reflect modern issues. Students might, for instance, introduce Bacon's discussion in "Of Revenge" in terms of current debates surrounding the death penalty. Or they might discuss "Of Studies" in terms of the discussions surrounding state standards. They might consider "Meditation" in terms of famous final letters, such as that of Senator John McCain. The final version hopefully will be a compelling combination of improved reading comprehension of archaic texts along with creative reflection on how an old text informs modern issues.

Lesson Plan 11.3

Brady and Woolf—A Woman's Place: Paired SOAPSTone

This activity encompasses Judy Brady's "I Want a Wife" and excerpts from Virginia Woolf's *A Room of One's Own.* In these two essays from very different eras, Brady and Woolf confront the stereotypes that face women, albeit from very different perspectives. Brady uses wit and humor, whereas Woolf uses syntactical acrobatics and richly convoluted argument to argue for a more favored status for women.

Activity: Comparing Brady and Woolf

At this point in the year, students have become accustomed to writing SOAPSTone analysis. For this activity, ask them to write the acronym SOAPSTone in the middle of their paper, leaving room on either side to write, like the following chart:

Woolf		Brady
	S	
	O	
	A	
	P	
	S	
	Tone	

For this activity, students should work in groups to read both essays, filling out the SOAPSTone chart on each essay, but in such a way that they can easily compare their findings.

After they have finished their SOAPSTone chart, students are to use the information in it to aid in writing an essay based on the following prompt:

> **In the passages, both Virginia Woolf and Judy Brady are interested in the relative position of women. Although they face this question at very different historical moments, certain themes emerge as being apparent in both essays. In a well-written essay, explore the similarities and differences in their arguments, tones, and use of language.**

Lesson Plan 11.4

Edwards and King—Rhetorical Analysis of the Great Preachers

This activity encompasses Jonathan Edwards's "Sinners in the Hands of an Angry God" and Martin Luther King, Jr.'s "Letter from Birmingham Jail." At first glance, it might seem strange to pair Edwards and King, but in terms of their voices, it is readily apparent they share a preaching quality. Both were ministers, and while Edwards's speech is, in fact, a sermon, King's letter also has many of the markings of a sermon.

Activity: Rhetorical Scavenger Hunt of "Sinners"

Jonathan Edwards's sermon is somewhat off-putting to many students. Not only is the intensity of the subject matter outside of most of their experiences, but the Puritan language is difficult to parse. However, the argument and rhetorical structure is clear and precise, an excellent opportunity for students to practice their skills with the all-important pre-20th century passage that appears on the AP Exam.

For this activity, have students complete a chart like the following for a rhetorical scavenger hunt of "Sinners in the Hands of an Angry God." (Photocopy the chart, or see **Chapter 11 online Teacher Resources, Lesson 11.4.**)

Device	Quotation	Connection to Meaning
Appeal to Pathos		
Appeal to Logos		
Appeal to Ethos		
Metaphor		
Allusion		
Powerful & Purposeful Diction		
What is Edwards's overall purpose?		
What do you think made his message so powerful?		

Activity: Rhetorical Scavenger Hunt of "Letter"

After students have worked through Edwards's speech, ask them to complete the same chart as an analysis tool for King's "Letter from Birmingham Jail."

Device	Quotation	Connection to Meaning
Appeal to Pathos		
Appeal to Logos		
Appeal to Ethos		
Metaphor		
Allusion		
Powerful & Purposeful Diction		
What is King's overall purpose?		
What do you think made his message so powerful?		

Class Closer

Ask students to consider the similarities and differences between the styles of the two preachers. How are they alike? How are they different?

Lesson Plan 11.5

Elizabeth, Hobbes, Machiavelli—Examining Ethics, Reason, and Power

This activity encompasses Queen Elizabeth I's "The Golden Speech," excerpts from Thomas Hobbes's *Leviathan,* and excerpts from Machiavelli's *The Prince.* In Queen Elizabeth's "The Golden Speech," the Queen defends herself against charges that she has inadequately guarded the interests of her subjects, instead showing favoritism to a small group of nobles who have taken advantage of her graces. In so doing, she turns the argument around, instead focusing on her love for her subjects and country. Taken as a whole, Hobbes's *Leviathan* and Machiavelli's *The Prince* share many similar ideas of what a leader or government should be. Machiavelli's treatise suggests that the power of the Prince can justify immoral means for obtaining his aims (i.e., the end justifies the means). While agreeing with the concept of a strong ruler, in the excerpts here Hobbes argues the importance of developing speech, reasoning, and logic in order to benefit mankind. In this lesson plan, we will ask students to read and analyze the arguments made by Hobbes and Machiavelli. Then students will apply that analysis to Queen Elizabeth's speech to determine which of Hobbes's and Machiavelli's ideals she embodies.

Activity: Reading and Summarizing

In order to apply the arguments in this lesson to a reading of "The Golden Speech," students first must read and understand the underlying principles each writer supports. In the selected passage from *The Prince*, Machiavelli addresses the question whether it is better to be loved or feared. Students should read the passage, writing at least three questions (each from a different page in the selection), and summarizing in 100 words the entire passage. They will undergo the same process for the Hobbes selection, focusing on speech, reason, and science. It is worth noting that the Hobbes selection is much longer, and you might choose to discuss Machiavelli before moving on to Hobbes. As students read Hobbes, whether after a discussion of Machiavelli or before, have them complete the same assignment as with Machiavelli—three discussion questions and a 100-word summary.

Activity: Applying the Principles

Now that students have an understanding of the principles, ask them to turn to "The Golden Speech." For this lesson, students should read the speech, selecting textual evidence that lends itself either to Hobbes's or to Machiavelli's ideas, or that combines both. Have them use a chart like the following to record their analysis (Photocopy the chart, or see **Chapter 11 online Teacher Resources, Lesson 11.5.**):

Elizabeth I says . . .	Hobbes/Machiavelli says . . .	Elizabeth I exemplifies the specific philosophy by . . .

Class Closer

After students have completed the chart, have them write an analysis essay of "The Golden Speech" in terms of Hobbes or Machiavelli or a combination of both.

Lesson Plan 11.6

Kennedy and Lincoln—Annotating Inaugural Addresses

This activity encompasses John F. Kennedy's "Inaugural Address" and Abraham Lincoln's "Second Inaugural Address." In addition to the fact that both men were assassinated, Kennedy and Lincoln have gone down in history as having delivered two of the greatest inaugural addresses of all time. Both men were faced with a nation in crisis. While Lincoln was facing the continuing Civil War, Kennedy was facing the very serious threat of the Cold War. Ask students to revisit their annotation skills as they analyze these speeches.

Activity: Annotation Practice

Annotation skills cannot be over-taught as students face the very real challenge of reading what appears as a speech and writing a rhetorical analysis essay within a 40-minute span. Have students read these speeches with specific purposes in mind. For this activity, you will need four colors of sticky notes. Assign a specific color to "diction," a specific color to "syntax," a specific color to "detail and imagery," and a specific color to "device." Give students three of each color of notes, and ask students to draw a line down the middle of each note. As they read the text, students should use the correct colored note to annotate for each given attribute. On one side of the line, they will write the example, and on the other side of the line, they will connect that example to the overall argument. For instance, in analyzing Kennedy's address, students might create a "device" note that looks like this:

Opens successive paragraphs with the word "to"	Addresses various contingencies and problems the presidency is facing; Kennedy makes clear that as president he will address each group directly, both friend and foe; Stylistically unifies the message and separates out the various groups

Activity: Annotation Practice

After students have completed their annotations, ask them to write an essay in which they group each specific color into a separate body paragraph. Their essay will be a rhetorical analysis essay that addresses the following prompt:

> **In their inaugural addresses, both John F. Kennedy and Abraham Lincoln faced the challenge of unifying a country that was at odds with itself. Choose one of the two inaugural addresses, and write an essay in which you analyze how the president used the resources of language to set a course for national unification.**

Lesson Plan 11.7

Didion, Mairs, Staples—Examining Marginalization Through Detail

This activity encompasses Joan Didion's "Marrying Absurd," Nancy Mairs's "On Being a Cripple," and Brent Staples's "Black Men and Public Space."

Class Opener

Ask students to define the term *marginalization* with a dictionary definition and an example. This is a term that may be new to many students, so consider being ready with examples of your own from the news.

Activity: Multiple-Entry Journaling of Details

Each of these essays deals with the nature of marginalization. Two of the authors, Mairs and Staples, draw from personal experience of being considered "other," while the third author, Didion, judges as absurd those who make certain choices related to marriage. Allow students to choose one of the essays for an analysis of marginalization.

Using a multiple-entry journal format, ask students to find specific details in their selected essay that lead to understanding that the subject or object is marginalized. Once they have their journals completed, group students according to the essay they chose to analyze. Allow these groups to discuss the issue of marginalization from the standpoint of their selected author/essay.

After your same-essay groups have discussed their work, mix the groups, making sure that each new group has at least one member who analyzed Staples, one who analyzed Didion, and one who analyzed Mairs. These new groups are tasked with completing this statement: *In these essays, the author established marginalization by providing details that. . . .*

Class Closer

This exercise allows for an excellent group essay. Now that students have written a thesis statement and analyzed the three essays, have students write an essay that synthesizes all three essays, using details from their multiple-entry journals and the thesis they created in the class closer.

Lesson Plan 11.8

The Things We Carry—A Creative Approach to Sentence Variety

This activity encompasses the excerpt from *The Things They Carried* by Tim O'Brien. A warning to teachers: If you have not taught this text before, keep in mind that O'Brien uses language of war, including profanity. If you feel this will be a problem within your class, you might elect to forego this selection.

Class Opener

In their groups, ask students to compose a list of at least two items each person in the group is currently carrying on their person. Have them add their group items to a classroom list on the board.

Activity: Analyzing Sentence Patterns

This particular excerpt establishes the extended metaphor upon which the title of the book is based. The description of the things soldiers carry includes both literal and figurative items. They carry things, but they also carry fears, ideals, and thoughts. Use this selection to have students classify sentences. Ask them to create a catalog of how O'Brien starts and ends his sentences. Ask them to compile a list of 10 sentence patterns he uses (i.e., Subject Verb Complement; Introductory Adverb Subject Verb Complement; Inverted Order, etc.).

Activity: Using Sentence Variety in Paragraphs

After they have compiled their lists, have students create a substantial paragraph for their group, defining the group by the things they carry. Their list should contain physical items, like the ones they "discovered" during the class opener, but they should also include the intangible characteristics those tangible objects connect to. Tell students they must use at least five of the sentence patterns they discovered in O'Brien's writing in their own paragraphs.

Class Closer

Ask groups to share their paragraphs. As a follow-up activity, ask groups to create a visual depiction of their paragraphs.

Lesson Plan 11.9

Orwell and Sedaris—A Study of Diction

This activity encompasses George Orwell's "Shooting an Elephant" and David Sedaris's "Me Talk Pretty One Day."

Class Opener

Explain that Orwell and Sedaris rely on diction—specific word choice and play on words—as their trademarks. Tell students to choose either essay for a diction study.

Activity: In-Class Essay

Regardless of the essay students choose, the goal is singular: Students are to focus on the specific word choices of the author and connect those word choices to other word choices and to an overall intent on the part of the essayist. Students will begin by reading the essay. They should annotate as they read, noting the words that stand out to them. Then they will complete the analysis outlined in the following numbered questions and chart. Remind students of the difference between connotation (feeling) and denotation (dictionary definition). In "Connection to Other Words," the student should connect the word choice to other words the author selects. In "Connection to Argument," the student should connect the word choice to the overall argument in question. If students need help with the thesis statement, you can provide the following template: *In his essay, "Me Talk Pretty One Day," the author uses [type of diction] to establish a tone that is marked with tone marker words.*

A STUDY IN DICTION

1. What is the main argument of the essay?
2. What is the author's purpose? (Note to students: It MUST be more than "to entertain.")
3. Choose 5 specific words the author uses and complete the following chart on those words.

Word	Connotation	Denotation	Connection to Other Words	Connection to Argument

4. Assume that you are writing an essay about how the author uses diction to establish a specific tone in this essay. Write the thesis statement.
5. Now, using your thesis statement to guide you, write two body paragraphs for the essay, each focused on a different manifestation of tone in the essay.

Swift—Recognizing and Analyzing Satire

This activity encompasses Jonathan Swift's "A Modest Proposal." Satire is one of the hardest topics we teach to AP Language students. It is rife with subtlety, and too often students become so mired in understanding the language that they lose the overall meaning. In the College Board's notes on the 2009 rhetorical analysis passage, teachers were advised that students be familiar with satirical forms in addition to Swift's "A Modest Proposal," suggesting that knowledge of "A Modest Proposal" is foundational. Additionally, the notes suggest that students "need to learn how to detect and explain irony, which is an essential element of most satire but is used in other genres as well."

Class Opener

To introduce satire, consider showing clips from *Saturday Night Live* (particularly the political coverage), *The Daily Show*, or *The Colbert Report* to help students grasp the nature of satire. Students often struggle with understanding that satire is not just sarcasm. Rather, it is a combination of wit with rhetoric in an attempt to effect change.

Activity: An Introduction to Satire

Satire appears with some regularity on the AP Exam. In 2005, the rhetorical analysis question presented a mock press release from the satirical newspaper *The Onion*. In 2009, a paired critique of environmentalists and "people-first" critics appeared, presenting the double whammy of comparison/contrast and satire. Swift's essay provides an excellent opportunity to introduce students to the ironic contrasts we find in Horatian satire, with its gentler tone and use of wit and humor.

Aristotelian or Rhetorical Triangle

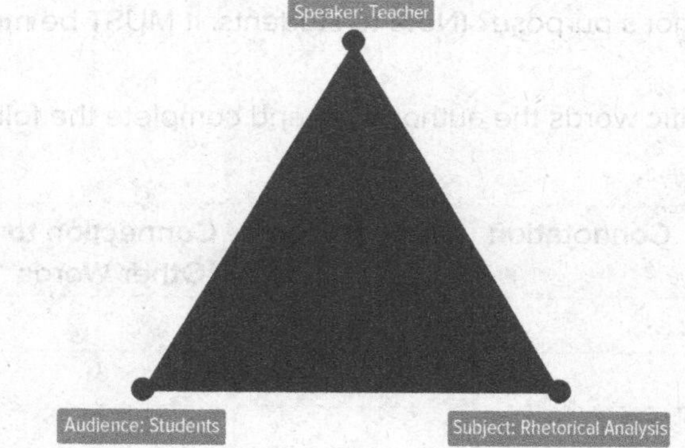

Traditionally, satire has been seen as a somewhat "less" sophisticated argumentation strategy because it maintains a level of personal attack. By its very nature, it incorporates and even embraces fallacious argument. In its attempt to sway the reader to a particular viewpoint, it presents the opposing view as not simply uninformed but cruel, ridiculous, stupid, or malicious. Although all of these arguments against satire ring true, we must not ignore the intrinsic complexity within the satiric model. Satire presents a **more** complicated argument, not a less complicated argument, something students realize when we examine the audience. Remind students that the traditional Aristotelian triangle presents an equal hegemony among the speaker, the audience, and the subject.

The complexity of satire has everything to do with how we define *audience*. In a straightforward argument, the audience will be multifaceted. The rhetorician is generally dealing with the audience from an assumption that he or she is manipulating language and argument in such a way as to bring the audience into the fold—to convince audience members to share the rhetorician's unique perspective.

The Satiric Audiences

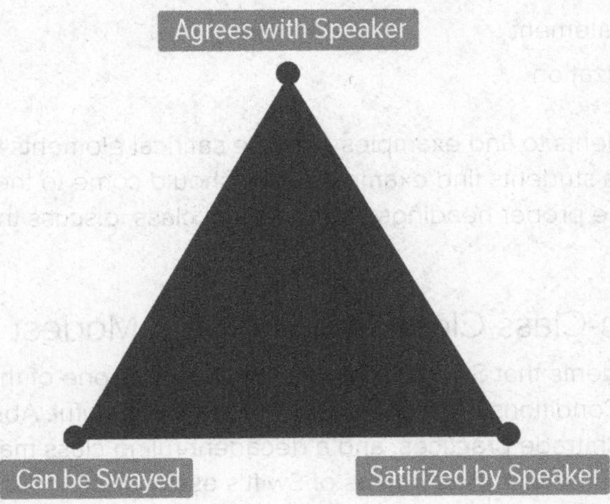

The satirist, however, has no such clear aim. Instead of aiming a single message with a single desired effect, the satirist is crafting a single message but with multiple purposes based on at least three distinct audiences.

A satirist can safely assume that some portion of the audience—most likely the majority—will agree with his position. In dealing with this audience, the satirist simply aims to maintain an intelligent position that will impress his supporters with wit, humor, and amusing rhetorical acrobatics.

A second audience emerges among those the satirist believes can be swayed—if only those intelligent souls can see how foolish the opposing viewpoint is. The satirist walks a fine line with this audience. If the arguments are too vicious or too punishing, they may push the fence-sitters over to the wrong side.

Finally, the satirist is addressing his opponent directly and often without much compassion. Ask students to consider how the opposition must feel when their positions and even their persons are attacked viciously through satire. Explain that, in order to sway the swayable, the satirist must show the opponent as holding views that are simply untenable.

Activity: Working with Satire

After clearly establishing what satire is and how it works, write the following elements of satire as headings on the board:

- Situational/Structural Irony
- Verbal Irony
- Hyperbole
- Understatement
- Generalization

Then ask students to find examples of these satirical elements within Swift's essay. Explain that as students find examples, they should come to the board and write them under the proper headings. At the end of class, discuss the examples they have written.

Activity: In-Class Close Reading of "A Modest Proposal"

Explain to students that Swift's "A Modest Proposal" is one of the most famous satires ever written. Conditions in Ireland during his life were awful. Absentee landlords, abusive English trade practices, and a decadent ruling class made life miserable for the mass of the Irish. The ironies of Swift's essay are famous and well known to you. Your students, however, may not find Swift's irony so obvious. One way that Swift undercuts his persona is by having him cite unreliable authorities. The "American" referred to is a cannibal and an Indian. That the speaker trusts a cannibal is suspicious. The Psalmanazar he refers to is George Psalmanazar (1679?–1763), a famous impostor, who claimed he was a Japanese convert to Christianity from Formosa. He published a history of Formosa (1704) and taught at Oxford until his hoax was discovered in 1706. Swift wrote "A Modest Proposal" in 1729.

There is probably no better way to study "A Modest Proposal" than by a deliberate, line-by-line, in-class close reading. This text is difficult for even the most astute student to fully understand; therefore, consider using the same think-along strategies you would use in a lower-level class with your AP students as they struggle with the language, the political climate, and the harsh Juvenalian nature of Swift's satire. As a whole group, determine what Swift's argument really is. Make sure students understand that Swift does not really want to impose cannibalism on the populace.

Activity: Debate "A Modest Proposal"

In groups, assign students to one of three potential Swiftian audiences: those who agree with Swift's political stance, those who disagree with Swift's political stance, and those who are not sure whether or not they agree with Swift's stance.

From the position they have been assigned, students should reread the text, looking for textual evidence they can use to further their position, or, in the case of the "unsure" group, crafting questions to pose to the debaters. After they have compiled their evidence, have a classroom debate. (Note that the debate will be between those who agree and those who disagree—the "fence-sitter" group, rather than compiling evidence, should compile questions to pose to the debaters that can be answered with textual evidence.

Lesson Plan 11.11

Thoreau—Fishbowl Discussion on the Politics of Transcendentalism

This activity encompasses Henry David Thoreau's "On the Nature of Civil Disobedience."

Class Opener

This particular lesson is based on a discussion of the transcendentalist texts and concludes with an in-class essay. Class openers can be based on a short quick-write or group definition of any of the topics listed below.

Activity: Fishbowl Discussion

Assign the text for reading at home and require students to write and submit for grading three questions per day of your discussion. In a standard 45–50 minute period, you should consider discussing this essay for at least two, if not three, class periods. Consider breaking the reading into manageable chunks and discussing the text in part rather than in whole. A workable breakdown, including discussion topics that should be discussed, could follow this schedule:

Class period 1—Paragraphs 1 through 16. Topics for discussion include the nature of government and Thoreau's claim that minimal government is to be desired, man as a machine, the right of revolution, Thoreau's discussion of slavery, and Thoreau's opinions on slavery.

Class period 2—Paragraphs 17 through 31. Topics for discussion include the nature of man's duty (wherein he seems to divest himself of any moral obligation regarding his objection to slavery), the series of rhetorical questions Thoreau poses in paragraph 19, response to unjust laws, the idea that just men belong in prison, and Thoreau's choice to go to jail.

Class period 3—Paragraph 32 to end. Topics for discussion include the response of Thoreau's neighbors to his civil disobedience, why we agree to pay taxes (is it only as Thoreau says in sympathy to the state?), Thoreau's complaints against the ineptitude of all legislators, and the idea that the government must have the sanction and consent of the governed.

Although individual experiences will vary, students seem to enjoy the philosophical weight of the essay. Thoreau expounds on deeply philosophical topics, and does so through the use of examples and narration, making his writing more accessible than we often give him credit for. Students' discussion of the selection helps them gain self-confidence in their ability to tackle older language and texts.

Activity: In-Class Essays

As an extension, provide students with the following in-class essay topic, asking them to draw at least some of their examples from their reading of transcendental philosophy.

> **Mark Twain once said, "It is our nature to conform; it is a force which not many can successfully resist."* In a well-reasoned essay, drawing on evidence from your reading and experience, defend, challenge, or qualify Twain's assertion.**

*From *Europe and Elsewhere* by Mark Twain. NY: Gabriel Wells, © 1923 by The Mark Twain Company.

Suggested Answers to Chapter 11 Essays

"Graduation" by Maya Angelou

Comprehension

1. What is the significance of the title?

Graduation is a landmark and centrally commands the actions of the story.

2. The graduation speaker, Mr. Edward Donleavy, praises recent graduates for their achievements. How do these achievements differ from the narrator's hopes for herself and her classmates?

Mr. Donleavy believes that the graduates' highest achievements are to become athletes or common laborers. Ms. Angelou dreams that she and her classmates will become much more successful than that. She was even considering the diploma as her ticket to become a teacher.

3. Why does the narrator initially admire Henry Reed? How does he come through for the community at the end?

She admires him because he is smart, unafraid, and courteous. He handles himself well with adults and children. Henry Reed's actions on the stage, leading the graduation audience in the Negro National Anthem, "Lift Ev'ry Voice and Sing," restores dignity and pride to the event.

Rhetorical Analysis

4. Look at the images in paragraph 47 and describe their effect on the narrator's feelings at the moment.

The narrator's feelings of frustration and dejection are shown by seeing the stereotypical characteristics of the Negroes, along with other cultural stereotypes, through the white person's eyes. She is frustrated because she cannot speak out in defense of her culture. She imagines all the cultures piled on top of one another in a funeral pyre with the white culture on the bottom. She is dejected about the inhumanity of humanity.

5. What are some of the details concerning dress in "Graduation" that give it a culturally historical feel? How does dress show Angelou's family's community status?

She mentions the "readymade clothes" from "Sears and Roebuck or Montgomery Ward" catalogs in paragraph 4, which would be ordered by those "who could afford it." Others would have the "best seamstresses" make the dresses or the "cut down secondhand pants." Her dress, described in paragraph 7, brings back the nostalgia of the 1940s era with the "butter-yellow pique dresses . . . crocheted cuff on the puff sleeves and a pointy crocheted collar." Still others would have to make do with what they had. Paragraph 28 describes "hair brushed back, legs oiled, new dresses and pressed pleats, fresh pocket handkerchiefs and little handbags," all homemade.

6. Explain the significance of the last two paragraphs on the overall effect of the essay.

The last two paragraphs show an inspired admiration for all the Black "poets" of the world who have given African Americans voice and courage. It is through their mutual voices of music, spirituality, and lyrical verse that they have "survived" achieving hope and a diverse type of freedom.

7. What is the purpose of intertwining objective and subjective narration in this essay? How does it change the effect of the essay?

The purpose is to achieve different lenses for the readers to look through as Angelou recounts this experience. Objective narration allows Angelou to step back and recount her local community's culture. Using this form of narration, the reader can see the whole spectrum of the Stamps, Arkansas community joining in the preparation and community experience of the graduation ceremony. Children are described as trembling "with visible anticipation," and the teachers ironically have now become "respectful of the now quiet and aging (high school) seniors." When she changes to subjective narration, Angelou separates herself from the community as a whole and defines her position within the community. By description, the reader can gather that Angelou's family owns a general store. Intellectually, she is at the top of her class with only Henry Reed receiving better grades than she. Subjective narration allows the reader to experience, along with Angelou, that feeling that she can be so much more than the typical graduate of Stamps.

8. What effects foreshadow Mr. Donleavy's speech?

In paragraph 27, when the people approach the school, "the school blazed without gaiety. The windows seemed cold and unfriendly." The school became a "now-strange building." The "usual assembly pattern" was askew with the band and principal's directions becoming misaligned, as described in paragraph 29, creating a "state of nervous tension."

9. Why was the graduation's response to the speaker described, in paragraph 36, like "rain through a ragged umbrella"?

The graduation attendees recognize that the speaker is demeaning. He methodically goes through his speech, giving no thought to the audience or their response. His mechanical speech represents the glaring differences between the Black and White cultures in Arkansas during that decade. He has determined who their heroes ought to be, and this assumption has deflated the audience.

“Of Revenge” by Francis Bacon

“Of Revenge” by Francis Bacon, third edition 1625. From *Bacon’s Essays and Wisdom of the Ancients*. Cambridge, Mass: The University Press. Copyright © 1884 by Little, Brown, and Company.

Comprehension

1. What is the primary theme of “Of Revenge”?

The primary theme is that private revenge is harmful, although Bacon advocates for “fortunate” public revenge, or state-sanctioned punishment.

2. According to Bacon, who and what get hurt when one takes revenge?

The person taking revenge and the law get hurt. Bacon argues that it is better to deal with the present wrongs and threat of future wrongs. He believes that letting past wrongs dominate one’s feelings is futile. The goal of our spiritual (moral) senses should be to try to influence the betterment of laws that address present and future wrongs where change can happen.

Rhetorical Analysis

3. Identify the logos in Bacon’s essay.

Bacon logically lays out his premise that private revenge, in any form, is detrimental to a person’s and society’s future. It puts “the law out of office.” It might even result in harm to the person who took revenge because the law might harm him or her (“two for one”). And it keeps the wound alive. Bacon points out that foregoing revenge results in a superior person.

4. Explain the metaphor in the opening statement, “Revenge is a kind of wild justice, which the more man’s nature runs to, the more ought law to weed it out.”

Bacon compares the human spirit to plants in a garden. He argues that we need to morally distinguish between the healthy plants and the weeds needing to be removed for the good of the garden. He recognizes that revenge is a natural desire, but argues that at various times it needs to be restrained for the good of the garden (humanity).

5. How does Bacon make use of pathos in his argument?

Bacon appeals to our sense of emotion by illustrating the point that private revenge is a useless waste of passionate reaction. He wants us to emotionally agree with him that our moral beliefs should guide our sense of retribution for the greater good. And, in order to do this, we must quell our natural human desire for revenge.

6. Explain the purpose of the imagery used in the following line: “But base and crafty cowards are like the arrow that flieth in the dark.”

Bacon explains that the lowest of those seeking revenge are the devious cowards who do not expose themselves but instead strike without identification. They are like “the arrow that flieth in the dark,” harming their enemy.

"Of Studies" by Francis Bacon

"Of Studies" by Francis Bacon, third edition 1625. From *Bacon's Essays and Wisdom of the Ancients*. Cambridge, Mass: The University Press. Copyright © 1884 by Little, Brown, and Company.

Comprehension

1. According to Bacon, what are the three main benefits of study? In Bacon's opinion, what danger can result from each benefit?

The benefits of study are delight—privateness and retiring; ornament—discourse; and ability—judgment and disposition of business. The danger of delight is sloth—to spend too much time in studies. The danger of ornament is affectation. The danger of ability is to make judgment wholly by one's own rules.

2. What is the proper attitude and purpose Bacon advises readers to take toward their books? What does this advice tell you about Bacon's attitude toward learning?

Bacon advises to read "not to contradict and confute, nor to believe and take for granted, nor to find talk and discourse, but to weigh and consider." He also believes "some books are to be tasted," or read only in parts; "others to be swallowed," or read without too much attentiveness; and "some few to be chewed and digested," or "read wholly, and with diligence and attention." Bacon believes books and studies can help one learn, but should not be the sole origination of learning.

Rhetorical Analysis

3. What analogy does Bacon make between different kinds of study and different kinds of physical exercise?

Bacon states that "as diseases of the body may have appropriate exercises," certain types of study can help improve one's wit. Studying mathematics will help one whose mind wanders. Studying medieval philosophers will help one who cannot "distinguish or find difference" (compare and contrast). Studying law will help one who has trouble debating and making deductions.

4. Find three examples of parallelism in "Of Studies." How does Bacon's use of parallelism help emphasize his ideas?

Bacon uses parallelism throughout most of this essay. The first sentence uses parallelism: "Studies serve for delight, for ornament, and for ability." The first part of sentence two (lines 1–3) also uses parallelism: "Their chief use . . . disposition of business." Lines 6–8 are another example of parallelism: "To spend too much time . . . humor of a scholar." Lines 21–25 show multiple forms of parallelism: "Reading maketh a full man . . . to know that he doth not." Using parallelism helps Bacon list his ideas as well as to compare and contrast.

5. Examine Bacon's diction in listing the benefits of studying history, poetry, mathematics, philosophy, logic, and rhetoric. How do his word choices affect the tone of the list?

Using one-word descriptions with connotations, such as "wise," "witty," "subtile" (subtle), "deep," and "grave" keeps Bacon's tone fast-moving and light.

"I Want a Wife" by Judy Brady

Judith E. Brady (Formerly Judith Syfers)

Comprehension

1. **Make a list of the wife's general expected duties.**

   Answers may include the following: Works to support the family so the husband can go back to school; Keeps the house clean; Takes care of all the children's needs, including babysitting arrangements; Sees to it that her husband's personal things are where he can find them when he needs them; Is sensitive to the husband's physical needs, but does not demand attention when he is not in the mood; Does not bother the husband by complaining about a wife's duties.)

2. **Were you surprised when you read this essay? Why or why not?**

   When it was first published, "I Want a Wife" had the humorous effect of surprising the reader. A woman was the one asking for a wife. In that era, women were expected to find happiness by taking care of their husbands and children.

Rhetorical Analysis

3. **What is the tone of the essay? Point out the irony in the essay.**

   The tone is humorous, satirical, and ironic, with an underlying desolation. In order to better his family, the husband is overburdening his wife.

4. **Explain the use of the rhetorical device anaphora in this essay.**

   Anaphora is a figure of speech in which the author uses a repetition of words. The repetition in this essay is "I want a wife." Brady uses this to make the point that husbands picture wives as subservient people who willingly want to do everything for their husbands. The author's repetition of these words reverberates with the reader and strengthens her point.

5. **How does the author successfully get the reader emotionally involved (pathos)?**

   She lists the jobs required of wives. After those jobs, she says, "My God, who *wouldn't* want a wife?" The reader clearly sees that tremendous inequity exists, and emotionally supports the argument.

"Marrying Absurd" by Joan Didion

Comprehension

1. Explain how the title relates to the essay.

Didion believes that the Las Vegas wedding business is a farce, because marriage should be held more sacred and not entered into so lightly.

2. Didion views Vegas weddings to be "the facsimile of proper ritual, to children who do not know how else to find it." Who are these "children" she mentions in paragraph 4?

Didion views some who use Las Vegas marriage services to be like children with the characteristics of being innocent, naïve, and unsophisticated.

3. What attracts people to the Las Vegas setting in order to get married?

It is almost like a faux Disneyland, full of bright lights and a flashy panorama. It is also relatively cheap to get married there, and people can get married quickly because there is no waiting period or blood test.

Rhetorical Analysis

4. Why is the last line in the essay so ironic?

When the bride states that her wedding was "just as nice as [she] hoped and dreamed it would be," the irony is that the girl is young (too young to drink legally), pregnant, and has just experienced a quick, cheap wedding. Her hopes and dreams are minimal, and the reader can infer that the rest of the girl's life will be full of minimal experiences as well.

5. Explain Didion's attitude about Las Vegas weddings and the people who participate in them. Give at least two specific examples to back up that attitude.

Didion disdains the practice of Las Vegas weddings. She reveals this through details highlighting the cheap element of the weddings [bored waiter, pink champagne, "on the house"] and also through the point made about the age of the pregnant bride. Details of another bride's flashy and cheesy orange mini dress, complete with "masses of flame-colored hair," accentuate the gaudiness of these types of weddings.

6. "Marrying Absurd" conveys more than Joan Didion's criticism of Las Vegas marriages. It also suggests something of Didion's attitude toward a larger world problem of what she describes in paragraph 2 as "venality" and "a devotion to immediate gratification." Explain what she means by this.

She believes the world has become a corrupt place where people are looking for instant fixes. Everyone is ready to stumble over everybody else to get what they immediately desire.

7. How does the craps metaphor in paragraph 3 add to this essay?

The metaphor ties marriage to Las Vegas, which is the overt theme of the essay. Craps is a game that she says should be played "when the table seems hot," making the game impulsive, unpredictable, and instinctive in a very delusional way—which is symbolic of the unpredictable futures of those married impulsively in Las Vegas.

8. In making her argument about Vegas weddings, Didion appeals to the reader's ethos (sense of character). She achieves this by making what points?

Didion makes the immediate point that she is merely observing these weddings, and that she would never participate in such a farce. By giving specifically ludicrous examples of several of these weddings and describing the Vegas environment, she is appealing to the reader's sense of character to agree that these weddings are not sacred ceremonies.

“Meditation (No Man Is an Island)” by John Donne

“Meditation” by John Donne, 1624. From “Devotions Upon Emergent Occasions” in *The Works of John Donne*, Vol. III. London: John W. Parker, West Strand. 1839.

Comprehension

1. In your opinion, what is Donne’s message in lines 1–4?

Responses will vary. Students may note that when people hear a bell tolling, their first response is to wonder why or for whom the bell is tolling, rarely realizing the bell applies to them.

2. In the last few lines, what does Donne think he will gain from “consideration of another’s danger”?

He will gain consideration for his own mortality and appeal to God, thus gaining security into heaven.

3. What purpose does the tolling bell serve?

The tolling bell represents death, an event experienced universally. It serves as a reminder that we are all part of a larger conceptual makeup. No one is truly independent of another. We are all joined together by the fact we are living and will one day die.

4. According to Donne, what act would be “an excusable covetousness”? Why?

The “excusable covetousness” is the “taking upon us the misery of our neighbours.” Bacon states that “affliction is a treasure” that brings one closer to God, and thus coveting others’ afflictions is understandable.

Rhetorical Analysis

5. What are some points of comparison Donne makes between humankind and “one volume” by “one author”? Is the comparison effective?

As the universal author, God will bind together various “translated” pages, each man a chapter, into a volume. In the new universal “library” of mankind, “every book shall lie open to one another.” We are all chapters in a volume that is in God’s library. Once again we are “bound” together.

6. According to Donne, in what ways are people like a “piece of the continent”?

No person is completely self-reliant. We are all dependent on one another in a larger sense. The context expands with “a part of the main,” meaning that all people are connected by some form of unity. The continent represents that unity.

7. Explain Donne’s metaphor when he states that when a man dies he is “translated into a better language.”

The person who dies from old age or sickness or war or justice will be made a better person or soul, and his or her “scattered leaves” will be brought back into God’s “library.”

8. Find several examples of alliteration in the essay. How do the examples affect the tone of the essay?

Examples include “death diminishes,” “none coined into current moneys,” and “Tribulation is treasure.” Alliteration—as well as repetition—creates a tone of steady seriousness.

"Sinners in the Hands of an Angry God" by Jonathan Edwards

"Sinners in the Hands of an Angry God" by Jonathan Edwards, 1741. From *Selected Sermons of Jonathan Edwards, Edited with Introduction and Notes* by H. Norman Gardiner. New York: The Macmillan Company and London: Macmillan & Co., Ltd. 1904.

Comprehension

1. What is the central idea Edwards delivers in this sermon?

He promises eternal damnation for people who do not take proper steps to avoid the wrath of God. His point is for repentance of those who are "sleeping" from negligence and those who are true sinners.

2. Edwards plays on a certain emotion from the congregation as he delivers this sermon. What emotion does he hope to draw from the congregation?

He hopes to draw fear, and he invokes fear through fire and brimstone.

3. Why does Edwards choose to use a variety of simple images that personify land and water?

He uses images of land and water to convey the power of God to the people of his congregation, many of whom are illiterate and can best respond to terms and ideas with which they are already familiar. The people, who lived off the land, had a respect for the land and the water, including its potentially violent nature.

4. Why does Edwards open his sermon with the Biblical text from Deuteronomy 32:35, "Their foot shall slide in due time"?

He wants to make the point to the congregation that life is a slippery surface, and a person walking on it has a very good chance of falling at some point. Eventually man will slip to destruction.

Rhetorical Analysis

5. What image of a great storm does Edwards use to describe the power of God, and why is it effective?

He compares divine fury to "black clouds . . . big with thunder." The congregation has experienced the reality of a violent thunderstorm. Farmers feared storms because they could damage crops, endangering a farmer's living. Those living in the villages and small towns feared thunderstorms because they could damage homes and businesses.

6. Edwards's rhetorical use of repetition is also effective. Give examples of this repetition and explain the intent of the repetition.

Answers will vary. Sample responses: Edwards repeats the word "nothing" several times throughout the sermon, emphasizing that there is nothing man can do on his own to save himself. His repetition of the term "slender thread" also is effective. The first states "it is easy for us to cut or singe a slender thread that anything hangs by." The second states "[you] hang by a slender thread, with the flames of divine wrath flashing about it." Both lines contain images of burning and fire, referring to the flames of Hell and the slender thread that man is on. Edwards hoped this connection would feed the fear of damnation and spur his congregation back to true faith and dependence upon God.

7. How do the Biblical references help the argument?

For congregations at this time in history, the Bible was the written authority of all power and might, thus establishing an appeal to all three persuasions of ethos, pathos, and logos.

8. **Edwards references fruit and the bearing of fruit twice. He views sin as a "bitter and poisonous fruit" and sees it to be like the "grapes of Sodom." What is the desired effect of these metaphors?**

Edwards is trying to teach his congregation that people get out of life the achievement of their efforts. If a person is righteous and obeys the word and law of God, God will grant His favor and a place in Heaven. If a person is sinful and denies God or His role in a man's salvation, he will earn God's wrath and be cast into Hell.

9. **What is the effect of the metaphor of God holding the souls of men over Hell "much as one holds a spider or some loathsome insect over the fire"?**

It ties together the ideas of man's reliance upon God, man's vulnerability to damnation, and the sheer power of the wrath of God. God is dangling the spider over the fire but he has not dropped it—yet.

10. **What sensory details does Edwards include in paragraph 4? What effect does this imagery have on the reader?**

The weight of sin will make the sinner fall; thus the images both frighten and intimidate the reader.

"The Golden Speech" by Queen Elizabeth I

"The Golden Speech" by Queen Elizabeth I, 1601. From *Cobbett's Parliamentary History of England*. Vol. I. London: Printed by T. Curson Hansard, Peterborough-Court, Fleet-Street. 1806

Comprehension

1. What was Elizabeth I's greatest challenge delivering this speech?

Although she had successfully reigned for 43 years, she was addressing an audience of the all-male Parliament. She had to appeal to their concerns, which no doubt also included the fact that she was now 68 years old. Her challenge was to show that she still remained a strong reigning sovereign.

2. Summarize what Elizabeth I is stating in paragraph 16.

She wants Parliament to see her only as an instrument of God. She is dismissing the idea that it is the trappings of the crown that make her such a person of authority. The crown is merely a symbol, as is the "glorious name of a king, or royal authority of a queen." She emphasizes that her role was given to her by God.

3. How does she use her gender, in her role as Queen, in a strongly affirmative manner?

She points out on several occasions, many great men have sat in her place in the role of King, but none were more loving and caring. This reminder serves as a remembrance that as a woman, she is a born nurturer.

Rhetorical Analysis

4. Considering that many connotations exist for the word *gold*, list other ways that Elizabeth and her speech could be considered "golden."

Elizabeth was known to wear strikingly red wigs, and ornate dresses, which gave her a shining and golden appearance. Her feisty, positive nature also projected her golden spirit. She ruled in the Golden Age of literature and commerce and exploration. She was known as "Good Queen Bess" and "Gloriana."

5. What tone does Elizabeth establish in the first 3 paragraphs of her speech?

With a tone a concern and self-deprecation, she lovingly acknowledges her respect for the members of Parliament and their concerns.

6. What persuasive strategies does Elizabeth use in her speech?

She acknowledges Parliament's grievances when she states in paragraph 11: "That my grants should be grievous to my people, and oppressions to be privileged under colour of our patents; our kingly dignity shall not suffer it; yea, when I heard it, I could give no rest to my thoughts until I had reformed it." Thus, she is quick to state that she had no knowledge of the problem, and she could not find peace until she had fixed it. She also asks her bowed audience to rise so she can speak to them directly. This strategy shows that she wants everyone to at least physically be on the same level. She further acknowledges members of Parliament by asking them to kiss her hand before they leave.

7. Analyze Elizabeth I's rhetoric of death in paragraphs 4 and 14.

She discusses that she desires "to live longer days" only to be able to see her subjects live in prosperity. She alludes to death again when she mentions the "last judgment day" when she is "judged to answer before a higher judge." Again she is referencing the fact that all she wants to do is leave her people in emotional and physical prosperity.

“Education” by Ralph Waldo Emerson

“Education” from *Lectures and Biographical Sketches* by Ralph Waldo Emerson. Boston: Houghton, Mifflin and Company, 1884

Comprehension

1. Why, in paragraph 5, does Emerson believe “[i]t is better to teach the child arithmetic and Latin than rhetoric or moral philosophy”?

The teachings of arithmetic and Latin require “exactitude of performance” and will make “certain that the lesson is mastered and that power of performance is worth more than knowledge.”

2. What are Emerson’s defining characteristics of an ideal education?

The “Drill” of a student’s mind, which goes hand in hand with “Genius,” needs to be armed with knowledge “in the very direction to which it points.” Emerson believes that one’s performance is almost as important, if not more important, than one’s actual knowledge. The final defining characteristic of an ideal education is that the student needs patience and devotion to the subject being taught.

3. In paragraph 10, why does Emerson criticize schools as bureaucratic institutions?

Schools abide by complicated, stagnant rules and must, by this reason, lower higher standards and serve to the lowest common denominator. In these institutions, those who teach have to work for the general outcomes of large classes as opposed to working for the outcomes of individuals. The focus is no longer on one particular student but rather it is now poised on the entire class. It seems to be bureaucratic because nobody is really allowed to be creative, do anything categorized as “different,” or be spontaneous. These schools expect students to do what is asked and not go against their imposed, rigid rules.

Rhetorical Analysis

4. How would you describe the overall tone of this essay?

The tone of this essay is convincingly philosophical. In order to achieve this tone, Emerson paints the idea of education with the use of analogies and metaphors. Thus, he discloses a deeply philosophical side to how he views education.

5. Emerson uses the rhetorical strategy of extended example in paragraph 4. What purpose does this example achieve?

He wants readers to see that the desire for and persistence of a subject will bring about a wealth of enlightening gifts. Using the example of his acquaintance, Sir Charles Fellowes, Emerson points out that Fellowes dogmatically followed his desires to learn all he could about sculptured Turkish ornaments. Fellowes followed many paths of learning not only to deliver a rare statue to the British Museum, but to achieve an “excellent education” forming a “college for himself.”

6. Explain the paradoxical relationship between “Genius and Drill” in paragraph 3.

The relationship between “Genius and Drill” is paradoxical because both are contradictory yet essential to education. A child is born with inspiration and enthusiasm for learning (Genius), but must adopt “the rules and instruments” (Drill) in order to join the “society of the lovers of the truth” (become educated).

7. What is Emerson’s point when he says “Nature loves analogies, but not repetitions”?

Every gift of nature might look similar, but each is actually different and unique. For example, while each snowflake looks similar on the surface, under the microscopic eye it is quite unique from the others. We can point to ourselves as human beings and make that same argument.

"Leviathan" by Thomas Hobbes

Leviathan by Thomas Hobbes, 1651. From *Thomas Hobbes Leviathan, Or the Matter, Forme & Power of a Commonwealth, Ecclesiasticall and Civill*. Edited by A.R. Waller. London: C. J. Clay and Sons, Cambridge University Press. 1904.

Comprehension

1. What, ultimately, is Hobbes's attitude about science?

Science has just rewards but should not be regarded by blind faith. The dogmatism that often results in scientific theory is blinded to other phenomena that have yet to be discovered or have been inexplicably ignored. Merely believing science to be true because one has read it in a book is not a valid enough reason to accept it unconditionally.

2. Hobbes uses the word *absurd* several times throughout this essay. Explain his definition of *absurd*.

Absurd means that an idea is taken at face value; it could even be read in a book or heard in a debate, but it has not passed the person's internal moral test. The idea has to come from spiritual ideals that further humanity in a positive direction.

Rhetorical Analysis

3. Explain what one could consider the irony in the last few sentences of paragraph 24.

Hobbes is telling people to not be fooled by rhetoric, and he shows the emptiness of words that are only being used for particular intentions. It is ironic since "Leviathan" is a strong example of rhetorical excellence.

4. What rhetorical skill does Hobbes use to dispute his sixth point in paragraph 38?

He uses religious words and allusions to argue that figurative language does not really ever tell the truth.

5. How does Hobbes further the arithmetic metaphor in paragraph 27?

Hobbes discusses summations and conclusions in this paragraph but questions the validity simply because it is so much agreed upon, without real questioning. He questions those who are quick to agree to the solution, and who actually are "unpracticed" in a particular mathematical quest.

6. Explain how using an anecdote in paragraph 28 furthers Hobbes's argument.

Hobbes is making the point that every step of the process must be taken into account if one is to believe the result. He talks about the master of a house who looks only at the final summation of his bills rather than examining each bill that contributed to this summation. He further compares it to someone who just agrees with an author's point without truly looking at the text that led up to that point. He draws a line between "knowing" and "believing."

7. What purpose does language serve, according to Hobbes? How does the language in the following statement fortify his belief: "To conclude, The Light of humane minds is Perspicuous Words, but by exact definitions first snuffed, and purged from ambiguity; *Reason* is the *pace*; Encrease of *Science*, the *way*; and the Benefit of man-kind, the *end*. And on the contrary, Metaphors, and senslesse and ambiguous words, are like *ignes fatui*; and reasoning upon them, is wandering amongst innumerable absurdities; and their end, contention, and sedition, or contempt."

He believes that language and solid definitions are the basis for all rationales, both scientific and philosophical. He also believes that they can come about objectively with universally accepted principles. He says that figurative language is basically senseless, ambiguous, and harmful. He calls for the purest language possible.

8. What is the overall tone of the passage?

The tone is stern, demanding, authoritarian, unrelenting, condemning, and elitist. Ask students to provide examples from the text to back up these responses.

John F. Kennedy's Inaugural Address

Inaugural Address of John F. Kennedy. Transcription courtesy of the John F. Kennedy Presidential Library and Museum. www.ourdocuments.gov

Comprehension

1. What foreign political experience is Kennedy addressing in paragraphs 8–11? How does his language affect his message?

Kennedy is addressing the Cold War and the spread of communism. He also has the imminent threat of nuclear war facing the country. He is clearly uncompromising to any other outcome but democracy when he states, "Let all our neighbors know that we shall join with them to oppose aggression or subversion anywhere in the Americas. And let every other power know that this Hemisphere intends to remain the master of its own house."

2. Paraphrase the following two famous statements: "And so, my fellow Americans: ask not what your country can do for you—ask what you can do for your country. My fellow citizens of the world: ask not what America will do for you, but what together we can do for the freedom of man."

It is our responsibility to actively maintain the standards of good American citizenry. We join with the rest of the world with the singular goal of maintaining the rights of freedom for all people.

3. What are Kennedy's goals, as articulated in this speech? How does he believe they can best be achieved?

He says (speaking for all Americans) that "we shall pay any price, bear any burden, meet any hardship, support any friend, oppose any foe, in order to assure the survival and the success of liberty." Thus, one goal is the continued pursuit of liberty for all human beings across the world. Another related goal is to help those who are persecuted and to not shrink away if challenged. These goals can best be achieved by everyone recognizing these fundamental rights and working together to make them a reality for everyone.

4. Who did Kennedy consider to be the audience of this speech?

This was not just a speech for those who attended his inauguration, nor was it a speech for the first audience to ever watch a presidential inauguration on television or those who listened to it on the radio. Kennedy's intended audience was the rest of the world, and he knew that in order to be heard by the world and future generations, his words would have to achieve ringing posterity.

Rhetorical Analysis

5. What rhetorical strategies are used in the opening paragraph of this speech?

The rhetorical strategies of parallelism, repetition, and juxtaposition are evident in the first paragraph.

6. This speech lasted approximately nine minutes. One of Kennedy's directives to Ted Sorenson, who helped him with this speech, was to eliminate the word "I" as much as possible. The word "we" is used approximately 33 times. What effect did Kennedy hope to achieve by this?

He wanted to emphasize to the nation that the speech was about the nation, not about Kennedy. He used the word "we" to show unified commitment to the betterment of this country. It emphasized what we as a nation could give rather than what the individual could receive. It also creates a stronger rapport with those who are listening to him.

7. **Explain the paradox in the statement, "Only when our arms are sufficient beyond doubt can we be certain beyond doubt that they will never be employed."**

   Upon a first reading, the statement appears contradictory. The first half indicates that we must own sufficient weaponry, which makes the country appear warmongering. But the second half explains that by owning sufficient weaponry, other countries will know that their offensive measures can be overturned, and they will hesitate to attack.

8. **What is the effect of the extended metaphor "Now the trumpet summons us again—not as a call to bear arms, though arms we need; not as a call to battle, though embattled we are—but a call to bear the burden of a long twilight struggle, year in and year out, 'rejoicing in hope, patient in tribulation'—a struggle against the common enemies of man: tyranny, poverty, disease, and war itself"?**

   This is an extended metaphor with a military theme. The trumpet signifies a military call to action, yet Kennedy points out that we are not being called to the military directives of "bear(ing) arms" or being "call(ed) to battle" but we are about to embark on a long struggle with the "common enemies of man: tyranny, poverty, disease, and war itself."

9. **How does Kennedy use juxtaposition to assure his audience "that the torch has been passed to a new generation of Americans—born in this century, tempered by war, disciplined by a hard and bitter peace"; further pointing out that "we observe today not a victory of party, but a celebration of freedom—symbolizing an end, as well as a beginning—signifying renewal, as well as change"?**

   He juxtaposes the words "war" and "peace" to recognize that we are a country who has engaged in revolutions to attain peace. He observes the ending of an era that, through renewal, can also have the benefit of change. This juxtaposition aids in creating a rich ethos of hope and change.

"Letter From Birmingham Jail" by Martin Luther King, Jr.

Comprehension

1. King begins this letter by addressing the eight clergymen who protested his actions in Birmingham as "unwise and untimely." How does his initial approach referring to common spiritual shared beliefs help to dissolve the clergymen's words?

He appeals to them on a common religious level, which makes it difficult for them to refute him because their response would be seen as hypocritical.

2. How does King address the clergymen's argument that he is basically an outsider?

He nationalizes the problem at home and explains that civil unrest cannot be separated by geographical location. This is a national problem, and he is not treading in a territory that only belongs to these religious leaders.

3. King eloquently pays respect to two unsung heroes in this time of civil unrest. He gives these examples to achieve what purpose?

He is building an argument that these people fought against racial strife by personal acts of civil disobedience that served to preserve the humanity of all people. These acts should be celebrated and not ignored.

4. How does King appeal to an academic audience who have turned deaf ears to the plight of black Americans?

He uses a quotation by Socrates to demonstrate that, philosophically, moderate whites and seemingly middle-class blacks are taking a stance that ignores what is spiritually right. He challenges the idea that ignorance is bliss and that silence protects people.

Rhetorical Analysis

5. In the last paragraph, King uses figurative language associated with how one views the sky and discrimination. Analyze the effectiveness of this metaphor.

King discusses effects on the sky, such as the "dark clouds of racial prejudice" and the "deep fog of misunderstanding" that can only be resolved by the "radiant stars of love and brotherhood." He aptly shows that clear skies equate to happiness and harmony.

6. Biblical allusions abound in his text. Explain the effectiveness of these allusions.

Examples include Shadrach, Meshach, and Abednego to emphasize their calling to a Higher Power that allowed for them to practice civil disobedience for the greater good of humanity. He uses other Christian allusions to further this point. He uses these appeals because he has addressed members of the clergy in Birmingham.

7. **Explain King's rhetorical goals when he genderizes the South of the 1960s by stating: "I have travelled the length and breadth of Alabama, Mississippi and all the other southern states. On sweltering summer days and crisp autumn mornings I have looked at her beautiful churches with their spires pointing heavenward. I have beheld the impressive outlay of her massive religious education buildings. Over and over again I have found myself asking: "Who worships here? Who is their God? Where were their voices when the lips of Governor Barnett dripped with words of interposition and nullification? Where were they when Governor Wallace gave the clarion call for defiance and hatred? Where were their voices of support when tired, bruised, and weary Negro men and women decided to rise from the dark dungeons of complacency to the bright hills of creative protest?"**

He sees the south as a nurturing mother who has been unfairly discredited through the words and actions of pretentious and unthinking male politicians. He is promoting the inhumanity that exists against a metaphorical "mother."

8. **In paragraph 26, King uses interesting terms such as "somebodiness" and "donothingism." Explain why he chose these colloquial terms.**

He uses simple, colloquial terms to better connect with his Black brotherhood as well as reviving political terms that celebrate the terminology of the everyman. These simple words express the concrete feelings that lay at the center of his argument.

9. **What purpose separates King's distinction between "just" and "unjust"?**

King acknowledges laws that determine civic behavior, but he questions the morality that distinguishes "just" from "unjust" laws. He argues that morals and ethics have been ignored in favor of laws that seemingly created a fair system. He points out that these laws need to be revisited as times become more modern and socio-cultural dynamics change with the passage of time.

10. **Identify a paragraph in this letter where King successfully uses repetition (and parallel structure) to his advantage.**

These rhetorical devices are basically inherent in every paragraph. Perhaps the best strategy is to pull out one paragraph and demonstrate the power of the repetitive style—how it beats a rhythm into the reader's mind.

Abraham Lincoln's Second Inaugural Address

Second Inaugural Address of Abraham Lincoln. www.ourdocuments.gov

Comprehension

1. **Knowing that Lincoln, in his Second Inaugural Address, reasoned with a country much different than that of his First Inaugural Address, explain the main points that had to dominate this particular inaugural speech.**

   The first inaugural speech had to center itself on the ills connected to the Civil War; the second occurred when the Civil War was drawing to an end. Lincoln's purpose had to focus on the reunification of the citizens of the states to move towards a positive form of democracy.

2. **The overall theme of Lincoln's references are Biblical. Why does Lincoln choose an evangelical theme?**

   At this period of time, it was essential for Lincoln to call on all citizens of the North and South to reconcile. His best argument was embedded with Christian references.

3. **Lincoln aptly does not the blame this war totally on the South. He brings up some historical realities that push forward the idea that everyone is to blame. What historical reality does he refer to?**

   He insinuates that the North has much fault to own up to when the issue of slavery is addressed. Although the North did not promote slavery overtly, Lincoln mentions the cotton industry and shows a correlation of the North's need for cotton and the South's management of meeting that need.

Rhetorical Analysis

4. **What rhetorical impact does paragraph 6 display?**

   Lincoln's plea uses repetition through opening phrases to unify all the citizenry under one umbrella. He figuratively pleads with his audience to medically "bind up the nation's wounds" including the mention of "widow and his orphan" in order to accentuate that every person has, in some sense, lost something to the disease of war.

5. **What does Lincoln hope to gain by using this statement: "let us judge not, that we be not judged"?**

   He knows these references will reverberate with a religious American public. By referring to man's fall from grace in Genesis and the Book of Matthew, he hopes to bind Americans together in a common goal. The reference highlights the hypocrisy of pointing moral fingers at people when one is also guilty of sinning.

6. **Explain the rhetorical genius behind Lincoln's brevity of response.**

   Lincoln made succinct, figurative, and demonstrably unarguable points about the plight of civil rights at that point in time. He wanted his response to be read as a pivotal sermon that uses Christianity as the cornerstone of why people should treat one another in a fair and civil manner.

"The Prince" by Machiavelli

The Prince by Nicolo Machiavelli. Translated by W.K. Marriott, F.R. Hist. S. From *Everyman's Library*, Edited by Ernest Rhys. London: J.M. Dent & Sons, Ltd. New York: E.P. Dutton & Co. 1908.

Comprehension

1. What is Machiavelli's main contention concerning respect?

If people do not fear your actions, they will not respect you. If they do not respect you, they will undermine your sense of justice.

2. Machiavelli gives historical reference as to why fear, love, and hatred have not worked. What are some of his major points given at the beginning of this passage?

He discusses the Borgia rule, describing it as corrupt but basically successful. He mentions the Florentine influence that will not historically be considered as very successful. At this point, Italy was divided into factions that were embedded in mistrust and deception. His references paved the way to many theories of successful political power.

3. Machiavelli points out an innate nature of man that one should never discount. What is that innate nature?

People basically look for instant gratification and often overlook the greater good in order to receive immediate satisfaction. Machiavelli warns that all leaders need to assume that this will happen and to approach people with that thought in mind.

Rhetorical Analysis

4. Why does Machiavelli consider many writers of Hannibal's famed acclaim to be "short-sighted"?

Many of Hannibal's historians did not truly understand that his actions had to be cruel in order to keep the respect of his armies who were of different cultures. In many ways, those who praised Hannibal's military tactics could never understand just how much he had to make cruel decisions that increased his power among his troops. They could never find a way to reconcile this fact.

5. How might females respond to Machiavelli's points of argument if he had been less gender-biased?

Although Machiavelli does address Virgil's comments about Dido's less-than-successful tenure as a person in power, he never acknowledges the fact that women were people who held powerful leadership roles even at that point in history. It would be easy to see how women could be dismissive of his male-biased views.

6. Discuss the irony of Machiavelli equally considering clemency and cruelty in terms of maintaining power.

Machiavelli distinguishes between the two that, on the surface, demonstrate different connotations. Clemency equates to forgiveness and benevolence. Cruelty defines the opposite. Yet what Machiavelli argues is that cruelty is justified only if it addresses the better, common good. Through cruelty, clemency can be achieved since it addresses the good of the general citizenry.

7. Machiavelli argues that "men more quickly forget the death of their father than the loss of their patrimony." What does this observation signify?

Heritage—and all the traditions and obligations that go with it—involves far more forceful emotions than merely coping with the loss of one person who represented that patrimony. This argument is obviously questionable and open to a healthy debate.

"On Being a Cripple" by Nancy Mairs

Comprehension

1. Mairs adamantly defends the viewpoint that she will define herself as a "cripple." Why does she use this specific term and not some other, more gentle term?

Mair detests euphemisms and wants to dispel the idea that her situation in life should be delicately addressed. She believes that being crippled is just another definition of her total makeup as a person who still has much to contribute to life.

2. Explain how the opening bathroom anecdote of Mairs's situates the rest of the tone of the essay.

Showing humor and self-awareness, she highlights the absurdity of the situation where she finds herself fallen down on the toilet seat. She imagines what exchange would have occurred had someone walked in finding her in that particular situation. She uses this anecdote as a way of affirming that living with what many would consider to be unfair detriments does not equate to a death sentence. She is living life by the terms she has been given.

3. List some areas of her life where Mairs considers herself fortunate.

She is grateful for family members who not only support her but do not tiptoe around her. She feels fortunate that she is able to write about this life-changing event in her life and to help others see her, and others like her, as humans who just had the misfortune to acquire diseases others pray that they will avoid. Her matter-of-factness allows the reader to look at her as an active woman who does not want to be pitied.

Rhetorical Analysis

4. Mairs's reference to several pop culture icons serves what purpose?

Those references show that she is staying current. She refers to the Rolling Stones song "You Can't Always Get What You Want" to emphasize the truth behind those words and how she takes them to heart. She also brings up other contemporary rock groups from her young adult years such as Creedence Clearwater Revival and Cream who were known for their protest songs.

5. Mairs's definition of herself as a "cripple" goes far beyond the word itself. What type of person does Mairs really want to show herself to be?

Her use of *cripple* and her attitude about the word is her way of showing others that she is strong, confident, and relevant. She is a contributing person equal to others.

6. Explain the irony is her observation that "as a cripple, I swagger."

The irony is evident because as one who is crippled, she cannot literally swagger. However she creates a swagger with her "take no prisoners" attitude. Her swagger is read by the attitude she projects, although on a closer look, students might be able to recognize the vulnerability she is trying to cover up.

7. Mairs shows a finesse for conveying sarcastic humor while making valid points. Look at paragraph 3 and discuss how this humor is expressed in her use of figurative language.

Her observation "And I certainly don't like 'handicapped,' which implies that I have deliberately been put at a disadvantage, by whom I can't imagine (my God is not a Handicapper General), in order to equalize chances in the great race of life," looks at living as a great horse race. She plays on the word *handicapped*, with which those in the horse-racing world are familiar (horses are handicapped by bettors' expectations for a horse to win a race), and wryly makes the connection of God as "Handicapper General" to the Surgeon General.

"The Things They Carried" by Tim O'Brien

Comprehension

1. What are your impressions of war after reading this story? Do you think this story is more about the physical or psychological realities of war?

As indicated by "the things they carry," the story is about both the physical and psychological realities of war. It is about the demands and dangers of marching through a war zone and the difficulties of living with fear and constant death.

2. In addition to the "necessities," what other tangible things do individual soldiers carry? Reread the second paragraph. What do these additional "things" reveal about the soldiers who carry them?

Other than "necessities," soldiers carry things that help them remain focused on surviving the war, and not yielding to death or perhaps insanity. They carry things, for instance, to remind them of their identity, fearful that in the chaos of war they might lose their core selves. David Jensen, a hygienist, carries vitamins and items associated with personal cleanliness; Kiowa, a Christian and Native American, carries a New Testament, his grandfather's old hatchet, and moccasins; Mitchell Sanders, thinking himself a womanizer, carries condoms. All these things represent how they define themselves, and remind them of who they really are and their individuality in an arena where no one much considers their selfhood. In addition, they carry things to remind them of home and to focus their attention on what they have to live for. For instance, Lieutenant Cross carries letters and pictures of the girl he loves; Henry Dobbins carries his girlfriend's pantyhose, sometimes around his neck; others carry candy, comics, a slingshot, and additional reminders of home and their life apart from war. To shore up their confidence, some carry superstitious trinkets: a good-luck pebble from a girlfriend or rabbit's foot, for instance. Norman Bowker carries a thumb cut from a Vietcong corpse. The thumb bolsters the confidence and machismo of Bowker, "a very gentle person."

3. What intangible things do the men carry?

"They all carried ghosts" and "the emotional baggage of men who might die. Grief, terror, love, longing." A close reading of the lengthy paragraph about cowardice would be a useful exercise. You might discuss the contrast in tone and content with the brief paragraphs preceding it.

4. How do the soldiers keep from being overwhelmed by the threat and reality of death?

The soldiers have several methods to help them survive the ever-present reality of death, but primarily they assume an identify much like an actor playing a role. Some acted "with a sort of wistful resignation, others with pride or stiff soldierly discipline or good humor or macho zeal . . . there were numerous such poses." The soldiers try to believe in the pose. Thus jokes and seeming callousness are survival techniques. Consider the soldiers' reactions to Lavender's death. Furthermore, the reader now understands the significance of those things they carry that reaffirm their true identifies.

Rhetorical Analysis

5. What irony does O'Brien reveal with the "moral" that Mitchell Sanders finds in the dead Vietcong boy in the irrigation ditch?

Initially, the moral is obscure. However, a few pages later, the moral is clarified. The soldiers fight and struggle to survive, yet ironically the peace they seek can be found in death. Nothing can hurt the dead Vietcong boy any longer and Lavender's corpse seems "incredibly tranquil," evincing a tranquility Lavender never found in his drugs.

6. **What is incongruous about "the great American war chest," which includes "sparklers of the Fourth of July [and] colored eggs for Easter"? Is there any bitterness in the narrative at this point? If so, at whom or what is it directed?**

At the point in the story in which O'Brien references "the great American war chest," there is an ironic bitterness. Consider the incongruity of giving soldiers "colored eggs" and "sparklers"—especially when we read that they often explode Claymore mines and grenades for fun. But the passage suggests that America is a great war-producing complex, with industrial and natural resources all available, designed, and cultivated for the purpose of war, and specifically in Vietnam, a war fraught with "ambiguities."

7. **What is the effect of O'Brien interrupting the essay with deliberate line spaces?**

The author allows the reader to take a breath and regroup.

8. **Point out an example of repetition O'Brien uses to add "weight" to the soldiers.**

Students should note that repetition and parallelism occur throughout the essay. Refer students to paragraph 39: "They carried diseases, among them malaria and dysentery. They carried lice and ringworm and leeches and paddy algae and various rots and molds. They carried the land itself—Vietnam, the place, the soil—a powdery orange-red dust that covered their boots and fatigues and faces. They carried the sky. The whole atmosphere, they carried it, the humidity, the monsoons, the stink of fungus and decay, all of it, they carried gravity."

"Shooting an Elephant" by George Orwell

Comprehension

1. Briefly summarize the events that take place in the essay.

Orwell is working as a police officer in Burma where he is called upon to shoot an elephant that is behaving in an aggressive manner. He reluctantly completes the task because he is expected by the locals to do the job. He does this against his better judgment, made worse by the creature's slow, painful death.

2. How does Orwell reconcile that his actions were correct?

He followed the law, even if he knew that the law might not be just.

3. In paragraph 8, Orwell gives several logical reasons for not killing the elephant. What are they, and are they believable?

He recognizes the "grandmotherly air" of the elephant, and sees that it should be far more valued as an acknowledged working animal rather than some type of rabid beast. The elephant did not project violent tendencies. Orwell realized that he had just become a part of the show the villagers wanted to see for their own entertainment.

4. What forces Orwell to carry out his duty?

He knows that he must appear in charge and authoritative in this land that the British occupy. He does it because British Imperialism calls for it.

Rhetorical Analysis

5. Orwell confesses that he is anti-Imperialist and emphasizes the damage done, through Imperialism, to both the conquered and the conqueror. How does the language in the last paragraph of this essay emphasize this belief?

He asks in the last sentence if "any of the others grasped that I had done it solely to avoid looking a fool." Both the conquered and conqueror are engaged in this strange cultural dance that often takes on ridiculous overtones.

6. In paragraph 12, how does Orwell use language to give dignity to the elephant's death?

It is a slow-dying death that is horrible to read. The elephant appears stoic and resigned through his "tortured breathing" that did not weaken. His blood appears "royally velvet" increasing his majestic passing. Orwell clearly shows that a well-respected beast of burden is leaving his presence.

7. Explain the paradox presented with Orwell's views of the "beasts" in this essay.

Orwell sees the Burmans as sub-human "little beasts" who are urging him to kill the elephant, a "great beast" admired in Orwell's eyes. He does succumb to the wishes of the "little beasts" and, with a resigned sadness, fulfills his duty, albeit an empty one.

8. Orwell sets the tone of this essay at the beginning by describing the setting as a "cloudy, stuffy morning at the beginning of the rains." How does this setting expand into the overall mood of what occurs?

The fact that the day begins as cloudy and stuffy while waiting for the rains to arrive is a premonition that no will see this day or its occurrences through clear daylight. The words "cloudy and stuffy" basically describe what was becoming the debacle of British Imperialism. A farce had descended on the proceedings, and the shooting of the elephant exemplified this overall element.

9. Describe rhetorical examples and assumptions in paragraph 7, using a short quote and analysis, that exemplify how Orwell views himself both as a magician and puppet of the people he supposedly controls.

In this paragraph he states that "They were watching me as they would watch a conjurer about to perform a trick. They did not like me, but with the magical rifle in my hands I was momentarily worth watching." In this observation he has become the magician who will perform for the people, thus making him a puppet, the source of entertainment, of this mass of people as well. His magical rifle allows him to fulfill the purpose of the people's entertainment on several levels.

"Allegory of the Cave" by Plato

From *The Republic* by Plato. Translated by Benjamin Jowett, M.A. New York: P.F. Collier & Son. Copyright 1902 by The Colonial Press.

Comprehension

1. What does Plato hope to convey to readers of his allegory?

Plato hopes to convey to his readers a sense of the nature of their own lives. He employs allegory to make this reality as vivid and dramatic as possible.

2. According to Plato, do human beings typically perceive reality? To what does he compare the world?

An interpretation of Plato's allegory appears in paragraph 35. Most of us are like people chained to the wall of a cave who see only the shadows of reality, not reality itself. Plato compares the world to a prison in a cave. For details of the cave, see paragraphs 1–13.

3. According to Plato, what often happens to people who develop a true idea of reality? How well do they compete with others? Who is usually considered superior? Why?

See paragraphs 15–33. When they first look at the light of the sun, people are painfully blinded (paragraphs 15–17). At first, they will long for the cave shadows. After a while they become used to the light of day. Then, if they return to the cave, they are blinded by the darkness (paragraph 31). Someone who has remained in the cave will win any contest with such a blinded person. In addition, ask your students to interpret the allegory. The cliché of an absent-minded professor is like the person who sees the light.

Rhetorical Analysis

4. Is the conversation portrayed here realistic? How effective is this conversational style at conveying information?

Plato believed that dialogue was the best way to discover truth. Notice, though, that Glaucon hardly does more than assent to Socrates's ideas. Anyone, though, talking with Socrates would lapse into awed assent.

5. How do you interpret such details of this allegory as the chains, the cave, and the fire? What connotations do such symbols have?

The cave and chains have negative connotations. Before they are "enlightened," people are virtually buried and enchained by their ignorance. The fire, a symbol of inspiration, warmth, and light, is a figure of the source of reality. Plato also uses this light to blind as well as inform.

6. How does Plato use conversation to develop his argument? What is Glaucon's role in the conversation?

Glaucon is a foil to Socrates. He grants Socrates's observations. When he says more than "yes," he summarizes Socrates's argument (see paragraphs 6, 26, and 30). In paragraph 36, Glaucon has a more humorous role to play. He is our representative, willing to agree but not sure he understands. By relating the allegory as a conversation, Plato adds a dramatic excitement to his allegory.

7. Note examples of transition words that mark contrasts between the real and the shadow world. How does Plato use contrast to develop his idea of the true real world?

There are numerous comparisons. There are certain words that mark the real world: light, upper, and real. The world of the cave is lower, shadowy, and a den. The outer world transforms perception. Reality becomes illusion; illusion becomes reality. Comparative expressions such as "clearer," "truer" (paragraphs 15, 17) can refer to either world. When he first ascends to the real world, a man believes that the shadow world appears clearer. After a while, the real world is clearer (paragraph 5). Finally, in paragraph 29, he does not value the world of shadows at all.

8. Plato uses syllogistic reasoning to derive human behavior from his allegory. Trace his line of reasoning, noting transitional devices and the development of ideas in paragraphs 5–14. Find and describe a similar line of reasoning.

Note the frequent use of "if": "if" they could move their heads (paragraph 6), "if" they conversed (paragraph 9). See also the use of "suppose" (paragraph 11). Paragraph 13 concludes the first part of the hypothetical syllogism. In paragraph 15 a similar pattern appears. Note the use of "naturally follow" and "if." What is missing from this syllogism is the second sentence. That appears in paragraph 35: We are like such people; therefore, we will act as they do.

9. In what paragraph does Plato explain his allegory? Why do you think he locates his explanation where he does?

By paragraph 35, Glaucon has accepted the allegory that we are like the men in the cave. This is another indication of Plato's dramatic sense.

"Me Talk Pretty One Day" by David Sedaris

Comprehension

1. Why does Sedaris use words that are unfamiliar to the vast majority of readers? What point is he trying to make?

He is showing that pronunciations of terms and thoughts do not automatically make sense to the person who is trying to learn the language or acclimate himself to the dialect. He uses these jumbled words to demonstrate how indifferent, humorous, and unimportant they can become.

2. In paragraph 28, Sedaris notes that, "Understanding doesn't mean that you can suddenly speak the language." What does he mean by this statement?

Sedaris points out that when one begins recognizing nuances of a new language, it paves the way of beginning to know and speak the language. More work with the language has to happen, but now an initial understanding of how the language works provides a template for how one can truly start to master the language.

Rhetorical Analysis

3. What makes this essay immediately appealing to the reader?

Sedaris does not talk in a pretentious tone, but merely addresses people in a matter-of-fact manner. This allows for readers to look at him as a contemporary.

4. What is significant about the title, and how does it successfully introduce the point of the essay?

The hopeful idea behind the title shows how great goals often do not successfully occur with the intended effect.

5. Sedaris compares his French class to a refugee camp in paragraphs 23–24. Why does his analogy seem realistic?

His French class is much like a refugee camp where everyone is trying to live day to day and weather every pitfall that presents itself to them. The "crying alone" admission shows the humorous desperation that surrounds the "refugees."

6. Describe how paragraphs 26–27 highlight the gloomily amusing situation of this French class.

The rain gives a comical melancholy backdrop to the situation of this class of nonnative speakers struggling to learn French from an arrogant and impatient teacher. Sedaris observes that the class "would now be scolded for the water dripping from our coats and umbrellas."

"Black Men and Public Space" by Brent Staples

Brent Staples writes editorials on politics and culture for *The New York Times* and is author of "Parallel Time," a memoir.

Comprehension

1. What was your reaction to the title of this essay?

Student responses will vary.

2. Staples determined (as related in paragraph 12) that whistling Beethoven and Vivaldi along with more "popular classical composers" was a therapeutic gesture. Elaborate on the intended purpose of that gesture.

He "warble[ed] bright, sunny sections so even the most "steely New Yorkers [would] relax," even sometimes joining in the tune. Classical music goes against the gangster connotations of more recent language.

3. What is Staples's main purpose in writing this essay?

He is trying to purge the uncomfortable idea that he is discriminated against based on his skin color. He finds it sadly unsurprising that the color of his skin rather than his morals define him.

Rhetorical Analysis

4. What image does the word *victim* conjure up in Staples's opening sentence?

He recognizes this woman as his first victim because she is the first person he noticed who was terrified by the color of his skin, his rougher appearance, and the fact that they were in a deserted section of a large city near nighttime. Sadly, Staples knows that this fear victimizes both the woman and himself.

5. What images and sounds does Staples use to describe the "language of fear" that had entered his awareness?

Staples mentions the sound of feet clopping away with increasing steps to get away from him and the "thunk-thunk-thunk" sound of doors locking. He discusses the women who "have set their faces on neutral, and with their purse straps strung across their chests bandolier-style, they forge ahead as though bracing themselves against being tackled."

6. Explain the irony of Staples's situation.

He is an intelligent young man who holds a professional job and is trying to make his way through life. The reactions of others to his physical appearance show a misjudgment of who he is. As a child, he grew up in a rough neighborhood but rejected violence.

7. Describe the alliterative effect used in some of Staples's sentences.

Several abound throughout the essay. It adds to his voice and gives a cadence to his narrative.

"A Modest Proposal" by Jonathan Swift

"A Modest Proposal" by Dr. Jonathan Swift, 1729. www.gutenberg.org/files/1080/1080-h/1080-h.htm

Comprehension

1. Who is Swift's audience for this essay? Defend your answer.

Swift was writing to delight his Irish audience and criticize his English audience.

2. Describe the persona in this essay. How is the unusual narrative personality (as distinguished from Swift's personality) revealed by the author in degrees? How can we tell that the speaker's opinions are not shared by Swift?

Make sure students are aware of this difference between Swift and his persona. Swift moves rapidly at times from satire to sincerity, but on the whole the persona is a ruthlessly reasonable man for whom human life has the same value as livestock and property. These two qualities, reason and brutality, characterize the persona. Swift exploits the shared morality between his readers and himself to distance himself from his persona. For example, the persona uses the word "good" in a "good fat child" to mean tasty (paragraph 14). For the reader, "good" is brutally misused here. As the essay proceeds, Swift explicitly criticizes Ireland and England. In paragraph 29 he offers his own plan for Ireland's reform. These proposals are quite different from the modest proposal of the persona.

3. What are the major propositions behind Swift's modest proposal? What are the minor propositions?

Swift's persona proposes that most of the children in Ireland be slaughtered when they are a year old. The major proposition of his argument is that because most of the Irish are either beggars in truth or beggars in effect, they cannot support their children. The major assertions that underlie Swift's proposal appear in paragraph 6, in which he describes in detail why raising children in Ireland is impossible. Selling them for slaughter to the country's wealthy and flaying their skin to make gloves will improve the country's economy. The persona also offers a number of other proposals, which he doubts will work. In paragraph 29, he proposes that absentee landlords should be taxed, goods should not be imported, patriotism should be encouraged, among other things. These proposals, though relegated to a subordinate position, are Swift's true proposals.

Rhetorical Analysis

4. Explain the importance of the word *modest* in the title. What stylistic devices does this "modesty" contrast with?

"Modest" has two meanings that are relevant here. Primarily it means of limited extent, humble, and not showy. It also means chaste and delicate. Both meanings are thoroughly inappropriate. The title, then, is another proof that the persona lacks sense or humanity. What he offers in "humility" is to slaughter children ruthlessly.

5. What is the effect of Swift's persistent reference to people as "breeders," "dams," "carcass," and the like? Why does he define *children* in economic terms? Find other words that contribute to this motif.

All such words show that the persona sees human beings as animals and commodities. Swift also calls children a "commodity" (paragraph 7) and "food" (paragraph 9). He calls the poor "our savages," and refers to children's arms and legs as "the fore or hind quarter" (paragraph 10). He praises "infant's flesh" and calls it "nutritive meat" (paragraph 14). In paragraph 32, he refers to people as "mouths and backs" and "creatures in human figure."

6. Analyze the purpose of the relatively long introduction, consisting of paragraphs 1–7. How does Swift establish his ironic-satiric tone in this initial section?

The introductory paragraphs describe the present situation in Ireland: They establish the problem the persona intends to solve. As he describes Ireland, though, he quickly shows his insensitivity. The first paragraph begins, "It is a melancholy object." The "object" he is referring to is the sight of starving people. Even in the first sentence, the speaker reduces people to objects and shows that he is more concerned with the effect the poor's appearance has on the rich than with the poor's plight. In the fourth paragraph, a poor woman is already a "dam" who "drops" children. The persona having already reduced people to things, his proposal is inevitable.

7. What contrasts and discrepancies are at the heart of Swift's ironic statement in paragraphs 9 and 10? Explain both the subtlety and savagery of the satire in paragraph 12.

In paragraph 9, Swift juxtaposes "young healthy child" with a gourmet's delight in food. Note also the use of the word "whole-some." Like many adjectives in this essay, this adjective has moral connotations. There is nothing wholesome about eating children. In paragraph 10, the word "humbly" is inappropriate, as are the analogy of men to cattle, the moral disapproval of children born out of wedlock, the advice to mothers to let their children "suck plentifully," and the claim that children will make "a reasonable dish." In paragraph 12, Swift expresses an important idea of the essay: because landlords have figuratively devoured their tenants, why not do it literally? Note also the ironically understated "somewhat dear."

8. Paragraphs 13–20 develop six advantages of Swift's proposal, while paragraphs 21–26 list them in enumerative manner. Analyze the progression of these propositions. What is the effect of the listing? Why is Swift parodying argumentative techniques?

His persona is supposed to be an enlightened, scientific, and reasonable man. Thus, an argumentative method is appropriate. The irony is that the substance of his proposal is so at odds with the style. Paragraphs 13–20 show why yearling children are the best "commodities." The second list begins with political and religious reasons, moves to economic reasons, then ends with moral reasons to support the proposal.

9. How does the author both sustain and suspend the irony in paragraph 29? How is the strategy repeated in paragraph 32? How does the concluding paragraph cap his satiric commentary on human nature?

Swift uses a classic rhetorical device, paraleipsis. He says that he rejects a series of remedies, which in fact are the only valid remedies in the essay. The denial is ironic. In paragraph 32, Swift again compares the brutality of his proposal with the brutality of conditions in Ireland and finds little difference between the two. The final irony is that the persona will not be affected by his proposal. He does not have children upon which to gain any profit.

"On the Duty of Civil Disobedience" by Henry David Thoreau

"On the Duty of Civil Disobedience" by Henry David Thoreau, 1849. From *Man or the State? A Group of Essays by Famous Writers*. Compiled and Edited by Waldo R. Browne. New York: B.W. Huebsch, 1919.

Comprehension

1. What issue grounds Thoreau's justification for civil disobedience?

He claims that the laws previously put into effect did not address future ramifications that consider the word of the law. He declares that civil disobedience is sometimes an action that has to address laws that did not consider how laws could be misinterpreted.

2. How would you define "civil disobedience" and how does it affect your own life? Give examples that better define your own term of civil disobedience.

The point is to make students aware of just laws and unjust laws that need to be questioned, giving new perspectives addressing these laws.

3. What does Thoreau think about the word *eloquence*?

He thinks it is nice to listen to but believes that people should not automatically equate eloquence with genius or brilliance of mind. He believes that people give eloquence far more credit as far as being a beacon of truth.

Rhetorical Analysis

4. One successful technique Thoreau employs is first person narration. How does this essay benefit from this point of view?

By using first person, Thoreau brings the reader closer into his reasons. He is able give first person accounts to situations that were unjust and called for action.

5. Another technique Thoreau uses is his repetition of terms to further emphasize his belief that it is a citizen's duty to question the government and the humans who comprise it. Thoreau writes, "*It* does not keep the country free. *It* does not settle the West. *It* does not educate." How does the repetition help make the point?

The pronoun he is referencing is obviously the government. He repeats this word to stress the government is an institution made up of humans. It is these humans who have kept it corrupt.

"A Room of One's Own" by Virginia Woolf

Comprehension

1. One of the most important points Woolf makes is why women have been limited by their lack of ways of making money. How does she make the argument that by lacking rooms of their own, women have been prevented from making money and being more of a literary force?

Women did not have the luxuries of privacy or financial independence. Their lives were often interrupted by being the caretaker of others' lives; thus, their literary desires were not as intensely approached as their male counterparts.

2. What do Woolf's musings about Shakespeare's sister and "Judith's" belief that she would not have been considered a genius, even if she shared the same mental capacities of her brother, prove in aiding Woolf's thesis?

Shakespeare's sister would never have been given the opportunity to prove her genius. The thought that she might have been a genius would never have entered anyone's thoughts.

3. What makes the one major character in this essay so uncanny?

The one major character in this essay is not Woolf, but the unnamed narrator. Woolf's point that it is not she alone who bemoans women's historical lack of adding to bodies of significant fiction—she is an Everywoman joining in many women's voices.

Rhetorical Analysis

4. What is the effect of the repetition of the word *without* when describing what life might be like today for Shakespeare's sister in the closing paragraph?

When Woolf ends with the statement, "As for her coming without that preparation, without that effort on our part, without that determination that when she is born again she shall find it possible to live and write her poetry, that we cannot expect, for that would be impossible," she is pointing out that a sense of history must exist that is not just "his" story, where she can be encouraged to write poetry and break out from the traditional feminine roles that bogged her, and others, down in the past. The repetition gives structure to Woolf's warning.

5. What does Woolf's rhetoric suggest about the literature women did write at the time and its connection to men?

She implies that women writers had to be like George Eliot and take a pseudonym so the literature would be accepted in a man's world, or the literature had to be like Jane Austen's, which played upon the male and female roles and could almost be considered deferring to certain men.

6. "A Room of One's Own," by the words alone, is a metaphor for independent and respected living. Come up with some other metaphors that have similar meanings.

Answers will vary.

7. Explain the irony presented in paragraph 7.

When Woolf talks about the composite of women, she calls it "very queer" that woman is imaginatively viewed as having highest importance, but on practical grounds she remains "completely insignificant."

CHAPTER 12
Sample Student Essays

The ubiquitous question students pose to writing teachers is always some version of "What do you want?" or "What should it look like?" or "What should I include?" This brief chapter offers you three real students' essays—well-written exemplars gathered from classrooms across the country. These essays will give you the opportunity to help your students break down what works and seek to imitate it.

Teaching the Chapter

Lesson Plan 12.1

Synthesis Essay

Class Opener

On a whiteboard, project **Question 1** of the **2009 Released Exam** from the College Board website as students come into the classroom. Together, read and discuss the prompt/introduction. Ask students to brainstorm what they already know about space exploration, and point them to the single sentence prompt. In particular, discuss with students the need to "take a position" and consider the issues surrounding that position.

Activity: Writing the Synthesis Essay

NOTE: This lesson works best on a block schedule rather than class periods. If you have less time and need to spread the activity over two days, consider doing all of the preliminary analysis on day one, and the writing itself on day two. You also may choose to do step 4 (analysis of the exemplar) before step 3 (writing the essay).

STEP ONE

Provide students with copies of the 2009 Released Exam, question 1, including the introductory/prompt page and all sources. Ask students to read each source and conduct the following actions for each:

1. Identify the author's main argument.
2. Identify three key ideas/topics/words the author discusses in the source.
3. Highlight three sentences or parts of sentences that seem most important to you upon first reading.

Provide students with 15 minutes to read and annotate the sources, using the three-step approach above.

STEP TWO

After students have completed their annotations, give them 5-10 minutes to work in groups to discuss their answers to question 2 in STEP ONE. Ask them to consolidate their lists.

When groups are done with their consolidated lists, make a list of the most commonly identified ideas/topics/ words on the whiteboard, noting which sources students identified. Make sure they see the connections between the ideas they have jotted down. (For example, you want them to recognize that protection of earth and ethics/ stewardship could be linked.) Your list might look something like this:

Government Spending (A, C, E)
Economy (A, C)
Quality of Life (A, C)
Protection of Earth (A, E)
Pride (B)
Nationalism (B)
Technological Expertise (B)
Health Services—no mention of space (D)
Other worthwhile uses of tax money (D)
Ethics/Stewardship (E)
Contamination (F)

Using the list that students have generated, create an outline for the essay:

- **I.** Introduction with strong thesis (2-3) sentences
- **II.** Government spending and the economy
  - **a.** Source A/C/E evidence
  - **b.** Commentary
  - **c.** Source A/C/E evidence
  - **d.** Commentary
- **III.** Protection of Earth/Stewardship of Space
  - **a.** Source A/E
  - **b.** Commentary
  - **c.** Source A/E
  - **d.** Commentary
- **IV.** Motivations for Space Exploration (Pride/Nationalism) vs. Other Spending
  - **a.** Source B
  - **b.** Commentary
  - **c.** Source D
  - **d.** Commentary
- **V.** Conclusion (or conclude in paragraph 4)

STEP THREE

Give students 40 minutes to write the essay they have outlined using the sources. Encourage students to practice paraphrasing some sources and to keep quoted material to 7 words or less (per quotation).

STEP FOUR

Some teachers prefer to have students analyze the exemplar on pages 652–653 of the textbook before writing their own essays; some prefer to have students analyze it after. Either approach works. To utilize the exemplar, have students identify which parts of the essay are argument (the thesis statement and each topic sentence), which parts are evidence (it is woven throughout the paragraphs much like in the outline above), and which parts are commentary (the student writer provides explanation and analysis after each quotation). Encourage your students to note the citations and the embedding of evidence.

Class Closer

End class by allowing students to discuss this writing process. What came easily? What was more difficult? What do they need to practice? If time allows, consider using additional exemplar essays from AP Central online.

Lesson Plan 12.2

Rhetorical Analysis Essay

Class Opener

Provide students with copies of **Question 2** of the **2017 Released Exam** from the College Board as they come into the classroom. Together as a class, read and unpack the prompt. Make sure students recognize the rhetorical situation of the prompt: Clare Boothe Luce is "preparing her audience" for her remarks; she is speaking to women journalists; and she is, herself, a journalist. Guide students to predict what sort of information and what sorts of strategies Luce might employ based on the statement, "In this speech, Luce went on to criticize the tendency of the American press to sacrifice journalistic integrity in favor of the perceived public demand for sensationalist stories."

Activity: Writing the Rhetorical Analysis Essay

STEP ONE

Have students read the Question 2 prompt, annotating it as they read. Suggest that in the margin by every new paragraph, students note the rhetorical mode Luce is employing in that paragraph. Suggest that students underline any use of **D**iction, **I**magery, **D**etail, figurative **L**anguage, and **S**yntax (DIDLS) they recognize, as well as any specific rhetorical devices they notice.

For the past several years, the rhetorical analysis prompt has called for students to recognize "rhetorical strategies" or even "strategies" employed by the writer. There is a strong push to move students away from simply listing devices and toward a more holistic understanding of the author's message, incorporating purpose, audience, and rhetorical situation.

Remind students that rhetorical modes are just methods or patterns of speaking and writing that help a writer develop his or her ideas. Point out that rhetorical modes are linked to the writer's purpose for writing. Review with students the following purposes and rhetorical modes:

Purpose	Rhetorical Mode
To narrate, to tell a story	Narration
To define, to explain what a term means	Definition
To describe	Description
To classify	Classification
To present a process; to show how something is done	Process Analysis
To give examples	Exemplification
To explain what causes a result	Cause and Effect
To compare and contrast	Comparison/Contrast
To analyze; to show how separate parts work to create the whole	Analysis
To convince or persuade	Persuasion; Argumentation

Rhetorical devices are tools the writer uses to create meaning. Refresh students' memory by reviewing several common rhetorical devices.

- **Alliteration** = repetition of the same sounds in neighboring words
- **Allusion** = reference to history or literature
- **Analogy** = relationship (A is to B in the same relationship as C is to D)
- **Diction** = word choice
- **Hyperbole** = great exaggeration
- **Imagery** = appeal to 5 senses
- **Irony** = contradiction between what is said and what is meant
- **Juxtaposition** = side-by-side
- **Metaphor and Simile** = comparison
- **Parallel structure** = same sentence patterns
- **Personification** = giving inanimate objects human characteristics
- **Repetition** = repeating a remark
- **Satire** = to ridicule in order to elicit change
- **Symbolism** = concrete items that represent abstract ideas
- **Syntax** = sentence structure

Finally, as an important part of their annotation, students should draw a line where they see shifts in the speech, "chunking" the speech into 3 or 4 sections.

STEP TWO

Discuss with students where they saw shifts in Luce's speech, and encourage them to organize an outline of their essay around those shifts. Discuss the annotations they noted, and encourage them to write using rhetorically significant verbs. (Point out to students that the difference between a score of a 4 or a 6 on the exam often hinges on the amount of explanation or commentary a student provides.) Students' paragraphs should be fully developed, aiming for 7-8 sentences rather than 4-5. Students' essay outlines might look something like this:

I. Introduction with strong thesis statement

II. Analysis of first section of text (to first shift)
- **a.** Evidence of author's choice
- **b.** Commentary that explains the effect of this choice by the author
- **c.** Second example of evidence of author's choice (can be a second choice connected to same topic sentence)
- **d.** Commentary that explains the effect of this choice by the author

III. Analysis of second section of text (to second shift)
- **a.** Evidence of author's choice
- **b.** Commentary that explains the effect of this choice by the author
- **c.** Second example of evidence of author's choice (can be a second choice connected to same topic sentence)
- **d.** Commentary that explains the effect of this choice by the author

IV. Analysis of third section of text (to third shift)
- **a.** Evidence of author's choice
- **b.** Commentary that explains the effect of this choice by the author
- **c.** Second example of evidence of author's choice (can be a second choice connected to same topic sentence)
- **d.** Commentary that explains the effect of this choice by the author

V. Conclusion (There is no set number of body paragraphs. Students do NOT have to write a 5-paragraph essay.)

STEP THREE

As with the synthesis essay, you may have your students analyze the exemplar on pages 654–655 of the textbook either before or after they write their own essays. To analyze the exemplar, have students identify which parts of the essay are claims (the thesis statement and each topic sentence), which parts are evidence (it is woven through the paragraphs much like in the outline above), and which parts are commentary (the student writer provides explanation and analysis after each quotation). Encourage your students to note the citations and the embedding of evidence.

Class Closer

End class by allowing students to discuss this writing process. What came easily? What was more difficult? What do they need to practice? If time allows, consider using additional exemplar essays from AP Central online.

Lesson Plan 12.3

Argument Essay

Class Opener

On a whiteboard, project **Question 3** of the **2005 Released Exam** from the College Board website as students come into the classroom. Point out to students that unlike some prompts, this prompt specifically requires them to examine both sides of the argument, yet pick which side they find more convincing.

Activity: Writing the Argument Essay

STEP ONE

Remind students of the HELPS ME mnemonic presented in Chapter 3 of the textbook, and discuss with them possible implications within these broad categories:

HELPS ME

History
Current **E**vents
Literature and Arts
Personal Experience
Science and Technology
Money
Ethics

Point out to students that evidence **HELPS ME** prove our arguments. Working individually or in groups, have students complete a T-chart, brainstorming possible evidence for both sides of the argument.

Pros of Singer's Argument	Cons of Singer's Argument

STEP TWO

Give students 40 minutes to write the argument essay. Stress that they need to **argue**, not **explain,** their position. Remind them of the information they learned in Chapter 3:

- Their thesis must state a clear argument. Even though they are evaluating both sides, they MUST take a position.

- Each topic sentence must further the argument in the thesis statement. (If you were to read only the thesis statement and the topic sentences, you should have a summary of the argument but without evidence.)

You may want to refresh students' understanding of the following argument terms:

- An *argument* is a series of statements intended to *justify* some opinion; any true argument has at minimum three parts, although one part or other may only be implied: a *claim*, some *evidence*, and some *interpretation*.
- A *claim* is an opinion that can be *justified* by further *evidence* and *interpretation*. The term *claim* usually refers to the *main idea*—the *point*, or the *thesis* you plan to present in an argument.
- A *counterargument* is an alternative interpretation of evidence that challenges rather than supports a claim.
- *Evidence* is that part of the argument that is *interpreted* in support of the claim. In argumentation, effective evidence should be acceptable to readers without further argument, based on facts, examples, statistics, credible narrative description, or on already-accepted opinions. Without adequate evidence, the audience will not accept your interpretations in support of your claim (your point or your thesis).
- A *fallacy* is a weak interpretation of evidence, as opposed to a valid, strong, or convincing interpretation of evidence. Common fallacies include (1) a strained analogy, (2) a hasty generalization from one skewed example, and (3) an inaccurate paraphrase of accepted opinions.
- *Interpretation* is the bridge you build between widely-accepted evidence and your widely-debated claims. Some refer to interpretation as the *warrant* or *backing* for your argument. Effective interpretations include (1) accurate analogies between evidence and claim, (2) accurate generalizations from evidence, and (3) accurate paraphrases of accepted opinions.
- *Justification* is what defines a claim as being something worth arguing about, that the claim requires some evidence and interpretation (*grounds*) in order to be believed, and the claim is not already accepted by likely readers.
- *Grounds* for an argument are the evidence and interpretation combined in support of your claim.
- A *warrant* is a stated or unstated belief, rule, or principle that underlies an argument. A *backing* is an even broader principle that serves as the foundation for a warrant.
- The *major proposition* is the main point of an argument, which is supported by the minor propositions.
- The *minor propositions* are the reasons you offer in support of the major proposition.
- A *fact* is a verifiable statement.
- A valid *opinion* is a judgment based on the facts and careful deductive or inductive reasoning.
- *Induction* is a process of reasoning by which you develop evidence in order to reach a useful generalization.

- *Deduction* is a process of reasoning that proceeds from the general to the particular.
- A valid *conclusion* of an argument derives logically from the major and minor propositions. The logical conclusion is termed the *inference,* in which you arrive at a decision by reasoning from the previous evidence.
- *Refutation* is the acknowledgment and handling of opposing viewpoints. You must anticipate opposing viewpoints and counter them effectively (what we term *rebuttal*) in order to convince or persuade readers.

A typical outline in argument is simply *not typical*. There is no real formula for success. Instead, students need to be always mindful that each component of the essay must move the argument forward. The key to argument is arguing thoroughly. Paragraphs should be fully developed and should work to a purpose. Students should avoid vague statements and clichés. A basic outline might look like this:

I. Introduction with strong thesis statement. The thesis will be the central argument.

II. Minor argument one—claim-based topic sentence

- **a.** Evidence in support of claim
- **b.** Commentary showing that evidence proves claim and that claim supports thesis

III. Minor argument two—claim-based topic sentence

- **a.** Evidence in support of claim
- **b.** Commentary showing that evidence proves claim and that claim supports thesis

IV. Minor argument three—claim-based topic sentence

- **a.** Evidence in support of claim
- **b.** Commentary showing that evidence proves claim and that claim supports thesis

V. Conclusion (or conclude in the final body paragraph). The essay does not have to be 5 paragraphs.

STEP THREE

As with the other essays, you may have your students analyze the exemplar on pages 656–657 of the textbook either before or after they write their own essays. To analyze the exemplar, have students identify which parts of the essay are claims (the thesis statement and each topic sentence), which parts are evidence (it is woven through the paragraphs), and which parts are commentary (the student writer provides explanation and analysis within each paragraph). Encourage your students to note the types of evidence used and the writer's development of that evidence.

Class Closer

End class by allowing students to discuss this writing process. What came easily? What was more difficult? What do they need to practice? If time allows, consider using additional exemplar essays from AP Central online.

CHAPTER 13
Writing a Research Paper

Teaching how to write a research paper in an AP English class is no different than teaching a research paper in any other English class. The same goals need to be met. First, students need to be taught to synthesize information from disparate sources. You also want to teach students to incorporate quoted material yet keep their focus on their individual argument rather than on that of the source(s). Next, students must learn to document their sources carefully and accurately, avoiding plagiarism and incorporating correct MLA-style parenthetical documentation. However, because this is an AP course, it is advantageous to prepare students for the AP Exam by incorporating timed synthesis writing. The following lesson plans combine writing a research paper and synthesis essays based on an earlier AP English Language and Composition prompt that forces students to select, narrow, research, and write about a controversial topic. Limit subject areas if necessary. Some topics require a certain level of maturity to handle, and you are the best judge of whether your students are able to write about these topics sensitively.

Teaching the Chapter

Lesson Plan 13.1

Finding a Research-Worthy Topic

Class Opener

Begin class by introducing the following prompt, which was included on the 2004 AP English Language Exam: "Contemporary life is marked by controversy. Choose a controversial local, national, or global issue with which you are familiar. Then, using appropriate evidence, write an essay that carefully considers the opposing positions on this controversy and proposes a solution or compromise." Explain that this prompt is the basis for students' research writing assignment.

Activity: Brainstorming Topics

Discuss with students Phase 1 of the research process: Defining Your Objective.

Phase I: Defining Your Objective

1. Choose a researchable topic.
2. Identify a problem inherent in the topic that gives you the reason for writing about the topic.

3. Examine the purpose of or the benefits to be gained from conducting research on the topic.
4. Think about the assumptions, interests, and needs of your audience.
5. Decide how you are going to limit your topic.
6. Establish a working hypothesis to guide and control the scope and direction of your research.

"Where do you get your ideas?" Anyone who has struggled to come up with a writing topic would like to know the answer to this question. If this writing assignment has students drawing a blank, tell them to try one of these strategies to get started.

Strategy	How to Do It
Create a question-and-answer chart	On paper, ask and answer questions about a general topic.
Browse the media	Browse newspapers, magazines, and the Internet to get ideas. Also try an encyclopedia or atlas.
Create a chain of word associations	Write keywords about a topic. For each word, write the first word that comes to mind, and then the next word until you have a chain of word associations.
Do a freewrite	Write your immediate thoughts about a topic. Do not worry about punctuation or grammar, and do not censor yourself.

Idea generation strategies such as freewriting and brainstorming can help students determine what they already know or believe about a topic. Students should take a few minutes to brainstorm potential controversial topics. Make sure that you have specified your ground rules for highly controversial/inflammatory topics. Consider allowing only one student in each class to write about any single topic. This will force students to do their own research and will make the final assignment more interesting.

Remind students that their audience does not want general information, a bland summary of the known and the obvious, or meditations on an issue or problem. Explain to students that their audience wants answers. Controversial topics that require both primary and secondary sources are advantageous because they will allow students to include others' interpretations into their own research papers.

Activity: Limiting Topics

Take students to the media center and allow them to spend a class period finding and narrowing their potential topics. Point out that one way to choose and limit a topic is to ask questions about it. Give students the following example: Suppose someone asked you "What do you know about Germany?" You might be too overwhelmed by the topic to answer. But what if the question were more limited: "What do you know about the reunification of East and West Germany?" You would probably have a better idea of where to begin. The same principle applies when you write a research report.

Explain that a topic web can also help one choose a research topic that is narrow enough in scope to cover fully. Here's how: First, enter your topic in the center of a web like the one shown below. Then ask questions such as: What different kinds of areas does my topic include? What events does it cover? What places does it include? What people or groups of people are involved? Tell students to use their answers to help fill in the groups of ovals. Circle the most interesting subject. Try to narrow it again by repeating these steps for the subtopic.

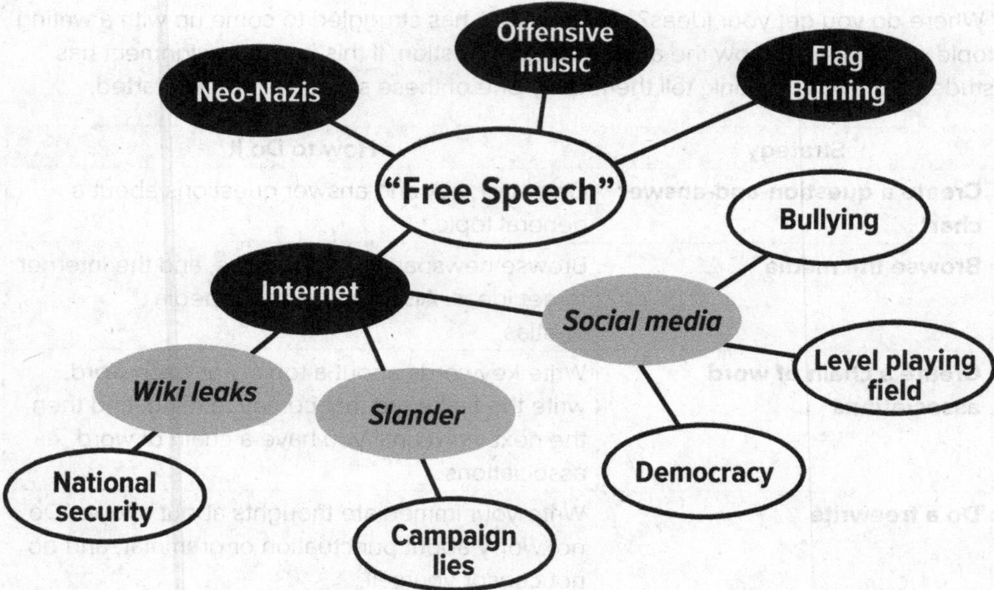

Class Closer

Using poster board or sticky notes, create a chart of all approved topics for research and post the chart in your classroom.

Lesson Plan 13.2

Conducting Research

Class Opener

Ask students to phrase their research topic as an **arguable question**. Questions starting with the word "should" are generally arguable. Your students will now be ready to move onto the process of researching.

Activity: Research and Documentation Guidelines

Briefly discuss with students what makes for good research for their "arguable questions." Point out that the timeline for relevant academic material is generally within the last five years, and explain that sites such as Wikipedia and personal blogs may provide some background information and opinions, but that they are not authentic sites that are acceptable sources in academic writing. Discuss Phase 2: Locating Your Sources.

Phase 2: Locating Your Sources

1. Decide on your methodology—the types or varieties of primary and secondary research you plan to conduct. Determine the method of collecting data.
2. Explore your library's online catalog to determine the viability of your topic, including how much secondary research has been done on your topic and whether your hypothesis is likely to stand up.
3. Develop a tentative working bibliography, a file listing sources that seem relevant to your topic.
4. Review your bibliography, and reassess your topic and hypothesis.

Activity: Creating a Synthesis Prompt

After you have set some parameters for research, give students the following *specific* requirement for research. Explain that, for this research paper, students will create their own synthesis prompt. Ultimately, you want students to find six to eight resources, each roughly one page in length. If students choose a longer resource, they must shorten it to a portion of the article or book that is no more than a page in length. At this point, however, explain to your students that they should conduct research and find as many sources as they can that represent both sides of the question they have posed in the Class Opener. Tell them that they will narrow the number of sources in the subsequent lesson. **Important note: Ask students to make two copies of every source they ultimately choose to use. They will annotate one copy. The other copy will be submitted to you for the final lesson plan in this chapter.**

Class Closer

Allow students to share their favorite research sites and resources. Research can be an intimidating practice for students, and sharing their findings helps lessen the burden. Instruct students to bring their research materials with them to the next class period.

Lesson Plan 13.3

Annotating Research

Class Opener

Introduce Phase 3: Gathering and Organizing Data.

Phase 3: Gathering and Organizing Data

1. Study your sources, taking notes on all information related directly to your thesis.
2. Analyze and organize your information. Design a preliminary outline with a tentative thesis if your findings support your hypothesis.
3. Revise your thesis if your findings suggest alternative conclusions.

Activity: Analyzing Annotations

As a class, read aloud the sample student research paper in the textbook paragraph by paragraph, stopping to read the annotations in the margins. Have students also note the parenthetical documentation.

Activity: Annotating Sources in Class

Although it is tempting to give this activity as a homework assignment, organizing and annotating in class for one or two days can promote and result in a scholarly response to research from your students. In class, discuss the guidelines below and on the next few pages before students begin narrowing their sources, annotating, and taking notes.

Have students gather and begin reading all of the sources they found earlier. After an initial read, have students decide whether the source is important enough to the topic to keep. If so, have students annotate and take notes on the sources they have chosen. Also consider having them write short analysis paragraphs for each source. Gerald Graff's "They Say/I Say" templates are popular among teachers and can be located with a quick Google search. Providing students with a way to broach academic writing within a protected framework (a template) yields predictable writing but also offers struggling academic writers a crutch.

Review annotation techniques with the class. Go over these annotating guidelines with students as they organize their data:

1. Read first; take notes later. First, do background reading, selecting the most general sources that provide an overview of the topic.
2. Skim what appear to be the chief sources. Learn what other writers on the topic consider the important facts, issues, and points of debate.
3. Do not highlight endlessly. Instead, carefully bracket material you want to use. Then write a note in the margin indicating how and where you might use that material.
4. Either download Internet sources or take careful notes on the material. Before preparing a note on content, be sure to copy all necessary information for documenting the material, including the date you accessed the website.
5. Initially mark key passages in books with sticky notes. Write on the sticky note how and where you might use the material. Alternatively, photocopy book pages and then annotate them. Be sure to record the source of all copied pages.
6. As you study and annotate, create labels for source materials that will help you organize your research paper. For example, put at the top of a photocopy or on a sticky note: "Facts FOR the topic" or "Opinions AGAINST the topic" or "Solutions for the problem."
7. Recognize that when you are working with many sources, note taking rather than annotating copies of sources is more helpful. Notes written on index cards provide an efficient method for collecting and organizing lots of information.

Remind students that it is essential that they record source information for *every* note that they take, whether that note is a summary, a paraphrase, or a direct quotation. Highlight the important information below that students should gather as they organize their sources.

Record the following information for a book:

- Name(s) of author(s)
- Title of book, italicized
- Place of publication
- Publisher's name
- Date of publication
- Call number or location in library
- URL or DOI and date of access online

Record the following information for an article in a periodical:

- Name(s) of author(s)
- Title of article, in quotation marks
- Title of periodical, italicized
- Volume number or issue number
- Date of publication
- Page numbers on which article appears
- Call number or location in library
- URL or DOI and date of access online

Discuss the following **guidelines for taking notes about your topic**:

1. Write the author's last name, the title of the source, and the page number at the top of each card or entry. (Complete information on the source should already be recorded on a card or in a file.)
2. Record only one idea or a group of closely related facts on each card or in each entry.
3. List a subtopic at the top of the card or entry. This will permit you to arrange your cards or entries from various sources into groups, and these groups can then serve as the basis of your outline.
4. List three types of information: (*a*) summaries of material, (*b*) paraphrases of material, in which you recast the exact words of the author, and (*c*) direct quotations, accurately transcribed.
5. Add your own ideas at the bottom of the card or following specific notes.

Class Closer

Have students narrow their sources to the best six to eight pieces for their topic. Tell students that they *must* bring these sources with them to the next class period.

Lesson Plan 13.4

Synthesizing the Sources

Class Opener

Write the 2004 AP English Language Exam prompt on the board again: "Contemporary life is marked by controversy. Choose a controversial local, national, or global issue with which you are familiar. Then, using appropriate evidence, write an essay that carefully considers the opposing positions on this controversy and proposes a solution or compromise."

Activity: Timed Essay

Explain to students that they are going to write a synthesis essay in class. Tell them to follow the College Board prompt and use their own sources to write a 40-minute timed essay. Students should be able to write their best essay of the year. After all, they chose the topic and the sources. Allow them to begin writing immediately.

Class Closer

Take time to unpack the prompt. Ask students what they learned about their sources. What worked well? What did not?

Lesson Plan 13.5

Peer Review

Class Opener

Lay the groundwork for peer reviewing essays. Explain to students how important it is that they help each other recognize both the strong points of each essay and the points that need to be addressed for additional work.

Activity: Peer Editing

Put students into groups of 3 or 4. Remind students of the holistic grading rubric (see Chapter 1 of the Teacher Manual). In their groups, ask students to read each other's essays, paying attention to only three areas of concern: the argument (How strong is the thesis?), the organization (Do topic sentences contribute to the thesis? Are paragraphs well developed?), and the evidence (Are the choices compelling? Does the author maintain control of the argument, rather than ceding control to the sources?). In their editing circles, students will "grade" each other and uncover areas for improvement.

Class Closer

Ask each student to reread his or her own paper. After rereading the essay and the peer reviewers' comments, students should write a bulleted list of 3 ideas they want to incorporate into their final research paper from the suggestions offered by the editing team.

Lesson Plan 13.6

Writing the Research Paper

Class Opener

Discuss with students your global notes about the students' synthesis essays. Did students lead with their own ideas and support those ideas with textual evidence? Did they rely too heavily on textual evidence? How were the thesis statements? Consider sharing one or two essays that really shined.

Activity: Drafting Research Papers

Allow students to use a computer lab, if possible, to prepare a draft of their research papers. They should base the paper on the draft they wrote as a timed essay, taking into consideration the peer editing suggestions. At this time, students should also prepare an MLA-formatted Works Cited page. If students do not have access to the full-scale MLA manual, refer them to the Student Edition, which lists proper parenthetical documentation as well as proper Works Cited documentation.

Point out that the MLA recommends that writers prepare their Works Cited page(s) *before* drafting. With this important information prepared correctly and next to students as they draft, they will be less likely to make errors in documentation that will result in plagiarism. Although students may believe that stopping to include parenthetical documentation as they write will cramp their writing, explain that it is difficult to try to insert documentation after completing the writing. The risk of failing to document accurately is too great to chance. Remind students that parenthetical documentation is brief, and they should listen to the experts: take the time to include documentation as they compose.

Remind students that all of **the following materials require documentation**:

- Direct quotations
- Paraphrased material
- Summarized material
- Any key idea or opinion adapted and incorporated into your paper
- Specific data (whether quoted, paraphrased, or tabulated in graphs, charts, lists, or tables)
- Visual media like illustrations, maps, photographs, or screenshots
- Disputed facts

Allow students as much time as possible to write. Depending on the length of the essays, the length of your teaching block, and the keyboarding speed of your students, you may need to allow for several days of drafting.

Activity: Revising Research Papers

Provide a deadline for students to complete the research paper. A day or two before the deadline, discuss with students **the criteria for revising their drafts**:

- Does your title illuminate the topic of the essay and capture the reader's interest?
- Have you created the proper tone to meet the expectations of your audience?

- Does your opening paragraph hook the reader? Does it clearly establish and limit the topic? Is your thesis statement clear, limited, and interesting?
- Does the order of body paragraphs follow the order of your thesis? Do all the body paragraphs support your thesis? Is there a single topic and main idea for each paragraph? Do you achieve unity, coherence, and proper development? Is there sufficient evidence in each paragraph to support the main idea?
- Are there clear and effective transitions linking your ideas within and between paragraphs?
- Have you selected the best strategies to meet the demands of the assignment and the expectations of your audience?
- Are your assertions clearly stated, defined, and supported? Do you use sound logic and avoid faulty reasoning? Do you acknowledge other people's ideas properly? Do you use signal phrases to introduce your sources when summarizing, paraphrasing, and quoting? Are all of your summaries, paraphrases, and quotations appropriately cited?
- Is your conclusion strong and effective?
- Are your sentences grammatically correct? Have you avoided errors in the use of verbs, pronouns, adjectives, and prepositions? Have you corrected errors of agreement?
- Are your sentences complete? Have you corrected all fragments, comma splices, and fused sentences?
- Have you varied your sentences effectively? Have you employed clear coordination and subordination? Have you avoided awkward constructions?
- If you include visual information, do you provide adequate context? Is the placement of the visual logical? Is the visual clearly reproduced?
- Are all words spelled correctly? Do your words mean what you think they mean? Are they specific? Are they concrete? Is your diction appropriate to academic writing? Is your language free of clichés, slang, jargon, and euphemism? Do you avoid needless abstractions? Is your usage sound?
- Have you carefully attended to such mechanical matters as apostrophes, capitals, numbers, and word divisions?
- Does your manuscript conform to acceptable guidelines?

Class Closer

Make sure students have turned in their extra copies of their six to eight source packets to you. You will need to staple these together and have them ready to distribute during the final lesson.

Lesson Plan 13.7

Writing a Surprise Synthesis Essay

Class Opener

Write the 2004 AP English Language Exam prompt on the board again: "Contemporary life is marked by controversy. Choose a controversial local, national, or global issue with which you are familiar. Then, using appropriate evidence, write an essay that carefully considers the opposing positions on this controversy and proposes a solution or compromise."

Activity: Synthesis Essays on Others' Sources

Students have already written their own response to this prompt on a subject that interests them. Explain that now they will write a second response to the prompt, this time using someone else's sources. Randomly distribute the source packets, making sure not to give any student his or her own research. Allow students 15 minutes to study the sources, and then 40 minutes to write this second synthesis essay.

Class Closer

Discuss with students the similarities of the circumstances surrounding the day's writing assignment with the AP Exam.

AP Language and Composition Practice Exam

Section I—Answers to Multiple Choice

After students have completed the Practice Exam in Part 5 of the Student Edition (pages 718-744), you may wish to spend a day discussing the feedback for each multiple choice question.

1. **Answer:** (B)
   Feedback: This question focuses on the author's purpose. Other choices provide supporting details offered by the author; however, B identifies the overall message provided by the comparison and contrast.
   Difficulty Level: Average

2. **Answer:** (E)
   Feedback: In the first paragraph, the author presents Tolkien's framework, which he is then able to use in discussing the various fairy tale exemplars. Although B is a tempting alternative, it does not provide an explanation of the "why." Tolkien is offered as an expert; therefore, his framework is useful.
   Difficulty Level: Average

3. **Answer:** (D)
   Feedback: In this paragraph, the author is not analyzing the stories as much as offering them as evidence in a somewhat glancing way, implying either that he will cover them in more depth later or that he expects the audience to be thoroughly familiar with these examples. In either case, the examples and brief explanation are provided as evidence of the author's claim.
   Difficulty Level: Average

4. **Answer:** (C)
   Feedback: The author's use of dashes makes the connection clear between the stories and the analysis. The dashes are a clear choice on the part of the writer, and they serve a rhetorical purpose. There is no implication that this is sloppy writing or poor thinking.
   Difficulty Level: Average

5. **Answer:** (C)
Feedback: The first paragraph provides Tolkien's framework for analyzing fairy tales; the second paragraph begins the application of that framework. The author's opinions are not unqualified (A); this is not an example of causal analysis (B); this is not an example of process analysis (D); choice E is tempting, but the second paragraph does not actually deal with the concrete.
Difficulty Level: Challenging

6. **Answer:** (C)
Feedback: Students need to recognize the polarizing effect of the word choices the author uses. The words exist in stark contrast to experienced reality and highlight the notion that children see the world as either good or bad with no room for human error.
Difficulty Level: Challenging

7. **Answer:** (D)
Feedback: This is a conclusion that the author's analysis has built to. Choice B is tempting (largely because students may be wooed by the words *extrinsic* and *intrinsic*), but it is incorrect. Choice E is incorrect because the final statement is more closely linked to the effect than to the cause.
Difficulty Level: Average

8. **Answer:** (D)
Feedback: This is a good time to review the difference between primary and secondary texts. Chesterton and Tolkien both represent primary texts, while Collier and Gaier is a secondary text.
Difficulty Level: Easy

9. **Answer:** (E)
Feedback: The author is not offering a definition in the parenthetical, but rather clarifying the concept by offering additional information.
Difficulty Level: Easy

10. **Answer:** (B)
Feedback: This should be an easy question. The passage is about children's psychological reactions to fairy tales. Although literary analysis is included, it is included in order to develop the ideas surrounding psychological response.
Difficulty Level: Easy

11. Answer: (A)
Feedback: Students may not immediately recognize the words "One may" as opening a concession, but in this case, they do. The author is suggesting that there is a different, reasonable interpretation of the information; however, he argues that this position is invalid.
Difficulty Level: Average

12. Answer: (A)
Feedback: The final paragraph provides specific examples that provide evidence of the claims offered previously. "Hansel and Gretel" and "The Goose Girl" are discussed briefly in terms of how they cement the author's claims.
Difficulty Level: Average

13. Answer: (E)
Feedback: Paragraph three offers rhetorical questions that serve to help develop the claim. The reference to Chesterton provides an example of children's reactions to a "bad" fairy tale. This builds the logical analysis.
Difficulty Level: Average

14. Answer: (B)
Feedback: This is a standard academic vocabulary list that students should be able to understand in context.
Difficulty Level: Basic

15. Answer: (C)
Feedback: This is a scientific article, and the reading itself is challenging. The writer opens the piece by defining the technology the article will discuss. Students should learn to recognize that definitions do not have to take the format "X is (definition)."
Difficulty Level: Challenging

16. Answer: (C)
Feedback: All of the choices except C are true. If students are confused by this answer, point out that just because the cited evidence begins in 1985, we cannot be sure the study of this phenomenon or this technology actually began in 1985 based on the references provided.
Difficulty Level: Average

17. Answer: (D)
Feedback: As part of establishing credibility with the topic, the author acknowledges that there is disagreement among researchers. The words to notice here are "However, others have argued. . . ."
Difficulty Level: Challenging

18. Answer: (D)
Feedback: While all of these are mentioned, the main idea the author continues to expound on is found in choice D. A good tip for students is to refer to the topic sentences of the body paragraphs to double-check their instincts.
Difficulty Level: Challenging

19. Answer: (D)
Feedback: Students should pay particular attention to the last sentence of the first paragraph, and the first half of the second paragraph. The author states "an issue" that has not been "previously addressed" in paragraph one, offering the purpose for the paper. He then offers examples of systems in place in Mexico and Japan in the second paragraph.
Difficulty Level: Challenging

20. Answer: (E)
Feedback: Students may be tempted to choose C because the author does describe contrasting beliefs among researchers. However, this is a minor element in the discussion. The correct answer is E, which again can be supported by the purpose statement at the end of paragraph one.
Difficulty Level: Average

21. Answer: (A)
Feedback: Students should recognize that in scientific research (or really in any research paper), the writer must establish that he or she is writing within the context of the broader community. You might want to point out to students that this author is "entering the conversation" by synthesizing sources.
Difficulty Level: Average

22. Answer: (C)
Feedback: In paragraph two, the author describes existing systems, acknowledging that the technology being described is already established in earthquake-prone areas of the world. This is done by discussing the basic technical overview of two systems and highlighting their relative successes in notifying people in advance of earthquakes. Although other statements may be supported by the text, they are tertiary ideas rather than the main idea.
Difficulty Level: Average

23. Answer: (E)

Feedback: Paragraph two discusses implementations; paragraph three describes research to this date. Students may be thrown by choice C, but it is actually the opposite of the order of information. They also might be thrown by B because paragraph two is based on case studies; it's worth noting to students that case studies are based on research.

Difficulty Level: Average

24. Answer: (D)

Feedback: This question asks students to consider the possible underlying flaws in this particular paper. Answer D is the only choice that can be supported with evidence from the text. It is worth pointing out to students that research that is 20 years old would be considered somewhat archaic in scientific fields.

Difficulty Level: Average

25. Answer: (B)

Feedback: In this case, students need to recognize the word *fault* as a scientific term related to earthquakes.

Difficulty Level: Average

26. Answer: (D)

Feedback: This question requires students to make strategic choices in a text to address a rhetorical situation (Rhetorical Situation—Writing); Skill 2.A: Write introductions and conclusions appropriate to the purpose and context of the rhetorical situation.

Difficulty Level: Average

27. Answer: (D)

Feedback: This question requires students to use organization and commentary to illuminate the line of reasoning in an argument (Reasoning and Organization—Writing); Skill 6.B: Use transitional elements to guide the reader through the line of reasoning of an argument.

Difficulty Level: Average

28. Answer: (B)

Feedback: This question requires students to use organization and commentary to illuminate the line of reasoning in an argument (Reasoning and Organization—Writing); Skill 6.A: Develop a line of reasoning and commentary that explains it throughout an argument.

Difficulty Level: Challenging

29. Answer: (E)

Feedback: This question requires students to analyze and select evidence to develop and refine a claim (Claims and Evidence—Writing); Skill 4.C: Qualify a claim using modifiers, counterarguments, or alternative perspectives.

Difficulty Level: Average

30. Answer: (C)

Feedback: This question requires students to use organization and commentary to illuminate the line of reasoning in an argument (Reasoning and Organization—Writing); Skill 6.C: Use appropriate methods of development to advance an argument.

Difficulty Level: Challenging

31. Answer: (E)

Feedback: This question requires students to analyze and select evidence to develop and refine a claim (Claims and Evidence—Writing); Skill 4.B: Write a thesis statement that requires proof or defense and that may preview the structure of the argument.

Difficulty Level: Challenging

32. Answer: (E)

Feedback: This question requires students to use organization and commentary to illuminate the line of reasoning in an argument (Reasoning and Organization—Writing); Skill 6.B: Use transitional elements to guide the reader through the line of reasoning of an argument.

Difficulty Level: Average

33. Answer: (C)

Feedback: This question requires students to select words and use elements of composition to advance an argument (Style—Writing); Skill 8.C: Use established conventions of grammar and mechanics to communicate clearly and effectively.

Difficulty Level: Average

34. Answer: (B)

Feedback: This question requires students to make strategic choices in a text to address a rhetorical situation (Rhetorical Situation—Writing); Skill 2.B: Demonstrate an understanding of an audience's beliefs, values, or needs.

Difficulty Level: Challenging

35. Answer: (C)

Feedback: This question requires students to select words and use elements of composition to advance an argument (Style—Writing); Skill 8.A: Strategically use words, comparisons, and syntax to convey a specific tone or style in an argument.

Difficulty Level: Challenging

36. Answer: (D)

Feedback: This question requires students to analyze and select evidence to develop and refine a claim (Claims and Evidence—Writing); Skill 4.A: Develop a paragraph that includes a claim and evidence supporting the claim.

Difficulty Level: Average

37. Answer: (A)

Feedback: This question requires students to make strategic choices in a text to address a rhetorical situation (Rhetorical Situation—Writing); Skill 2.A: Write introductions and conclusions appropriate to the purpose and context of the rhetorical situation.

Difficulty Level: Average

38. Answer: (D)

Feedback: This question requires students to analyze and select evidence to develop and refine a claim (Claims and Evidence—Writing); Skill 4.A: Develop a paragraph that includes a claim and evidence supporting the claim.

Difficulty Level: Challenging

39. Answer: (C)

Feedback: This question requires students to make strategic choices in a text to address a rhetorical situation (Rhetorical Situation—Writing); Skill 2.B: Demonstrate an understanding of an audience's beliefs, values, or needs.

Difficulty Level: Average

40. Answer: (E)

Feedback: This question requires students to use organization and commentary to illuminate the line of reasoning in an argument (Reasoning and Organization—Writing); Skill 6.C: Use appropriate methods of development to advance an argument.

Difficulty Level: Average

41. Answer: (D)

Feedback: This question requires students to analyze and select evidence to develop and refine a claim (Claims and Evidence—Writing); Skill 4.B: Write a thesis statement that requires proof or defense and that may preview the structure of the argument.

Difficulty Level: Challenging

42. Answer: (B)

Feedback: This question requires students to select words and use elements of composition to advance an argument (Style—Writing); Skill 8.B: Write sentences that clearly convey ideas and arguments.

Difficulty Level: Challenging

43. Answer: (C)

Feedback: This question requires students to analyze and select evidence to develop and refine a claim (Claims and Evidence—Writing); Skill 4.C: Qualify a claim using modifiers, counterarguments, or alternative perspectives.

Difficulty Level: Challenging

44. Answer: (E)

Feedback: This question requires students to use organization and commentary to illuminate the line of reasoning in an argument (Reasoning and Organization—Writing); Skill 6.A: Develop a line of reasoning and commentary that explains it throughout an argument.

Difficulty Level: Average

45. Answer: (D)

Feedback: This question requires students to analyze and select evidence to develop and refine a claim (Claims and Evidence—Writing); Skill 4.C: Qualify a claim using modifiers, counterarguments, or alternative perspectives.

Difficulty Level: Challenging

Section II—Scoring Rubrics for Essays

An Overview of Scoring

Scoring essays can be intimidating—especially when your goal is to assign scores that match the scores students will receive on the overall AP Exam. It helps to keep in mind a few thoughts:

- All AP essays are scored holistically based on a 9-point scoring guide.
- Scores fall into four categories with variations based on the strength of the essay.
- Students had only 40 minutes to complete this draft of the essay. Score with that in mind.

To score effectively, do NOT begin by thinking of all 9 score points. Start with the four most important breaks, and consider the language that appears on the College Board's scoring guide:

8 Effective: Appropriate, convincing, coherent, well developed, consistent, control, *not* flawless. (A **9** is a strong **8**.)

6 Adequate: Appropriate, sufficient, adequately developed, coherent, (may contain) lapses, clear. (A **7** is a strong **6**.)

4 Inadequate: Inappropriate, insufficient, less convincing, inadequately developed, lapses in coherence, less consistent control. (A **3** is a weak **4**.)

2 Little Success: May misunderstand, may substitute a simpler task, tangential, unrelated, inaccurate, inappropriate, consistent weakness, grammatical problems, lack of development, lack of organization, lack of coherence, lack of control (A **1** is a weak **2**.)

Scores of 6 or above (upper half) could be considered college-level writing; scores of 4 or below (lower half) do not rise to that level. The 5 is an anomaly. A 5 has elements of both college-level writing and high school level writing. The scoring guide highlights that essays scoring a 5 are uneven, inconsistent, or limited. When assigned a 5, keep in mind that this is not a mid-point score. Instead, it is a score that simply has elements of both upper and lower half writing. AP scorers strongly dislike giving a score of 5. It is frustrating not to be able to declare *for certain* that a student is definitely an upper-level writer or definitely needs additional instruction and work to reach that level.

Earlier in this Teacher Manual, we discussed the QOEGV method for scoring—see page 9. As you are internalizing the scoring guide and learning to assign fully holistic grades, QOEGV is still an excellent method for helping students see their areas of strength and weakness, and for having them self-assess.

The following rubrics also provide a way for students to self-assess their essays. They offer a breakdown of specific feedback based on these areas of development: Answering the Prompt (correlates to Q); Providing Concrete Examples (correlates to E); and Re-Reading the Topic Sentences and Concluding Sentences (correlates to O). The rubrics include helpful samples as well. Provide copies to students.

Question 1: Scoring Your Synthesis Essay

A total score of 9 is the goal.

Answering the Prompt

On a scale of 1-3, how well did you respond to the question? Remember that for all practical purposes, a synthesis essay is simply an argument essay with sources. For this question in particular, did you evaluate a specific series of factors that must be addressed by school systems (not parents or students) when considering school start times? If you did not have a thesis statement, do not give yourself any points. Restating the prompt does not provide an adequate argument.

Examples of Arguments And Their Scores

Teenagers need more sleep than they get.

0 *(This statement does not really answer the prompt, which specifically references school systems.)*

School systems need to take into consideration all of the needs of students when determining school start times.

1 *(This statement offers little analysis. It is too narrow.)*

In order to enact policies that are beneficial to the community, school systems must work to establish a start time that meets the needs of students and parents and is scientifically supportable.

2 *(This statement is a good start, but it is overly vague.)*

The issue of school start times is one that affects all of the members of a community. From parents who must plan their mornings around both work and school arrival to community members who avoid morning traffic to school system employees themselves, there are many practical concerns in this debate. Although change is always difficult, the scientific community has weighed in with research suggesting heavily that existing models may not be best for learning. When deciding the best time of day to begin school for high school students, school systems must consider a variety of factors, including both practical community-driven needs and scientific formulations in order to establish a policy that provides the most conducive environment for learning.

3 *(This thesis/introduction evaluates multiple points of view and promises further development of suggestions.)*

Providing Concrete Examples

On a scale of 1-3, how well did you support your argument? For this question in particular, did you synthesize specific information from the text? Did you embed your quotations appropriately? Were your examples relevant to your argument? Have you "nodded" to the opposing side of the argument, showing that you understand there are at least two reasonable positions to take?

Examples of Evidence And Their Scores

The Academy of Sleep Medicine claims that "later high school start times are associated with positive outcomes among teens." This is important because it proves that high schools should start later.

1 *(Although this is correctly embedded, the quotation it is too long, there is little commentary offered, and the argument lacks depth.)*

Later school day start times present many positive outcomes, including fewer car accidents and longer sleep durations for teenagers. (Source A) While it may not be immediately clear to teenagers or their parents that sleep duration is an important consideration, there is no doubt that reducing the number of car accidents is important. Whether this factor is related to the additional sleep attained by students or simply the reduction in traffic congestion which occurs slightly later in the day, the clear answer is simply to delay school start times.

3 *(Notice that the writer refers glancingly to the source as part of her own argument. She did not directly quote and she is not letting the sources control her essay.)*

Re-Reading the Topic Sentences and Concluding Sentences

On a scale of 1-3, how well did you organize your response? Do your topic sentences further your argument? Go back through your essay and read only the thesis statement and the first sentence of each paragraph. Does the paper flow logically? Do your topic sentences provide "punch" in proving your argument? Look for words that indicate contrast (*however*, *although*, *instead*, etc.) to make sure you have adequately explored the opposing viewpoint. Review the concluding sentences of your body paragraphs. Have you clearly shown that the evidence proves your argument?

*Give yourself a **1** if your topic sentence review does NOT reveal a clear argument.*
*Give yourself a **2** if your topic sentence review reveals an EMERGING argument.*
*Give yourself a **3** if your topic sentence review reveals a SOLID, CLEAR argument.*

Academy of Sleep Medicine. "Review Suggests that Teens Benefit from Later High School Start Times." Press release. Dec. 14, 2016. Available from: https://aasm.org.

Question 2: Scoring Your Rhetorical Analysis Essay

A total score of 9 is the goal.

Answering the Prompt

On a scale of 1-3, how well did you respond to the question? For this question in particular, did you articulate a clear argument related to how the author crafts his argument (rhetoric)? Did your thesis statement adequately and concisely convey *what* the author's message is, *how* he crafts it, and *why* he is writing? If you did not have a thesis statement, do not give yourself any points. Restating the prompt does not provide an adequate analysis. (An effective thesis statement may be more than one sentence.)

Examples of Arguments And Their Scores

Walt Whitman wrote the preface to *Leaves of Grass* in 1855 to characterize the United States.

0

Walt Whitman wrote the preface to *Leaves of Grass* in 1855 to characterize the United States as being different and "more poetical" than other countries.

1

Walt Whitman's preface to *Leaves of Grass* characterizes the United States through comparison and contrast.

2

Employing the same lyrical language he uses in his poetry, Walt Whitman's imagery creates a stirring portrayal of the United States as a land of beauty and ideals. In describing the nation as a poem, Whitman is crafting an idealized version of both the land and the people who have inspired his writing.

3

Providing Concrete Examples

On a scale of 1-3, how well did you support your argument? For this question in particular, did you provide solid concrete examples from the text that proved your thesis? Were your quotations short yet effective? Did you tie your textual evidence to your analysis of the author's intent?

Examples of Evidence And Their Scores

Whitman says, "The Americans of all nations at any time upon the earth, have probably the fullest poetical nature." Whitman calls Americans "poetical" in order to reference his poetry and his inspiration.

1 *(Explain why this is important. Shorten the quotation and answer the "so what?" question.)*

Whitman refers to the American nature as "poetical," suggesting that there is a parallel to be drawn between poetry, ostensibly his own, and the nature of being American. He continues his analysis by describing the United States as "the greatest poem." In so doing, he continues the parallel, suggesting that the characteristics he ascribes to his county also be applied to his poetry.

3 *(This provides a framework using Whitman and allows for a thread of analysis.)*

Re-Reading the Topic Sentences and Concluding Sentences

On a scale of 1-3, how well did you organize your response? Do your topic sentences further your argument? Go back through your essay and read only the thesis statement and the first sentence of each paragraph. Does the paper flow logically? Do your topic sentences provide "punch" in proving your argument? Look for words that indicate contrast (*however*, *although*, *instead*, etc.) to make sure you have adequately explored the opposing viewpoint. Review the concluding sentences of your body paragraphs. Have you clearly shown that the evidence proves your argument?

*Give yourself a **1** if your topic sentence review does NOT reveal a clear argument.*

*Give yourself a **2** if your topic sentence review reveals an EMERGING argument.*

*Give yourself a **3** if your topic sentence review reveals a SOLID, CLEAR argument.*

Preface to *Leaves of Grass* by Walt Whitman. Brooklyn, New York: 1855.

Question 3: Scoring Your Argument Essay

A total score of 9 is the goal.

Answering the Prompt

On a scale of 1-3, how well did you respond to the question? For this question in particular, did you articulate a clear argument related to the impact of the question for power on the individual? If you did not have a thesis statement, do not give yourself any points. Restating the prompt does not provide an adequate argument.

Examples of arguments and their scores:

Many people say that power corrupts.

0 *(There is no argument.)*

Power and individualism can coexist; I believe that if people strive for power it has an impact on them.

1 *(This is a restatement of the prompt with a little opinion thrown in.)*

Being focused on power keeps an individual from being their true self because they are focused more on control than is healthy.

2 *(This restates the prompt, then gives a rather simple, unqualified argument.)*

History has suggested that power and, more importantly, the desire for power has a corrupting influence on the individual; however, society also cannot succeed within a power vacuum. There is, therefore, a significant tension that exists between society's need for leadership and the over-development of power within any given individual. To address this tension, society must offer a series of checks and balances on any individual's power—whether that power exists within the political arena or a corporate or religious setting—to ensure that leadership exists outside of the cult of personality that can emerge when an individual's quest for power becomes all-consuming.

3 *(This thesis offers plenty of room to grow the argument.)*

Providing Concrete Examples

On a scale of 1-3, how well did you support your argument? For this question in particular, did you provide solid concrete examples that proved your thesis? Were your examples relevant? Were they substantial? Have you "nodded" to the opposing side of the argument, showing that you understand there are at least two reasonable positions to take? (i.e., an example about an experience with bullying, a discussion of the importance of individualism in the perpetuation of the arts) Generalized platitudes do not count as evidence.

Examples of Evidence And Their Scores:

Suggesting that power has always been a problem, but not offering examples
0

Power corrupts. Absolute power corrupts absolutely.
1 *(This is a platitude. You could choose to work with this, but it is not evidence on its own.)*

A situation where a student ran for school office and either lost her individuality because of it or became a stronger individual
3

An allusion to a historical moment significantly impacted by a seemingly charismatic and popular leader being corrupted
3

A literary example of power's corrupting influence on a character (Make sure the focus is on what the author was trying to convey; for example, "In Hamlet, Shakespeare suggests. . . .")
3

Re-Reading the Topic Sentences and Concluding Sentences

On a scale of 1-3, how well did you organize your response? Do your topic sentences further your argument? Go back through your essay and read only the thesis statement and the first sentence of each paragraph. Does the paper flow logically? Do your topic sentences provide "punch" in proving your argument? Look for words that indicate contrast (*however*, *although*, *instead*, etc.) to make sure you have adequately explored the opposing viewpoint. Review the concluding sentences of your body paragraphs. Have you clearly shown that the evidence proves your argument?

*Give yourself a **1** if your topic sentence review does NOT reveal a clear argument.*
*Give yourself a **2** if your topic sentence review reveals an EMERGING argument.*
*Give yourself a **3** if your topic sentence review reveals a SOLID, CLEAR argument.*